THE POETICAL WORKS

OF

WILLIAM DRUMMOND

OF HAWTHORNDEN

Etc.

II

PLATE I.—PORTRAIT FROM THE (?) 1614 EDITION OF THE *POEMS*.

Frontispiece.

THE POETICAL WORKS

OF

WILLIAM DRUMMOND
Of Hawthornden

With ' A Cypresse Grove'

Edited by

L. E. Kastner, M.A.
Professor of French Language and Literature

Volume the Second

HASKELL HOUSE PUBLISHERS Ltd.
Publishers of Scarce Scholarly Books
NEW YORK. N. Y. 10012
1968

First Published 1856

HASKELL HOUSE PUBLISHERS LTD.
Publishers of Scarce Scholarly Books
280 LAFAYETTE STREET
NEW YORK, N. Y. 10012

Library of Congress Catalog Card Number: 68-24906

Haskell House Catalogue Item # 157

Printed in the United States of America

CONTENTS.

II

PLATE 2.—PANEL-PORTRAIT AT HAWTHORNDEN.

Facing page vii.

ICONOGRAPHY.

THE Drummond portraits seem to us to fall naturally into three distinct groups :

GROUP A.

I. Unsigned oval-shaped engraving (reproduced for the first time in plate 1, Frontispiece to Vol. II.), measuring $3\frac{4}{5} \times 3\frac{1}{3}$ inches ; half length to right, in lace-edged collarette and sash.

This portrait, roughly executed, probably by a local artist, has so far remained unnoticed, and is of the greatest importance in determining the genuineness and the relationship of the various portraits said to represent the poet William Drummond.

It occurs for the first time in the Bodleian advance issue of the *Poems* (? 1614), mounted on a blank leaf, between the title-page and the commencement of the *Poems*. It is also contained in the Bodleian copy of the regular edition of the *Poems* (1616), mounted on the back of the title-page of *Madrigalls and Epigrammes* ; and likewise in the Edinburgh University copy of the *Poems* (1616), mounted on a blank leaf facing p. 96. In the Aberdeen University copy of the *Poems* (1616), the blank leaf in the same place is extant, but the engraving itself has disappeared. All these copies of the *Poems* are original editions, bound in a contemporary binding, and in all three cases the blank leaf on which is mounted the portrait forms part of a sheet sewn in with the rest of the sheets when the volume was made up by the binder. Thus there can be no doubt that this portrait was inserted by Drummond's authority, and that we are in presence of an undoubtedly genuine picture of the poet, however unskilled the artist may have been. If, as we may reasonably suppose, the engraving was executed expressly for the advance issue of the *Poems*, which appeared in 1614 or 1615, it represents Drummond at the age of twenty-nine or thirty. We should say that it was probably copied from a picture.

II. Signed panel-portrait (reproduced for the first time in plate 2, facing p. vii); three-quarter length to left, in stiff collar, cloak and sash.

This portrait is now hung in the dining-room at Hawthornden. It was acquired, some twenty years ago, at an auction sale in Edinburgh. In an estimate, dated 1892, from a Mr. Halkerston, a picture-restorer of Edinburgh, mention is made of a panel-picture at Hawthornden. This would tend to show that the picture in question was restored at that date. It certainly bears traces of having been touched up at least once. Notwithstanding, it undeniably bears a close resemblance to No. I., and in its original state was perhaps the model of the latter.

III. Signed oval-shaped etching, with arms of Drummond (reproduced in plate 3, facing p. viii), measuring $6 \times 4\frac{5}{8}$ inches; half length to right, in lace-edged collarette, cloak and sash, by Richard Gaywood (*c*. 1630–*c*. 1711), a pupil and imitator of Wenceslaus Hollar.

This engraving figures as frontispiece to the first edition ($165\frac{4}{5}$) of Drummond's *History of Scotland*. A copy of this (measuring $3\frac{1}{4} \times 2\frac{2}{5}$ inches), reversed, appears as frontispiece to Phillips's edition of the *Poems* (1656), and, in a modified form, in the 1681, 1682, and 1683 editions of the *History of Scotland*. Another copy of Gaywood's first attempt, also facing right, but very coarsely executed, constitutes the frontispiece of the folio edition (Edinburgh, 1711) of Drummond's *Works*.

PLATE 3.—PORTRAIT AFTER THE ENGRAVING BY GAYWOOD.

Facing page viii.

However unsatisfactory the execution of Gaywood's engraving may appear—we confess that it leaves a great deal to be desired—there is no reason to doubt its genuineness. The *History of Scotland* and the *Poems* of 1656 were both published with the approval and concurrence of Sir John Scott of Scotstarvet,[1] Drummond's brother-in-law, who was a man of literary tastes, and with whom Drummond was on terms of the most intimate friendship. It is not likely, under the circumstances, that Scott of Scotstarvet would have allowed the London publisher, who, it may be recalled, dedicated the *Poems* of 1656 to Sir John, to insert a portrait of Drummond which had no claim to authenticity. The same argument holds good of the editors of the folio edition of the *Works*; they give us clearly to understand in the preface that they were in close touch with Sir William, the poet's son. Moreover, the Gaywood engraving bears a close resemblance to Nos. I. and II., except in one unimportant particular—the length and shape of the moustache. In our opinion Nos. I., II., and III. undoubtedly belong to the same group, and confirm one another's genuineness. Probably No. III. was copied from No. I., or possibly from No. II., and perhaps No. II., in its original state, served as the model for No. I.

The Gaywood engraving is also reproduced in :

(*a*) David Masson, *Drummond of Hawthornden*. London, 1873—as frontispiece, in embellished form by C. H. Jeens.

(*b*) W. M. C. Ward, *The Poems of William Drummond of Hawthornden*. London and New York, 1894—as frontispiece to the first volume.

(*c*) R. Garnett and E. Gosse, *History of English Literature*. London, 1903, vol. ii. p. 296—a poor reproduction.

(*d*) Chambers, *Cyclopædia of English Literature* (new edition). London and Edinburgh, 1903, vol. i. p. 510—from the engraving prefixed to the *Works*, but embellished.

---

[1] See our Bibliography, vol. i. p. lxxxiv.

IV. Miniature, formerly at Hawthornden, but now apparently lost (reproduced, according to the copy in *Effigies Poeticæ*, in plate 4, facing p. x).

Though this miniature cannot be said to bear any close resemblance to those already described, we are not indisposed to believe that it may represent Drummond, at a more advanced age, however, than the three foregoing. In it several of the characteristic features of Nos. I., II., and III. are traceable—the hair advancing to a point over the high forehead and receding on both sides, leaving the temples quite free, the large superciliary arches, the eyes deep-set, the cheek-bones projecting slightly, etc. The collar, too, is of the same type.

Reproduced in :

(*a*) [B. W. Proctor], *Effigies Poeticæ : or the Portraits of the British Poets.* London, 1824, vol. i. plate 39.
It is there said to be in the possession of Captain Drummond.

(*b*) The Maitland Club edition of Drummond's *Poems.* Edinburgh, 1832—as frontispiece, with the addition at the foot of Drummond's autograph.

It is important to lay stress on the fact that the autograph of Drummond has no connection with the miniature.

(*c*) W. B. Turnbull, *The Poetical Works of William Drummond of Hawthornden.* London, 1856 (reprinted in 1890) —as frontispiece, according to the copy of the Maitland Club edition, but reduced and embellished.

V. Unsigned portrait (reproduced for the first time in plate 5, facing p. xii) ; half length to right, in lace-edged collarette.

This portrait, a beautiful work of art, is at Hawthornden, and has been there for a considerable time. When, some hundred years ago, John Gibson Lockhart visited Hawthornden, he had no doubt as to the authenticity of the portrait in question ; in the following passage of

II

PLATE 4.—PORTRAIT FROM THE MINIATURE FORMERLY AT
HAWTHORNDEN.

Facing page x.

his *Peter's Letters to his Kinsfolk*, he gives a beautiful
and withal remarkably accurate description of it : " Mr.
G—— carried me into the house, chiefly to show me the
original portrait of Drummond, which is preserved there ;
and, in truth, I am obliged to him for having done so.
The picture represents him at about the age of forty—
the best of all ages, perhaps, for taking a man's portrait,
if only one is to be taken of him—when the substance of
the face is in all its firmness and vigour, and the fire of
youth has been tempered, but not obscured, by the
gravity of manhood.   Drummond's features are singularly
fine and expressive—and the picture is an admirable one,
and in perfect preservation, so that we see them exactly
as they were the day they were painted.   His forehead
is clear, open, and compact, with the short black hair
combed back in dark glossy ringlets, in the true Italian
style—as we see it in the pictures of Venetian Nobles,
by Titian.   The nose is high and aquiline, and the lips
rich and full, like those in the statues of Antinous.   His
eyes are black as jet (and so are his eyebrows), but the
dazzle of their brilliancy is softened by a melancholy
wateriness, which gives to the whole visage an inexpress-
ible air of pensive delicacy and sentiment." [1]   Since
Lockhart's days, however, the portrait described by him
has been all but forgotten,[2] and most of the authorities
to whom it has been submitted are agreed that it does
not represent the poet Drummond.   We confess, in all
humility, that we are not prepared to be quite so positive,
and that if full allowance is made for the difference
between a finished work of art and the rather crude
effigies represented by Nos. I., II., and III., it is not
impossible to trace some connection between these three
and the present portrait.

[1] See *Peter's Letters to his Kinsfolk*, second edition (1819), vol. iii.
pp. 128-9.
[2] Mr. J. L. Caw (in his *Scottish Portraits*.   Edinburgh, 1902) confuses
it with No. II.

GROUP B.

I. Panel-portrait (reproduced in plate 6, facing p. xiv, according to the mezzotint by J. Finlayson, from the Earl of Home's picture), measuring $23\frac{1}{4} \times 18\frac{1}{2}$ inches ; half length to right, in standing lace collarette.

This portrait, as already indicated, is in the possession of the Earl of Home. It bears no date, contrary to what Mr. J. L. Caw (*op. cit.*) says ; it has painted upon the wood at the back, " Sir William Drummond of Hathornden. C. Janson. Pinx^t." Above this inscription is stuck a piece of paper, apparently in the handwriting of the present Earl's father, to this effect : " Exhibited in the National Portrait Exhibition of South Kensington, 1866. Supposed by Mr. Scharf and others to be painted by G. Jamieson."

Personally, we are convinced that this portrait does not represent the poet Drummond, despite the fact that Mr. J. L. Caw (*op. cit.*) is against us, as is also, we understand, Professor Holmes, the director of the National Portrait Gallery, London. Mr. Caw believes that it bears " so close a resemblance " to Nos. II. and III. in Group A (No. I. of Group A was then unknown to him) that it may be accepted as reliable ; and Professor Holmes is apparently of opinion that it represents the same person as No. I. in Group A—that No. I. in Group A is probably a rough copy of the Home picture, and that the occurrence of No. I. in Group A with the ?1614 issue of the *Poems* confirms the genuineness of the Home portrait. He also thinks that the picture cannot be attributed to Cornelius Jansen or Jonson (?1590–1665), chiefly because of certain technical differences between the Home picture and the rest of Jansen's work. Possibly it is by D. Mytens, who painted a picture of Henry Prince of Wales, or by P. Van Somer, to whom is due a portrait of James I. Leaving aside the question of the artist who may be responsible for this portrait, we have been

II

PLATE 5.—PORTRAIT AT HAWTHORNDEN.

Facing page xii.

unable, though we have kept a perfectly open mind in the matter, to trace any resemblance whatever between the face depicted in the Home picture and that represented in Nos. I., II., and III. of Group A. Our view is that the Home portrait depicts a totally different man, whose open humorous face contrasts strikingly with the pensive somewhat melancholy countenance of Nos. I., II., and III. of Group A, which one associates naturally with the poet Drummond. Further, if it be supposed that the Home picture is genuine, how can it be explained— its artistic superiority would give it an exclusive recommendation—that it was not chosen either for Drummond's *History of Scotland* or for the 1656 edition of the *Poems*, or for the folio edition of the *Works* in 1711? It may also be recalled that the Home picture has painted upon the wood at the back, "*Sir* William Drummond of Hathornden," a title which the poet Drummond never possessed. From this one might be tempted to conclude that the Home portrait may represent the poet's son, who was *Sir* William, but the dress, especially the collar, makes such a conclusion impossible.

Reproduced also in :

(*a*) *The Poems of William Drummond of Hawthornden.* London, 1791—as frontispiece.

(*b*) J. Pinkerton, *The Scottish Gallery*. London, 1799, plate 29.

(*c*) R. Chambers, *A Biographical Dictionary of Eminent Scotsmen*. Glasgow, Edinburgh, and London, 1835—as frontispiece to the second volume.

(*d*) H. Drummond, *Histories of Noble British Families*. London, 1846, vol. i. p. 120.

(*e*) J. L. Caw, *Scottish Portraits*. Edinburgh, 1902, portfolio 2, plate xxviii.

(*f*) R. Garnett and E. Gosse, *History of English Literature*. London, 1903, vol. ii. p. 298—a poor reproduction.

(*g*) A. H. Bullen, *A Cypress Grove, by Wm. Drummond of Hawthornden*. Stratford-on-Avon, 1907—as frontispiece.

II. Portrait (reproduced in plate 7, facing p. xvi), measuring 8⅞ × 7⅝ inches, in the National Portrait Gallery, London, attributed to George Jamesone (c. 1588–1644), the famous Scottish portrait-painter, whose name has already been mentioned in connection with the Home portrait.

Except that it shows the left profile and not the right profile, this portrait is not unlike that in the possession of the Earl of Home. The forehead has the same ampleness, and is framed in like manner by a luxuriant mass of hair, which in both portraits covers the ear almost entirely; the nose is firm, the upper lip is full and slightly projecting, and the chin round. Besides, in both the collar is of the same type, though not identical. We are inclined to believe that both the portrait in question and the Home portrait may be by George Jamesone ; that they may represent the same person, and that this person is not the poet Drummond.

Group C.

So little can be said in favour of the portraits of this group that they may be dismissed more summarily.

I. Panel-picture, measuring 22 × 17 inches, in the Warden's house at All Souls College, Oxford, of which there is a copy at Hawthornden.

Practically all authorities are agreed that this portrait does not represent Drummond. It may possibly be a likeness of John Drummond, second Earl of Perth, judging by the portraits of the latter that are extant.

A brief technical description of this portrait is given in the Illustrated Catalogue of the Oxford Exhibition of Historical Portraits for 1905.

II. Portrait, bearing the inscription " Peryſera | Æta : 23. | 1600 ", formerly in the possession of Mr. A. Muirhead of Edinburgh.

II

PLATE 6.—PORTRAIT AFTER THE PICTURE ATTRIBUTED TO C. JANSEN.

Facing page xiv.

This portrait was bought by Mr. Muirhead at a sale held at Hawthornden some forty years ago, when several properties belonging to Hawthornden were disposed of in mistake, along with a lot of more or less valueless articles. It was recently acquired by the authorities of the National Portrait Gallery of Edinburgh at a sale of Mr. Muirhead's effects. It represents a man with hair brushed back high, a thin beard, and a generally mournful appearance. If the inscription " Æta : 23. 1600 " be authentic, this portrait cannot possibly represent Drummond, who in that year was only fifteen years of age. However that may be, it appears to bear no relationship to any of the portraits that possess any pretence to authenticity.

III. Miniature, at Montagu House, Whitehall, the town residence of the Duke of Buccleuch, famous for its noble collection of English miniatures. At the foot is fixed a small plate bearing the inscription : " William Drummond." The artist is generally supposed to be Isaac Olivier or Oliver (?1556–1617).

This miniature, as far as we can see, has no affinity to any of the other portraits, and probably represents a William Drummond, of which there were several, belonging to another branch of the family.

Reproduced in :

G. C. Williamson, *History of Portrait Miniatures.* London, 1904, vol. i. plate 12, fig. 6.

II

PLATE 7.—PORTRAIT AFTER THE PICTURE ATTRIBUTED TO
GEORGE JAMESONE.

Facing page xvi.

LIST OF ILLUSTRATIONS.

xvii

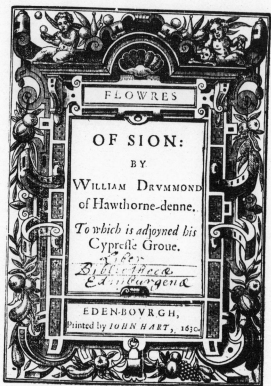

𝒴.

Giuen to king James His Colledge in Eden-Bourgh by the Author 1630.

PLATE 8.—FACSIMILE OF TITLE-PAGE.

Flowres of Sion.

Reprinted from the Edition of 1630.

B

FLOWRES OF SION:

OR

SPIRITVALL POEMES,

BY

W. D.

[i]

[The Instabilitie of Mortall Glorie.]

Riumphant Arches, Statues crown'd with
    Bayes,
    Proude Obeliskes, Tombes of the vastest
    frame,
    Colosses, brasen *Atlases* of Fame,
    Phanes vainelie builded to vaine Idoles
    praise ;
5 States, which vnsatiate Mindes in blood doe raise,
From the Crosse-starres vnto the Articke Teame,
Alas ! and what wee write to keepe our Name,
Like Spiders Caules are made the sport of Dayes :
All onely constant is in constant Change,
10 What done is, is vndone, and when vndone,
Into some other figure doeth it range ;
Thus moues the restlesse World beneath the Moone :
    Wherefore (my Minde) aboue Time, Motion, Place,
    Thee raise, and Steppes, not reach'd by Nature trace.

With the exception of *An Hymne of the Fairest Faire* and *The Shadow of the Iudgement*, the titles of the several pieces are wanting in I, and in the two issues of J they occur in the " Table " of contents only.   They are also wanting in NO.
  I. This sonnet is wanting here in O.
  ³ N. Brazen Colosses *Atlases* of Fame   ⁴ I. Phanes vainelie builded [N. And Temples builded] to vaine Deities praise   ⁶ N. From Southerne Pole unto   ⁷ N. And even what   ¹² IN. Thus rolles   ¹⁴ N. Aspire, and Steps

5

[ii]

[Humane Frailtie.]

A Good that neuer satisfies the Minde,
  A Beautie fading like the Aprile flowres,
A Sweete with floodes of Gall that runnes combind,
A Pleasure passing ere in thought made ours,
5 A Honour that more fickle is than winde,
A Glorie at Opinions frowne that lowres,
A Treasurie which Bankrout Time deuoures,
A Knowledge than graue Ignorance more blind :
A vaine Delight our equalles to command,
10 A Stile of greatnesse, in effect a Dreame,
A fabulous Thought of holding Sea and Land,
A seruile Lot, deckt with a pompous Name,
  Are the strange endes wee toyle for heere below,
  Till wisest Death make vs our errores know.

[i]

[The Permanencie of Life.]

L Ife a right shadow is,
  For if it long appeare,
Then is it spent, and Deathes long Night drawes neare ;
Shadowes are mouing, light,
5 And is there ought so mouing as is this ?
When it is most in Sight,
It steales away, and none can tell how, where,
So neere our Cradles to our Coffines are.

II. 7 INO. banckrupt   11 I. A fabling Thought NO. A swelling
Thought
   I. 7 NO. *and none knows how or where*

[iii]

[No Trust in Tyme.]

LOoke how the Flowre, which lingringlie doth fade,
The Mornings Darling late, the Summers Queene,
Spoyl'd of that Iuice, which kept it fresh and greene,
As high as it did raise, bowes low the head :
5 Right so my Life (Contentments beeing dead,
Or in their Contraries but onelie seene)
With swifter speede declines than earst it spred,
And (blasted) scarce now showes what it hath beene.
As doth the Pilgrime therefore whom the Night
10 By darknesse would imprison on his way,
Thinke on thy Home (my Soule) and thinke aright,
Of what yet restes thee of Lifes wasting Day :
  Thy Sunne postes Westward, passed is thy Morne,
  And twice it is not giuen thee to bee borne.

[iv]

[Worldes Ioyes are Toyes.]

THe wearie Mariner so fast not flies
An howling Tempest, Harbour to attaine,
Nor Sheepheard hastes, when frayes of Wolues arise,
So fast to Fold to saue his bleeting Traine :
5 As I (wing'd with Contempt and just Disdaine)
Now flie the World, and what it most doth prize,
And Sanctuarie seeke, free to remaine
From wounds of abject Times, and Enuies eyes.
Once did this World to mee seeme sweete and faire,
10 While Senses light Mindes prospectiue keept blind,
Now like imagin'd Landskip in the Aire,
And weeping Raine-bowes, her best Ioyes I finde :
  Or if ought heere is had that praise should haue,
  It is a Life obscure, and silent Graue.

III. ¹ NO. Look as ⁵ NO. Right so the pleasures of my Life being
dead [*In the copy of* I *containing the signature of the Earl of Lauderdale,
the brackets enclosing the words* Contentments . . . seene *are put in in
ink.*] ⁹ INO. Therefore as doth the Pilgrime [O. Pilgrims] ¹⁰ NO.
Hast darkly to imprison ¹² NO. Of what's yet left thee
    IV. ¹ N. so far ⁹ INO. To mee this World did once ¹⁰ I. Whiles
¹⁴ NO. an obscure Life

[v]

[Nature must yeelde to Grace.]

TOo long I followed haue on fond Desire,
    And too long painted on deluding Streames,
Too long refreshment sought in burning Fire,
Runne after Ioyes which to my Soule were Blames;
5 Ah! when I had what most I did admire,
And prou'd of Lifes delightes the last extreames,
I found all but a Rose hedg'd with a Bryer,
A nought, a thought, a show of golden Dreames.
Hence-foorth on Thee (mine onelie Good) I thinke,
10 For onelie Thou canst grant what I doe craue,
Thy Nailes my Pennes shall bee, thy Blood mine Inke,
Thy winding-sheete my Paper, Studie Graue:
    And till that Soule from Bodie parted bee,
    No hope I haue, but onelie onelie Thee.

[vi]

[The Booke of the World.]

OF this faire Volumne which wee World doe name,
    If wee the sheetes and leaues could turne with care,
Of Him who it correctes, and did it frame,
Wee cleare might read the Art and Wisedome rare?
5 Finde out his Power which wildest Pow'rs doth tame,
His Prouidence extending euerie-where,
His Iustice which proud Rebels doeth not spare,
In euerie Page, no, Period of the same:
But sillie wee (like foolish Children) rest
10 Well pleas'd with colour'd Velame, Leaues of Gold,
Faire dangling Ribbones, leauing what is best,
On the great Writers sense nee'r taking hold;
    Or if by chance our Mindes doe muse on ought,
    It is some Picture on the Margine wrought.

V. This sonnet is wanting here in NO.
[3] I. midst burning   [11] I. my Inke
VI. [10] I. Velumne   [13] INO. we stay our Mindes

[vii]

[The Miserable Estate of the World before
the Incarnation of God.]

THe Griefe was common, common were the Cryes,
　　Teares, Sobbes, and Groanes of that afflicted
　　　　Traine,
Which of Gods chosen did the Summe containe,
And Earth rebounded with them, pierc'd were Skies ;
5 All good had left the World, each Vice did raigne,
In the most hideous shapes Hell could deuise,
And all degrees, and each Estate did staine,
Nor further had to goe, whom to surprise :
The World beneath the Prince of Darknesse lay,
10 In euerie Phane who had himselfe install'd,
Was sacrifiz'd vnto, by Prayers call'd,
Responses gaue, which (Fooles) they did obey :
　　When (pittying Man) God of a Virgines wombe
　　Was borne, and those false Deities strooke dombe.

VII. ⁶ INO. In the most monstrous sorts ¹⁰ NO. And in each
Temple had ¹⁴ O. struck

[viii]

[The Angels for the Natiuitie of our Lord.]

R Vnne (Sheepheards) run where *Bethleme* blest
     appeares,
Wee bring the best of newes, bee not dismay'd,
A Sauiour there is borne, more olde than yeares,
Amidst Heauens rolling hights this Earth who stay'd ;
5 In a poore Cotage Inn'd, a Virgine Maide
A weakling did him beare, who all vpbeares,
There is hee poorelie swadl'd, in Manger lai'd,
To whom too narrow Swadlings are our Spheares :
Runne (Sheepheards) runne, and solemnize his Birth,
10 This is that Night, no, Day growne great with Blisse,
In which the power of *Sathan* broken is,
In Heauen bee glorie, Peace vnto the Earth.
     Thus singing through the Aire the Angels swame,
     And Cope of Starres re-echoed the same.

VIII. ⁴ INO. Amidst the rolling Heauen ⁷ I. There is hee swadl'd
in Cloathes NO. There he in Cloathes is wrapt [*In the Edinburgh
University copy of* I, *presented by Drummond,* There is hee poorlie
swadl'd *is pasted in over the original reading on a printed slip in
type similar to the rest of the text, presumably by Drummond himself.
This process is repeated in several other instances, and in nearly every
case the reading pasted in is that adopted in the second edition* (J) *of
" Flowres of Sion."*] ¹⁰ O. Bless ¹⁴ NO. And all the Stars

[ix]
[For the Natiuitie of our Lord.]

O Than the fairest Day, thrice fairer Night !
  Night to best Dayes in which a Sunne doth rise,
Of which that golden Eye, which cleares the Skies,
Is but a sparkling Ray, a Shadow light :
5 And blessed yee (in sillie Pastors sight)
Milde Creatures, in whose warme Cribe now lyes
That Heauen-sent Yongling, holie-Maide-borne Wight,
Midst, end, beginning of our Prophesies :
Blest Cotage that hath Flowres in Winter spred,
10 Though withered blessed Grasse, that hath the grace
To decke, and bee a Carpet to that Place.
  Thus sang, vnto the Soundes of oaten Reed,
    Before the Babe, the Sheepheards bow'd on knees,
    And Springs ranne Nectar, Honey dropt from Trees.

[x]
[Amazement at the Incarnation of God.]

TO spread the azure Canopie of Heauen,
  And make it twinkle with those spangs of Gold,
To stay this weightie masse of Earth so euen,
That it should all, and nought should it vp-hold ;
5 To giue strange motions to the Planets seuen,
Or Ioue to make so meeke, or Mars so bold,
To temper what is moist, drie, hote, and cold,
Of all their Iarres that sweete accords are giuen :
LORD, to thy Wisedome nought is, nor thy Might ;
10 But that thou shouldst (thy Glorie laid aside)
Come meanelie in mortalitie to bide,
And die for those deseru'd eternall plight,
  A wonder is so farre aboue our wit,
  That Angels stand amaz'd to muse on it.

IX. ³ N. the golden ¹² NO. Thus singing to the ¹³ NO. their
knees
   X. This sonnet is wanting here in O.
    ³ IN. To stay the pondrous globe   ⁹ IN. to thy Wisdome's
nought, nought to thy Might ¹² *In the Errata of the second issue of* J,
eternallie *is corrected to* eternall.

[xi]
[For the Baptiste.]

THe last and greatest Herauld of Heauens King,
   Girt with rough Skinnes, hyes to the Desarts wilde,
Among that sauage brood the Woods foorth bring,
Which hee than Man more harmlesse found and milde :
5 His food was Blossomes, and what yong doth spring,
With Honey that from virgine Hiues distil'd ;
Parcht Bodie, hollow Eyes, some vncouth thing
Made him appeare, long since from Earth exilde.
There burst hee foorth ; All yee, whose Hopes relye
10 On GOD, with mee amidst these Desarts mourne,
Repent, repent, and from olde errours turne.
Who listned to his voyce, obey'd his crye ?
   Onelie the Ecchoes which hee made relent,
   Rung from their Marble Caues, repent, repent.

[xii]
[For the Magdalene.]

THese Eyes (deare Lord) once Brandons of Desire,
   Fraile Scoutes betraying what they had to keepe,
Which their owne heart, then others set on fire,
Their traitrous blacke before thee heere out-weepe :
5 These Lockes, of blushing deedes the faire attire,
Smooth-frizled Waues, sad Shelfes which shadow deepe,
Soule-stinging Serpents in gilt curles which creepe,
To touch thy sacred Feete doe now aspire.
In Seas of Care behold a sinking Barke,
10 By windes of sharpe Remorse vnto thee driuen,
O let mee not expos'd be Ruines marke,
My faults confest (LORD) say they are forgiuen.
   Thus sigh'd to IESVS the Bethanian faire,
   His teare-wet Feete still drying with her Haire.

XI. ⁴ NO. Which he more harmlesse found than man ⁵ INO. His
food was Locusts, and what there doth spring ¹⁴ INO. flintie Caues
   XII. ¹ NO. Tapers of Desire ³ *In the Errata of the second issue of*
J, than *is corrected to* then. ⁵ INO. the gilt attire ⁶ INO. Waues
curling, wrackfull shelfes to shadow deepe ⁷ INO. Rings wedding
Soules to Sinnes lethargicke sleepe ¹¹ NO. O let me not be Ruines
aym'd-at marke

[xiii]
[For the Prodigall.]

I Countries chang'd, new pleasures out to finde,
But *Ah !* for pleasure new I found new paine,
Enchanting pleasure so did Reason blind,
That Fathers loue, and wordes I scorn'd as vaine :
5 For Tables rich, for bed, for frequent traine
Of carefull seruants to obserue my Minde,
These Heardes I keepe my fellowes are assign'd,
My Bed a Rocke is, Hearbes my Life sustaine.
Now while I famine feele, feare worser harmes,
10 Father and Lord I turne, thy Loue (yet great)
My faults will pardon, pitty mine estate.
This, where an aged Oake had spread its Armes,
Thought the lost Child, while as the Heardes hee led,
Not farre off on the ackornes wilde them fed.

[xiv]
[For the Passion.]

IF that the World doth in a maze remaine,
To heare in what a sad deploring mood,
The Pelican powres from her brest her Blood,
To bring to life her younglinges backe again ?
5 How should wee wonder of that soueraigne Good,
Who from that Serpents sting (that had vs slaine)
To saue our liues, shed his Lifes purple flood,
And turn'd in endlesse Ioy our endlesse Paine ?
Vngratefull Soule, that charm'd with false Delight,
10 Hast long long wandr'd in Sinnes flowrie Path,
And didst not thinke at all, or thoughtst not right
On this thy Pelicanes great Loue and Death,
Heere pause, and let (though Earth it scorne) Heauen see
Thee powre forth teares to him powr'd Blood for thee.

XIII. [1] NO. I changed Countries new delights to find [2] NO. I
did find   [5] INO. following traine [*In the Edinburgh University copy of*
I, comelie Traine *is pasted over the original reading on a printed slip, as
described.*]   [8] I. Rocke is my Bed, and Herbes NO. My Bed's a Rock,
and Herbs   [14] NO. And pin'd with hunger on wild Acorns fed
XIV. [1] INO. in amaze   [5] NO. at that   [8] NO. turn'd to

[i]

[An Hymne of the Passion.]

IF, *when farre in the East yee doe behold*
Foorth from his Christall Bed the Sunne to rise,
With rosie Robes and Crowne of flaming Gold ?
If gazing on that Empresse of the Skies,
5   *That takes so many Formes, and those faire Brands,*
Which blaze in Heauens high Vault, Nights watchfull
eyes ?
If Seeing how the Seas tumultuous Bands
Of bellowing Billowes haue their course confin'd,
How vnsustain'd the Earth still steadfast stands :
10 *Poore mortall Wights, yee e're found in your Minde*
A thought, that some great King did sit aboue,
Who had such Lawes and Rites to them assign'd ;
A King who fix'd the Poles made Spheares to moue,
All Wisedome, purenesse, Excellence, and Might,
15   *All Goodnesse, Greatnesse, Iustice, Beauty, Loue ?*
With feare and wonder hither turne your Sight,
See, see (alas) Him now, not in that State
Thought could fore-cast Him into Reasons light.
Now Eyes with teares, now Hearts with griefe make great,
20   *Bemoane this cruell Death and dreary case,*
If euer plaints iust Woe could aggrauate ?
From Sinne and Hell to saue vs, humaine Race,
See this great King naill'd to an abiect Tree,
An obiect of reproach and sad disgrace.
25 *O vnheard Pitty, Loue in strange degree !*
Hee his owne Life doth giue, his Blood doth shed,
For Wormelings base such Excellence to see.
Poore Wightes, behold His Visage pale as Lead,
His Head bow'd to His Brest, Lockes sadlie rent,
30   *Like a cropt Rose that languishing doth fade.*

I. ¹ NO. *If in the East when you do there behold* ¹⁰ NO. *you e're*
¹⁴ INO. *Excellency, Might* ²⁰ NO. *and ruthfull case* ²⁷ NO. *such*
Worthinesse

Weake Nature weepe, astonish'd World lament,
   Lament, yee Windes, you Heauen that all containes,
   And thou (my Soule) let nought thy Griefe relent.
Those Hands, those sacred Hands which hold the raines
35   *Of this great All, and kept from mutuall warres*
   The Elements, beare rent for thee their Veines :
Those feete which once must trade on golden Starres,
   For thee with nailes would bee pierc'd through and torne,
   For thee Heauens King from Heauen himselfe debarres.
40 *This great heart-quaking Dolour waile and mourne,*
   Yee that long since Him saw by might of Faith,
   Yee now that are, and yee yet to bee borne.
Not to behold his great Creators Death,
   The Sunne from sinfull eyes hath vail'd his light,
45   *And faintly iourneyes vp Heauens saphire Path.*
And, cutting from her Browes her Tresses bright,
   The Moone doth keepe her Lords sad Obsequies,
   Impearling with her Teares this Robe of Night.
All staggering and lazie lowre the Skies,
50   *The Earth and elemental Stages quake,*
   The long since dead from bursted Graues arise.
And can things wanting sense yet sorrow take,
   And beare a Part with him who all them wrought ?
   And Man (though borne with cries) shall pitty lacke ?
55 *Thinke what had beene your state, had hee not brought*
   To these sharpe Pangs himselfe, and priz'd so hie
   Your Soules, that with his Life them life Hee bought.
What Woes doe you attend, if still yee lie
   Plung'd in your wonted ordures, wretched Brood,
60   *Shall for your sake againe GOD euer die ?*
O leaue deluding shewes, embrace true good,
   Hee on you calles, forgoe Sinnes shamefull trade,
   With Prayers now seeke Heauen, and not with Blood.
Let not the Lambes more from their Dames bee had,
65   *Nor Altars blush for Sinne ; liue euery thing,*
   That long time long'd-for sacrifice is made.

32 NO. *you Winds*   33 NO. *Griefes*   37 O. tread   48 NO. *her Robe*

All that is from you crau'd by this great King
*   Is to beleeue, a pure Heart Incense is,*
*   What gift (alas) can wee him meaner bring ?*
70 *Haste sinne-sicke Soules, this season doe not misse,*
*   Now while remorselesse time doth grant you space,*
*   And GOD inuites you to your only Blisse.*
Hee who you calles will not denie you Grace,
*   But low-deepe burie faults, so yee repent,*
75 *   His armes (loe) stretched are you to embrace.*
When Dayes are done, and Lifes small sparke is spent,
*   So yee accept what freely here is giuen,*
*   Like brood of Angels, deathlesse, all-content,*
Yee shall for euer liue with him in Heauen.

[xv]
[To the Angels for the Passion.]

COme forth, come forth yee blest triumphing Bands,
Faire Citizens of that immortall Towne,
Come see that King which all this All commands,
Now (ouercharg'd with Loue) die for his owne ;
5 Looke on those Nailes which pierce his Feete and Hands,
What a sharpe Diademe his Browes doth crowne ?
Behold his pallid Face, his Eyes which sowne,
And what a Throng of Theeues him mocking stands.
Come forth yee empyrean Troupes, come forth,
10 Preserue this sacred Blood that Earth adornes,
Those liquid Roses gather off his Thornes,
O ! to bee lost they bee of too much worth :

For streams, Iuice, Balm they are, which quĕch,
kils, charms
Of GOD, Death, Hel, the wrath, the life, the harmes.

70 *In the copy of* I *containing the signature of the Earl of Lauderdale,*
a redundant " doe " before " doe " is erased in ink. 74 *In the copy of* I
containing the signature of the Earl of Lauderdale, " burie " is pasted in
on a printed slip between " low-deepe " and " faults." 77 NO. *So you*
XV. 7 NO. *his heavy frown* 11 INO. *Gather those liquid Roses*

[ii]
[Faith aboue Reason.]

SOule, which to Hell wast thrall,
Hee, Hee for thine offence,
Did suffer Death, who could not die at all.
O soueraigne Excellence,
5 O Life of all that liues,
Eternall Bounty which each good thing giues,
How could Death mount so hie ?
No wit this hight can reach,
Faith only doth vs teach,
10 For vs Hee died, at all who could not dye.

[xvi]
[Vpon the Sepulcher of our Lord.]

LIfe to giue life depriued is of *Life*,
And Death displai'd hath ensigne against *Death* ;
So violent the Rigour was of *Death*,
That nought could daunt it but the Life of *Life* :
5 No Power had Pow'r to thrall Lifes pow'r to *Death*,
But willingly Life hath abandon'd *Life*,
Loue gaue the wound which wrought this work of *Death*,
His Bow and Shafts were of the Tree of *Life*.
Now quakes the Author of eternall *Death*,
10 To finde that they whom earst he reft of *Life*
Shall fill his Roome aboue the listes of *Death* :
Now all reioyce in Death who hope for *Life*.
Dead IESVS lies, who Death hath kill'd by *Death*,
His Tombe no Tombe is, but new Source of *Life*.

II. ¹ NO. *Soule, whom Hell did once inthrall* ⁸ INO. *this Point*
¹⁰ NO. *He died for us*
XVI. ² *In the Edinburgh University copy of* I, *and in that containing
the signature of the Earl of Lauderdale,* displayeth *is pasted in on a
printed slip, as described, between* Death *and* Ensigne ⁵ INO. Pow'rs
to *Death* ⁶ INO. Life down hath layd *Life* [O. his *Life*] [*In the
Edinburgh University copy of* I, hath abandon'd Life *is pasted in on
a printed slip over the original reading.*] ¹⁰ NO. late he reft ¹⁴ INO.
No Tombe his Tombe is

[ii]

[An Hymne of the Resurrection.]

R Ise from those fragrant Climes thee now embrace,
  Vnto this world of ours O haste thy Race,
Faire Sunne, and though contrary-wayes all yeare
Thou hold thy course, now with the highest Spheare
5 Ioyne thy swift Wheeles, to hasten time that lowres,
And lazie Minutes turne in perfect Houres ;
The Night and Death too long a league haue made,
To stow the world in Horrors vgly shade.
Shake from thy Lockes a Day with saffron Rayes
10 So faire, that it out shine all other dayes ;
And yet doe not presume (great Eye of light)
To be that which this Day shall make so bright :
See, an eternall Sunne hastes to arise,
Not from the Easterne blushing Seas or Skies,
15 Or any stranger Worlds Heauens Concaues haue,
But from the Darknesse of an hollow Graue :
And this is that all-powerfull Sunne aboue,
That crownd thy Browes with Rayes, first made thee moue.
Lights Trumpetters, yee neede not from your Bowres
20 Proclaime this Day, this the angelike Powres
Haue done for you ; But now an opall hew
Bepaintes Heauens Christall, to the longing view
Earths late hid Colours glance, Light doth adorne
The World, and (weeping Ioy) foorth comes the Morne ;
25 And with her, as from a Lethargicke Transe
Breath (com'd againe) that Bodie doth aduance,
Which two sad Nights in rocke lay coffin'd dead,
And with an iron Guard inuironed,
Life out of Death, Light out of Darknesse springs,
30 From a base Iaile foorth comes the King of kings ;
What late was mortall, thrall'd to euery woe,
That lackeyes life, or vpon sence doth grow,

II. ⁴ O misprints Share for Spheare   ⁵ INO. thy blew Wheeles
⁶ NO. turn to   ¹² INO. must make   ²⁶ NO. The breath returned [O
also has the misprint Bodies for Body]

Immoi tall is, of an eternall Stampe,
Farre brighter beaming than the morning Lampe.
35 So from a blacke Ecclipse out-peeres the Sunne :
Such [when a huge of Dayes haue on her runne,
In a farre forest in the pearly East,
And shee her selfe hath burnt and spicie Nest]
The lonlie Bird with youthfull Pennes and Combe,
40 Doth soare from out her Cradle and her Tombe :
So a Small seede that in the Earth lies hidde
And dies, reuiuing burstes her cloddie Side,
Adorn'd with yellow Lockes, of new is borne,
And doth become a Mother great with Corne ;
45 Of Graines brings hundreths with it, which when old
Enrich the Furrowes with a Sea of Gold.
  Haile holy Victor, greatest Victor haile,
That Hell dost ransacke, against Death preuaile,
O how thou long'd for comes ! with Iubeling cries,
50 The all-triumphing Palladines of Skies
Salute thy rising ; Earth would Ioyes no more
Beare, if thou rising didst them not restore :
A silly Tombe should not his flesh enclose,
Who did Heauens trembling Tarasses dispose ;
55 No Monument should such a Iewell hold,
No Rocke, though Rubye, Diamond, and Gold.
Thou onely pittie didst vs, humane Race,
Bestowing on vs of thy free giuen Grace
More than wee forfaited and loosed first,
60 In Edens Rebell when wee were accurst.
Then Earth our portion was, Earths Ioyes but giuen,
Earth and Earths Blisse thou hast exchang'd with Heauen.
O what a hight of good vpon us streames
From the great splendor of thy Bounties Beames !
65 When wee deseru'd shame, horrour, flames of wrath,
Thou bled our wounds, and suffer didst our Death ;

36 NO. [when her course of Daies   45 I. hundredths   NO. hundreds
46 NO. which do float with gold   49 NO. com'st with joyfull cries   57 NO.
Thou didst lament and pitty humane Race   60 NO. Rebells   62 O. Bless
66 NO. bledst

But *Fathers Iustice pleas'd, Hell, Death o'rcome,*
In triumph now thou risest from thy Tombe,
With Glories which past Sorrowes contervaile,
70 *Haile holy Victor, greatest Victor haile*
    Hence humble sense, and hence yee Guides of sense,
Wee now reach Heauen, your weake intelligence
And searching Pow'rs, were in a flash made dim,
To learne from all eternitie, that him
75 *The Father bred, then that hee heere did come*
(His Bearers Parent) in a Virgins Wombe;
But then when sold, betray'd, scourg'd, crown'd with Thorne,
Naill'd to a Tree, all breathlesse, bloodlesse, torne,
Entomb'd, him rising from a Graue to finde,
80 *Confounds your Cunning, turnes like Moles you blinde.*
Death, thou that heretofore still barren wast,
Nay, didst each other Birth eate vp and waste,
Imperious, hatefull, pittilesse, vniust,
Vnpartiall Equaller of all with dust,
85 *Sterne Executioner of heauenly doome,*
Made fruitfull, now Lifes Mother art become,
A sweete releife of cares, the Soule molest,
An Harbinger to Glory, Peace and Rest,
Put off thy mourning Weedes, yeeld all thy Gall
90 *To daylie sinning Life, proud of thy fall,*
Assemble thy Captiues; bid all hast to rise,
And euerie Corse in Earth-quakes where it lies,
Sound from each flowrie Graue, and rockie Iaile,
Haile holy Victor, greatest Victor haile.
95   *The World, that wanning late and faint did lie,*
Applauding to our ioyes thy Victorie,
To a yong Prime essayes to turne againe,
And as ere soyl'd with Sinne yet to remaine,
Her chilling Agues shee beginnes to misse,

⁷⁷ INO. *crown'd, scourg'd* [*In the Edinburgh University and Haigh Hall copies of* I, *as well as in that containing the signature of the Earl of Lauderdale,* " *Scourg'd, crown'd with Thorne,*" *is pasted in on a printed slip, over the original reading.*] ⁷⁹ INO. *risen* ⁸⁴ O. Impartial ⁹¹ NO. *Assemble all thy Captives, haste to rise*

100 *All Blisse returning with the* Lord *of Blisse.*
With greater light Heauens Temples opened shine,
Mornes smiling rise, Euens blushing doe decline,
Cloudes dappled glister, boisterous Windes are calme,
Soft Zephires doe the Fields with sighes embalme,
105 *In ammell blew the Sea hath husht his Roares,*
And with enamour'd Curles doth kisse the Shoares.
All-bearing Earth, like a new-married Queene,
Her Beauties hightenes, in a Gowne of Greene
Perfumes the Aire, Her Meades are wrought with Flowres,
110 *In colours various, figures, smelling, powres ;*
Trees wanton in the Groues with leauie Lockes,
Her Hilles empampred stand, the Vales, the Rockes
Ring Peales of ioy, her Floods her christall Brookes
(The Meadowes tongues) with many maz-like Crookes,
115 *And whispering murmures, sound vnto the Maine,*
That Worlds pure Age returned is againe.
The honny People leaue their golden Bowres,
And innocently pray on budding Flowres ;
In gloomy Shades, pearcht on the tender Sprayes,
120 *The painted Singers fill the Aire with Layes :*
Seas, Floods, Earth, Aire, all diuerslie doe sound,
Yet all their diuerse Notes haue but one ground,
Re-ecchoed here downe from Heauens azure Vaile,
Haile holy Victor, greatest Victor haile.
125 *O Day! on which Deathes Adamantine Chaine*
The Lord *did breake, ransacking* Satans *Raigne,*
And in triumphing Pompe his Trophees rear'd,
Bee thou blest euer, hence-foorth still endear'd
With Name of his owne Day ; the Law to Grace,

---

100 O. Bless **102** O *misprints* Morn's *and* Even's *for* Morns *and* Evens **105** NO. *In silent calmes the Sea hath husht her* **112** NO. *enamell'd stand* **113** INO. *Floods, and pratling Brookes* [*In the Edinburgh University copy of* I, " *her christall Brookes* " *is pasted in after* " *Floods* " *on a printed slip, over the original reading.*] **114** INO. (*Starres liquid Mirrors*) *with serpenting Crookes* [*In the Edinburgh University copy of* I, " (*The Meadowes Tongues*) *with many Maze-like Crookes,*" *is pasted in on a printed slip, as described.*] **116** NO. *The Golden Age* **122** INO. *hath but* **126** NO. *did ransack*

130 *Types to their Substance yeelde, to Thee giue place*
The olde New-Moones, with all festiuall Dayes,
And what aboue the rest deserueth praise
The reuerent Saboth *; what could else they bee,*
Than golden Heraulds, telling what by thee
135 *Wee should enjoy ? Shades past, now shine thou cleare,*
And hence-foorth bee thou Empresse of the Yeare ;
This Glorie of thy 'Sisters sex to winne,
From worke on thee, as other Dayes from sinne,
That Man-kind shall forbeare, in euerie place
140 *The Prince of Planets warmeth in his race ;*
And farre beyond his Pathes in frozen Climes :
And may thou bee so blest to out-date Times,
That when Heauens Quire shall blaze in accents lowd,
The manie mercies of their soueraigne Good,
145 *How hee on thee did sinne, Death, Hell destroy,*
It may bee aye the Antheme of their Ioy.

[iii]

[An Hymne of the Ascension.]

BRight *Portalles of the Skie,*
Emboss'd with sparkling Starres,
Doores of Eternitie,
With diamantine barres,
5 *Your Arras rich vp-hold,*
Loose all your bolts and Springs,
Ope wyde your Leaues of gold ;
That in your Roofes may come the King of kings.
Scarff'd in a rosie Cloud,
10 *Hee doth ascend the Aire,*
Straight doth the Moone him shrowd
With her resplendant Haire ;
The next enchristall'd Light

146 INO. *It may bee aye* [NO. *still*] *the Burthen*
III. This piece first appeared in J, and is wanting in N.

Submits to him its Beames,
15   And hee doth trace the hight
    Of that faire Lamp which flames of beautie streames.
   Hee towers those golden Bounds
    Hee did to Sunne bequeath,
    The higher wandring Rounds
20   Are found his Feete beneath ;
    The milkie-way comes neare,
    Heauens Axell seemes to bend,
    Aboue each turning Spheare
    That roab'd in Glorie Heauens King may ascend.
25 O Well-spring of this All,
    Thy Fathers Image viue,
    Word, that from nought did call
    What is, doth reason, liue ;
    The Soules eternall Foode,
30   Earths Ioy, Delight of Heauen ;
    All Truth, Loue, Beautie, Good,
    To Thee, to Thee bee praises euer giuen.
   What was dismarshall'd late
    In this thy noble Frame,
35   And lost the prime estate,
    Hath re-obtain'd the same,
    Is now most perfect seene ;
    Streames which diuerted were
    (And troubled strayed vncleene)
40   From their first Source, by Thee home turned are.
   By Thee that blemish old,
    Of Edens leprous Prince,
    Which on his Race tooke hold,
    And him exyl'd from thence,
45   Now put away is farre ;
    With Sword, in irefull guise,
    No Cherub more shall barre
    Poore man the Entries into Paradise.
   By Thee those Spirits pure,
50   First Children of the Light,

Now *fixed stand and sure,*
In their eternall Right ;
Now humane Companies
Renew their ruin'd Wall,
55 *Fall'n man as thou makst rise,*
Thou giu'st to Angels that they shall not fall.
By Thee that Prince of Sinne,
That doth with mischiefe swell,
Hath lost what hee did winne,
60 *And shall endungeon'd dwell ;*
His spoyles are made thy pray,
His Phanes are sackt and torne,
His Altars raz'd away,
And what ador'd was late, now lyes a Scorne.
65 *These Mansions pure and cleare,*
Which are not made by hands,
Which once by him joy'd were,
And his (then not stain'd) Bands
(Now forefait'd, dispossest,
70 *And head-long from them throwne)*
Shall Adams Heires make blest,
By Thee their great Redeemer made their owne.
O Well-spring of this All,
Thy Fathers Image viue,
75 *Word, that from nought did call,*
What is, doth Reason, liue ;
Whose worke is, but to will,
Gods coeternall Sonne,
Great Banisher of ill,
80 *By none but Thee could these great Deedes bee done.*
Now each etheriall Gate,
To him hath opened bin ;
And glories King in state,
His Pallace enters in ;
85 *Now com'd is this high Prest,*
In the most holie Place,

Not without Blood addrest,
With Glorie Heauen the Earth to crowne with Grace.
Starres which all Eyes were late,
90   And did with wonder burne,
His Name to celebrate,
In flaming Tongues them turne ;
Their orbye Christales moue
More actiue than before,
95   And entheate from aboue,
Their Soueraigne Prince laude, glorifie, adore.
The Quires of happie Soules,
Wakt with that Musicke sweete,
Whose Descant Care controules,
100   Their Lord in Triumph meete ;
The spotlesse Sprightes of light,
His Trophees doe extole,
And archt in Squadrons bright,
Greet their great victor in his Capitole.
105 O Glorie of the Heauen,
O sole Delight of Earth,
To Thee all power bee giuen,
Gods vncreated Birth ;
Of Man-kind louer true,
110   Indeerer of his wrong,
Who dost the world renew,
Still bee thou our Saluation and our Song.
From Top of Oliuet such notes did rise,
When mans Redeemer did transcend the Skies.

110 O. Endurer

[xvii]

[Mans Knowledge, Ignorance in the Misteries of God.]

BEneath a sable vaile, and Shadowes deepe,
Of Vnaccessible and dimming light,
In Silence ebane Clouds more blacke than Night,
The *Worlds great King* his secrets hidde doth keepe :
5 Through those Thicke Mistes when any Mortall Wight
Aspires, with halting pace, and Eyes that weepe,
To pore, and in his Misteries to creepe,
With Thunders hee and Lightnings blastes their Sight.
O Sunne invisible, that dost abide
10 Within thy bright abysmes, most faire, most darke,
Where with thy proper Rayes thou dost thee hide ;
O euer-shining, neuer full seene marke,
    To guide mee in Lifes Night, thy light mee show,
    The more I search of thee, The lesse I know.

XVII. ⁴ INO. great Minde [*In the Edinburgh University copy of* I,
King *is pasted in on a printed slip between* great *and* his]   ⁷ INO. To
prye

[xviii]

[Contemplation of Inuisible Excellencies aboue, by the Visible below.]

IF with such passing Beautie, choise Delights,
  The Architect of this great Round did frame
This Pallace visible (short listes of Fame,
And sillie Mansion but of dying Wights)
5 How many Wonders, what amazing Lights
Must that triumphing Seat of Glorie clame,
That doth transcend all this great Alls vaste hights,
Of whose bright Sunne ours heere is but a Beame ?
O blest abod ! O happie dwelling-place !
10 Where visiblie th' Invisible doth raigne,
Blest People which doe see true Beauties Face,
With whose farre Dawnings scarce he Earth doth daigne :
  All Ioy is but Annoy, all Concord Strife,
  Match'd with your endlesse Blisse and happie life.

[iii]

[The Difference betweene Earthlie and Heauenlie Loue.]

L *Oue which is heere a Care,*
  That Wit and Will doth marre,
Vncertaine Truce, and a most certaine Warre ;
A shrill tempestuous Winde,
5 *Which doth disturbe the minde,*
And like wilde Waues our designes all commoue :
Among those Powres aboue,
Which see their Makers Face,
It a contentment is, a quiet Peace,
10 *A Pleasure voide of Griefe, a constant Rest,*
Eternall Ioy, which nothing can molest.

XVIII. 7 all this Alls vaste [O. vastest] hights 12 INO. farre
Shadowes [*In the Edinburgh University copy of* I, dawnings *is pasted
in on a printed slip between* farre *and* scarce]
III. 6 NO. *all our designes*

[xix]

[Earth and all on it Changeable.]

T^Hat space, where raging Waues doe now diuide
　 From the great Continent our happie Isle,
Was some-time Land, and where tall Shippes doe glide,
Once with deare Arte the crooked Plough did tyle :
5 Once those faire Bounds stretcht out so farre and wide,
Where Townes, no, Shires enwall'd, endeare each mile,
Were all ignoble Sea, and marish vile
Where *Proteus* Flockes danc'd measures to the Tyde.
So Age transforming all still forward runnes,
10 No wonder though the Earth doth change her face,
New Manners, Pleasures new, turne with new Sunnes,
Lockes now like Gold grow to an hoarie grace ;
　　 Nay, Mindes rare shape doth change, that lyes despis'd
　　 Which was so deare of late and highlie pris'd.

[iv]

[The World a Game.]

T^*His world a Hunting is,*
　 The Pray poore Man, the Nimrod *fierce is Death,*
His speedie Grei-hounds are,
Lust, sicknesse, Enuie, Care,
5 *Strife that neere falles amisse,*
With all those ills which haunt vs while wee breath.
Now, if (by chance) wee flie
Of these the eager Chase,
Old Age with stealing Pace,
10 *Castes vp his Nets, and there wee panting die.*

　　 XIX. [1] NO. curled Waves　 [3] INO. and now where Shippes doe
glide　 [4] INO. Once with laborious Art the Plough did tyle　 [8] J *has
the misprint* thee *before* Tyde.
　　 IV. [10] O. *Casts on*

[xx]

[The Court of True Honour.]

WHy (worldlings) do ye trust fraile honours dreams ?
 And leane to guilted Glories which decay ?
Why doe yee toyle to registrate your Names
On ycie Pillars, which soone melt away ?
5 True Honour is not heere, that place it clames,
Where blacke-brow'd Night doth not exile the Day,
Nor no farre-shining Lamp diues in the Sea,
But an eternall Sunne spreades lasting Beames :
There it attendeth you, where spotlesse Bands
10 Of Spirits, stand gazing on their Soueraigne Blisse,
Where yeeres not hold it in their canckring hands,
But who once noble, euer noble is.
  Looke home, lest hee your weakned Wit make thrall,
  Who *Edens* foolish Gardner earst made fall.

[xxi]

[Against Hypocrisie.]

AS are those Apples, pleasant to the Eye,
 But full of Smoke within, which vse to grow
Neere that strange Lake, where God powr'd from the Skie
Huge showres of Flames, worse flames to ouer-throw :
5 Such are their workes that with a glaring Show
Of humble Holinesse, in Vertues dye,
Would colour Mischiefe, while within they glow
With coales of Sinne, though none the Smoake descrie.
Ill is that Angell which earst fell from Heauen,
10 But not more ill than hee, nor in worse case,
Who hides a traitrous Minde with smiling face,
And with a Doues white feathers maskes a Rauen :
  Each Sinne some colour hath it to adorne,
  Hypocrisie All-mighty GOD doth scorne.

XX. [10] O. Bless
XXI. [9] NO. Bad is that Angell that [10] NO. But not so bad as
he [12] NO. cloaths a Raven

[v]

[Change should breede Change.]

NEw doth the Sunne appeare,
The Mountaines Snowes decay,
Crown'd with fraile Flowres foorth comes the Babye yeare.
My Soule, Time postes away,
5 And thou yet in that Frost
Which Flowre and fruit hath lost,
As if all heere immortall were, dost stay :
For shame thy Powers awake,
Looke to that Heauen which neuer Night makes blacke,
10 And there, at that immortall Sunnes bright Rayes,
Decke thee with Flowers which feare not rage of Dayes.

[xxii]

[The Praise of a Solitarie Life.]

THrice happie hee, who by some shadie Groue,
Farre from the clamorous World, doth liue his owne,
Though solitarie, who is not alone,
But doth conuerse with that Eternall Loue :
5 O ! how more sweete is Birds harmonious Moane,
Or the hoarse Sobbings of the widow'd Doue ;
Than those smooth whisperings neere a Princes Throne,
Which Good make doubtfull, doe the euill approue ?
O ! how more sweet is Zephires wholesome Breath,
10 And Sighes embalm'd, which new-borne Flowrs vnfold,
Than that applause vaine Honour doth bequeath ?
How sweete are Streames to poison drunke in Gold ?
The World is full of Horrours, Troubles, Slights,
Woods harmelesse Shades haue only true Delightes.

V. ² O. Snow ³ NO. *the Infant yeare* ⁷ O. doth
XXII. ¹² N. dranke in Gold

[xxiii]
[To a Nightingale.]

SWeet Bird, that sing'st away the early Howres,
Of Winters past or comming void of Care,
Well pleased with Delights which Present are,
Faire Seasones, budding Sprayes, sweet-smelling Flowers :
5 To Rocks, to Springs, to Rils, from leauy Bowres
Thou thy Creators Goodnesse dost declare,
And what deare Gifts on thee hee did not spare,
A Staine to humane sence in sinne that lowres.
What Soule can be so sicke, which by thy Songs
10 (Attir'd in sweetnesse) sweetly is not driuen
Quite to forget Earths turmoiles, spights, and wrongs,
And lift a reuerend Eye and Thought to Heauen ?
    Sweet Artlesse Songstarre, thou my Minde dost raise
    To Ayres of Spheares, yes, and to Angels Layes.

[xxiv]
[Content and Resolute.]

AS when it hapneth that some louely Towne
Vnto a barbarous Besieger falles,
Who there by Sword and Flame himselfe enstalles,
And (Cruell) it in Teares and Blood doth drowne ;
5 Her Beauty spoyl'd, her Citizens made Thralles,
His spight yet so cannot her all throw downe,
But that some Statue, Arch, Phan of renowne,
Yet lurkes vnmaym'd within her weeping walles :
So after all the Spoile, Disgrace, and Wrake,
10 That Time, the World, and Death could bring combind,
Amidst that Masse of Ruines they did make,
Safe and all scarre-lesse yet remaines my Minde :
    From this so high transcending Rapture springes,
    That I, all else defac'd, not enuie Kinges.

XXIII. [13] NO. Songster
XXIV. [3] NO. Who both by Sword and Flame [O. Flames] [4] INO.
And (shamelesse) [6] INO. yet can not so her [7] NO. Statue, Pillar of
renown

[xxv]

[Deathes Last-Will.]

MOre oft than once, Death whisper'd in mine Eare,
Graue what thou heares in Diamond and Gold,
I am that Monarch whom all Monarches feare,
Who hath in Dust their farre-stretch'd Pride vproll'd.
5 All all is mine beneath Moones siluer Spheare,
And nought, saue Vertue, Can my power with-hold :
This (not belieu'd) Experience true Thee told,
By Danger late when I to Thee came neare.
As Bugbeare then my Visage I did show,
10 That of my Horrours thou right Vse mightst make,
And a more sacred Path of liuing take :
Now still walke armed for my ruthlesse Blow,
    Trust flattering Life no more, Redeeme Time past,
    And Liue each Day as if it were thy Last.

[xxvi]

[The Blessednesse of Faithfull Soules by Death.]

LEt vs each day enure our selues to dye,
If this (and not our Feares) be truely Death ;
Aboue the Circles both of Hope and Faith
With faire immortall pinniones to flie ?
5 If this be Death our best Part to vntie
(By ruining the Iaile) from Lust and Wrath,
And euery drowsie languor heere beneath,
It turning deniz'd Citizen of Skie ?
To haue, more knowledge than all Bookes containe,
10 All Pleasures euen surmounting wishing Powre,
The fellowship of Gods immortall Traine,
And these that Time nor force shall er'e deuoure ?
    If this be Death ? what Ioy, what golden care
    Of Life, can with Deaths ouglinesse compare ?

XXV. This sonnet first appeared in J, and is wanting in N.
4 O. have
XXVI. 8 NO. To be made deniz'd Citizen

[iv]

[An Hymne of True Happinesse.]

A Midst the azure cleare
   Of Iordans *sacred Streames,*
  Iordan *of* Libanon *the of-spring deare ;*
  When Zephires Flowers vnclose,
5   *And Sunne shines with new Beames,*
  With graue and stately Grace a Nimphe arose.
Vpon her Head she ware
   Of Amaranthes a Crowne,
  Her left hand Palmes, her right a Brandon bare,
10 *Vnvail'd Skinnes whitenesse lay,*
   Gold haires in Curles hang downe,
  Eyes sparkled Ioy, more bright than Starre of Day.
The Flood a Throne her rear'd
   Of Waues, most like that Heauen
15 *Where beaming Starres in Glorie turne ensphear'd ;*
  The Aire stood calme and cleare,
   No Sigh by Windes was giuen,
  Birdes left to sing, Heards feed, her voyce to heare.
World-wandring sorrie Wights,
20 *Whom nothing can content*
  Within those varying listes of Dayes and Nights,
   Whose life (*ere knowne amisse*)
  In glittering Griefes is spent,
  Come learne (*said shee*) *what is your choisest Blisse.*
25 *From Toyle and pressing Cares*
   How yee may respit finde,
  A Sanctuarie from Soule-thralling Snares,
   A Port to harboure sure
  In spight of waues and winde,
30 *Which shall when Times Houre-glasse is runne endure.*
Not happie is that Life
  Which yee as happie hold,

IV. ⁷ O. *wore* ⁹ NO. *her right a Torch did beare* ²¹ INO. *these*
³⁰ NO. *Times swift Glass* ³² N. *Which you*

No, but a Sea of feares, a field of Strife,
  Charg'd on a Throne to sit
35 With Diadems of Gold,
  Preseru'd by Force, and still obseru'd by Wit :
Huge Treasures to enioy,
  Of all her Gemmes spoyle Inde,
  All Seres silke in Garments to imploy,
40 Deliciously to feed,
  The Phenix plumes to finde
To rest vpon, or decke your purple Bed.
  Fraile Beautie to abuse,
  And (wanton Sybarites)
45 On past or present touch of sense to muse ;
  Neuer to heare of Noise
  But what the Eare delites,
  Sweet musicks Charmes, or charming Flatterers voice.
Nor can it Blisse you bring,
50 Hidde Natures Depthes to know,
  Why Matter changeth, whence each Forme doth spring ;
  Nor that your Fame should range,
  And after-Worlds it blow
From Tänäis to Nile, from Nile to Gange.
55 All these haue not the Powre
  To free the Minde from feares,
  Nor hideous horror can allay one howre,
  When Death in steele doth glance,
  In Sicknesse lurke or yeares,
60 And wakes the Soule from out her mortall Trance.
No, but blest Life is this,
  With chaste and pure desire,
  To turne vnto the Load-starre of all Blisse,
  On GOD the Minde to rest,
65 Burnt vp with sacred Fire,
  Possessing him, to bee by him possest.
When to the baulmie East
  Sunne doth his light impart,

[42] J has the misprint "deckt" [58] NO. Death in stealth [50] NO. lurks

Or When hee diueth in the lowlie West,
70   *And rauisheth the Day,*
  With spotlesse Hands and Hart
  Him chearefully to praise and to him pray.
 To heed each action so,
  As euer in his sight,
75   *More fearing doing ill than passiue woe ;*
  Not to seeme other thing
  Than what yee are aright,
  Neuer to doe what may Repentance bring :
 Not to bee blowne with Pride,
80   *Nor mou'd at Glories breath,*
  Which Shadow-like on wings of Time doth glide ;
  So Malice to disarme,
  And conquere hastie Wrath,
  As to doe good to those that Worke your harme :
85 *To hatch no base Desires*
  Or Gold or Land to gaine,
  Well pleas'd with what by Vertue one acquires,
  To haue the Wit and Will
  Consorting in one Straine,
90   *Than what is good to haue no higher skill.*
 Neuer on Neighbours well,
  With Cocatrices Eye
  To looke, and make an others Heauen your Hell ;
  Not to be Beauties Thrall,
95   *All fruitlesse Loue to flie,*
  Yet louing still a Loue transcending all.
 A Loue which while it burnes
  The Soule with fairest Beames,
  In that vncreated Sunne the Soule it turnes,
100   *And makes such Beautie proue,*
  That (if Sense saw her Gleames ?)
  All lookers on would pine and die for loue.
 Who such a life doth liue,

---

[87] NO. *with that which Vertue faire acquires*   [91] NO. *Neighbours Goods*   [93] O. *nor make*   [99] O. To that increated

Yee happie euen may call,
105   *Ere ruthlesse Death a wished end him giue,*
And after then when giuen,
More happie by his fall,
For Humanes, Earth, enioying Angels, Heauen.
Swift is your mortall Race,
110   *And glassie is the Field,*
Vaste are Desires not limited by Grace ;
Life a weake Tapper is,
Then while it light doth yeeld
Leaue flying ioyes, embrace this lasting Blisse.
115 *This when the Nimph had said,*
Shee diu'd within the Flood,
Whose Face with smyling Curles long after staid.
Then Sighes did Zephyres presse,
Birdes sang from euery Wood,
120   *And Ecchoes rang, this was true Happinesse.*

[104] NO. You   [105] *In the Edinburgh University copy of* I, *" wished"
is pasted in on a printed slip between " a " and " end "*   [106-7] *In the
ordinary copies of* J, *these two lines are printed in reversed order. In the
Errata of the second issue of* J, *they appear in the correct order ; and in
the Edinburgh University copy of* J, *they are pasted in on a printed slip.*

AN HYMNE OF THE
FAIREST FAIRE.

[v]
[An Hymne of the Nature, Atributes,
and Workes of God.]

I Feele my Bosome glow with wontlesse Fires,
    Rais'd from the vulgar prease my Mind aspires
    (Wing'd with high Thoghts) vnto his praise to clime,
From deepe Eternitie who call'd foorth Time ;
5 That Essence which not mou'd makes each thing moue,
Vncreat'd Beautie all-creating Loue :
But by so great an object, radient light,
My Heart appall'd, enfeebled restes my Sight,
Thicke Cloudes benighte my labouring Ingine,
10 And at my high Attempts my Wits repine.
If thou in mee this sacred Rapture wrought,
My Knowledge sharpen, Sarcells lend my thought ;
Grant mee (Times Father, world-containing King)
A Pow'r, of Thee in pow'rfull Layes to sing,
15 That as thy Beautie in Earth liues, Heauen shines,
So it may dawne, or shadow in my Lines.
    As farre beyond the starrie walles of Heauen,
    As is the loftiest of the Planets seuen

V. ² NO. *presse* ⁶ O. Uncreate ¹¹ NO. *this sacred heat hast*
wrought ¹⁶ IN. *It dawning may or shadow* [*In the Edinburgh University*
copy of I, " *So it may dawne* " *is stuck in on a printed slip before* "*or* "]

37

Sequestred from this Earth, in purest light,
20 Out-shining ours, as ours doth sable Night,
Thou, All-sufficient, Omnipotent,
Thou euer-glorious, most excellent,
GOD various in Names, in Essence one,
High art enstalled on a golden Throne,
25 Out-reaching Heauens wide Vastes, the Bounds of nought,
Transcending all the Circles of our Thought :
With diamantine Scepter in thy Hand,
There thou giu'st Lawes, and dost this World command,
This world of Concords rais'd vnliklie-sweete,
30 Which like a Ball lyes prostrate to thy Feete.
     If so wee may well say (and what wee say,
Heere wrapt in flesh, led by dimme Reasons ray,
To show by earthlie Beauties which wee see
That spirituall Excellence that shines in Thee,
35 Good Lord forgiue) not farre from thy right Side,
With curled Lockes *Youth* euer doth abide ;
Rose-cheeked *Youth*, who garlanded with Flowres,
Still blooming, ceasleslie vnto thee powres
Immortall Nectar, in a Cuppe of Gold,
40 That by no darts of Ages Thou grow old,
And as ends and beginnings Thee not clame,
Successionlesse that Thou bee still the same.
     Neare to thy other side resistlesse *Might*,
From Head to Foote in burnisht Armour dight,
45 That ringes about him, with a wauing Brand,
And watchfull Eye, great Sentinell doth stand ;
That neither Time nor force in ought impaire
Thy workmanshippe, nor harme thine Empire faire,
Soone to giue Death to all againe that would
50 Sterne *Discord* raise which thou destroy'd of old ;
Discord that Foe to order, Nurse of Warre,
By which the noblest things dimolisht are :
But (Catife) Shee no Treason doth deuise,

[25] NO. *Out-stretching Heavens wide bespangled vault*   [30] NO. *prostrate at*   [44] O. armour bright

When *Might* to nought doth bring her enterprise,
55 Thy All-vpholding *Might* her Malice raines,
And her in Hell throwes bound in iron Chaines.

With Lockes in waues of Gold that ebbe and flow
On yuorie necke, in Robes more white than Snow,
Truth stedfastlie before thee holdes a Glasse,
60 Indent'd with Gemmes, where shineth all that was,
That is, or shall bee : heere, ere ought was wrought,
Thou knew all that thy Pow'r with Time forth-brought,
And more, Things numberlesse which thou couldst make,
That actuallie shall neuer beeing take :
65 Heere, thou beholdst thy selfe, and (strange) dost proue,
At once the Beautie, Louer and the Loue.

With Faces two (like Sisters) sweetlie faire,
Whose Blossomes no rough Autumne can impaire,
Stands *Prouidence*, and doth her lookes disperse
70 Through euerie Corner of this Vniuerse :
Thy *Prouidence* at once which generall Things
And singulare doth rule, as Empires Kings ;
Without whose care this world (lost) would remaine,
As Shippe without a Maister in the Maine,
75 As Chariot alone, as Bodies proue
Depriu'd of Soules by which they bee, liue, moue.

But who are They which shine thy Throne so neare ?
With sacred countenance, and looke seuere,
This in one hand a pondrous Sword doth hold,
80 Her left stayes charg'd with Ballances of Gold ;
That with Browes girt with Bayes, sweete-smiling Face,
Doth beare a Brandon, with a babish grace
Two milke-white Winges him easilie doe moue,
O Shee thy *Iustice* is, and this thy *Loue* !
85 By this thou brought this Engine great to light,
By that it fram'd in Number, Measure, Weight,
That destine doth reward to ill and good ;
But Sway of *Iustice* is by *Loue* with-stood,

---

[56] NO. *to Hell*   [76] NO. *whereby*   [82] O. *with a Infant Grace*   [85] NO. *brought'st*

Which did it not relent and mildlie stay,
90 This World ere now had had its funerall Day.
 What Bands (enclustred) neare to these abide,
Which into vaste *Infinitie* them hide ?
Infinitie that neither doth admit,
Place, Time, nor Number to encroach on it :
95 Heere *Bountie* sparkleth, heere doth *Beautie* shine,
Simplicitie, more white than Gelsemine,
Mercie with open wings, ay-varied *Blisse*,
Glorie, and *Ioy*, that *Blesses* darling is.
 Ineffable, All-pow'rfull GOD, All-free,
100 Thou onelie liu'st, and each thing liues by Thee,
No Ioy, no, nor Perfection to Thee came
By the contriuing of this Worlds great Frame ;
Ere Sunne, Moone, Starres beganne their restlesse race,
Ere paint'd with purple Light was Heauens round Face,
105 Ere Aire had Clouds, ere Clouds weept down their showrs,
Ere Sea embraced Earth, ere Earth bare Flowres,
Thou happie liu'd ; World nought to Thee supply'd,
All in thy selfe thy selfe thou satisfy'd :
Of Good no slender Shadow doth appeare,
110 No age-worne tracke, in Thee which shin'd not cleare ;
Perfections Summe, prime-cause of euerie Cause,
Midst, end, beginning, where all good doth pause.
Hence of thy Substance, differing in nought
Thou in Eternitie thy Sonne foorth brought,
115 The onelie Birth of thy vnchanging Minde,
Thine Image, Paterne-like that euer shin'd,
Light out of Light, begotten not by Will,
But Nature, all and that same Essence still
Which thou thy selfe ; for thou dost nought possesse
120 Which hee hath not, in ought nor is hee lesse
Than Thou his great Begetter ; of this Light,

90 NO. *had found*   98 INO. *Blisses*   104 NO. *Ere painted was with light Heavens pure Face*   107 NO. *liv'dst*   110 IN. *which shin'd in thee* 111 O. *has the misprint* Sun *for* Sum.   121 IN. *Than Thee* [*In the Edinburgh University and Haigh Hall copies of* I, *as well as in that containing the signature of the Earl of Lauderdale, "* Thou *" is pasted in on a printed slip between "* Than *" and "* his *"*]

Eternall, double, kindled was thy Spright
Eternallie, who is with Thee the same,
All-holie Gift, Embassadour, Knot, Flame :
125 Most sacred, Triade, O most holie One,
Vnprocreat'd Father, euer-procreat'd Sonne,
Ghost breath'd from both, you were, are, aye shall bee
(Most blessed) Three in One, and One in Three,
Vncomprehensible by reachlesse Hight,
130 And vnperceiued by excessiue Light.
So in our Soules, three and yet one are still,
The Vnderstanding, Memorie, and Will ;
So (though vnlike) the Planet of the Dayes,
So soone as hee was made begate his Rayes,
135 Which are his Of-spring, and from both was hurl'd
The rosie Light which comfort doth the World,
And none fore-went an other : so the Spring,
The Well-head, and the Streame which they foorth bring,
Are but one selfe-same Essence, nor in ought
140 Doe differ, saue in order, and our Thought
No Chime of time discernes in them to fall,
But three distinctlie bide one Essence all.
But these expresse not Thee ; who can declare
Thy beeing ?   Men and Angels dazel'd are :
145 Who force this Eden would with wit or sence,
A Cherubin shall finde to barre him thence.
    Alls Architect, Lord of this Uniuerse,
Wit is ingulph'd that would thy greatnesse pierce ;
Ah ! as a Pilgrime who the *Alpes* doth passe,
150 Or *Atlas* Temples crown'd with winters glasse,
The ayrie *Caucasus*, the *Apennine*,
Pyrenès cliftes where Sunne doth neuer shine,
When hee some heapes of Hilles hath ouer-went,
Beginnes to thinke on rest, his Iourney spent,

---

122 O. double-kindled   126 O. Unprocreate Father, ever procreate
127 NO. are, [O. *has the misprint* eare] *still shall be*   136 NO. *which con-
solates*   142 O. 'bide   145 NO. *Who would this* Eden *force*   147 NO.
Great Architect   148 I. *Ingulph'd is Wit would in thy* NO. *That light is
blinded would thy*   150 INO. *with winter glasse*   153 NO. *some craggy Hills*

155 Till mounting some tall Mountaine hee doe finde,
More hights before him than hee left behinde :
With halting pace, so while I would mee raise
To the vnbounded Circüits of thy praise,
Some part of way I thought to haue o're-runne,
160 But now I see how scarce I haue begunne,
With wonders new my Spirits range possest,
And wandring waylesse in a maze them rest.
    In those vaste Fieldes of Light, etheriall Plaines,
Thou art attended by immortall Traines
165 Of Intellectuall Pow'rs, which thou brought forth
To praise thy Goodnesse, and admire thy Worth ;
In numbers passing other Creatures farre,
Since most in number noblest Creatures are,
Which doe in Knowledge vs no lesse out-runne,
170 Than Moone doth Starres in light, or Moone the Sunne ;
Vnlike, in Orders rang'd and manie a Band,
(If Beautie in Disparitie doth stand ?)
Arch-Angels, Angels, Cherubes, Seraphines,
And what with name of Thrones amongst them shines,
175 Large-ruling Princes, Dominations, Powres,
All-acting Vertues of those flaming Towres :
These fred of Vmbrage, these of Labour free,
Rest rauished with still beholding Thee,
Inflam'd with Beames which sparkle from thy Face,
180 They can no more desire, farre lesse embrace.
    Low vnder them, with slow and staggering pace
Thy hand-Maide *Nature* thy great Steppes doth trace,
The Source of second Causes, golden Chaine
That linkes this Frame, as thou it doth ordaine ;
185 *Nature* gaz'd on with such a curious Eye
That Earthlings oft her deem'd a Deitye.

---

[158] NO. *unbounded limits*   [163] INO. *In these*   [165] NO. *broughtst*
[168] IN. *Since Creatures most noble maniest are [In the Edinburgh
University copy of* I, " *Since most in number noblest Creatures are* " *is
pasted in on a printed slip over the original reading.*]   [170] INO. *in light
doth Starres [O. has also the misprint* Noon *for* Moon]   [184] O. *thou
doth it

By *Nature* led those Bodies faire and greate
Which faint not in their Course, nor change their State,
Vnintermixt, which no disorder proue,
190 Though aye and contrarie they alwayes moue ;
The Organes of thy Prouidence diuine,
Bookes euer open, Signes that clearelie shine,
Times purpled Maskers, then doe them aduance,
As by sweete Musicke in a measur'd Dance.
195 Starres, Hoste of heauen, yee Firmaments bright Flowrs,
Cleare Lampes which ouer-hang this Stage of ours,
Yee turne not there to decke the Weeds of Night,
Nor Pageant-like to please the vulgare Sight,
Great Causes sure yee must bring great Effectes,
200 But who can descant right your graue Aspects ?
Hee onlie who You made deciphere can
Your Notes, Heauens Eyes, yee blinde the Eyes of Man.
  Amidst these saphire farre-extending Hights,
The neuer-twinkling euer-wandring Lights
205 Their fixed Motions keepe ; one drye and cold,
Deep-leaden colour'd, slowlie there is roll'd,
With Rule and Line for times steppes measur'd euen,
In twice three Lustres hee but turnes his Heauen.
With temperate qualities and Countenance faire,
210 Still mildelie smiling sweetlie debonnaire,
An other cheares the World, and way doth make
In twice sixe Autumnes through the Zodiacke.
But hote and drye with flaming lockes and Browes
Enrag'd, this in his red Pauillion glowes :
215 Together running with like speede if space,
Two equallie in hands atchieue their race ;
With blushing Face this oft doth bring the Day,
And vsheres oft to statelie Starres the way,
That various in vertue, changing, light,

---

[204] *In the Edinburgh University copy of* I, " *euer-wandring lights* "
is pasted in on a printed slip over the original reading. [207] INO. *meating*
euen [*In the Edinburgh University copy of* I, " *measur'd euen* " *is pasted
in on a printed slip after* " *steppes* "] [209] O. *has the misprint* Quality's

220 With his small Flame engemmes the vaile of Night.
   Prince of this Court, the Sunne in triumph rides,
   With the yeare Snake-like in her selfe that glides ;
   Times Dispensator, faire life-giuing Source,
   Through Skies twelue Posts as hee doth runne his course,
225 Heart of this All, of what is knowne to Sence
   The likest to his Makers Excellence :
   In whose diurnall motion doth appeare
   A Shadow, no, true pourtrait of the yeare.
   The Moone moues lowest, siluer Sunne of Night,
230 Dispersing through the World her borrow'd light,
   Who in three formes her head abroad doth range,
   And onelie constant is in constant Change.
     Sad Queene of Silence, I neere see thy Face,
   To waxe, or waine, or shine with a full grace,
235 But straight (amaz'd) on Man I thinke, each Day
   His state who changeth, or if hee find Stay,
   It is in drearie anguish, cares, and paines,
   And of his Labours Death is all the Gaines.
   Immortall Monarch, can so fond a Thought
240 Lodge in my brest ? as to trust thou first brought
   Heere in Earths shadie Cloister wretched Man,
   To sucke the Aire of woe, to spend Lifes span
   Midst Sighes and plaints, a stranger vnto Mirth,
   To giue himselfe his Death rebuking Birth ?
245 By sense and wit of Creatures Made King,
   By sense and wit to liue their Vnderling ?
   And what is worst, haue Eaglets eyes to see
   His owne disgrace, and know an high degree
   Of Blisse, the Place, if thereto hee might clime,
250 And not liue thralled to imperious Time ?
   Or (dotard) shall I so from Reason swerue,
   To deeme those Lights which to our vse doe serue,
   (For thou dost not them need) more noblie fram'd
   Than vs, that know their course, and haue them nam'd ?

255 No, I neere thinke but wee did them surpasse
As farre, as they doe Asterismes of Glasse,
When thou vs made ; by Treason high defil'd,
Thrust from our first estate wee liue exil'd,
Wandring this Earth, which is of Death the Lot,
260 Where he doth vse the Pow'r which he hath got,
Indifferent Umpire vnto Clownes and Kings,
The supreame Monarch of all mortall things.
  When first this flowrie Orbe was to vs giuen
It but in place disualu'd was to Heauen,
265 These Creatures which now our Soueraignes are,
And as to Rebelles doe denounce vs warre,
Then were our Uassalles, no tumultuous Storme,
No Thunders, Quakings, did her Forme deforme,
The Seas in tumbling Mountaines did not roare,
270 But like moist Christall whispered on the Shoare,
No Snake did met her Meads, nor ambusht lowre
In azure Curles beneath the sweet-Spring Flowre ;
The Nightshade, Henbane, Naple, Aconite,
Her Bowels then not bare, with Death to smite
275 Her guiltlesse Brood ; thy Messengers of Grace,
As their high Rounds did haunte this lower Place :
O Ioy of Ioyes ! with our first Parents Thou
To commune then didst daigne, as Friends doe now :
Against thee wee rebell'd, and iustly thus,
280 Each Creature rebelled against vs,
Earth, reft of what did chiefe in her excell,
To all became a Iaile, to most a Hell,
In Times full Terme vntill thy Sonne was giuen,
Who Man with Thee, Earth reconcil'd with Heauen.
285   Whole and entire all in thy Selfe thou art,
All-where diffus'd, yet of this *All* no part,
For infinite, in making this faire Frame,
(Great without quantitie) in all thou came,
And filling all, how can thy State admit,
290 Or Place or Substance to be voide of it ?

268 NO. Earthquakes 271 NO. did trace her Meads

Were Worlds as many, as the Raies which streame
From Heauens bright Eyes, or madding Wits do dreame,
They would not reele in nought, nor wandring stray,
But draw to Thee, who could their Centers stay ;
295 Were but one houre this World disioyn'd from Thee,
It in one houre to nought reduc'd should bee,
For it thy shaddow is, and can they last,
If seuer'd from the Substances them cast ?
O only blest, and Author of all blisse,
300 No Blisse it selfe, that all-where wish'ed is,
Efficient, exemplarie, finall Good,
Of thine owne Selfe but onely vnderstood ;
Light is thy Curtaine, thou art Light of Light,
An euer-waking Eye still shining bright,
305 In-looking all, exempt of passiue powre,
And change, in change since Deaths pale shade doth lowre.
All Times to thee are one, that which hath runne,
And that which is not brought yet by the Sunne,
To thee are present, who dost alwayes see
310 In present act, what past is or to bee.
Day-liuers wee rememberance doe losse
Of Ages worne, so Miseries vs tosse,
(Blinde and lethargicke of thy heauenly Grace,
Which sinne in our first Parents did deface,
315 And euen while Embryones curst by iustest doome)
That wee neglect what gone is, or to come :
But thou in thy great Archieues scrolled hast
In parts and whole, what euer yet hath past,
Since first the marble wheeles of Time were roll'd,
320 As euer liuing, neuer waxing old,
Still is the same thy Day and Yesterday,
An vn-diuided *Now*, a constant *Ay*.
   O King, whose Greatnesse none can comprehend,
Whose boundlesse Goodnesse doth to all extend,
325 Light of all Beautie, Ocean without ground,
That standing flowest, giuing dost abound,

<hr />

292 INO. *From Dayes bright Lamp* 293 O. in ought

Rich palace, and Indweller euer blest,
Neuer not working euer yet in Rest ;
What wit cannot conceiue, words say of Thee,
330 Heere where as in a Mirrour wee but see,
Shadowes of shadowes, Atomes of thy Might,
Still owlie eyed when staring on thy Light,
Grant that released from this earthly Iaile,
And fred of Clouds which heere our Knowledge vaile,
335 In Heauens high Temples, where thy Praises ring,
I may in sweeter Notes heare Angels sing.

[vi]
[A Prayer for Mankinde.]

GReat *GOD, whom wee with humble Thoughts adore,*
Eternall, infinite, Almightie King,
Whose Dwellings Heauen transcend, whose Throne before
Archangells serue, and Seraphines doe sing ;
5 *Of nought who wrought all that With wondring Eyes*
Wee doe behold within this spacious Round,
Who makes the Rockes to rocke, to stand the Skies,
At whose command Clouds dreadfull Thunders sound :
Ah ! spare vs Wormes, weigh not how wee (alas !)
10 *(Euill to our selues) against thy Lawes rebell,*
Wash of those Spots which still in Mindes cleare Glasse
(Though wee be loath to looke) wee see to well.
Deseru'd Reuenge, O doe not doe not take,
Doe thou reuenge what shall abide thy blow ?
15 *Passe shall this World, this World which thou didst make,*
Which should not perish till thy Trumpet blow.

330 INO. *Heere where wee as but in a Mirrour see* 334 NO. *freed from*
336 NO. *In sweeter Notes I may.*
    VI. 1 IN. *humbled* 6 INO. *various Round* 8 INO. *peales of Thunder*
11 INO. *in Conscience Glasse* [*In the Edinburgh University copy of I,*
" *in Minds cleare Glass* " *is pasted in on a printed slip over the original*
reading after " *still* "] 13 I *has the misprint of for* O [*In the Edinburgh*
University copy of I, "O" *is pasted in on a printed slip between* " *Reuenge* "
and " *doe* " ; *in the Haigh Hall copy, and in that containing the signature*
of the Earl of Lauderdale, " *of* " *is corrected in ink to* " O "] 14 INO.
If thou reuenge what [O. *who*]

What Soule is found whom Parents Crime not staines ?
Or what with its owne Sinne destaind is not ?
Though Iustice Rigor threaten (ah) her Raines
20 *Let Mercy guide, and neuer bee forgot.*
*   Lesse are our Faults farre farre than is thy Loue,*
O What can better seeme thy Grace diuine,
Than They that plagues deserue thy Bounty proue,
And where thou showre mayst Vengeance faire to shine ?
25 *Then looke and pittie, pittying forgiue*
Vs guiltie Slaues, or Seruants, now in thrall,
Slaues, if (alas) thou looke how wee doe liue ;
Or doing ill Or doing nought at all ?
Of an vngratefull Minde a foule Effect !
30 *But if thy Giftes which amplie heretofore*
Thou hast vpon vs powr'd thou dost respect,
Wee are thy Seruants, nay, than Seruants more ;
Thy Children, yes, and Children dearely bought,
But what strange Chance vs of this Lot bereaues,
35 *Poore worthles Wights how lowlie are wee brought,*
Whom Grace made Children Sinne hath turned Slaues ?
Sinne hath turn'd Slaues, but let those Bands Grace breake,
That in our Wrongs thy Mercies may appeare,
Thy Wisedome not so meane is, Pow'r so weake,
40 *But thousand wayes they can make Worlds thee feare.*
*   O Wisedome boundlesse ! O miraculous Grace !*
Grace, Wisedome which make winke dimme Reasons Eye,
And could Heauens King bring from his placelesse Place,
On this ignoble Stage of Care to die :
45 *To dye our Death, and with the sacred Streame*
Of Bloud and Water, guishing from his Side,
To put away each odious act and Blame,
By vs contriu'd, or our first Parents Pride.
Thus thy great Loue and Pitty (heauenly King)

---

18 INO. *with its owne Sinne* [NO. *Sins*] *defyl'd is not*   19 NO. *yet her Raines*   23 NO. *they who*   24 INO. *thou showre mayst* [O. mayst show'r] *Vengeance there to shine*   30 INO. *largelie heretofore*   31 I. *thou doe*   47 INO. *To make vs cleane of that contagious Blame*   48 INO. *First on vs brought by our first Parents Pride*

50 *Loue, Pitty, which so well our Losse preuent,*
  Of Euill it selfe (loe !) could all Goodnesse bring,
  And sad Beginning cheare with glad Euent.
  O Loue and Pitty ! ill-knowne of these Times,
  O Loue and Pittie ! carefull of our neede,
55 *O Bounties ! Which our execrable Crimes*
  (Now numberlesse) contend neere to exceed.
  Make this excessiue Ardour of thy Loue,
  So warme our Coldnesse, so our Lifes renew,
  That wee from sinne, Sinne may from vs remoue,
60 *Wit may our will, Faith may our Wit subdue.*
  Let thy pure Loue burne vp all worldly Lust,
  Hells pleasant Poison killing our best part,
  Which makes vs ioye in Toyes, adore fraile Dust
  In stead of Thee, in Temple of our Heart.
65   *Grant when at last our Soules these Bodies leaue,*
  Their loathsome Shops of Sinne, and Mansions blinde,
  And Doome before thy royall Seat receaue,
  They may a Sauiour, not a Iudge thee finde.

[55] INO. *which our horride Acts and Crimes*   [56] INO. *(Growne number-lesse)*   [60] NO. *Wisdome our Will, Faith*   [62] INO. *candi'd Poison*   [68] NO. *A Saviour more than Judge they thee may find*

THE SHADOW
OF THE IVDGEMENT.

[vii]

[An Essay of the Great and Generall Iudgement
of the World.]

Aboue those boundlesse Bounds where Starrs do
   moue,
The Seeling of the christall Round aboue,
And Raine-bow-sparkling Arch of Diamond cleare,
Which crownes the azure of each vnder Spheare,
5 In a rich Mansion radiant with light,
To which the Sunne is scarce a Taper bright,
Which, though a Bodie, yet so pure is fram'd,
That almost spirituall it may bee nam'd ;
Where Blisse aboundeth, and a lasting May
10 All Pleasures heightning flourisheth for ay,
The King of Ages dwells. About his Throne
(Like to those Beames Days golden Lamp hath on)
Angelike Splendors glance, more swift than ought
Reueal'd to sence, nay, than the winged Thought,
15 His will to practise : here doe Seraphines
Burne with immortall loue, there Cherubines
With other noble people of the Light,
As Eaglets in the Sunne, delight their Sight :
Heauens ancient Denizones, pure actiue Powres,
20 Which (fred of death) that Cloister high embowres,

VII. This piece first appeared in J, and is wanting in N.
¹² O. these

50

Etheriall Princes, euer-conquering Bandes,
Blest Subjectes acting what their King commandes ;
Sweet Quiristers, by whose melodious Straines
Skies dance, and Earth vntyr'd their Brawle sustaines.
25 Mixed among whose sacred legiones deare
The spotlesse Soules of Humanes doe appeare,
Deuesting Bodies which did Cares deuest,
And there liue happie in eternall Rest.
   Hither, sure-charg'd with griefe, fraught with Annoy,
30 (Sad Spectacle into that place of Ioy)
Her Haire disordered dangling o're her Face,
Which had of pallid Violets the grace,
The Crimsin Mantle wont her to adorne
Cast loose about, and in large peeces torne,
35 Sighes breathing forth, and from her heauie Eyne
Along her Cheekes distilling christall Brine,
Which downe-wards to her yuorie Brest was driuen,
And had bedewed the milkie-Way of Heauen,
Came *Pietie :* at her left hand neare by
40 A wailing Woman bare her Company,
Whose tender Babes her snowie Necke did clip,
And now hang on her Pappe now by her Lip :
Flames glanc'd her Head aboue, which once did glow,
But late looke pale (a Poore and ruthfull Show !)
45 Shee sobbing shrunke the Throne of God before,
And thus beganne her Case to him deplore.
   Forlorne, wretch'd, desolate, to whom should I
My Refuge haue, below or in the Skie,
But vnto thee ? see (all beholding Kinf)
50 That Seruant, no, that Darling thou diast bring
On Earth, lost Man to saue from Hells Abisme,
And raise vnto these Regiones aboue Tyme ;
Who made thy Name so truelie bee implor'd,
And by the reuerent Soule so long ador'd,
55 Her banisht now see from these lower Boundes,
Behold her Garments Shreedes her Bodies woundes ;

37 O. downward   52 O. those

VOL. II   E

Looke how her Sister *Charitie* there standes,
Proscrib'd on Earth, all maim'd by wicked Handes :
Mischeefe there mountes to such an high degree,
60 That there, now none is left who cares for mee.
There dwelles Idolatrie, there Atheisme raignes,
There Man in dombe, yet roaring, sinnes him staines ;
So foolish, that hee Puppets will adore
Of Mettall, Stone, and Birds, Beastes, Trees, before
65 Hee once will to thy hollie seruice bow,
And yeelde the Homage : Ah alas ! yee now
To those black Sprightes which thou dost keepe in
      chaines
Hee vowes Obedience, and with shamefull paines
Infernall Horroures courtes ; Case fond and strange !
70 To Bane than Blisse desiring more the Change.
Thy *Charitie* of Graces once the Cheife,
Did long tyme find in Hospitalls reliefe ;
Which now lye leuell'd with the lowest Ground,
Where sad memorialls scarce are of them found.
75 Then (Vagabounding) Temples her receau'd,
Where my Poore Cells afforded what she crau'd ;
But now thy Temples raz'd are, humane Blood
Those Places staines, late where thy Altares stood :
Tymes are so horrid, to implore thy Name,
80 That it is held now on the Earth a Blame.
Now doth the Warriour with his Dart and Sword
Write lawes in blood, and vent them for thy word ;
Relligion, Faith pretending to make knowne,
All haue all Faith, Religion quite o'rthrowne,
85 Men awlesse, lawlesse liue (most woefull case !)
Men, no more men, a GOD-contemning Race.
    Scarce had shee said, when from the neither World,
(Like to a Lightning through the Welken hurl'd,
That scores with Flames the way, and euerie eye
90 With Terrour dazelles as it swimmeth by)
Came *Iustice :* to whom Angels did make place,

60 O. that cares   66 O. yet now

And *Truth* her flying foote-steppes straight did trace.
Her Sword was lost, the precious Weights shee bare,
Their Beame had torne, Scales rudlie bruised were :
95 From off her head was reft her golden Crowne,
In ragges her Vaile was rent and starre-spangl'd Gowne,
Her teare-wette Lockes hange o're her Face, which made
Betweene her and the mightie King a Shade.
Iust wrath had rais'd her colour (like the Morne
100 Portending Clouds moist Embryones to bee borne)
Of which shee taking leaue, with Heart swollen great,
Thus stroue to plaine before the Throne of State.
 Is not the Earth thy worke-man-ship (great King)
Didst Thou not all this *All* from nought once bring
105 To this rich Beautie which doth on it shine :
Bestowing on each Creature of thine
Some Shadow of thy Bountie ? Is not Man
Thy Vassall, plac'd to spend his lifes short Span
To doe Thee Homage : and then didst not Thou
110 A Queene installe mee there, to whom should bow
Thy Earths Endwellers, and to this effect
Put in my hand thy Sword ? O high Neglect !
Now wretched Earthlings, to thy great disgrace,
Peruerted haue my Pow'r, and doe deface
115 All reuerent trackes of Iustice ; now the Earth,
Is but a Frame of Shame, a funerall Harth,
Where euerie Vertue hath consumed beene,
And nought (no not their dust) restes to bee seene
Long hath it mee abhor'd, long chased mee,
120 Expelled last, heere I haue fled to Thee,
And foorth-with rather would to Hell repaire,
Than Earth, sith Iustice execute is there.
All liue on Earth by Spoyle, the Host his Guest
Betrayes, the Man of her lyes in his Brest
125 Is not assured ; the Sonne the Fathers death
Attempts, and Kinred Kinred reaue of Breath

---

 [97] O. hang'd [100] O *has the misprint* Embryo's [120] O. Expell'd
at last [122] O. since

By lurking meanes, of such Age few makes sicke,
Since Hell disgorg'd her banefull Arsenicke.
Whom Murthers, foule Assasinates defile,
130 Most who the harmelesse Innocent beguile,
Who most can rauage, robe, ransacke, blasphame,
Is held most vertuous, hath a Worthies name ;
So on emboldned Malice they relye,
That (madding) thy great Puissance they defye :
135 Earst man resembl'd thy Pourtrait soyl'd by Smooke,
Now like thy Creature hardlie doth hee looke.
Olde *Nature* heere (Shee pointed where there stood
An aged Ladie in a heauie Mood)
Doth breake her Staffe, denying humane Race
140 To come of Her, Things borne to her disgrace !
The Doue the Doue, the Swan doth loue the Swan,
Nought so relentlesse vnto man as Man.
O ! if thou madst this World, gouern'st it all,
Deserued vengeance on the Earth let fall ;
145 The Periode of her standing perfect is,
Her Houre-glasse not a Minute short doth misse.
The End (O LORD) is come, then let no more
Mischiefe still triumph, Bad the Good deuoure,
But of thy Word sith Constant, true, Thou art,
150 Giue Good their Guerdon, wicked due Desart.
　　　Shee said : Through out the shining Palace went
A Murmure soft, such as a farre is sent
By musked Zephires Sighes along the Maine,
Or when they curle some flowrie Lea and Plaine ;
155 One was their Thought, one their Intention, Will,
Nor could they erre *Truth* there residing still :
All (mou'd with zeale) as one with cryes did pray,
Hasten (O LORD) O hasten the last Day.
　　　Looke how a generous Prince, when hee doth heare,
160 Some louing Citie and to him most deare,
Which wont with Giftes, and Showes him intertaine
(And as a Fathers did obey his Raigne)

130 O, Innocents　　131 O. blaspheme　　149 O. since

A rout of Slaues and rascall foes to wracke,
Her Buildings ouer-throw, her Richesse sacke,
165 Feeles vengefull Flames within his bosome burne,
And a just rage all Respects ouer-turne :
So seeing Earth, of Angels once the Inne,
Mansion of Saintes, deflowred all by sinne,
And quite confus'd, by wretches heere beneath,
170 The worlds great Soueraigne moued was to Wrath.
Thrice did hee rouse himselfe, thrice from his Face,
Flames sparkle did throughout the heauenlie place.
The Starres, though fixed, in their Rounds did quake,
The Earth, and Earth-embracing Sea did shake :
175 *Carmell* and *Hæmus* felt it, *Athos* Topes
Affrighted shrunke, and neare the *Æthiopes*
Atlas, the *Pyrenèes*, the *Appennine*,
And loftie *Grampius*, which with Snow doth shine.
Then to the Synode of the Sprights hee swore,
180 Mans care should end, and Tyme should bee no more ;
By his owne Selfe hee swore of perfect worth,
Straight to performe his word sent Angels forth.
      There lyes an Island, where the radiant Sunne,
When hee doth to the northerne Tropicke runne,
185 Of sex long Monethes makes one tedious Day,
And when through southerne Signes he holds his way,
Sex Monethes turneth in one loathsome Night
(Night neither heere is faire, nor Day hote-bright,
But halfe white and halfe More) where sadlie cleare
190 Still coldlie glance the Beames of either Beare,
The frostie *Groen-land*.   On the lonlie Shore
The Ocean in Mountaines hoarse doth roare,
And ouer-tumbling, tumbling ouer Rockes,
Castes various Raine-bowes, which in Froth he choakes ;
195 Gulfes all about are shrunke most strangelie steepe,
Then *Nilus* Cataractes more vaste and deepe.
To the wilde Land beneath to make a shade,
A Mountaine lifteth vp his crested Head :

184 O. Tropicks   196 O. Than

His Lockes are yce-sheekles, his Browes are Snow,
200 Yet, from his burning Bowelles deepe below,
Cometes, farre-flaming Pyramides are driuen
And pitchie Meteores, to the Cope of Heauen.
No Summer heere the Ioulie Grasse forth bringes,
Nor Trees, no, not the deadlie Cypresse springes.
205 Caue-louing Eccho Daughter of the Aire,
By humane voyce was neuer wakned heere :
In stead of nights blake Birdes, and plaintfull Owle,
Infernall Furies heere doe yell and howle.
A Mouth yawnes in this Hight so blacke obscure
210 With vapours, that no eye it can endure :
Great *Ætnas* Cauernes neuer yet did make
Such sable dampes, though they bee hideous blacke,
Sterne Horroures heere eternallie doe dwell,
And this Gulfe destine for a Gate to Hell.
215 Forth from this place of dread (Earth to appall)
Three Furies rushed at the Angels call.
One with long Tresses doth her Visage maske,
Her Temples clouding in a horrid Caske,
Her right Hand swinges a Brandon in the Aire,
220 Which Flames and Terrour hurleth euery where ;
Ponderous with Darts, her left doth beare a Shield,
Where *Gorgones* Head lookes grimme in sable Field :
Her eyes blaze Fire and Blood, each haire stilles Blood,
Blood trilles from either pappe, and where shee stood
225 Bloods liquid Corrall sprang her feete beneath,
Where shee doth streach her Arme is Blood & Death.
Her stygian Head no sooner shee vpreares,
When Earth of Swords Helmes Lances straight appeares
To bee deliuered, and from out her Wombe
230 In Flame-wing'd Thunderes Artellerie doth come,
Floodes siluer streames doe take a blushing Dye,
The Plaines with breathlesse Bodies buried Iye ;
Rage, Wronge, Rapte, Sacriledge doe her attend,
Feare, Discorde, Wracke, & Woes which haue none end :

235 Towne is by Towne, and Prince by Prince with-stood,
Earth turnes an hideous Shambles a Lake of Blood.
   The next with Eyes, sunke hollow in her Braines,
Lane face, snarl'd haire, with blacke and emptie Veines,
Her dry'd-vp Bones scarce couered with her Skinne,
240 Bewraying that strange structure built within,
Thigh-Bellilesse, most gastlie to the sight,
A wasted Skeliton resembleth right.
Where shee doeth roame in Aire faint doe the Birdes,
Yawne doe Earths ruthlesse brood & harmelesse Heards,
245 The Woods wilde Forragers doe howle and roare,
The humid Swimmers dye along the shoare ;
In Townes, the liuing doe the dead vp-eate,
Then dye themselues, Alas ! and wanting meate,
Mothers not spare the Birth of their owne Wombes,
250 But turne those Nestes of life to fatall Tombes.
   Last did a saffron-colour'd Hagge come out,
With vncomb'd Haire, Browes banded all about
With duskie cloudes, in ragged Mantle cled,
Her breath with stinking Fumes the Aire be-spred,
255 In either Hand shee held a Whip, whose Wyres,
Still'd poyson, blaz'd with phlegethontall Fyres.
(Relentlesse) Shee each state, sex, age defiles,
Earth streames with goares, burnes with inuenom'd
   Biles ;
Where Shee repaires, Townes doe in Desartes turne,
260 The liuing haue no pause the dead to mourne,
The friend (Ah !) dares not locke the dying Eyes
Of his belou'd, the Wyfe the Husband flies ;
Men Basiliskes to men proue, and by Breath,
Then Lead or Steale, bring worse and swifter Death :
265 No Cypresse, Obsequies, no Tombe they haue,
The sad Heauen mostlie serues them for a Graue.
   These ouer Earth tumultuouslie doe runne,
South, North, from rising to the setting Sunne ;
They some time parte, yet than the windes more fleete,

<hr />

236 O. Shamble   238 O. Lean   253 O. clad   258 O. Boils

270 Forth-with together in one place they meete.
   Great *Quinzai* yee it know, *Susanias* pride,
   And you Where statelie *Tibers* streames doe glide,
   Memphis, Parthenopè yee too it know,
   And where *Euripus* seuen-folde Tyde doth flow :
275 Yee know it Empresses on *Tames, Rosne, Seine,*
   And yee faire Queenes by *Tagus Danube Reine.*
   Though they doe scoure the Earth, roame farre & large,
   Not thus content the Angels leaue their Charge :
   Wee of her wracke these slender Signes may name,
280 By greater they the Iudgement doe proclame.
     This Centers Center with a mightie Blow
   One bruiseth, whose crackt Concaues lowder low,
   And rumbel, than if all the Artellerie
   On Earth discharg'd at once were in the Skie ;
285 Her Surface shakes, her Mountaines in the Maine
   Turne topsiturnie, of Heights making plaine :
   Townes them ingulfe, and late where Towres did stand,
   Now nought remaineth but a waste of Sand.
   With turning Eddyes Seas sinke vnder Ground,
290 And in their floting Depthes are Valleyes found ;
   Late where with foamie Crestes waues tilted waues,
   Now fishie Bottomes shine and mossie Caues.
   The Mariner castes an amazed eye
   On his wing'd Firres, which bedded hee findes lye,
295 Yet can hee see no Shore ; but whilst hee thinkes,
   What hideous Creuesse that hudge Current drinkes,
   The Streames rush backe againe with storming Tyde,
   And now his Shippes on cristall mountaines glyde ;
   Till they bee hurl'd farre beyond Seas and Hope,
300 And setle on some Hill or Palace Tope :
   Or by triumphant Surges ouer-driuen,
   Show Earth their Entrailles and their Keeles the Heauen.
     Skies clowdie Tables some doe paint, with Fights
   Of armed Squadrones, justling Steedes and Knights,
305 With shining Crosses, Iudge, and saphire Throne ;

---

[283] O. th' Artillery   [286] O. topsy-turvy

Arraigned Criminelles to howle and groane,
And plaintes send forth are heard : New-worlds seeme
    shine,
With other Sunnes and Moones, false Starres decline,
And diue in Seas ; red Comets warme the Aire,
310 And blaze, as other Worlds were judged there.
Others the heauenlie Bodies doe displace,
Make Sunne his Sisters stranger Steppes to trace ;
Beyond the course of Spheares hee driues his Coach,
And neare the cold *Arcturus* doth approach ;
315 The Scythian amaz'd is at such Beames,
The Mauritanian to see ycie Streames ;
The Shadow which ere-while turn'd to the West,
Now wheeles about, then reeleth to the East :
New starres aboue the eight Heauen sparkle cleare,
320 *Mars* chopes with *Saturne, Ioue* claimes *Marses* spheare,
Shrunke nearer Earth, all blackned now and Broone,
In Maske of weeping Cloudes appeares the Moone.
There are noe Seasons, Autumne, Summer, Spring,
Are all sterne Winter, and no birth forth bring :
325 Red turnes the Skies blew Curtaine o're this Globe,
As to propine the Iudge with purple Robe.
    At first (entraunc'd) with sad and curious Eyes
Earths Pilgrimes stare on those strange Prodigies :
The Starre-gazer this Round findes truely moue
330 In partes and whole, yet by no Skill can proue
The Firmaments stay'd firmenesse.   They which dreame
An euerlastingnesse in worlds vaste Frame,
Thinke well some Region where they dwell may wracke,
But that the whole nor Time nor Force can shake ;

---

307 O. New Worlds seen shine [*This, with the addition of a comma
after* seene, *and of a hyphen between* New *and* worlds *is the reading of
the first issue of* J, *which in the Errata of the second issue is corrected to*
New worlds seeme shine   *In the Edinburgh University copy of the
second issue of* J, *the correction, made in* (?) *ink, also appears in the text
itself, except that the comma between* seeme *and* shine *has not been
deleted.*]   315 *In the Errata of the second issue of* J, Sythian *is corrected
to* Scythian.   317 J *has the misprint* thee *for the before* West   318 J
has the misprint thee *before* East   319 O. Eighth   321 O. brown   324 O.
All are   328 O *has the misprint* Pilgrim's

335 Yet (franticke) muse to see Heauens statly Lights,
    Like Drunkards, waylesse reele amidst their Heights.
    Such as doe Nationes gouerne, and Command
    Vastes of the Sea and Emperies of Land,
    Repine to see their Countries ouer-throwne,
340 And find no Foe their Furie to make knowne :
    Alas (say they) what bootes our toyles and Paines,
    Of Care on earth is this the furthest Gaines ?
    No Richesse now can bribe our angrye Fate,
    O no ! to blaste our Pride the Heauenes do threate :
345 In dust now must our Greatnesse buried lye,
    Yet is it comfort with the World to dye.
    As more and more the warning Signes encrease,
    Wild dread depriues lost *Adames* Race of Peace ;
    From out their Grandame Earth They faine would flie,
350 But whither know not, Heauens are farre and hie ;
    Each would bewaile and mourne his owne Distresse,
    But publicke Cryes doe priuate Teares suppresse,
    Lamentes plaintes shreekes of woe disturbe all Eares,
    And Feare is equall to the Paine it feares.
355   Amidst this Masse of Crueltie and Slights,
    This Galley full of God-despising Wights,
    This Iaile of Sinne and Shame, this filthie Stage
    Where all act folly miserie and rage ;
    Amidst those Throngs of old prepar'd for Hell,
360 Those Numbers which no *Archimede* can tell,
    A silly Crue did lurke, a harmelesse Rout
    Wandring the Earth, which God had chosen out
    To liue with Him (Few Roses which did blow
    Among those Weedes Earthes Garden ouer-grow ;
365 A deaw of Gold still'd on Earths sandy Mine,
    Small Diamondes in Worlds rough Rocks which shine)
    By purple Tyrants which persued and chas'd,
    Liu'd Recluses, in lonlie Islands plac'd ;
    Or did the Mountaines haunte, and Forests wild,
370 Which they than Townes more harmelesse found and mild :
    Where many an Hymne they to their Makers praise

Teacht Groues and Rocks, which did resound their Layes.
Nor Sword nor Famine nor Plague poisoning Aire,
Nor Prodigies appearing euery where,
375 Nor all the sad Disorder of this *All*,
Could this small handfull of the World appall ;
But as the Flowre, which during winters Cold
Runnes to the Roote, and lurkes in Sap vp-rol'd,
So soone as the great Planet of the Yeare
380 Beginnes the Twinnes deare Mansion to cleare,
Liftes vp its fragrant Head, and to the Field
A Spring of Beauty and Delight doth yeeld :
So at those Signes and Apparitiones strange
Their thoughts lookes gestures did beginne to change,
385 Ioy makes their Hands to clap, their Hearts to dance,
In Voice turnes Musicke in their Eyes doth glance.
    What can (say They) these Changes else portend
Of this great Frame saue the approaching End ?
Past are the Signes, all is perform'd of old
390 Which the Almighties Heraulds vs fore-told.
Heauen now no longer shall of Gods great Power
A turning Temple be, but fixed Tower,
Burne shall this mortall Masse amidst the Aire,
Of diuine Iustice turn'd a Trophee faire ;
395 Neare is the last of Dayes, whose light enbalmes
Past Griefes, and all our stormy Cares becalmes.
O happy Day ! O chearefull holy Day !
Which Nights sad Sables shall not take away !
Farewell Complaintes, and yee yet doubtfull Thought,
400 Crown now your Hopes with comforts long time sought ;
Wypt from our Eyes now shall be euerie Teare,
Sighes stopt ; since our Saluation is so neare.
What long wee long'd for, God at last hath giuen
Earths chosen Bands to ioyne with those of Heauen ;
405 Now noble Soules a Guerdon just shall finde,

---

399 *In the Errata of the second issue of* J, Thoughts *is corrected to*
Thought   *In some copies of* J *the* s *of* Thoughts *has been scraped out,
and along with it the punctuation presumably.*

And Rest and Glorie bee in one combinde,
Now, more than in a Mirrour, by these Eyne
Euen Face to face our Maker shall be seene ;
O Welcome Wonder of the Soule and Sight !
410 O Welcome Obiect of all true Delight !
Thy Triumphes and Returne wee did expect,
Of all past Toyles to reape the deare Effect :
Since thou art iust, performe thy holy Word,
O come still hop'd for, come long Wish'd for Lord.
415   While thus They pray, the Heauens in Flames appeare,
As if they shew Fires elementall Spheare,
The Earth seemes in the Sunne, the Welken gone,
Wonder all hushes ; straight the Aire doth grone
With Trumpets, which thrice-lowder Sounds doe yeeld
420 Than deafening Thunders in the airie Field.
Created Nature at the Clangor quakes,
Immur'd with Flames Earth in a Palsey Shakes,
And from her wombe the Dust in seuerall Heapes
Takes life, and mustereth into humane Shapes :
425 Hell burstes, and the foule prisoners there bound
Come howling to the Day, with Serpentes crown'd.
Milliones of Angels in the loftie Hight,
Cled in pure Gold and the Electar bright,
Ushering the way still where the Iudge should moue,
430 In radiant Raine-bowes vaulte the Skies aboue ;
Which quickly open, like a Curtaine driuen,
And beaming Glorie show the KING OF HEAVEN.
    What Persian Prince, Assirian most renown'd,
What Scythian with conquering Squadrones Crown'd,
435 Entring a breached Citie, where conspire
Fire to drie Blood, and Blood to quench out Fire ;
Where cutted Carcasses quicke Members reele,
And by their ruine blunte the reeking Steele,
Resembleth now the euer-liuing King ?
440 What Face of *Troy* which doth with yelling ring,

---

428 O. Clad   **434** *In the Errata of the second issue of* J, Sythian *is
corrected to* Scythian.

And grecian Flames transported in the aire,
What dreadfull Spectacle of *Carthage* faire ?
What Picture of rich *Corinthes* tragicke wracke,
Or of *Numantia* the hideous sacke,
445 Or These together showne, the Image, Face
Can represent of Earth, and plaintfull case ;
Which must lye smoaking in the Worlds vast Wombe,
And to it Selfe both fewell be and Tombe ?
　　Neare to that sweet and odoriferous Clime,
450 Where the all-cheering Emperour of Tyme
Makes spring the Casia, Narde, and fragrant Balmes,
And euerie Hill, and Collin Crownes with Palmes ;
Where Incense sweats, where weeps the precious Mirre,
And Cedars ouer-tope the Pine and Firre ;
455 Neare where the aged Phœnix, ty'rd of Breath
Doth build her Nest, and takes new life in Death :
A Valley into wide and open Feildes
Farre it extendeth, 　　*　　*　　*　　*　　*

The rest is desired.

PLATE 9.—FACSIMILE OF HALF-TITLE PAGE.

A
CYPRESSE GROVE.

HOVGH it hath beene doubted, if there bee in the Soule such imperious and superexcellent Power, as that it can, by the vehement & earnest working of it, deliuer knowledge to an other without bodilie Organes, and by onelie Conceptions and Ideas produce reall Effects; yet it hath beene euer, and of all, held, as infalible and most certaine, that it often (either by outward inspiration or some secret motion in it selfe) is Augure of its owne Misfortunes, and hath shadowes of approaching Dangers presented vnto it before they fall forth. Hence so manie strange Apparitions and signes, true Visions, vncouth heauinesse, and causelesse languishings: Of which to seeke a reason, vnlesse from the sparkling of GOD in the Soule, or from the God-like sparkles of the Soule, were to make Reason vnreasonable, by reasoning of things transcending her reach.

Hauing when I had giuen my selfe to rest in the quiet Solitarinesse of the Night, found often my imagination troubled with a confused feare, no, sorrow or horror,

---

This prose essay is wanting in N.
⁶ MO by the onely ⁷ IMO. ideas of it ¹⁴ IO *insert* vncomfortable *after* causelesse ¹⁹⁻²⁰ IMO. Hauing often and diuerse times . . . found my imagination ²¹ O. or Sorrow

which interrupting Sleepe, did astonish my Senses, and
rouse mee, all appalled and transported in a sudden
Agonie and amazednesse ; of such an vnaccustomed
25 Perturbation, not knowing, nor beeing able to diue into
any apparent cause, carried away with the streame of my
(then doubting) Thoughts, I beganne to ascribe it, to
that secret fore-knowledge and presaging power of the
profeticke Minde, and to interpret such an Agonie to bee
30 to the Spirit, as a sudden faintnesse and vniuersall weari-
nesse vseth to bee to the Bodie, a signe of following
Sicknesse, or, as Winter Lightninges, Earth-quakes, and
Monsteres proue to Common-wealthes and great Cities,
Herbingers of wretched euents, and Emblemes of their
35 hidden Destinies.

Heerevpon, not thinking it strange if whatsoeuer is
humaine should befall mee, knowing how Prouidence
ouer-commeth Griefe, and discountenances Crosses : And
that as wee should not despaire in Euills which may
40 happen vs, wee should not bee too confident, nor too
much leane to those goods wee enjoye, I beganne to turne
ouer in my remembrance all that could afflict miserable
Mortalitie, and to fore-cast euerie accident which could
beget gloomie & sad apprehensions, and with a maske of
45 horrour shew it selfe to humaine eyes. Till in the end (as
by vnities & points Mathematicians are brought to great
numbers, and huge greatnesse) after manie fantasticall
glances of the woes of Mankind, and those encombrances
which follow vpon life, I was brought to thinke, and
50 with amazement, on the last of humaine Terrors, or as
one tearmed it, the last of all dreadfull and terrible euils
Death : For to easie Censure it would appeare, that the
Soule, if it can fore-see that diuorcement which it is to

---

[30] IM *omit* sudden *before* faintnesse   [32-34] IMO. or Earth-quakes are
to Commonwealthes and great Cities, Herbingers of more wretched
euents   [33] O. Monsters are to   [34-35] IM *omit* and . . . destinies, *and*
O *replaces* hidden *by* sudden   [38] MO. overcoms   [39] IM. of euills
[40] MO. to us   [40-41] IMO. nor leane much to   [43] IMO. euery thing that
[O. which]   [43-44] IM *omit* could beget . . ., and   [53] IM *omit* can *before*
fore-see

haue from the Bodie, should not without great reason
55 bee thus ouer-grieued, and plunged in inconsolable and
vn-accustumed Sorrow; considering their neare Vnion,
long Familiaritie and Loue, with the great Change, Paine,
vglinesse, which are apprehended to bee the inseperable
attendants of Death.
60   They had their beeing together, partes they are of
one reasonable Creature, the harming of the one is the
weakning of the working of the other; what sweete contentments doeth the Soule enjoye by the senses, They
are the Gates and Windowes of its Knowledge, the Or-
65 ganes of its Delight? If it bee tideous to an excellent
Player on the Lute to endure but a few Monethes the
want of one, how much more must the beeing without
such noble Tooles and Engines bee plaintfull to the
Soule? And, if two Pilgrimes, which haue wandred
70 some little peece of ground together, haue an hearts-
griefe when they are neare to parte, what must the
sorrow bee at the parting of two so louing Friendes and
neuer-loathing Louers as are the Bodie and Soule?
     Death is the sade Estranger of acquantance, the eternall
75 Diuorcer of Mariage, the Rauisher of the Children from
their Parentes, the stealer of Parents from the Children,
the Interrer of Fame, the sole cause of Forgetfulnesse, by
which the liuing talke of those gone away as of so manie
Shadowes, or fabulous Paladines: all Strength by it is
80 enfeebled, Beautie turned in deformitie and rottennesse,
Honour in contempt, Glorie into basenesse, it is the vnreasonable breaker off of all the actions of Vertue; by
which wee enjoye no more the sweete pleasures on Earth,
neither contemplate the statelie reuolutions of the Hea-
85 uens; Sunne perpetuallie setteth, Starres neuer rise vnto

66 IMO. to abide   68 O. painful   70 IMO. some few miles together, haue a   72 O *omits* the *before* parting   74 IMO. violent
Estranger   76 IMO. the Parentes . . . from their Children   79 IMO.
or age-worne Stories   80 IMO. into deformitie   81 O. into Contempt
81-83 it is the reasonlesse breaker off of all actions; by which   83 IMO.
of Earth   84 IM. nor gaze vpon the   O. nor contemplate the   85 O.
The Sun

vs ; It in one moment depriueth vs of what with so great
toyle and care in manie yeeres wee haue heaped together :
By this are Successions of Linages cut short, Kingdomes
left Heirelesse, and greatest States orphaned : It is
90 not ouercome by Pride, smoothed by gawdie Flatterie,
tamed by Intreaties, bribed by Benefites, softned by
Lamentations, diuerted by Time, Wisedome, saue this,
can alter and helpe anie thing.   By Death wee are exiled
from this faire Citie of the World ; it is no more a World
95 vnto vs, nor wee anie more People into it.   The Ruines of
Phanes, Palaces, and other magnificent Frames, yeeld a
sad Prospect to the Soule : And how should it consider the
wracke of such a wonderfull Maister-piece as is the Bodie
without Horrour ?

100   Though it cannot well and altogether bee denyed but
that Death naturallie is terrible and to bee abhorred ; it
beeing a Priuation of life, and a not beeing, and euerie
priuation beeing abhorred of Nature and euill in it selfe,
the feare of it too beeing ingenerate vniuersalie in all
105 Creatures ; yet I haue often thought that euen naturallie,
to a Minde by onelie Nature resolued and prepared,
it is more terrible in conceite than in veritie, and at the first
glance than when well pryed into ; and that rather by the
weaknesse of our Fantasie, than by what is in it ; and
110 that the marble Colours of obsequies, weeping, and
funerall pompe (with which wee our selues limne it forth)
did adde much more Gastlinesse vnto it than otherwayes
it hath.   To auerre which conclusion when I had recol-
lected my ouer-charged spirits I began thus with my selfe.
115   If on the great Theater of this Earth, amongst the

---

86 IMO. robbeth vs   **90** IMO *omit* gawdie *before* flatterie, *and* O
replaces smoothed *by* soothed   **91-92** IM *omit* tamed . . . Lamentations, *and in* **92** O *has* nor diverted   **93** IMO. can preuent and helpe
euery thing   **95** MO. nor we no [O. any] more a people vnto it   **97-99**
IMO. And how should it without horrour view   **100-101** IMO. That
Death naturally is terrible and to be abhorred, it can not well and
altogether be denied   **104** O. ingenerated   **106** O. by Nature only
111 IM. (which wee our selues cast ouer it)   O. (which we our selves
paint it with)   **113-14** IMO. when I had gathered my wandring thoughts

numberlesse number of Men, *To die* were onelie proper
to thee and thine, then vndoubtedlie thou hadst reason
to grudge at so seuere and partiall a Law.   But since it is
a necessitie, from the which neuer an Age by-past hath
120 beene exempted, and vnto which these which bee, and
so manie as are to come, are thralled (no consequent
of life beeing more common and familiar) why shouldst
thou, with vnprofitable and nothing auailing stubburn-
nesse, oppose to so vneuitable and necessarie a Condition ?
125 This is the high-way of mortalitie, our generall Home :
behold, what millions haue trode it before thee, what
multitudes shall after thee, with them which at that same
instant runne ! in so vniuersall a Calamitie (if Death be
one) priuate complaints cannot bee heard : With so manie
130 royall Palaces, it is small lose to see thy poore Caban
burne.   Shall the Heauens stay their euer-rolling Wheeles
(for what is the motion of them but the motion of a
swift & euer-whirling wheele, which twinneth forth and
againe vp-windeth our life ?) and hold still Time, to pro-
135 long thy miserable dayes, as if the highest of their working
were to doe homage vnto thee ?   Thy Death is a peece of
the order of this *All*, a part of the Life of this World ; for
while the world is the world, some creatures must dye,
and others take life.   Eternall things are raised farre aboue
140 this Orbe of generation and corruption, where the first
Matter, like a still-flowing and ebbing Sea, with diuerse
Waues, but the same Water, keepeth a restlesse and
neuer-tyring Current ; what is below in the Vniuersality
of the kind, not in it selfe, doeth abide ; *Man* a long line of
145 yeeres hath continued, *This Man* euerie hundreth is swipt
away.   This aire-encircled Globe is the sole Region of
Death, the Graue, where euerie thing that taketh life must

117-18 IMO. reason to repine   119 O. from which   120 IMO. they which
bee   123 IMO. nought-auailing   124 O. oppose so   130 IMO. no lose
O. Cabin   134 IMO. vprolleth   [*In the Edinburgh University copy of* I,
vpwindeth *is pasted in on a printed slip between* againe *and* our]   136 O.
Pace   140 IMO. Spheare of generation and corruption   141 IMO. euer-
flowing   145 MO. hundred   146 IMO. This globe enuironed with aire

rotte, the Listes of Fortune and Change, onelie glorious
in the inconstancie and varying Alterationes of it ;
150 which though manie, seeme yet to abide one, and being
a certaine entire one, are euer manie. The neuer-agree-
ing bodies of the elementall Brethren turne one in another,
the Earth changeth her countenance with the Seasons,
some-times looking colde and naked, other tymes hote
155 and flowrie : Nay, I can not tell how, but euen the
lowest of those celestiall Bodies, that Mother of Moneths,
and Empresse of Seas, and moisture, as if shee were a
Mirrour of our constant mutabilitie, appeareth (by her
great nearnesse vnto vs) to participate of our alterations,
160 neuer seeing vs twice with that same Face, now looking
blacke, than pale and wanne, sometimes againe in the
perfection and fulnesse of her beautie shining ouer vs.
Death heere no lesse than Life doth acte a part ; the taking
away of what is olde beeing, the making way for what
165 is young. This Earth is as a Table Booke, and men are
the Notes, the first are washen out, that new may be written in. They which forewent vs did leaue a Roome
for vs, and should wee grieue to doe the same to these
which should come after vs ? who beeing admitted to
170 see the exquisite Rarities of some Antiquaries Cabinet is
grieued, all viewed, to haue the Courtaine drawen, and
giue place to new Pilgrimes ? And when the LORD
of this Vniuerse hath shewed vs the various wonders of
his amazing Frame, should wee take it to heart, when
175 hee thinketh time to dislodge ? This is his vnalterable
and vncuitable Decree ; as wee had no part of our will
in our entrance into this Life, wee should not presume
of anie in our leauing it, but soberlie learne to will that
which hee wills, whose verie willing giueth beeing to

---

[148] IMO. the Stage of [149] IM. vnconstancie [152] O. into another
[158-59] IMO. (by her too great . . .) [159] IMO. our changes [163] IMO.
Death no lesse than life doth heere [165-67] IM *omit* This Earth . . .
written in. [167] O. They who [168] IMO. to those [169-70] IMO. beeing
suffered to see [170] IMO. of an Antiquaries [170-72] IMO. is grieued
that the curtaine bee drawne and to giue [173-74] IMO. the amazing
wonders of his various frame [179] MO. whose very will

180 all that it wills, and adoring the Orderer, not repine at
the Order and Lawes, which all-where, and all-wayes, are
so perfectlie established, that who would essay to alter
& amend anie of them, hee should either make them worse,
or desire thinges beyond the leuell of possibilitie : all that
185 is necessarie and conuenient for vs they haue bestowed
vpon vs, and freelie granted, and what they haue not
bestowed nor granted vs, neither is it necessarie, nor
conuenient that wee should haue it.

If thou doest complaine, that there shall bee a time
190 in the which thou shalt not bee, why doest thou not too
grieue, that there was a time in the which thou wast
not, and so that thou art not as olde, as that enlifening
Planet of Time ? For, not to haue beene a thousand
yeeres before this moment, is as much to bee deplored,
195 as not to bee a thousand after it, the effect of them both
beeing one : that will bee after vs which long long ere
wee were was. Our Childrens children haue that same
reason to murmure that they were not young men in our
dayes, which wee now, to complaine that wee shall not
200 be old in theirs. The Violets haue their time, though they
empurple not the Winter, & the Roses keepe their season,
though they discouer not their beautie in the Spring.

Empires, States, Kingdomes, haue by the Doome of the
Supreame prouidence their fatall Periods, great Cities lye
205 sadlie buried in their dust, Artes and Sciences haue not
onelie their Ecclipses, but their wainings & deathes ; the
gastlie Wonders of the World, raised by the ambition of
Ages, are ouerthrowne and trampled ; some Lights aboue
(deseruing to bee intitled Starres) are loosed and neuer
210 more seene of vs ; the excellent fabrike of this Vniuerse
it selfe shall one day suffer ruine, or a change like a ruine,
and poore Earthlings thus to bee handled complaine !

180 IMO. and reuerencing   182-83 IMO. essay to correct & amend
183 IM *omit* hee *before* should   184-88 IM *omit* all that . . . haue it
185 O. He hath bestow'd   186 O. and what He hath not   190-91 O. also
grieue   192 O. thou was   195 MO. as not to live   199 IMO. which we
haue, to complaine   202 IMO. they disclose not   209 IMO. (not idlie
intitled Starres)   212 O. and should poor Earthlings . . . ?

But is this Life so great a good, that the lose of it should bee so deare vnto Man ? if it be ? the meanest
215 creatures of Nature thus bee happie, for they liue no lesse than hee : If it bee so great a felicitie, how is it esteemed of man himselfe at so small a rate, that for so poore gaines, nay, one disgracefull Word, hee will not stand to loose it ? What excellencie is there in it, for the which hee should
220 desire it perpetuall, and repine to bee at rest, and returne to his olde Grand-mother Dust ? Of what moment are the Labours and Actions of it, that the interruption and leauing off of them should bee to him so distastfull, and with such grudging lamentations receiued ?
225 Is not the entring into Life weaknesse ? the continuing Sorrow ? in the one hee is exposed to all the injuries of the Elementes, and like a condemned Trespasser (as if it were a fault to come to light) no sooner borne than fast manacled and bound, in the other hee is restlesslie, like
230 a Ball, tossed in the Tinnise-court of this world ; when hee is in the brightest Meridiane of his glorie, there needeth nothing to destroy him, but to let him fall his owne hight : A reflexe of the Sunne, a blast of winde, nay, the glance of an Eye is sufficient to vndoe him : Howe can
235 that be anie great matter, of which so small instrumentes and slender actions are maisters ?

His Bodie is but a Masse of discording humours, composed and elemented by the conspiring influences of superior Lights, which though agreeing for a trace of tyme,
240 yet can neuer be made vniforme & keept in a just proportion. To what sickenesse is it subject vnto, beyond those of the other sensitiue Creatures ? no parte of it beeing which is not particularlie infected and afflicted by some

---

215 O. are happy   223 M omits so before distastfull   224 M. receive ?
228 IMO. (. . . to the [I. thee] light)   IMO also omit fast before manacled   231 IM. there mistereth   235-36 IMO omit of before which and insert of after maisters   237-38 IM. humours, boyled together by
242 IM omit sensible before creatures and in the Errata of the second issue of J, sensible is corrected to sensitiue.

one, nay, euerie part with many, yea, so many, that the
245 Maisters of that Arte can scarce number or name them.
So that the life of diuerse of the meanest Creatures of
Nature, hath with great reason by the most Wise, beene
preferred to the naturall life of Man : And wee should
rather wonder how so fragill a matter should so long
250 endure, than how so soone dissolue, and decay.

Are the Actiones of the most part of men, much
differing from the Exercise of the Spider, that pitcheth
toyles, & is tapist, to pray on the smaller Creatures, and
for the Weauing of a scornefull Webbe euiscerateth it selfe
255 manie dayes, which when with much Industerie finished,
a little Puffe of Winde carrieth away both the worke and
the worker ?   Or are they not, like the playes of Children ?
Or (to hold them at their highest rate) as is a May-Game,
a Maske, or what is more earnest, some studie at Chesse ?
260 Euerie day wee rise and lye downe, apparrell our Bodies
and disapparrell them, make them Sepulchers of dead
Creatures, wearie them, & refresh them ; which is a Circle
of idle Trauells, and Laboures (like *Penelopes* Taske) vn-
profitablie renewed.   Some time wee are in a Chase after
265 a fading Beautie ; now wee seeke to enlarge our Boundes,
increase our Treasure, liuing poorelie, to purchase what
wee must leaue to those wee shall neuer see, or (happelie)
to a Foole, or a prodigall Heire ; raised with the wind of
Ambition, wee courte that idle name of Honour, not
270 considering how They mounted aloft in the highest
Ascendant of earthlie Glorie, are but tortured Ghostes,
wandring with golden Fetters in glistering Prisones,
hauing Feare and Danger their vnseparable Executioners,
in the midst of Multitudes rather guarded than regarded.

244-45 IM *omit* yea . . . name them.   249 O. so frail   250 IM *omit* dissolue
after soone   254 M *has the misprint* euiscreateth   256 IM. a tempestuous
Puffe   259 IMO *omit* a Maske   260-62 IMO. apparell and disapparrell our
selues, wearie our bodies and refresh them   266 IMO. feeding poorelie
[*In the Edinburgh University copy of* I, liuing *is pasted in on a printed
slip between* treasure, *and* poorlie]   267 IMO. wee neuer saw   270 O.
who are mounted   271 IMO. are but like   273 IMO. danger

275 They whom opacke imaginations, and inward Thought-
fulnesse, haue made wearie of the worlds Eye, though
they haue with-drawne themselues from the course of
Vulgare Affaires, by vaine Contemplationes, curious
Searches, thinke their life away, are more disquieted, and
280 liue worse than others, their Wit beeing too sharpe
to giue them a true taste of present Infelicities, and
to agrauate their woes ; while they of a more shallow
and blunt Conceit, haue want of Knowledge and Ignorance
of themselues, for a remedie and Antidote against all
285 the Greeuances and incombrances of Life.

What *Camelion*, what *Euripe*, what *Raine-bow*, what
Moone doth change so oft as Man ?   hee seemeth not the
same person in one & the same day, what pleaseth him in
the Morning, is in the Euening distastfull vnto him. Yong
290 hee scorneth his childish Conceits, and wading deeper in
Yeeres (for Yeeres are a Sea, into which hee wadeth
vntill hee drowne) hee esteemeth his Youth vnconstancie,
Rashnesse, Follie ; Old, hee beginneth to pittie himselfe,
plaining because hee is changed, that the World is changed,
295 like those in a Ship, which when they launce from the
Shore, are brought to thinke the Shore doeth flie from
them.   Hee hath no sooner acquired what hee did desire,
but hee beginneth to enter into new Cares, and desire
what hee shall neuer bee able to acquire.   When hee
300 seemeth freed of euill in his owne estate, hee grudgeth
and vexeth himselfe at the happinesse and fortunes of
others.   Hee is pressed with Care for what is present,

275-76 IMO. inward melancholie   276 MO. of the world, though   278 O.
and curious   279 IMO *omit* thinke . . . away   280 IMO. liue a life
worse   281 IMO. taste of their   282 IMO. to increase   283 IMO. simple
Conceit   284-85 IMO. against all the calamities of Life [*In the Edinburgh
University copy of* I, Greeuances of life *is pasted in on a printed slip
after the words* against all the]   286 IM *omit* what " *Raine-bow* "
289 IMO. vnto him distastfull   290 IMO. hee scornes   293 IMO. hee
beginnes   O. Rashness and Folly   294 O. complaining   297-99 IM *omit*
Hee hath . . . to acquire   300 IMO. is fred . . ., he grudges

with Griefe, for what is past, with Feare for what is to come,
nay, for what will neuer come ; And as in the Eye one
305 Teare draweth another after it, so maketh hee one Sorrow
follow vpon a former,. and euerie day lay vp stuffe of
Griefe for the next.

The Aire, the Sea, the Fire, the Beasts bee cruell
Executioners of Man ; yet Beastes, Fire, Sea and Aire, are
310 pittifull to Man in comparison of man, for moe men are
destroyed by men, than by them all. What Scornes,
Wrongs, Contumelies, Imprisonmentes, Torments, Poy-
sons receiueth Man of Man ? What Ingines and new
workes of Death are daylie found out by Man against man ?
315 What Lawes to thrall his Libertie, Fantasies and Bug-
beares, to infatuate and inueigle his reason ? Amongst
the Beastes is there anie that hath so seruile a Lot in
anothers behalfe as Man, yet neither is content, nor hee
who raigneth, nor hee who serueth ?
320 The halfe of our Life is spent in Sleepe ; which hath
such a resemblance to Death, that often it separates the
Soule from the Bodie, and teacheth it a sort of beeing
aboue it, making it soare beyond the Spheare of sensuall
Delightes, and attaine to Knowledge, vnto which, while
325 the Bodie did awake, it dared scarce aspire. And who
would not rather than remaine chained in this loathsome Galley of the World, Sleepe euer (that is dye)
hauing all thinges at one stay, bee free from those Vexa-
tiones, Disasteres, Contempts, Indignities, and manie
330 manie Anguishes, vnto which this Life is enuassalled
and made thrall ? and, well looked vnto, our greatest
Contentment and Happinesse heere seemeth rather to

303 IMO. with sorrow 304 O. come, as in the eye 304-5 IMO. one
teare forceth out another, so makes hee 308 O. are cruel 310 MO.
more men 312-13 O. and Poysone 314 IM. found forth 315 O. Fancies
315-16 IM. and scarbugs to inveigle his reason 321 IMO. separates
as it were 324 IMO. attaine Knowledge 325 IMO. it could scarce
326 IMO. than abide chained in his [O. in this] 328 O. and be free
329 IM *replace* Disasteres *by* misadventers 331 IMO. and subdued ?
M *has also the misprint* and when looking into, *and* O *reads* And, if
well, etc.

consist in an absence of Miserie, than in the enjoying
of any great Good.

335 What haue the dearest Fauorites of the World, created
to the Paternes of the fairest Ideas of Mortalitie to
glorie in? Is it Greatnesse? Who can bee great
on so small a Round as is this Earth, and bounded with
so short a course of time? How like is that to Castles or
340 imaginarie Cities raised in the Skies by chaunce-meeting
Cloudes? or to Gyantes modelled (for a sport) of Snow
which at the hoter lookes of the Sunne melt away and
lye drowned in their owne moisture? Such an impetuous
√ Vicissitude towseth the Estate of this World! Is it Know-
345 ledge? But wee haue not yet attained to a perfect
Vnderstanding of the smallest Flower, and why the Grasse
should rather bee greene than red. / The Element of Fire
is quite put out, the Aire is but Water rarified, the Earth
is found to moue, and is no more the Center of the
350 Vniuerse, is turned into a Magnes; Starres are not fixed,
but swimme in the etheriall Spaces, Cometes are mounted
aboue the Planetes; Some affirme there is another World
of men and sensitiue Creatures, with Cities and Palaces
in the Moone; the Sunne is lost, for, it is but a Light made
355 of the conjunction of manie shining Bodies together, a
Clift in the lower Heauens, through which the Rayes of
the highest defuse themselues, is obserued to haue Spots;
Thus, Sciences by the diuerse Motiones of this Globe of
the Braine of Man, are become Opiniones, nay, Errores,
360 and leaue the Imagination in a thousand Labyrinthes.
What is all wee knowe compared with what wee knowe
not? Wee haue not yet agreed about the chiefe Good
and Felicitie. It is (perhaps) artificiall Cunning, how

333 IMO. in the beeing released from [*In the Edinburgh University
copy of* I, in an absence of miserie *is pasted in on a printed slip
between* consist *and* than] 335-37 IMO. What haue the most eminent
of mortalls to glorie in? 344 IMO. the estates 349 IMO. moueth
353 IMO *omit* sensitiue *before* Creatures, *and replace* Palaces *by* towers
354-55 IM *omit* a Light . . . together 356-57 IMO. through which the
light of the highest shines 357 IMO *omit* is obserued . . . Spots
359-60 IM *omit* nay, . . . Labyrinthes

manie Curiosities bee framed by the least Creatures of
365 Nature (who like a wise Painter showeth in a small
Pourtrait more ingine than in a great) vnto which the
industrie of the most curious Artizanes doeth not attaine?
Is it Riches? What are they, but the Idoles of Fooles,
the casting out of Friendes, Snares of Libertie, Bandes to
370 such as haue them, possessing rather than possessed,
Mettalles which Nature hath hidde (fore-seeing the great
Harmes they should occasion) and the onelie Opinion of
Man, hath brought in estimation? They are like to
Thornes which laid on an open hand are easilie blowne
375 away, and wound the closing and hard-gripping, Prodigalls
mis-spend them, Wretches mis-keepe them; when wee
haue gathered the greatest aboundance, wee our selues
can enjoye no more of them, than so much as belonges
to one man: They take not away Want, but occasione
380 it, what great and rich men doe by others, the meaner
and more contented sort doe by themselues. Will some
talke of our pleasures? It is not (though in the Fables)
told out of purpose, that *Pleasure* beeing called vp to
Heauen, to disburthen her selfe and become more light,
385 did heere leaue her Apparrell, which *Sorrow* (then naked,
forsaken, and wandring) finding, did afterwards attire her
selfe with: And if wee would say the truth of most of our
Ioyes, wee must confesse them to bee but disguised
Sorrowes; Remorse euer ensueth them, and (beeing the
390 Heires of Displeasure) seldome doe they appeare, except
Sadnesse and some wakning Griefe hath reallie preceded
and fore-went them. Will some Ladies vaunt of their

---

364 O. are framed   365-66 IMO *omit* (who . . . great)   368 IM *omit*
the Idoles of Fooles   369 IMO. the snares   372 IMO. (. . . harme
. . .)   373-74 IMO. Like Thornes   374-75 IMO. may bee blowne away,
and on a closing and hard gripping, wound it   378 IMO. no more
thereof   379-80 IM *omit* They take . . . occasione it   381 IMO *omit*
and more contented *and* IM by *before* themselues   382 O. (. . . Fable)
383 IMO. Pleasure in hast   384 IM *omit* to disburthen . . . more
light   385-87 IMO. forget her Apparell, which Sorrow thereafter finding
(to deceiue the world) attired herself with   388-92 IMO. confesse
that they are but disguised Sorrowes; the drames of their Honney
are sowred in pounds of Gall; Remorse euer enseweth them [I. and

Beautie ? That is but Skin-thicke of two Senses onelie
knowne, short euen of marble Statues and Pictures ; not
395 the same to all Eyes, dangerous to the Beholder, and
hurtfull to the Possessour, an Enemie to Chastitie, a
Frame made to delight others more than those which haue
it, a superficiall Varnish hiding Bones and the Braines,
thinges fearefull to bee looked vpon : Growth in Yeares
400 doeth blast it, or Sicknesse, or Sorrow preuenting them ;
Our Strength, matched with that of the vnreasonable
Creatures, is but Weaknesse. All wee can set our eyes
vpon in these intricate mazes of Life is but Alchimie,
vaine Perspectiue, and deceiuing Shadowes, appearing
405 farre other wayes afarre off, than when enjoyed, and
looked vpon at a neare Distance. O ! who if before hee
had a beeing, hee could haue knowledge of the manie-fold
Miseries of it, would enter this woefull Hospitall of the
World, and accept of life vpon such hard conditiones ?
410   If Death bee good, why should it bee feared ? and if
it bee the worke of Nature, how should it not bee good ?
for, Nature, is an Ordinance Disposition and Rule, which
GOD hath established in creating this Vniuerse, as is
the Lawe of a King, which can not erre : For, how
415 should the Maker of that Ordinance erre ? Sith in Him
there is no impotencie and weaknesse, by the which hee
might bring forth what is vnperfect, no peruersenesse
of Will, of which might proceede any vicious action,
no Ignorance, by the which hee might goe wrong in
420 working ; beeing most Powerfull, most Good, most Wise,

---

neuer doe they exist but by their opposite sadnesse] nay, in some
they haue no effect at all if some wakning griefe hath not pre-
ceeded and forewent them   393 IMO. skin-deepe   396 97 IMO. a
thing made   398 IM. a superficiall luster   402-3 IMO. eyes on, *and
omit* Alchimie   405-6 IMO. and gazed vpon in [O. at]   406-9 IM
omit O ! `. . . conditiones ?   406-7 O. O ! who before he had a Being,
could he haue a Knowledge of   412 IMO *omit* Disposition   413 IM.
in the creating   414-15 M *omits* For . . . erre ?   415 O *replaces*
sith *by* since *as always, in the* " *Cypresse Grove.*"   416 O. by which
417 O. imperfect   419 O. by which

nay, All-Wise, All-Good, All-Powerfull : Hee is the
first Orderer, and marshelleth euerie other Order, the
highest Essence, giuing Essence to all other thinges,
of all Causes the Cause : Hee worketh powerfullie,
425 bounteouslie, wiselie, and maketh Nature (his artificiall
Organ) doe the same. How is not Death of Nature ?
Sith what is naturallie generate, is subject to Corruption,
and sith such an Harmonie (which is Life) arising of
the mixture of the foure Elementes, which are the
430 ingredientes of our Bodies, can not euer endure ; the
contrarieties of their qualities (as a consuming rust in the
baser Metalles) beeing an inward cause of a necessarie
dissolution. O of fraile and instable Thinges the constant,
firme, and eternall Order ! For euen in their changes they
435 keepe euer vniuersall auncient and vncorruptible Lawes.

Againe, how can Death bee euill ; sith it is the Thaw
of all these vanities which the Frost of Life bindeth
together ? If there bee a Sacietie in Life, then must there
not bee a Sweetenesse in Death ? Man were an intoller-
440 able thing, were hee not mortall ; The Earth were not
ample enough to containe her Of-spring, if none dyed :
in two or three Ages (without Death) what an vn-
pleasant and lamentable Spectacle were the most flow-
rishing Cities ? For, what should there bee to bee seene in
445 them, saue Bodies languishing and courbing againe into
the Earth, pale disfigured Faces, Skelitones in steade of
Men ? And what to bee heard, but the Exclamationes
of the Yong, Complaintes of the Old, with the pittifull
cryes of sicke and pining Persons ? there is almost
450 no infirmitie worse than Age.

If there bee anie euill in Death, it would appeare to
bee that Paine and torment, which wee apprehend to

425-26 IMO. and maketh [M. makes] (his artificiall Organ) Nature
428 IMO omit sith   428-29 IMO. rising from the mixture   431 MO. con-
trariety [In the Edinburgh University copy of I, contrarietie is pasted
in on a printed slip between The and of their qualities]   431-32 O. (. . .
in baser Mettals)   433-35 IMO omit O . . . Lawes   436 IMO. how is
not Death good   437 IMO. all those   439-40 IM omit Man . . . mortell
445-46 O. and curbing again into the Earthly Pale, disfigured Faces

arise from the breaking of those strait Bands which keepe
the Soule & Bodie together ; which, sith not without great
455 struggling and motion, seemeth to proue it selfe vehement
and most extreame. The Senses are the onelie cause of
paine, but before the last Trances of Death they are so
brought vnder, that they haue no (or verie little) strength,
and their strength lessening the strength of Paine too must
460 bee lessened. How should wee doubt but the weaknesse
of Sense lesseneth Paine, sith wee know, that weakned
and maimed partes which receiue not nourishment, are a
great deale lesse sensible than the other partes of the
Bodie : And see, that olde strengthlesse, decrepit Persons
465 leaue this World almost without paine, as in a Sleepe ? If
Bodies of the most sound & wholesome constitution bee
these which most vehementlie feele paine, it must then
follow that they of a distempered & crasie Constitution,
haue least feeling of Paine ; and by this reason, all weake
470 and sicke Bodies should not much feele Paine ; for if they
were not distempered and euill complexioned, they would
not bee sicke. That the *Sight, Hearing, Taste, Smelling,*
leaue vs without Paine, & vn-awares, we are vndoubtedlie
assured : And why should wee not thinke the same of the
475 *Feeling* ? That, by which wee are capable of Feeling, is
the vitall Spirits animated by the Braine, which in a Man
in perfect Health, by veines & arteres are spred & extended through the whole bodie, and hence it is that the
whole Bodie is capable of paine : But, in dying Bodies wee
480 see, that by pauses and degrees those partes which are
furthest remoued from the Heart, become cold, and beeing
depriued of naturall heate, all the paine which they feele, is
that they doe feele no paine. Now, euen as ere the sicke
bee aware, the vitall Spirits haue with-drawne themselues
485 from the whole extension of the Bodie, to succour the

453 O. Bonds   455 IMO. seemes   458 *In* J, *the two words* or verie *only,
are enclosed in the bracket.*   464 IMO *omit* strengthlesse   468 IM. dis-
temperate   475-76 IM. That which is capable of feeling are the vitall
spirits, which in a Man   477 M. in a perfit health O. of perfect Health
IMO *omit* by veines & arteres   480 IMO. the partes   483-84 even as
before the sick are aware

Heart (like distressed Citizens which finding their Walles
battered downe, flie to the defence of their Cittadell)
so doe they abandonne the Heart without any sensible
touch : As the flame, the Oyle failing, leaueth the Weeke,
490 or as the light the Aire which it doeth inuest.   As to those
shrinking motions, and convultions of Sinewes & Members, which appeare to witnesse great paine, let one represent to himselfe the Stringes of an high-tuned Lute,
which breaking, retire to their naturall windings, or a
495 peece of Yce, that without any out-ward violence, cracketh
at a Thaw : No otherwise doe the Sinewes of the Bodie,
finding themselues slacke and vnbended from the
Braine, & their wonted labours & motions cease, struggle,
and seeme to stirre themselues, but without either
500 paine or sense.   Sowning is a true pourtrait of Death, or
rather it is the same, beeing a Cessation from all action,
motion, and function of Sense and Life : But in Sowning
there is no paine, but a silent rest, and so deepe and sound
a sleepe, that the naturall is nothing in comparison of it ;
505 What great paine then can there bee in Death, which is
but a continued Sowning, a sweete ignorance of Cares,
and a neuer againe returning to the workes and dolorous
felicitie of Life ? The wise and all prouident Creator
hath made Death by many signes of paine appeare terrible,
510 to the effect, that if Man, for reliefe of miseries and
present euills, should haue vnto it recourse, it beeing
(apparantlie) a worser, hee should rather constantlie
indure what hee knoweth, than haue refuge vnto that
which hee feareth and knoweth not, the Terrours of
515 Death seeme the Gardianes of Life.
    Now although Death were an extreame Paine, sith
it comes in an Instant, what can it bee ? why should
wee feare it ? for, while wee are, it commeth not, and
it beeing come, wee are no more.   Nay, though it were

490 IMO. As to the   MO. or as Light the Air   500 MO. Swoning
502 MO. Swoning   506 MO. Swowning   IM omit a sweete . . . of cares
508-15 IM omit The wise . . . Gardianes of Life.   512 O. worse   513 O.
he knows   516-17 MO. sith [O. since] it is in

520 most painefull, long continuing, and terrible-vglie, why
should wee feare it ? Sith Feare is a foolish passion but
where it may preserue ; but it can not preserue vs from
Death, yea, rather Feare maketh vs to meete with that
which wee would shunne, and banishing the Comfortes
525 of present Contentmentes bringeth Death more neare
vnto vs : That is euer terrible which is vnknowne ; so
doe little Children feare to goe in the darke, and their
Feare is increased with Tales.

But that (perhaps) which anguisheth Thee most, is to
530 haue this glorious Pageant of the World remoued from
Thee, in the Prime and most delicious Season of thy life ;
for, though to dye bee vsuall, to dye young may appeare
extraordinarie. If the present Fruition of these things bee
vnprofitable and vaine, what can a long Continuance of
535 them bee, If GOD had made Life happier, hee had also
made it longer ? Stranger and newe Halcyon, why
wouldst thou longer nestle amidst these vnconstant and
stormie Waues ? Hast thou not alreadie suffred enough
of this World, but thou must yet endure more ? To
540 liue long, is it not to bee long troubled ? But number thy
Yeares, which are now ( ) and thou shalt find,
that where as ten haue ouer-liued Thee, thousands haue
not attained this age. One yeare is sufficient to behold
all the magnificence of Nature, nay, euen one Day and
545 Night ; for more, is but the same brought againe : This
Sunne, that Moone, these Starres, the varying Dance of
the Spring, Summer, Autumne, Winter, Is that verie
same which the golden Age did see. They which haue
the longest time lent them to liue in, haue almost no
550 part of it at all, measuring it, either by that space of time
which is past, when they were not, or by that which is
to come : Why shouldst thou then care, whether thy
Dayes bee manie, or few, which when prolonged to the

---

520 M. terrible, ugly O *omits* terrible   523-26 IMO. rather the feare
of it, banishing the comfortes of present contentments makes Death
to aduance and approach the more neare vnto vs   531 IMO. in the
Spring and   535-36 IM *omit* If GOD . . . longer ?   537 MO. would thou

vttermost, proue, paralel'd with Eternitie, as a Teare is to
555 the Ocean ? To dye young, is to doe that soone, and
in some fewer dayes, which once thou must doe ; it is
but the giuing ouer of a Game that (after neuer so manie
hazardes) must bee lost. When thou hast liued to that Age
thou desirest, or one of *Platos* yeares, so soone as the last
560 of thy dayes, riseth aboue thy Horizon, thou wilt then as
now demand longer Respite, and expect more to come,
the oldest are most vnwilling to dye. It is Hope of
long life, that maketh Life seeme short. Who will
behold, and with the eyes of judgement behold, the manie
565 Changes depending on humaine affaires, with the after-
claps of Fortune, shall neuer lament to dye yong. Who
knoweth what alterations and sudden disasters, in outward estate, or inward contentments, in this Wildernesse
of the World, might haue befallen him who dyeth yong,
570 if hee had liued to bee olde ? Heauen, fore-knowing im-
minent harmes, taketh those which it loueth to it selfe,
before they fall foorth : Death in Youth is like the leauing
a supperfluous Feast, before the drunken Cups be presented
and walke about. Pure and (if wee may so say) Virgine
575 Soules carrie their bodies with no small Agonies, and delight not to remaine long in the dregs of humane corruption, still burning with a desire to turne backe to the
place of their Rest ; for this World is their Inne, and not
their Home. That which may fall foorth euerie houre, can
580 not fall out of time. Life is a Iourney in a dustie Way, the
furthest Rest is Death, in this some goe more heauilie
burthened, than others : Swift and actiue Pilgrimes
come to the end of it in the Morning, or at Noone, which
Tortoyse-paced Wretches, clogged with the fragmentarie
585 rubbige of this World, scarce with great trauell crawle
vnto at Mid-night. Dayes are not to bee esteemed after the
number of them, but after the goodnesse : more Compasse

556-57 M. it is the giving over   564 IM. with eyes of aduice   O. with
the Eye of Yudgment   565 M. attending on   O. attending   567 IMO.
knowes   571 IO. loues   572-74 IM *omit* Death . . . walke about   O
omits and walke about   585 O. Rubbish

maketh not a Spheare more compleate, but as round is a
little, as a large Ring ; nor is that Musician most praise-
590 worthie who hath longest played, but hee in measured
Accents who hath made sweetest Melodie ; to liue long
hath often beene a let to liue well.   Muse not how many
yeares thou mightst haue enjoyed Life, but how sooner thou
mightst haue lossed it ; neither grudge so much that it is
595 no better, as comfort thy selfe that it hath beene no worse:
let it suffice that thou hast liued till this day; and (after the
course of this World) not for nought; thou hast had some
smiles of Fortune, fauours of the worthiest, some friendes,
and thou hast neuer beene disfauoured of the Heauen.
600   Though not for Life it selfe, yet that to after-worlds thou
mightst leaue some Monument that once thou wast, hap-
pilie in the cleare light of Reason, it would appeare that
Life were earnestly to be desired : for sith it is denyed vs
to liue euer (said one) let vs leaue some worthy Remem-
605 brance of our once heere beeing, and drawe out this
Spanne of Life to the greatest length & so farre as is
possible.   O poore Ambition ! to what (I pray Thee) mayst
thou concreded it ?   Arches and stately Temples, which one
Age doth raise, doth not another raze ?   Tombes and
610 adopted Pillars, lye buried with those which were in them
buried : Hath not Auarice defaced, what Religion did
make glorious ?   All that the hand of man can vpreare, is
either ouer-turned by the hand of man, or at length by
standing and continuing consumed : as if there were a
615 secret opposition in Fate (the vneuitable Decree of the
Eternall) to controule our industry, and conter-checke
all our deuices and proposing.   Possessions are not en-
during, Children lose their Names, Families glorying
(like Marigolds in the Sunne) on the highest top of
620 Wealth and Honour (no better than they which are
not yet borne) leauing off to bee. So doeth Heauen
confound, what wee endeauour by Labour and Arte to

<hr>

599 O. of Heaven   608 O. concredit   610 O. adapted   615 O. inevitable
617 O. Proposals   618 O *omits* Families

distinguish. That Renowne by Papers, which is thought
to make men immortall, and which nearest doth ap-
625 proach the Life of these eternall Bodies aboue, how
slender it is, the very word of Paper doth import ; and
what is it when obtained, but a flowrish of Words, which
comming Tymes may scorne ?   How many millions neuer
heare the Names of the most famous Writers, and
630 amongst them to whom they are known, how few turne
ouer their Pages, and of such as doe, how many sport
at their Conceits, taking the Verity for a Fable, and oft
a Fable for Veritie, or (as wee doe Pleasants) vse all for
recreation? Then the arising of more famous, doth darken,
635 put downe, and turne ignoble the Glorie of the former,
being held as Garments, worne out of fashion.   Now
when thou hast attained what Praise thou couldst desire,
and thy fame is emblazoned in many Stories, neuer after
to bee either shadowed or worne out, it is but an Eccho,
640 a meere Sound, a Glow-worme, which seene a farre,
casteth some cold beames, but approached is found
nothing, an imaginarie happinesse, whose good dependes
on the opinion of others.   Desert and Vertue for the
most part want Monuments and Memorie, seldome are
645 recorded in the Volumes of Admiration, nay, are often
branded with Infamie, while Statues and Trophees are
erected to those, whose names should haue beene buried
in their dust, and folded vp in the darkest clowds of obliuion : So doe the rancke Weeds in this Garden of the
650 World choacke & ouer-run the swetest Flowres.   Applause,
whilst thou liuest, serueth but to make Thee that faire
Marke against which Enuye and Malice direct their
Arrowes, and when thou art wounded, all Eyes are turned
towards thee (like the Sunne which is most gazed on
655 in an Ecclipse) not for Pittie or Praise but Detraction ;

[627] IMO. a multitude of Words   [628] O. future Times   [635] O omits
put downe   [638 39] IM omit neuer after . . . worne out, and O omits
either before shadowed   [644] O. and seldom   [645] In the Errata of J,
Volumnes is corrected to Volumes.   [645-46] IM omit nay, . . . infamie,
and O reads they are often, etc.   [653-55] IM omit and when . . .
detraction

at the best, it but resembleth that Siracusianes Spheare of
Christall not so faire as fraile : and, borne after thy death,
it may as well bee ascribed, to some of those were in the
Trojan Horse, or to such as are yet to bee borne an hun-
660 dreth yeares heareafter, as to Thee, who nothing knowes,
and is of all vnknowne.   What can it auaile thee to bee
talked of, whilst thou art not ?   Consider in what Bounds
our Fame is confined, how narrow the Listes are of humane
Glorie, and the furthest shee can stretch her winges.
665 This Globe of the Earth and water, which seemeth huge to
vs, in respect of the Vniuerse, compared with that wide
wide Pauillion of Heauen, is lesse than little, of no sensible quantitie, and but as a Point : for the Horizon which
boundeth our sight, deuideth the Heauen as in two halfes,
670 hauing alwaies sixe of the Zodiacke Signes aboue, and as
many vnder it, which if the Earth had any quantitie compared to it, it could not doe.   More, if the Earth were not
as a point, the Starres could not still in all parts of it appeare to vs as of a like greatnes; for where the Earth raised
675 it selfe in Mountaines, wee beeing more neare to Heauen,
they would appeare to vs of a greater quantity, and where
it is humbled in Vallies, wee beeing further distant, they
would seeme vnto vs lesse : But the Starres in all partes of
the Earth appearing of a like greatnesse, and to euery part
680 of it, the Heauen imparting to our sight the halfe of its
inside, wee must auouch it to bee but as a Point.   Well
did One compare it to an Ant-hill, and men (the Inhabitants) to so manie Pismires, and Grashoppers, in the toyle
and varietie of their diuersified studies.   Now of this
685 small indiuisible thing, thus compared, how much is
couered with Waters ?   how much not at all discouered ?
how much vn-inhabited and desart ?   and how many
millions of millions are they, which share the remnant
amongst them, in Languages, Customes, diuine Rites differ-

<hr>

656 IMO. at the best [O. at best] is [O. it is] liked   657 I. as faire as
fraile   MO. as frail as fair   O. and being, born   659-60 MO. hundred
661 O. and art   666 IMO. & compared   681 J has the misprint is for it
before to bee   687 IM. vnhabited   689 O. and divine

690 ing, and all almost to others vnknowne ?   But let it bee
granted that Glorye and Fame are some great matter, are
the life of the dead, and can reach Heauen it selfe, sith they
are oft buried with the honoured, and passe away in so fleet
a Reuolution of time, what great good can they haue in
695 them ?   How is not Glorie temporall, if it increase with
yeares and depend on time ?   Then imagine mee (for what
cannot Imagination reach vnto ?) one could bee famous in
all times to come, and ouer the whole World present,
yet shall hee bee for euer Obscure and ignoble to those
700 mightie Ones, which were onely heere-tofore esteemed
famous, amongst the Assyrians, Persians, Romans.   Againe,
the vaine Affectation of man is so suppressed, that though
his workes abide some space, the Worker is vnknowne :
the huge Egyptian Pyramides, and that Grot in *Pausilipo*,
705 though they haue wrestled with Time, and worne vpon
the vaste of dayes, yet are their Aúthores no more known,
than it is knowne by what strange Earth-quackes, and
Deluges, Yles were diuided from the Continent, or Hilles
bursted foorth of the Vallies.   Dayes, Monthes, and
710 Yeares, are swallowed vp in the great Gulfe of Tyme (which
puts out the eyes of all their Glorie) and onelie a fattall
obliuion remaines :   Of so manie Ages past, wee may well
figure to our selues some likelie Apparances, but can affirme
little Certaintie.
715   But (my Soule) what aileth thee, to bee thus backward
and astonished, at the remembrance of Death, sith it doth
not reach Thee, more than Darknesse doth those farre-
shinning Lampes aboue ?   Rouse thy selfe for shame, why
shouldst thou feare to bee without a Bodie, sith thy Maker,
720 and the spirituall and supercelestiall Inhabitantes haue
no Bodies ?   Hast thou euer seene any Prisoner, who
when the Iaile Gates were broken vp, and hee enfranchised
and set loose, would rather plaine and sit still on his Fetters,

691-92 IMO *omit* are the . . . dead   699 O. shall he ever be obscure
706 IMO. the waste of dayes   715 IMO. ailes   723 O. complain and sit
still in

than seeke his freedome ?   Or any Mariner, who in the
725 midst of Stormes arriuing neare the Shore, would launch
forth againe vnto the Maine, rather than stricke Saile and
joyfullie enter the leas of a saue Harbour ?   If thou rightlie
know thy selfe, thou hast but small cause of anguish ;
for, if there bee any resemblance of that which is infinite,
730 in what is finite (which yet by an infinite imperfection is
from it distant) If thou bee not an Image, thou art a
Shadow of that vnsearchable Trinitie, in thy three essentiall Powers, Vnderstanding, Will, Memorie; which though
three, are in Thee but one, and abiding one, are distinctly
735 three :   But in nothing more comest thou neare that
Soueraigne Good, than by thy Perpetuitie, which who
striue to improue, by that same doe it proue :   Like those
that by arguing themselues to bee without all reason, by
the verie arguing, show how they haue some.   For, how
740 can what is whollie mortall more thinke vpon, consider,
or know that which is immortall, than the Eye can
know Soundes, or the Eare discerne of Coloures ; if none
had Eyes, who would euer dispute of light or shadow ?
And if all were deafe, who would descant of Musicke ?
745 To Thee nothing in this visible world is comparable ;
thou art so wonderfull a Beautie, and so beautifull a
Wonder, that if but once thou couldst be gazed vpon by
bodily Eyes, euery heart would be inflamed with thy loue,
and rauished from all seruile basenesse and earthlie desires.
750 Thy being dependes not on Matter ; hence by thine Vnderstanding dost thou dyue into the being of euerie other
thing ; and therein art so pregnant, that nothing by Place,
Similitude, Subject, Time, is so conjoyned, which thou
canst not separate ; as what neither is, nor any wayes can

[726] O. again into   [737] O. strive to disprove, by that same do prove
jt   [738] MO. without reason   [740-41] IMO *omit* thinke . . . consider, or
[742-43] IM. question about coloures   [*In the Edinburgh University and
Haigh Hall copies of* I, *and likewise in that containing the signature of
the Earl of Lauderdale,* discerne of *is pasted in on a printed slip between*
eare *and* colours]   [743] IMO. descant of light or shadow [M. Sorrow O.
Colours]   [744] IM *omit* and if . . . of musicke   [753] O. or Time   [754] O.
any way

755 exist, thou canst faine, & giue an abstract being vnto.
Thou seemest a World in thy selfe, containing Heauen,
Starres, Seas, Earth, Floodes, Mountaines, Forestes, and all
that liues : Yet rests thou not satiate with what is in thy-
selfe, nor with all in the wide Vniuerse (because thou
760 knowest their defectes) vntill thou raise thy selfe, to the
contemplation of that first illuminating Intelligence, farre
aboue Time, and euen reaching Eternitie it selfe, into which
thou art transformed, for, by receiuing thou (beyond all
other thinges) art made that which thou receiuest. The
765 more thou knowest the more apt thou art to know, not
being amated with any object that excelleth in predomin-
ance, as Sense by objectes sensible. Thy Will is vncom-
pellable, resisting Force, daunting Necessitie, despising
Danger, triumphing ouer Affliction, vnmoued by Pittie, and
770 not constrained by all the toyles and disasters of Life.
What the Artes-Master of this Vniuerse is in gouerning this
Vniuerse, thou art in the Bodie ; and as hee is whollie in
euerie part of it, so art thou whollie in euerie part of the
Bodie : Like vnto a Mirrouer, euerie small parcell of which
775 a parte, doeth represent and doe the same, what the whole
did enteire & together. By Thee Man is that Hymen of
eternall and mortall thinges, that Chaine, together binding
vnbodied and bodilie Substances, without which the
goodlie Fabricke of this World were vnperfect. Thou
780 hast not thy beginning from the fecunditie, power,
nor action of the elementall qualities, beeing an immediate
Master-piece of that great Maker : Hence hast Thou
the Formes and Figures of all thinges imprinted in Thee
from thy first originall. Thou onelie at once art capable of
785 contraries, of the three partes of Time, Thou makest but
one, thou knowest thy selfe so separate, absolute, & diuerse
an essence from thy Bodie, that Thou disposest of it
as it pleaseth Thee, for in Thee there is no passion so weake

[758] IMO. liueth O. not satiated with what is thy self [759-60] IM *omit*
(because . . . defectes) [765-66] O. not being amazed with any objects
[774-76] IM *omit* like vnto . . . together [779] O. imperfect [787] O. that
thou art dispossessed of it

which mastereth not the feare of leauing it. Thou shouldst
790 bee so farre from repining at this separation, that it should
bee the chiefe of thy desires ; Sith it is the passage, and
meanes to attaine thy perfection and happinesse. Thou
art heere, but as in an infected and leprous Inne, plunged
in a flood of humours, oppressed with Cares, suppressed
795 with Ignorance, defiled and destained with Vice, retrograd
in the course of Vertue ; Small thinges seeme heere great
vnto Thee, and great thinges small, Follie appeareth Wisedome and Wisedome Follie. Fred of thy fleshlie Care,
thou shalt rightlie discerne the beautie of thy selfe, and
800 haue perfect Fruition of that All-sufficient and All-suffizing
Happinesse, which is GOD himselfe ; to whom thou
owest thy beeing, to Him thou owest thy well beeing ;
Hee and Happinesse are the same. For, if GOD had not
Happinesse, Hee were not GOD, because Happinesse is the
805 highest and greatest Good : If then GOD haue Happinesse,
it can not bee a thing differing from Him, for, if there were
any thing in Him differing from Him, Hee should bee an
Essence composed & not simple. More, what is differing
in any thing, is either an accident or a part of it selfe ; In
810 GOD Happinesse can not bee an accident, because Hee is
not subject to any accidents ; if it were a part of Him (since
the part is before the whole) wee should bee forced to
grant, that something was before GOD. Bedded & bathed
in these earthlie ordures, thou canst not come neare this
815 soueraigne Good, nor haue any glimpse of the farre-off
dawning of his vn-accessible Brightnesse, no, not so much
as the eyes of the Birds of the night haue of the Sunne.
Thinke then by Death, that thy Shell is broken, and thou
then but euen hatched; that thou art a Pearle, raised from
820 thy Mother, to bee enchaced in Gold, and that the death-
day of thy bodie, is thy birth-day to Eternitie.

Why shouldst thou bee feare-stroken ? and discom-
forted, for thy parting from this mortall Bride, thy Bodie ;

[809] O. or a Part it self   [816] IMO. vncessable [O. inaccessible] brightnesse

sith it is but for a tyme, and such a tyme, as shee
825 shall not care for, nor feele any thing in, nor thou haue
much neede of her? Nay, sith thou shalt receiue her
againe, more goodlie and beautifull, than when in her
fullest Perfection thou enjoyed her; beeing by her
absence made like vnto that Indian Christall, which after
830 some Reuolutions of Ages, is turned into purest Diamond.
If the Soule bee the Forme of the Bodie, and the Forme
seperated from the Matter of it, can not euer so continue,
but is inclined and disposed to bee reunited thereinto;
What can let and hinder this desire, but that some time
835 it bee accomplished, and obtaining the expected end,
rejoyne it selfe againe vnto the Bodie? The Soule separate
hath a desire, because it hath a will, and knoweth
it shall by this reunion receiue Perfection: too, as the
Matter is disposed, and inclineth to its Forme when it
840 is without it, so would it seeme that the Forme should
bee towards its Matter in the absence of it. How is not
the Soule the Forme of the Bodie, sith by it it is, sith it
is the beginning and cause of all the actions and functions
of the Bodie: For though in excellencie it passe euerie
845 other Forme, yet doeth not that excellencie take from it
the Nature of a Forme. If the abiding of the Soule from
the Bodie bee violent, then can it not bee euerlasting, but
haue a regresse: How is not such an estate of beeing and
abiding not violent to the Soule, if it bee naturall to it to
850 bee in its Matter, and (seperate) after a strange manner,
many of the powers and faculties of it (which neuer leaue
it) are not duelie exercised? This Vnion seemeth not
aboue the Horizon of naturall reason, farre lesse impossible
to bee done by GOD: and though Reason can not eui-
855 dentlie heere demonstrate, yet hath shee a mistie and
groping notice. If the Bodie shall not arise, how can the
onelie and Soueraigne Good bee perfectlie and infinitlie
good? For, how shall Hee be just, nay, haue so much

---

833 O. thereunto 837 IMO. knowes 838 O omits too 842-44 IMO.
sith [O. since] by it it is, and is the beginning . . . of it

justice as man, if he suffer the euill & vicious to haue a
860 more prosperous and happie life, than the followers of
Religion and Vertue, which ordinarlie vseth to fall forth in
this life ?   For, the most wicked are Lords and Gods of this
Earth, sleeping in the lee port of Honour, as if the spacious
habitation of the World had beene made onelie for them,
865 and the Vertuous and good, are but forlorne cast-awayes,
floting in the surges of distresse, seeming heere either of
the Eye of Prouidence not pittied, or not reguarded :
beeing subject to all dishonours, wrongs, wrackes; in their
best estate passing away their dayes (like the Dazies in
870 the Field) in silence and contempt.   Sith then Hee is most
good, most just, of necessitie, there must bee appointed by
Him an other time and place of retribution, in the which
there shall be a Reward for liuing well, and a Punishment
for doing euill, with a life where-into both shall receiue
875 their due ;   and not onelie in their Soules diuested, for,
sith both the parts of man did acte a part in the right or
wrong, it carrieth great reason with it, that they both
(inteire man) bee araigned before that high Iustice, to
receiue their owne :   Man is not a Soule onlie, but a Soule
880 and Bodie, to which either Guerdon or punishment is
due.   This seemeth to bee the Voice of Nature in almost
all the Religions of the World ;   this is that generall Testi-
monie, charactered in the minds of the most barbarous and
saluage people ;   for, all haue had some rouing Guesses at
885 Ages to come, and a Glow-worme light of another life,
all appealing to one generall Iudgement Throne.   To what
else could serue so many expiations, sacrifices, prayers,
solemnities, and misticall Ceremonies ?   To what such
sumptuous Temples, & care of the dead ? to what all
890 Religion ?   If not to showe, that they expected a more

860 O *omits* and happie *before* life   868 O. and Wracks   871 O. and
most just   872 O. in which   873 I. for leauing well [*In the Edinburgh
University copy of* I, liuing *is pasted in on a printed slip between* for *and*
well, *and in that containing the signature of the Earl of Lauderdale the
word* leauing *is altered in ink to* liuing]   874 O. a Life wherein   878 IMO
omit (inteire man)   885 IMO. dimme-duskish light

excellent manner of being, after the Nauigation of this life did take an end. And who doeth denie it, must denie that there is a Prouidence, a GOD ; confesse that his worshippe, and all studie and reason of vertue are vaine ; and not

895 belieue that there is a World, are creatures, and that Hee Himselfe is not what Hee is.

But it is not of Death (perhaps) that we complaine, but of Tyme, vnder the fatall shadow of whose winges, all things decay and wither : This is that Tyrant, which exe-

900 cuting against vs his diamantine lawes, altereth the harmonious constitution of our Bodies, benuming the Organes of our knowledge, turneth our best Senses sencelesse, makes vs loathsome to others, and a burthen to our selues; Of which euills Death releiueth vs. So that, if wee could

905 bee transported (O happy colonie !) to a place exempted from the Lawes and conditiones of Time, where neither change, motion, nor other affection of materiall and corruptible things were, but an immortall, vnchangeable, impassible, all-sufficient kinde of life, it were the last of things

910 wisheable, the tearme and center of all our Desires. Death maketh this transplantation ; for the last instant of Corruption, or leauing off of any thing to bee what it was, is the first of Generation, or being of that which succeedeth ; Death then beeing the end of this miserable transitory

915 life, of necessity must bee the beginning of that other all excellent and eternall : And so causeleslie of a vertuous Soule it is either feared or complained on.

AS those Images were limned in my minde (the morning Starre now almost arising in the East) I

920 found my thoughts in a mild and quiet calme ; and not long after, my Senses one by one forgetting their vses, began to giue themselues ouer to rest, leauing mee in a still

---

893 O. and a God   897-917 *are omitted in* MO.   899 I. wether [*In the Edinburgh University copy of* I, wither *is pasted in on a printed slip between* decay *and* and : This *and in that containing the signature of the Earl of Lauderdale, the word* wether *is corrected in ink to* wither]   917 *In the Edinburgh University copy of* I, is it *is pasted in on a printed slip between* Soule *and* either   918 IMO. were pourtraited

and peaceable sleepe ; if sleepe it may bee called, where
the Minde awaking is carried with free wings from out
925 fleshlie bondage ? For heauy lids, had not long couered
their lights, when mee thought, nay, sure I was, where I
might discerne all in this great *All* ; the large compasse of
the rolling Circles, the brightnesse and continuall motion
of those Rubies of the Night, which (by their distance)
930 heere below can not bee perceiued ; the siluer countenance of the wandring Moone, shining by anothers light,
the hanging of the Earth (as enuironed with a girdle of
Christall) the Sunne enthronized in the midst of the
Planetes, eye of the Heauens, Gemme of this precious
935 Ring the World. But whilst with wonder and amazement I gazed on those celestiall Splendors, and the
beaming Lampes of that glorious Temple (like a poore
Countrie-man brought from his solitarie Mountaines and
Flockes, to behold the magnificence of some great Citie)
940 There was presented to my sight a MAN, as in the
spring of His yeares, with that selfe same Grace, comelie
feature, majesticke Looke which the late (   ) was
wont to haue : on whom I had no sooner fixed mine
eyes, when (like one Planet-stroken) I become amazed :
945 But Hee with a milde demeanour, and voyce surpassing
all humane sweetnesse appeared (mee thought) to say,
    What is it doth thus paine and perplexe thee ?   Is it the
remembrance of Death, the last Period of wretchednesse,
and entrie to these happie places ; the Lanterne which
950 lighteneth men to see the Misterie of the blessednesse of
Spirites, and that Glorie which transcendeth the Courtaine
of things visible ? Is thy Fortune below on that darke
Globe (which scarce by the smalnesse of it appeareth

---

⁹³⁴ O. and Gem   ⁹³⁷⁻³⁹ M *omits* (like a . . . great citie)   ⁹⁴² O. and
Majestick   ⁹⁴³⁻⁴⁴ IMO. set mine eyes   ⁹⁴⁴ IMO. became   ⁹⁴⁶ IMO. I
thought   [*In the Edinburgh University copy of* I, mee *is pasted in on a
printed slip between* appeared *and* thought]   ⁹⁴⁷ IMO. thus anguish and
trouble thee ?   [*In the Edinburgh University and Haigh Hall copies of*
I, *as well as in that containing the signature of the Earl of Lauderdale,*
paine and perplex thee ? *is pasted in on a printed slip between* thus
and Is it]

here) so great, that thou art heart-broken and dejected
955 to leaue it ? What if thou wert to leaue behinde thee a
(   ) so glorious in the eye of the World (yet but a
mote of dust encircled with a pond) as that of mine, so
louing (   ) such great Hopes, these had beene apparant
occasions of lamenting, & but apparant ? Dost thou
960 thinke thou leauest Life too soone? Death is best young;
things faire and excellent, are not of long indurance
vpon Earth. Who liueth well, liueth long ; Soules most
beloued of their Maker are soonest releeued from the
bleeding cares of Life, & with almost a sphericall swift-
965 nesse wafted through the Surges of Humane miseries.
Opinion (that great Enchantresse and Peiser of things,
not as they are, but as they seeme) hath not in any thing
more, than in the conceit of Death, abused Man : Who
must not measure himselfe, and esteeme his estate, after
970 his earthlie being, which is but as a dreame : For, though
hee bee borne on the Earth, hee is not borne for the
Earth, more than the Embryon for the mothers wombe.
It plaineth to bee releeued of its bands, and to come to
the light of this World, and Man waileth to bee loosed
975 from the Chaines with which hee is fettered in that Valley
of vanities : it nothing knoweth whither it is to goe,
nor ought of the beauty of the visible works of God,
neither doth Man of the magnificence of the intellectuall
World aboue, vnto which (as by a Mid-wife) hee is directed
980 by Death. Fooles, which thinke that this faire and
admirable Frame, so variouslie disposed, so rightly
marshalled, so strongly maintained, enriched with so
many excellencies, not only for necessity, but for ornament
and delight, was by that Supreme Wisedome brought
985 forth, that all things in a circulary course, should bee and
not bee, arise and dissolue, and thus continue, (as if they
were so many Shadowes careleslie cast out and caused by

963-65 IMO. from the [O. their] bleeding cares of life, and most swiftlie
wafted 966 O. Poiser 971-72 J has thee *for* the *before* Earth 972 O.
Embryo 973 MO. It [O. complaineth] to be delivered of 974 O. bewaileth
985 O. circular 987 IMO *omit* careleslie

the encountring of those superiour celestiall Bodies,
changing onelie their fashion and shape, or fantasticall
990 Imageries, or shades of faces into Christall) But more
They, which beleeue that Hee doth no other-wayes regard
this his worke than as a Theater, raised for bloudy Sword-
playeres, Wrastlers, Chasers of timorous and Combatters
of terrible Beastes, delighting in the daily torments
995 Sorrowes distresse and Miserie of Mankind. No, no, the
Eternall Wisedome, did make Man an excellent Creature,
though hee faine would, vnmake himselfe, and
returne vnto nothing : And though hee seeke his felicity
among the reasonlesse Wights, he hath fixed it aboue.
1000 Hee brought him into this world as a Master to a sumptuous well-ordered and furnished Inne, a Prince to a
populous and rich Empirie, a Pilgrime and Spectator to a
Stage full of delightfull Wonders and wonderfull Delightes.
And as some Emperour or great Monarch, when hee hath
1005 raised any stately City, the worke beeing atchieued, is
wont to set his Image in the midst of it, to bee admired
and gazed vpon : No otherwise did the Soueraigne of this
World, the Fabricke of it perfected, place Man (a great
Miracle) formed to his owne Paterne, in the midst of this
1010 spacious and admirable Citie, by the diuine splendor of
his Reason to bee an Interpreter and Trunchman of his
Creation, and admired and reuerenced by all his other
Creatures. GOD containeth all in Him, as the beginning
of all, Man containeth all in Him, as the midst of all ;
1015 inferiour things bee in Man more noblie than they exist,
superiour thinges more meanely, celestiall thinges fauour
him, earthly thinges are vassaled vnto him, hee is the
knot and Band of both ; neither is it possible but that

988 IMO. these   989 J *has* there *for* their *before* fashion   990 or
printes of faces   990-95 IMO *omit* but more . . . of mankind
996 IMO. hath made Man [*In the Errata of the second issue of* J,
created *is corrected to* did make]   998 IMO. to nothing   1000-3 IM *omit*
Hee brought . . . delightes   1004 IMO. Looke how some Prince or
great King on the Earth, when hee   1007-8 IMO. of this "*All*"   1010-13 IM
omit by the diuine . . . creatures   1011 O. the Interpreter   1018 IMO
omit knot and *and* O *has* Bond *instead of* Band

both of them haue peace with Man, if Man haue peace
1020 with Him who made the Couenant betweene them and
Him. Hee was made that hee might in the Glasse of the
World behold the infinite Goodnesse, Power, Magnificence,
and Glorie of his Maker, and beholding know, and knowing
Loue, and louing enioy, and to hold the Earth of him as
1025 of his Lord Paramount, neuer ceasing to remember and
praise Him. It exceedeth the compasse of Conceit, to
thinke that that Wisedome which made euerie thing so
orderlie in the partes, should make a confusion in the
whole, and the chiefe Master-piece ; how bringing forth
1030 so manie excellencies for Man, it should bring forth Man
for basenesse and miserie. And no lesse strange were it,
that so long life should bee giuen to Trees, Beastes, and
the Birds of the Aire, Creatures inferiour to Man, which
haue lesse vse of it, and which can not judge of this goodlie
1035 Fabricke, and that it should bee denyed to Man : Vnlesse
there were another manner of liuing prepared for him,
in a Place more noble and excellent.

But alas ! (said I) had it not beene better that for the
good of his Countrie A (   ) endued with so many peer-
1040 lesse Giftes, had yet liued vpon Earth : How long will yee
(replyed hee) like the Ants, thinke there are no fairer
Palaces, than their Hills ; or like to pore-blind Moles, no
greater light, than that little which they shunne ? As if
the Maister of a Campe, knew when to remoue a Sentinell,
1045 and Hee who placeth Man on the Earth, knew not how
long hee had neede of him ? Life is a Gouernement and
Office, wherein Man is so long continued, as it pleaseth
the Installer ; of the administration and charge of which,
and what hath passed during the tyme of his Residence,
1050 hee must rander an account, so soone as his Tearme

1019 IM. peace with him   1019-20 IM. if he haue, and M *omits* if man
. . . with him   1022 IMO *omit* Magnificence   1029 O. that bringing forth
1039 IMO. natiue Countrie   1040 IMO *omit* vpon Earth   1046-55 *In* I,
this passage is omitted and replaced by : Euerie one commeth there to
act his part of this Tragicomedie called Life, which done, the Courtaine
is drawne, and hee remouing, is said to dye, *and in* O *the passage quoted
is intercalated after* . . . made Roome for others.

expyreth, and hee hath made Roome for others.   As mens
Bodies differ in stature, which none can make more long
or short after their desire ; So doe they varie in that
length of Tyme which is appointed for them to liue vpon
1055 the Earth.   That Prouidence which prescriueth Causes
to euerie Euent, hath not onlie determined a definite &
certaine number of dayes, but of actions, to all men, which
they can-not goe beyond.

Most (   ) then (answered I) Death is not such
1060 an euill and paine, as it is of the Vulgare esteemed.   Death
(said hee) nor painefull is, nor euill (except in contemplation of the cause) beeing of it selfe as in-different as Birth ;
Yet can it not bee denyed, but amidst those Dreames
of earthlie pleasures, the vncouthnesse of it, with the
1065 wrong apprehension of what is vnknowne in it, are
noysome ; But the Soule sustained by its Maker, resolued,
and calmlie retired in it selfe, doeth find that Death (sith
it is in a moment of Time) is but a short, nay, sweete Sigh;
and is not worthie the remembrance, compared with the
1070 smallest dram of the infinite Felicitie of this Place.   Heere
is the Palace Royall of the Almightie KING, in which
the vncomprehensible comprehensiblie manifesteth Himselfe ; in Place highest, in Substance not subject to any
corruption or change, for it is aboue all motion, and solide
1075 turneth not ; in Quantitie greatest, for, if one Starre,
one Spheare bee so vast, how large, how hudge in ex-
ceeding demensions, must those boundes bee, which doe
them all containe ?   In Qualitie most pure and Orient,
Heauen heere is all but a Sunne, or the Sunne all
1080 but a Heauen.   If to Earthlinges the Foote-stoole of
GOD, and that Stage which Hee raised for a small course
of Tyme, seemeth so Glorious and Magnificent ; How
highlie would They prize (if they could see) his eternall
Habitation and Throne ? and if these bee so dazeling, what

1067 O. into it self   1074 O. and being solid   1082-83 IMO. what
estimation would they make (if they could see) of his [O omits the
bracket and of before his]   1084 IMO. bee so wonderfull

1085 is the sight of Him, for whom, and by whom all was
created ? of whose Glory to behold the thousand thousand
part, the most pure Intelligences are fully satiate, and
with wonder and delight rest amazed ; for the Beauty of
His light & the Light of his Beauty are vncomprehensible.
1090 Heere doth that earnest appetite of the Vnderstanding,
content it selfe, not seeking to know any more ; For it
seeth before it, in the vision of the Diuine essence (a
Mirour in the which not Images or shadowes, but the true
and perfect Essence of euery thing created, is more cleare
1095 and conspicuous, than in it selfe) all that is knowne or
vnderstood : And where as on Earth our senses show vs
the Creator by his Creatures, heere wee see the Creatures
by the Creator. Heere doth the Will pause it selfe, as in
the Center of its eternall rest, glowing with a feruent
1100 Affection of that infinite and all-sufficient Good ; which
beeing fully knowne, cannot (for the infinite motiues and
causes of loue which are in Him) but bee fully and perfectly
loued : As hee is onely true and essentiall Bountie so is
Hee onelie essentiall and true Beauty, deseruing alone all
1105 loue and admiration, by which the Creatures are onely in
so much faire and excellent, as they participate of his
Beauty and excelling Excellencies. Heere is a blessed
Company, euery one joying as much in anothers Felicity,
as in that which is proper, because each seeth another
1110 equallie loued of GOD ; Thus their distinct joyes are
no fewer, than the Co-partners of the joye : And as the
Assemblie is in number answerable to the large capacitie
of the Place, so are the Ioyes answerable to the numberlesse number of the Assemblie. No poore and pittifull
1115 Mortall, confined on the Globe of Earth, who hath neuer
seene but Sorrow, or interchangablie some painted superficiall Pleasures, and had but Guesses of contentment, can
rightlie thinke on, or be sufficient to conceiue the tearme-

1087 O. satiated   1089 O. incomprehensible   1095 IMO. may bee knowne
1096-98 IM *omit* and where . . . Creator [J *has* thee *for* the *before* Will]
1099-1100 IM. firie affection   1103 O. the true   1104 O. the onely   1115 O.
confined to   1117 IM *omit* and . . . contentment

lesse Delightes, of this Place. So manie Feathers moue
not on Birdes, so manie Birds dint not the Aire, so manie
Leaues tremble not on Trees, so manie Trees grow not
in the solitarie Forestes, so manie Waues turne not
in the Ocean, and so manie graines of Sand limit not
those Waues; as this triumphant Court hath varietie
of Delights, and Ioyes exempted from all comparison.
Happinesse at once heere is fullie knowne and fullie enjoyed, and as infinite in continuance as extent. Heere is
flourishing and neuer-fading Youth without Age, Strength
without Weaknesse, Beautie neuer blasting, Knowledge
without Learning, Aboundance without Lothing, Peace
without Disturbance, Participation without Enuy, Rest
without Labour, Light without rising or setting Sunne,
Perpetuitie without Momentes, for Time (which is the
Measure of Motion) did neuer enter in this shining
Eternitie. Ambition, Disdaine, Malice, difference of
Opinions, can not approach this Place, resembling those
foggie mists, which couer those Lists of sublunarie things.
All Pleasure, paragon'd with what is heere, is paine, all
Mirth Mourning, all Beautie Deformitie : Here one dayes
abiding is aboue the continuing in the most fortunate
Estate on the Earth manie yeeres, and sufficient to con-
teruaile the extreamest tormentes of Life. But, although
this Blisse of Soules bee great, and their Ioyes many, yet
shall they admit addition, and bee more full and perfect, at
that long wished and generall Reunion with their Bodies.

Amongst all the wonders of the great Creator, not
one appeareth to bee more wonderfull, nor more dazell
the Eye of Reason (replied I) than that our Bodies should
arise, hauing suffered so manie changes, and Nature
denying a returne from Privation to a Habit.

Such power (said hee) beeing aboue all that the Vnderstanding of Man can conceaue, may well worke such

---

[1134] IM. (. . . measure of endurance O. (. . . Measure of Duration)
did never [1136] O. And resembling [1143] O. Bless [1145] IMO. meeting
with [1147-48] IMO *omit* nor more . . . reason [1151] *In* J, that *is
repeated after* all

wonders ; For, if Mans vnderstanding could comprehend all the Secrets & Counselles of that Eternall Maiestie
1155 it would of necessity bee equall vnto it. The Author of
Nature, is not thralled to the Lawes of Nature, but
worketh with them, or contrarie to them, as it pleaseth
Him : What Hee hath a will to doe, Hee hath power to
performe. To that Power, which brought all this round
1160 *All* from nought, to bring againe in one instant any
Substance which euer was into it, vnto what it was once,
should not be thought impossible ; For, who can doe
more, can doe lesse : and His power is no lesse, after that
which was by Him brought forth is decayed & vanished,
1165 than it was before it was produced ; beeing neither re-
strained to certaine limits, or Instrumentes, or to any
determinate and definite manner of working : where the
power is without restraint, the work admitteth no other
limits, than the workers will. This World is as a Cabinet
1170 to GOD, in which the small things (how euer to vs hide
and secret) are nothing lesse keeped, than the great.
For, as Hee was wise and powerfull to create, so doth
His Knowledge comprehend His own Creation ; yea,
euery change and variety in it, of which it is the verie
1175 Source. Not any Atome of the scattered Dust of Mankinde, though dayly flowing vnder new Formes, is to him
vnknowne : and His Knowledge doth distinguish and
discerne, what once His power shall awake and raise vp.
Why may not the Arts-master of the World, like a
1180 Molder, what hee hath framed in diuers Shapes, confound
in one Masse, and then seuerally fashion them againe out
of the same ? Can the Spagericke by his Arte restore for
a space to the dry and withered Rose, the naturall Purple
and Blush : And cannot the Almightie raise and refine the
1185 body of Man, after neuer so many alterations in the
Earth ? Reason her selfe findes it more possible for
infinite power, to cast out from it selfe a finite world, and

---

1155 IMO. must of necessity 1158 IMO. a power 1159-60 IMO. all this
"*All*" 1167 O. determined 1178 IM. shall waken 1182 IM. Spargiricke

restore any thing in it, though decayed and dissolued,
to what it was first ; than for Man a finit peece of reason-
1190 able miserie, to change the forme of matter made to his
hand : the power of GOD neuer brought forth all that it
can, for then were it bounded and no more infinit. That
Time doth approach (O haste yee Times away) in which
the Dead shall liue, and the Liuing bee changed, and of all
1195 actions the Guerdon is at hand ; Then shall there bee an
end without an end, Time shall finish, and Place shall bee
altered, Motion yeelding vnto Rest, and another World
of an Age eternall and vnchangeable shall arise : Which
when Hee had said (mee thought) Hee vanished, and I
1200 all astonished did awake.

1195 J *has* their *for* there *after* shall

On the Report of the
Death of the Author.

IF that were true, which whispered is by Fame,
That Damons *light no more on Earth doth burne,*
His Patron Phœbus *physicke would disclame,*
And cloath'd in clowds as earst for Phaeton *mourne ?*

5 Yea, Fame by this had got so deepe a Wound,
That scarce Shee could haue power to tell his Death,
Her Wings cutte short ; who could her Trumpet sound,
Whose Blaze of late was nurc't but by His breath ?

That Spirit of His which most with mine was free,
10 By mutuall trafficke enterchanging Store,
If chac'd from Him it would haue com'd to mee,
Where it so oft familiare was before.

Some secret Griefe distempering first my Minde,
Had (though not knowing) made mee feele this losse :
15 A Sympathie had so our Soules combind,
That such a parting both at once would tosse.

Though such Reportes to others terrour giue,
Thy heauenly Vertues who did neuer spie,
I know, Thou, that canst make the dead to liue,
20 Immortall art, and needes not feare to die.

Sir WILLIAM ALEXANDER.

This piece is wanting in N.
[11] MO. have come.

To S. *W. A.*

THough I haue twice beene at the Doores of *Death*,
  And twice found shoote those Gates which euer
    mourne,
This but a lightning is, Truce tane to Breath,
For late borne Sorrowes augure fleete returne.

5 Amidst thy sacred Cares, and courtlie Toyles,
Alexis, when thou shalt heare wandring Fame
Tell, *Death* hath triumph'd o're my mortall Spoyles,
And that on Earth I am but a sad Name ;

If thou e're helde mee deare, by all our Loue,
10 By all that Blisse, those Ioyes Heauen heere vs gaue,
I conjure Thee, and by the Maides of *Ioue*,
To graue this short Remembrance on my Graue.
    Heere *Damon* lyes, whose Songes did some-time grace
    The murmuring *Eske*, may Roses shade the place.

In N, this sonnet is entitled " *To Sir* W. A.," and in O, " *To Sir*
William Alexander."
  2 MNO. shut

To the Memorie of the
most excellent Ladie, IANE
Countesse of *Perth*.

THis Beautie, which pale *Death* in Dust did turne,
And clos'd so soone within a Coffin sad,
Did passe like Lightning, like to Thunder burne;
So little Life so much of Worth it had !

5 Heauens but to show their Might heere made it shine,
And when admir'd, then in the Worlds Disdaine
(O Teares, O Griefe !) did call it backe againe,
Lest Earth should vaunt Shee kept what was Diuine.

What can wee hope for more ? what more enjoy ?
10 Sith fairest Thinges thus soonest haue their End ;
And, as on Bodies Shadowes doe attend,
Sith all our Blisse is follow'd with Annoy ?
　Shee is not dead, Shee liues where shee did loue,
　Her Memorie on Earth, Her Soule aboue.

In NO, this sonnet is entitled " *On the Death of a young Lady.*"
13 IM. Yet She's not

To the obsequies of the
blessed Prince, IAMES,
King of great Britaine.

LEt holie *Dauid*, *Salomon* the Wise,
    That King, Whose Brest *Ægeria* did inflame,
    Augustus, *Helenes* Sonne, Great in all Eyes,
Doe Homage low to thy mausolean Frame ;
5 And bow before thy Laurell Anadeame
Let all Those sacred Swannes, which to the Skies
By neuer-dying Layes haue rais'd their Name,
From North to South, where Sunne doth set and rise.

Religion, orphan'd, waileth o're thine Vrne,
10 Out *Iustice* weepes her Eyes, now truely Blind ;
In *Niobèes* the remnant *Vertues* turne :
Fame, but to blaze thy Glories, liues behind.
    The World, which late was Golden by thy Breath,
    Is Iron turn'd, and horrid by thy Death.

This sonnet is wanting in IM.
5 NO. thy Laurels 6 O. Set all 9 O. Thy Urn 10 NO. Justice
weeps out 11 NO. To *Niobes* 12 NO. staies behind 13 NO. I' th'
World

FINIS.

The Entertainment
of King Charles.

Reprinted from the Edition of 1633.

THE
ENTERTAINMENT
OF THE HIGH AND
MIGHTY MONARCH
CHARLES
KING of *Great Britaine*,
France, and *Ireland*,

Into his auncient and royall City of
EDINBVRGH, the fiftcenth
of *Iune,* 1 6 3 3.

Printed at EDINBVRGH by *Iohn Wreittoun.* 1633.

II

PLATE 10.—FACSIMILE OF TITLE-PAGE.

Page III.

The entertainement of the High
and Mighty Monarch, Prince CHARLES,
King of great Brittaine, *France* and
Ireland, into his ancient and Royall
Citie of *Edenbourgh*, the 15.
of Iune. 1633.

ITHOVT the Gate which is towards the
West, where the streete ascendeth to
Heroites Hospitall, did an Arch arise
of height . . . . of breadth . . . . square
with the battlements and inmost side
of the towne-wall, the face looking to
the Castle, represented a Citie situated on a rock, which
with pointed Clifts, Shrubs, Trees, Herbs, and Verdure,
did appeare in perspectiue upon the battlements ; in
great Letters was written,

ΠΤΕΡΩΤΑ ΣΤΡΑ-
ΤΟΠΕΔΑ.

As *Ptolomeus* nameth it : in a lesse and different
Character was written

In both N and O, the title of this work differs considerably from
that of the original edition, as will be seen from a reference to the
detailed Bibliography of Drummond's poetical works. Of the prose
passages, one only, that extending from ll. [61-105], is contained in N.
They are all wanting in O.

¹⁵   *Castra Puellarum.*

And under that in a different colour *M. Edenbourgh :*
The Rocke was inscribed *Montagna de diamant,* after two
Italians which gaue that name to the greatest Rocke
neere *Edenborourgh,* and *Cardan,* who in his booke,
20 *De rerum varietate,* highly priseth the Diamond of the
Rocke.

In the Freeze under the Towne was written

Ingredere ac nostris succede penatibus.

Vpon one side of the Towne was drawne the flood
25 *Lithus,* in a Mantle of sea-greene or water-colour, a Crowne
of sedges and reeds on his head with long locks ; his
arme leaned upon an earthen pot, out of which water and
fishes seemed to runne forth, in his hand hee held a bundle
of flowers, over him was written

30   *Picciol Ma famoso.*

On the other side of the Towne appeared *Neptune*
bestriding his *Hippocampius,* the *Nereides* about him, his
Trident in his hand, the word over him was,

Adsum Defensor vbiq ; .

35   The Theater under the Arch was a Mountaine, upon
which appeared the *Genius* of the towne represented by
a Nimph ; shee was attired in a sea-greene velvet Mantle,
her sleeves and under roabe of blew tissue, with blew
Buskins on her feete, about her necke shee wore a chaine
40 of Diamonds, the dressing of her head represented a Castle
with turrets, her locks dangled about her shoulders ;
upon her right hand stood *Religion* all in white taffeta,
with a blew Mantle seeded with starres, a Crowne of starres
on her head, to shew from whence she is, shee leaned her
45 on a Scutcheon, where upon was a Crosse with the word,

Cælo descendet ab alto.

Beneath her feete lay *Superstition* trampled, a woman
blind, in old and worne garments, her Scutcheon had—
Vltra Sauromatas.   On the left-hand of this Nymph stood
50 *Iustice*, a woman in a red damaske Mantle, her under-
garments Cloth of silver, on her head a Crowne of Gold,
on a Scutcheon she had Ballances and a Sword drawn.
The word was,

Fida regnorum Custos.

55   Beneath the feet of *Iustice* lay *Oppression* trampled,
a persón of a fierce aspect, in armes, but broken all and
scattered.   The word was,

Tenente Carolo Terras.

The Mountaine at the approach of the Kings Majestie
60 moved, and the Nymph thus spake unto him.

Sir, If nature could suffer Rockes to move, and abandon
their naturall places, this Towne founded on the strength
of Rockes (now by all cheering rayes of your Majesties
presence, taking not onely motion, but life) had with her
65 Castles, Temples, and Houses moved towards you, and be-
sought you to acknowledge her yours, and her indwellers
your most humble and affectionate Subjects, and to beleeve
how many soules are within her circuits, so many lives
are devoted to your sacred Person and C owne ; and here
70 *Sir*, she offers by me, to the Altar of your glorie, whole
Hecatombes of most happy desires, praying all things
may prove prosperous unto you, that every vertue and
heroicke grace which make a Prince eminent, may with a
long and blissed government attend you ; your King-

⁶¹⁻¹⁰⁵ In N, this prose passage is entitled " An intended Speech at
the West Gate."
    ⁶⁵ N. toward you   ⁶⁶ N. Inhabitants   ⁷⁴ N. blessed Government

75 domes flourishing abroad with Bayes, at home with Olives.
Presenting you *Sir*, (who art the strong key of this litle
world of Great Brittaine) with these keyes, which cast up
the gates of her affectioun, and designe you power to open
all the springs of the hearts of these her most loyal citizens.
80 Yet this almost not necessary, for as the Rose at the
farre appearing of the Morning Starre displayeth and
spreadeth her purples, so at the very noyse of your happy
returne to this your native country their hearts (if they
could have shined without their breasts) were with joy
85 and faire hopes made spatious, nor did they ever in all
parts feele a more comfortable heate, then the glorie of
your presence at this time darteth upon them.

The old forget their age, and looke fresh and young
at the sight of so gracious a Prince, the young bear
90 a part in your welcome, desiring many yeares of life, that
they may serue you long, all have more joyes then
tongues ; for as the words of other Nations farre goe
beyond and surpasse the affection of their hearts ; So in
this Nation the affection of their hearts is farre above
95 all they can expresse by words. Daigne then, *Sir*, from
the highest of Majestie, to looke downe on their low-
nesse, and embrace it, accept the homage of their humble
minds, accept their gratefull zeale, and for deeds, accept
that great good-will which they have ever carried to
100 the high deserts of your Ancestors, and shall ever to your
owne, and your Royall race, Whilst these Rocks shall
bee overshadowed with buildings, these buildings
inhabited by men, and while men bee endued either with
counsell or courage, or enioy any peece of reason, sense, or
105 life.

The keyes being delivered in a bason of silver, and
his Majestie received by the Majestrates, under a Pale of
state, where the streete ascendeth proudest, beginning

[81] N. Morning Sun   [82] N. very Report   [83-4] N. (as might be
apparent, if they could have shined through their Breasts)   [86] N.
than the Glory   [91-2] N. than Tongues

to turne towards the Gate of the old Towne, hee meeteth
110 with an Arch, the height of which was . . . . the breadth
. . . . the frontispice of this represented, in Land-skip, a
countrey wild, full of Trees, Bushes, Bores, white Kine,
along the which appeared one great Mountaine to extend
it selfe, with the word upon it,

115   *Grampius.*

In some parts was seene the Sea enriched with Corrall,
and the Mussell that conceiveth the pearle ; farther off in
an Iland appeared a flaming Mountaine with the word,

Tibi serviet vltima Thule.

120   On the Chapter was a Lyon rampant, the word

Imperat ipse sibi.

On the Land-skip was *Caledonia* in great Letters written,
and part represented a number of men in Armes flying
and retiring with *S. P. Q. R.* on their Ensignes, which
125 shew them to bee Romanes ; an other part had a number
of naked persons flying and enchayned, with the figures
of the Sunne, Moone, and Starres, drawne on their skins,
and shapes of flowers, which represented the Picts, under
the Romanes, and under-written,

130   *Fracti bello fatisquè repulsi.*

A Courten falling, the Theater discovered a Lady attired
in tissue, her haire was dressed like a *Cornucopia*, two
chaynes, one of gold, another of pearle baudricke wayes,
hung downe her shoulders, a Crowne of gold hung from
135 the Arch before her, shee represented the *Genius* of
Caledonia ; neere unto her stood a woman with an Olive-
coloured maske, long blacke Locks waving over her backe,

her attyre was of divers coloured feathers, which shew her
to bee an *American*, and to represent new *Scotland*, the
140 Scutcheon in her hand bare the Armes of new *Scotland*,
with this word,

Auspicijs CAROLE *magne tuis.*

His Majestie comming neere, was welcomed with these
verses by *Caledonia*.

[i]

THe heavens have heard our vowes, our just desires
   Obtained are, no higher now aspires
Our wishing thoughts, since to his native clime
The flower of Princes, honour of his time,
5 Encheering all our Dales, Hills, Forrests, streames,
(As *Phœbus* doth the Summer with his beames)
Is come, and radiant to us in his traine
The golden age and vertues brings againe;
Prince so much longed for, how thou becalm'st
10 Mindes easelesse anguish, every care embalm'st
With the sweet odours of thy presence! now
In swelling tydes joyes every where doe flow
By thine approach, and that the world may see
What unthought wonders doe attend on thee,
15 This Kingdomes Angel I, who since that day
That ruthlesse Fate thy Parent reft away,
And made a Starre, appear'd not any where,
To gratulate thy comming, saving here.
   Haile Princes Phœnix, Monarch of all hearts,
20 Soveraigne of love and justice, who imparts
More then thou canst receive; to thee this Crowne

I. In NO, these verses are entitled " The Speech of Caledonia, representing the Kingdom."
   ³ O. Thought   ¹⁸ NO. thy comming, come am here   ²¹ NO. More
than

Is due by birth ; but more, it is thine owne
By just desert ; and ere another brow
Then thine should reach the same, my flood[s] should flow
25 With hot vermilian gore, and every Plaine
Levell the hills with Carcases of slaine,
This Ile become a red Sea : Now how sweet
Is it to me, when love and Lawes thus meet
To girt thy Temples with this Diadem,
30 My nurselings sacred feare, and dearest Gemme.
No Roman, Saxon, Pict by sad alarmes
Could this acquire and keepe ; the heavens in armes
From us repelld all perills, nor by warres
Ought here was wonne but gaping wounds and scarres,
35 Our Lions Clymaterick now is past,
And crown'd with Bayes, he rampant's free at last.

Heere are no Serean fleeces, Peru gold,
Auroras gemmes, nor wares by Tyrians sold ;
Townes swell not here with Babilonian walles,
40 Nor *Nero's* sky-resembling gold-seel'd halles,
Nor Memphis spires, nor Quinzayes arched frames,
Captiving Seas, and giving Lands their names :
Faith (milke-white *Faith*) of old belov'd so well,
Yet in this corner of the World doth dwell
45 With her pure Sisters, *Truth, Simplicitie ;*
Heere banish'd *Honour* beares them company,
A *Mars*-adorning brood is heere, their wealth
Sound mindes, and bodies of as sound a health :
Walles heere are men, who fence their Cities more
50 Then Neptune when he doth in mountaines roare,
Doth guard this Isle, or all those Forts and Towres
Amphions Harpe rais'd about *Thebes* bowres,
Heavens arch is oft their roofe, the pleasant shed

---

24 NO. Than thine   29 O. To wreath   31 O. Nor Roman   33 NO.
repell   34 NO. or gaping wounds and scars   36 NO. he rampeth free at
last   48 K *reads* Sound mindes and bodies, and of as sound a health—
which haraly makes satisfactory sense. The reading of NO *has accordingly
been adopted.*   50 NO. Than *Neptune*   53 K *has the misprint of* for oft

Of Oake and Plaine oft serves them for a bed.
55 To suffer want, soft pleasure to despise,
Runne over panting Mountaines crown'd with Ice,
Rivers orecome, the wastest Lakes appall
(Being to themselves, Oares, Steerers, ship and all)
Is their renowne ; a brave all-daring race
60 Couragious, prudent, doth this Climate grace :
Yet the firme Base on which their glory stands,
In peace true hearts, in warres is valiant hands,
Which here (great King) they offer up to thee,
Thy worth respecting as thy pedegree :
65 Though much it be to come of Princely stemme,
More is it to deserve a Diadem.

Vouchsafe blest people, ravisht here with me,
To thinke my thoughts, and see what I doe see,
A Prince all gracious, affable, divine,
70 Meeke, wise, just, valiant, whose radiant shine
Of vertues (like the Starres about the Pole
Guilding the night) enlightneth every soule,
Your Scepter swayes, a *Prince* borne in this age
To guard the innocents from Tyrants rage,
75 To make *Peace* prosper, *Iustice* to reflowre,
In desert hamlet as in Lordly bowre ;
A *Prince,* that though of none he stand in awe,
Yet first subjects himselfe to his owne law,
Who joyes in good, and still, as right directs
80 His greatnesse measures by his good effects,
His Peoples pedestall, who rising high
To grace this throne makes *Scotlands* name to flie
On *Halcyons* wings (her glory which restores)
Beyond the Ocean to *Columbus* shores,
85 Gods sacred picture in this man adore,
Honour his *valour, zeale,* his *piety* more,

[59] O. Is their Renown—*which has been adopted, the reading of* KN,
as, *being obviously wrong.* [65] NO. Though it be much [77] O. he stands
[82] K *reads* make

High value what ye hold, him deep ingrave
In your hearts heart, from whom all good ye have :
For as Moones splendor from her brother springs,
90 The peoples welfare streameth from their Kings.
Since your loves object doth immortall prove,
O love this *Prince* with an eternall love,

   Pray that those Crownes his Ancestors did weare,
His temples long (more orient) may beare,
95 That good he reach by sweetnesse of his sway,
That even his shadow may the bad affray,
That heaven on him what he desires bestow,
That still the glory of his greatnesse grow,
That your begunne felicities may last,
100 That no *Orion* doe with stormes them blast,
That victory his brave exployts attend,
East, West, or South doe he his Forces bend,
Till his great deeds all former deeds surmount,
And quaile the *Nimbrot* of the Hellespont ;
105 That when his well-spent care all care becalmes,
He may in peace sleepe in a shade of Palmes ;
And rearing up faire Trophees, that heavens may
Extend his life to worlds extreamest day.

145   The other face of the arch shew men, women, and
children, dauncing after diverse postures with many
Musicall Instruments, the worde above them in great
Characters was,

HILARITATI PVBLICÆ.

150   *S. P. Q, E. P.*

Where the great streete divideth it selfe in two, upon the
old Foundations, inhabited by the Goldsmiths and Glovers,

87 NO. you hold   102 NO. where he his Force shall bend

did an Arch arise of height . . . of breadth . . . upon
the Chapter of this Arch was a Crowne set with this word

155   *Nec primam visa est similem, nec habere secundam.*

The face of the Arch had an *Abacke* or Square with this
inscription,

*Carolo, Mag. Brit. Reg. Jacobi filio
Princi: optimo, maximo, libert. vin-*
160   *dici. Restauratori legum, fundatori
quietis, Conservatori Ecclesiæ,
Regni vltra Oceanum in Americam
Promotori. S. P. Q. E. P.*

Amidst flourishes of Armes, as Helmes, Lances, Corslets,
165 Pikes, Muskets, Bowes, Cannons, at the one side of the
abacke stood *Mars*, the word by him was,

Patrium cognoscite Numen.

At the other side, amongst flourishes of instruments of
peace, as Harpes, Lutes, Organs, Cisseres, Hauboises, stood
170 *Minerva*, her word,

Quo sine me.

Vpon each side was Armes of the two Kingdomes, and
an Intertexture of Crownes with a word,

Nexus fœlix.

175   Vpon the *Freeze* was written

. . . *Genus immortale manet, multosq; per annos
stat fortuna domus & avi numerantur avorum.*

At the approach of the King, the Theater (a Courten drawne) manifested *Mercury*, with his feathered hat, and 180 his *Caduceus*, with an hundred and seven Scottish Kings, which hee had brought from the Elisian fields, *Fergus* the first had a speech in Latine, which is here desired.— Vpon the Crosse of the Towne was a shew of *Panisques*, *Bacchus* crowned with Ivie, and naked from the shoulders 185 up, bestroad a Hogshead, by him stood *Silenus, Silvanus, Pomona, Venus, Ceres* in a straw coloured mantle, embrodered with eares of Corne, and a dressing of the same on her head, should have delivered a speech to the King but was interrupted by the Satyres ; shee bare a 190 Scutcheon, upon which was,

Sustulit exutis vinclis. ad sydera palmas.

Meaning by the King shee was free of the great abuse of the Tithes in this Countrey.

In the midst of the streete, there was a Mountaine 195 dressed for *Parnassus*, where *Apollo* and the *Muses* appeared, and ancient Worthies of Scotland, for learning was represented ; such as *Sedullius, Ioannes Duns*, Bishop *Elphistoun* of *Aberdeen, Hector Boes, Ioannes Major,* Bishop *Gawen Douglasse*, Sir *David Lindsay, Georgius* 200 *Buchananus ;* the word over them was

Fama super æthera noti.

The *Muses* were clad in varying taffetas, cloath of silver and purle ; *Melpomene*, though her under vesture was blacke, yet her Buskines and Mantle were crimson, 205 they were distinguished by the Scutcheons they bare, and more properly then by their flats ; every one had a word, the first was Clio, who bare

Si vis omnia tibi subjici, subjice te rationi.

Which was the kings *Simbole* when hee was *Prince*.

210 *Melpomene* had the Simbole of King *Iames*,

> *Parcere subiectis, & debellare superbos.*

Thalia had that of Queene *Anna*,

> *Mia Ma grandezza del excelso.*

Euterpe had the word of Prince *Henry*,

215 > *Fax gloria mentis honestæ.*

TERPSICHORE.

Regni clementia custos.

ERATO.

Parendo imperat.

220 ## CALLIOPE.

Aurea sors regum est, & velle & posse beare.

VRANIA.

Non vinci potis est neq ; fingi regia virtus.

POLYHYMNIA.

225 *Patiens sit principis auris.*

Apollo sitting in the midst of them was clad in Crimson
taffeta, covered with some purle of gold, with a bowdricke
like the Raine-bow, a Mantle of tissue knit together
above his left shoulder, his head was crowned with

230 Laurell, with locks long and like gold ; hee presented
the King with a booke.

Where the great streete contracteth it selfe, at the
descent of the Easterne Gate of the Towne, did an Arch
arise of height .... of breadth .... the face of this
235 represented a Heaven, into the which appeared his
Majesties ascendant *Virgo*, shee was beautified with sixe
and twenty starres, after that order that they are in their
constellatioune.

One of them being of the first magnitude, the rest of
240 the third and fourth ; by her was written

Habet quantum æther habebat.

Beneath on the earth lay the *Titanes* prostrate, with
Mountaines over them, as when they attempted to bandy
against the gods ; their word was on the *Freeze.*

245 *Moniti ne temnite divos.*

The Chapter shew the three *Parcæ*, where was written,

Thy life was kept till these three Sisters spunne
Their threads of gold, and then thy life begunne.

The Stand discovered the seven Planets sitting on a
250 Throne, and *Endymion.* *Saturne* in a sad blew Mantle
embrodered with golden flames, his Girdle was like a
Snake byting his tayle, his Scutcheon bare

Spondeo digna tuis ingentibus omnia cœptis.

Iupiter was in a Mantle of silver, embrodered with
255 Lillies and Violets, his Scutcheon bare

Sat mihi sit Cœlum, post hæc tua fulmina sunto.

Mars, his haire and beard red, a Sword at his side, had
his robe of deepe crimson Taffeta, embroidered with

Wolves and Horses, his head bare a Helmet, and his
260 Scutcheon,

Per tela, per hostes.

The *Sunne* had a Crowne of flowers on his head, as
Marigolds, and Panses, and a Tissue Mantle, his Scutcheon
bare,
265   *Jmperium sine fine dedi.*

Venus had the attire of her head rising like parts in a
Coronet, and roses, shee was in a mantle of greene Damaske
embroidered with Doves, instead of her *Cæstus* she wore
a scarfe of diverse colours, her word

270   *Nullas recipit tua gloria metas.*

Mercury had a Dressing on his head of parti-coloured
flowers, his Mantle parti-coloured, his word

Fata aspera rumpes.

The Moone had the attyre of her head, like an halfe
275 Moone or Cressant of pearle ; her Mantle was sad Damasse
Frenzend with silver, embrodered with Chamelions and
Gourdes, her word

Consequitur quodcunq; petit

At a corner of the Theater, from out a Verdant Groue
280 came *Endymion*, hee was apparelled like a Shepheard in a
long Coat of crimson velvet comming over his knee ; hee
had a wreath of flowers upon his head, his haire was curled,
and long ; in his hand he bare a Sheep-hooke, on his legs
were Buskins of gilt Leather : These before the King had
285 this actioune.

[ii]

Endymion.

R Ows'd from the Latmian Cave, where many years
That Empresse of the lowest of the Sphæres,
Who cheeres the night, and kept me hid, apart
From mortall wights, to ease her love-sicke heart,
5 As young as when she did me first inclose,
As fresh in beauty as the Maying rose,
Endymion; that whilome kept my Flockes
Vpon *Ionas* flowry hills and rockes,
And warbling sweet layes to my *Cynthea's* beames,
10 Out-sang the *Swannets* of *Meanders* streames ;
To whom (for Guerdon) she heavens secret barres
Made open, taught the paths and powers of Starres ;
By this deare Ladies strict commandement
To celebrate this day I here am sent :
15 But whether is this heaven, which starres doe crowne,
Or are heavens flaming splendors here come downe,
To beautify this neather world with me ?
Such state and glory did e're Shepheard see ?
My wits my sense mistrust, and stay amaz'd,
20 No eye on fairer objects ever gaz'd,
Sure this is heaven, for every wandring starre,
Forsaking those great orbes where whirl'd they are,
All dismall sad aspects abandoning,
Are here assembled to greet some darling ;
25 Nor is it strange if they heavens hight neglect,
Vnwonted worth produceth like effect,
Then this it is, thy presence (royall youth)
Hath brought them here within an Azymuth,

In NO, the verse-pieces that follow are entitled, apart from their
separate titles which are as in the original, " The Speeches of the
Horoscopall Pageant by the Planets."
II. ³ NO. did keep me hid, apart ⁶ NO. as the morning Rose ⁹ NO.
And sweet Layes warbling ¹⁰ NO. Out-sang the Cignets ²⁴ NO. Are
here met to salute some gracious King ²⁶ NO. It of undoubted worth
is the effect

To tell by me (their Herauld) comming things,
30 And what each Fate to her sterne distaffe sings ;
Heavens volume to unclaspe, wast pages spread,
Mysterious golden cyphers cleere to reade,
Heare then the augur of the future dayes
And all the starry Senate of the Sayes ;
35 For what is firme decreed in heaven above
In vaine on earth strive mortalls to improve.

[iii]

Saturne.

TO faire hopes to give reines now is it time,
    And soare as high as just desires may climbe ;
O *Halcyonean*, cleere, and happy day,
From sorry wights let sorrow flie away,
5 And vexe Antarticke climes, great Britaines woes
Evanish, joy now in her *Zenith* glowes,
The old *Leucadian* Syth-bearing Sire
(Though cold) for thee feeles flames of sweet desire,
And many lusters at a perfect height
10 Shall keep thy Scepters majestie, as bright
And strong in power and glory every way,
As when thy peerelesse Parent did it sway,
Nere turning wrinkled in times endlesse length,
But one in her first beauty, youthfull strength,
15 Like thy rare mind, which stedfast as the Pole
Still fixed stands, however Sphæres doe role ;
More, to inhaunce thy favours, this thy raigne
His age of gold he shall restore againe,
Love, Iustice, Honour, Innocence renew,
20 Mens spirits with white simplicity indue,
Make all to live in plenties ceaselesse store

³³ NO. of thy future daies   ³⁵ NO. And what
III. ¹ O. it is Time   ⁶ NO. Vanish, for joy   ¹⁴ K. But on   ¹⁷ K
reads More, to inchant thy favours, this thy raigne—*which gives no
satisfactory sense.   The reading of* NO *has accordingly been adopted.*
¹⁸ O. he doth restore   ²¹ O. endless Store

With equall shares, not wishing to have more ;
Then shall not cold the Plow-mens hopes beguile,
On earth shall skie with lovely glances smile,
25 Vntill'd, which shall each flower and hearbe bring forth,
And with faire gardens make of equall worth ;
Life (long) shall not be thrall'd to mortall dates,
Thus heavens decree, so have ordain'd the Fates.

[iv]

Iove.

DElight of heaven, sole honour of the earth,
Iove (courting thine ascendant) at thy birth
Proclaimed thee a King, and made it true,
That Emperies should to thy worth be due,
5 He gave thee what was good, and what was great,
What did belong to love, and what to state,
Rare gifts whose ardors turne the hearts of all,
Like tunder when flint attomes on it fall ;
The *Tramontane* which thy faire course directs,
10 Thy counsells shall approve by their effects ;
Iustice kept low by grants, and wrongs, and jarres,
Thou shalt relieve, and crowne with glistering starres,
Whom nought save law of force could keepe in awe
Thou shalt turne Clients to the force of law,
15 Thou armes shalt brandish for thine owne defence,
Wrongs to repell, and guard weake innocence,
Which to thy last effort thou shalt uphold,
As Oake the Ivy which it doth infold ;
All overcome, at last thy selfe orecome,

---

22 NO. none wishing to haue more 23 NO. No more shall cold
24 NO. Skies shall on Earth 25 NO. Which shall untill'd 26 NO. And
Lands to Gardens turne of equall worth 27 K *has* deats *for* dates
    IV. 4 NO. That to thy worth great Monarchies are due 7 NO.
burne the hearts of all 8 NO. flints atoms 9 K *has the misprint*
" *Taramont* " 10 K *reads* Shall counsells be, approv'd by their effects ;
—*which is hardly satisfactory. The reading of* NO *has accordingly been
adopted.* 11 NO. Justice kept low by Giants, wrongs, and jars

20 Thou shalt make passion yield to reasons doome :
For smiles of fortune shall not raise thy mind,
Nor dismall most disasters turne declin'd,
True *Honour* shall reside within thy Court,
Sobrietie, and *Truth* there still resort,
25 Keepe promis'd faith thou shalt, Supercheries
Detest, and beagling Marmosets despise,
Thou, others to make rich, shalt not make poore
Thy selfe, but give that thou mayst still give more ;
Thou shalt no Paranymph raise to high place,
30 For frizl'd locks, quaint pace, or painted face ;
On gorgeous rayments, womanising toyes,
The workes of wormes, and what a Moth destroyes,
The Maze of fooles, thou shalt no treasure spend,
Thy charge to immortality shall tend,
35 Raise *Pallaces,* and *Temples* vaulted high,
Rivers ore arch, of hospitality,
Of Sciences the ruin'd Innes restore,
With walls and ports incircle *Neptunes* shore,
To new found worlds thy Fleets make hold their course,
40 And find of *Canada* the unknowne Sourse,
People those Lands which passe *Arabian* fields
In fragrant Wood and Muske which *Zephyre* yields ;
Thou fear'd of none, shalt not thy people feare,
Thy peoples love thy greatnesse shall up-reare,
45 Still rigour shall not shine, and mercy lower,
What love can doe thou shalt not doe by power,
New and vast taxes thou shalt not extort,
Load heavy those thy bounty should support,
By harmlesse *Iustice* graciously reforme,
50 Delighting more in calme then roaring storme,

---

²² NO. Nor shall disasters make it ere declin'd ²⁵ NO. thou shalt
all treacheries ²⁶ NO. Detest, and fawning Parasites despise ²⁸ K
reads Thy selfe, but if that thou mayst still give more—*which hardly
gives satisfactory sense. The reading of* NO *has been adopted.* ³⁰ K *reads*
For frizl'd leape, *instead of* For frizl'd locks *of* NO. ³⁷ NO. And
Sciences ⁴⁰ O. th' unknown ⁴⁸ O. that Bounty *The two following verses
are here inserted by* NO : Thou shalt not strike the Hinge nor Master
Beame | Of thine Estate, but errours in the same. ⁵⁰ NO. calme than

Thou shalt governe in *peace* as did thy *Sire*,
Keepe, save thine owne, and kingdomes new acquire,
Beyond *Alcides* Pillars, and those bounds
Where *Alexanders* fame till now resounds,
55 Till thou the greatest be among the Greats ;
Thus heavens ordaine, so doe decree the Faits.

[v]
Mars.

SOnne of the Lyon, thou of loathsome bands
Shalt free the earth, and what e're thee withstands
Thy noble pawes shall teare, the God of *Thrace*
Shall be the second, and before thy face,
5 To *Truth* and *Iustice*, whilst thou Trophees reares,
Armies shall fall dismayd with *Pannick* feares,
As when *Aurora* in skies azure lists
Makes shaddowes vanish, doth disperse the mists,
And in a twinckling with her opall light,
10 Nights horrours checketh, putteth starres to flight,
More to inflame thee to this noble taske,
To thee he here resignes his *Sword* and *Caske*,
A wall of flying Castles, armed Pines
Shall bridge thy sea, like heaven with steele that shines,
15 To aide earths tennants by foule yoakes opprest,
And fill with feares the great King of the West :
To thee already *Victory* displayes
Her garlands twin'd with Olive, Oake, and Bayes,
Thy triumphs finish shall all old debates ;
20 Thus Heavens decree, so have ordain'd the Fates.

[vi]
Sunne.

WEalth, *Wisedome, Glory, Pleasure,* stoutest hearts,
Religion, Lawes, Hyperion imparts
To thy just Raigne, which shall farre farre surpasse,

54 NO. Where *Alexander* gain'd the Easterne Crowns
V. 4 NO. thy second   10 NO. putting   19 O. Thy Triumph

Of Emperours, Kings, the best that ever was ;
5 Looke how hee dims the starres ; thy glories rayes,
So darken shall the lustre of these dayes :
For in faire vertues Zodiacke thou shalt runne,
And in the heaven of worthies be the *Sunne*.
No more contemn'd shall haplesse *Learning* lie ;
10 The maids of *Pindus* shall be raysed high ;
For Bay and Ivie which their browes enroll'd,
Thou shalt them decke with gems and shining gold ;
Thou open shalt *Parnassus* Cristall gates,
Thus heavens ordaine, so doe decree the Fates.

[vii]

Venus.

THe *Acidalian* Queene amidst the Bayes
    Shall twine her mirtles, grant thee pleasant dayes ;
She did make cleare thy house, and with her light
Of cheerelesse starres, put backe the dismall spight.
5 Thy Hymenean bed faire brood shall grace,
Which on the earth continue shall their race,
While *Floras* treasure shall the Meads endeare,
While sweete *Pomona* Rose-cheek't fruits shall beare,
While *Phœbes* beames her brothers emulates :
10 Thus Heavens decree, so have ordain'd the Fates.

[viii]

Mercury.

GReat *Atlas* Nephew, shall the workes of peace,
    (The workes of plenty) *Tillage*, *Trades* encrease,
And *Arts* in times gulfes lost againe restore,
To their *Perfection* ; nay, find many more,
5 More perfect artists, *Ciclopes* in their forge

VII. [1] K *has the misprint* "*Alcidanian*"   [4] K *has the misprint*
churelesse NO. churlish
VIII. [2] NO. (The Springs of plenty)   [4] K *reads* to cheere Perfection
—*which is obviously wrong. We have adopted the reading of* NO.

Shall mould those brasen *Tiphones*, which disgorge
From their hard bowels mettall, flame and smoake,
Mufling the ayre up in a sable cloake :
The Sea shrinkes at the blow, shake doth the ground,
10 The worlds West corners doth the sound rebound,
The *Stygian* Porter leaveth off to barke,
Black *Ioue* appall'd doth shrow'd him in the darke ;
Many a *Typhis* in adventures lost
By new found skill shall many mayden coast,
15 With thy sayle-winged *Argoses* find out,
Which like the Sunne shall runne the earth about,
And farre beyond his pathes score wavie wayes,
To *Cathayes* Lands by Hyperborean Seas,
Hee shall endue thee both in peace and warre,
20 With *Wisedome*, which then *Strength* is better farre,
Wealth, Honour, Armes, and *Arts* shall grace thy states :
Thus Heavens ordaine, so doe decree the Fates.

[ix]

The Moone.

O How the faire Queene with the golden maids,
  The Sunne of night, thy happy fortunes aids,
Though turban'd Princes for a badge her weare,
To them shee wain'd, to thee would full appeare ;
5 Her Hand-maid *Thetis* daily walkes the round
About the *Delos* that no force it wound,
Then when thou left it and abroad did stray
(Deare Pilgrim) shee did straw with flowers the way,
And turning forraine force and counsell vaine,
10 Thy Guard and Guid return'd thee home againe ;
To thee she *Kingdomes, Yeares, Blisse* did divine,

---

8 NO *add here the two following verses :* Geryons, Harpyes, Dragons,
Sphinges (*sic !*) strange | Wheele, where in spacious gires the Fume doth
range   10 NO. The Worlds vast Chambers doth the sound rebound   13 O.
in Adventures tost   14 NO. many a   15 O. With thy fil-winged *Argoses*
and out (*sic !*)   18 K *omits* To *before* " Cathayes "   20 NO. than Strength
    IX. 4 NO. she waine   6 NO. About thy *Delos*   7 N. Than when
O. thou left'st it   8 NO. thy way

Quailing *Medusas* grim Snakes with her shine,
Beneath thee raigne Discord (fell mischiefes forge,
The bane of peoples, state and kingdomes scourge)
15 Pale Envie (with the Cockatrices eye,
Which seeing kils, but seene doth forthwith dye·:)
Malice, Deceit, Rebellion, Impudence
Beyond the *Garamants* shall packe them hence,
With every Monster that thy glory hates,
20 Thus Heavens decree, so haue ordayn'd the Fates.

[x]

Endymion.

THat heretofore to thy heroicke mind
Haps, (hopes not answer'd as they were design'd :)
O doe not thinke it strange, times were not come,
And these faire starres had not pronounc'd their doome;
5 The destinies did on that day attend,
When to this Northren Region thou should lend
Thy cheering presence, and charg'd with Renowne,
Set on thy browes the *Caledonian* Crowne ;
Thy vertues now thy just desire shall grace,
10 Sterne *Chance* shall change, and to *Desert* give place ;
Let this be knowne to all the Fates admit
To their grave Counsell, and to every Witt
That spies Heavens inside ; this let *Sibilles* know,
And those mad *Corybants* which dance and glow
15 On *Dindimus* high tops with franticke fire :
Let this bee knowne to all *Apollo's* Quire,
And people let it not be hid from you,
What Mountaines noyse and Floods proclaime as true :
Where ever fame abroad his prayse shall ring,
20 All shall observe, and serve this blessed King.

[12] O. Quelling   [13] NO. Beneath thy raigne   [14] N. and Kingdome
Scourge
X. [2] NO. Hopes did not answer as they were design'd   [7] NO. Thy
cheerful presence   [13] NO. That courts Heavens inside   [14] NO. who
dance

The backe face of this Arch towards the East, had the three Graces drawen upon it, which were naked and in others hands ; they were crowned with eares of Corne, Flowers and Grapes to signifie fecunditie ; their word

290   *Læto testamur Gaudia plausu.*

By them was *Argos* full of eyes ; his word

Vt videam.

Vnder all was written,

Tales Roma fuit quondam admirata triumphos.

295 The Emperour *Iustinian* appoynted that the Shewes and Spectacles made to Princes, should be seaven for the East ; on the Battlements of the East Gate, in a Coat all full of eyes and tongues, with a Trumpet in her hand (as if shee would sound) stood Fame, the wings of the Bat at 300 her feete, a Wreath of gold on her head, and by her, Honour a person of a reverend countenance in a blew Mantle of the colour of silver, his haire broydered with silver shaddowing in waves his shoulders, they were aboue the statue of King *Iames*, under which was written

305   *Placida populos in pace regebat.*

[xi]

A T length we see those eyes,
  which cheere both over earth and skies,
Now ancient *Caledon*
   thy beauties highten, richest robes put on,
5   and let young joyes to all thy parts arise.

XI. In NO, this piece is entitled " The Song of the Muses at *Parnassus.*", and in O, it is placed immediately after the verses of " *Caledonia.*"   ² NO. *both Earth and Skies*

Here could thy Prince still stay,
 each moneth should turne in May,
We need not starre nor Sunne,
 save him to lengthen dayes and joyes begunne,
10 sorrow and night to farre climes hast away.

Now Majestie and Love
 combin'd are from above,
Prince never Scepter swayd.
 lov'd subjects more, of subjects more obey'd,
15 which may indure whilst heavens great orbs do move.

Ioyes did ye alwayes last,
 lifes sparke ye soone would wast,
Griefe followes sweet delight,
 as day is shaddowed by sable night,
20 yet shall remembrance keep you still, when past.

[xii]

EPIGRAMME.

ILlustrious *Top-bough of Heroicke Stemme,*
Whose head is crown'd with glories Anademe,
My shallow Muse, not daring to draw neere
Bright Phœbus *burning flames in his careere ;*
5 *Yet knowing surely that Apollo shines*
Vpon the Dung-hill, as on golden Mines :
And knowing this, the bounty of best Kings,
To marke the giver, not the gifted things,
Doth boldly venture in this pompous throng
10 *To greet thy greatnesse with a wel-come Song ;*
And with the Pye doth Ave Cæsar *sing,*
While graver wits doe greater Offrings bring.

---

7 NO. *turne to* 8 N. *We need nor Star, nor Sun* 16 K. Ioyes did
thee   NO. *Joyes did you* 17 NO. *you soon*
XII. This piece is wanting in NO.

To the Exequies, etc.

Reprinted from the Editions of
1638 and 1656.

TO THE
EXEQUIES

OF THE HONOVRABLE,
Sᵗ.
ANTONYE ALEXANDER,
KNIGHT, &c.

A Paſtorall Elegie.

EDINBVRGH,
Printed in King *James* his College,
by *George Anderſon*, 1638.

A Pastorall Elegie on the Death of S. A[ntonye] A[lexander.]

IN sweetest prime and blooming of his Age,
Deare *Alcon* ravish'd from this mortall Stage,
The Shepheards mourn'd as they him lov'd before :
Among the Rout him *Idmon* did deplore,
5 *Idmon*, who, whether Sun in East did rise
Or dive in West, pour'd Torrents from his Eyes
Of liquid Chrystall, under Hawthorne shade ;
At last to Trees and Rocks this plaint he made :
Alcon, delight of heaven, desire of Earth,
10 Off-spring of *Phœbus*, and the Muses birth,
The Graces Darling, *Adon* of our Plaines,
Flame of the fairest Nymphs the Earth sustaines,
What Power of thee hath us bereft ? What Fate
By thy untimely fall would ruinate
15 Our hopes ? O Death ! what treasure in one houre
Hast thou dispersed ? How dost thou devoure
What we on earth hold dearest ? All things good,
Too envious Heavens, how blast ye in the Bud ?

The unique but imperfect copy of this elegy, consisting of the title-page and of the last twenty-seven lines of the text only, formerly preserved in the library of the University of Edinburgh, is now lost. It was utilized by the editors of the Maitland Club edition of Drummond's poetical works, whose text we have accordingly followed for the latter part of this composition. We also had no other alternative but to reproduce, for this piece, the title-page of the Maitland Club edition.

In N, the piece is entitled " A Pastorall Elegie on the Death of S. W. A.," and in O, " *A Pastoral Elegy on the Death of* Sir William Alexander."

The Corne the greedy Reapers cut not down
20 Before the Fields with golden Eares it crown,
Nor doth the verdant Fruits the Gardener pull,
But thou art cropt before thy yeares were full.
　　With thee (sweet youth) the Glories of our Fields
Vanish away, and what contentments yields ;
25 The Lakes their silver look, the woods their shades,
The Springs their Christall want, their Verdure Meads,
The yeares their early seasons, cheerfull Dayes ;
Hills gloomy stand now desolate of Rayes,
　Their amorous whispers *Zephires* not us bring,
30 Nor do Aires Quiresters salute the Spring ;
The freezing winds our Gardens do defloure.
Ah, Destinies ! and you whom Skies embow'r,
To his faire Spoiles his Spright againe yet give,
And like another *Phœnix* make him live.
35 The Herbs, though cut, sprout fragrant from their stems,
And make with Crimson blush our Anadems ;
The Sun when in the West he doth decline,
Heavens brightest Tapers at his Funeralls shine ;
His Face, when washt in the *Atlantick* Seas,
40 Revives, and cheeres the *Welkin* with new Raies :
Why should not he, since of more pure a Frame,
Returne to us againe, and be the same ?
But wretch, what wish I ? To the winds I send
These Plaints and Prayers, Destines cannot lend
45 Thee more of Time, nor Heavens consent will thus
Thou leave their starry World to dwell with us ;
Yet shall they not thee keep amidst their Spheares
Without these lamentations and Teares.
　　Thou wast all Vertue, Courtesie, and Worth,
50 And as Suns light is in the Moon set forth,
Worlds supreame Excellence in thee did shine ;
Nor, though eclipsed now, shalt thou decline,
But in our Memories live, while Dolphins streames
Shall haunt, whilst *Eaglets* stare on *Titans* beames,

---

[48] O. Without those　　[54] O. whilst Eagles stare on *Titan* beams

55 Whilst Swans upon their Christall Tombes shall sing,
Whilst Violets with Purple paint the Spring.
A gentler Shepheard Flocks did never feed
On *Albions* Hills, nor sung to oaten Reed :
While what she found in Thee my Muse would blaze,
60 Griefe doth distract Her, and cut short thy Praise.
How oft have we, inviron'd by the Throng
Of tedious Swaines, the cooler shades among,
Contemn'd Earths glow-worme Greatnesse, and the Chace
Of Fortune scorn'd, deeming it disgrace
65 To court unconstancy ? How oft have we
Some *Chloris* Name graven in each Virgin Tree,
And finding Favours fading, the next Day
What we had carv'd we did deface away ?
Woefull Remembrance ! Nor Time nor Place
70 Of thy abodement shadows any Trace,
But there to me Thou shin'st : late glad Desires,
And ye once Roses, how are ye turned Bryers ?
Contentments passed, and of Pleasures Chiefe,
Now are ye frightfull Horrours, Hells of Griefe.
75 When from thy native Soyle Love had Thee driven,
(Thy safe returne Prefigurating) a Heaven
Of flattering Hopes did in my Fancy move,
Then little dreaming it should Atomes prove.
These Groves preserve will I, these loved Woods,
80 These Orchards rich with Fruits, with Fish these flouds :
My *Alcon* will returne, and once againe
His chosen Exiles he will entertaine ;
The populous City holds him, amongst Harmes
Of some fierce *Cyclops*, *Circe's* stronger Charmes.
85 These Bankes (said I) he visit will and Streames,
These silent shades ne're kist by courting Beames ;
Far, far off I will meet him, and I first
Shall him approaching know, and first be blest
With his Aspect ; I first shall heare his voice,
90 Him find the same he parted, and rejoyce

55 O. Whilst Swains   59 O. Whilst   63 O. Condemn'd

To learne his passed Perills, know the Sports
Of forraine Shepheards, Fawns, and Fairy Courts.
No pleasure to the Fields ; an happy State
The Swaines enjoy, secure from what they hate :
95 Free of proud Cares they innocently spend
The Day, nor do black Thoughts their ease offend ;
Wise Natures Darlings they live in the World,
Perplexing not themselves how it is hurld.
These Hillocks *Phœbus* loves, *Ceres* these Plaines,
100 These Shades the *Sylvans*, and here *Pales* straines
Milke in the Pailes, the Maids which haunt the Springs
Daunce on these Pastures, here *Amintas* sings ;
Hesperian Gardens, *Tempe's* shades are here,
Or what the Easterne *Inde*, and West hold deare.
105 Come then, deare Youth, the Wood-nymphs twine thee
          Boughs
With Rose and Lilly, to impale thy Brows.
Thus ignorant, I mus'd, not conscious yet
Of what by Death was done, and ruthlesse Fate :
Amidst these Trances Fame thy losse doth sound,
110 And through my Eares gives to my Heart a wound ;
With stretched-out Armes I sought thee to embrace,
But clasp'd (amaz'd) a Coffin in thy Place ;
A Coffin ! of our Joyes which had the Trust,
Which told that thou was come, but chang'd in Dust.
115 Scarce, even when felt, could I believe this wrake,
Nor that thy Tyme and Glory Heavens would break.
Now since I cannot see my *Alcons* Face,
And finde nor Vowes nor Prayers to have place
With guiltie Starres, this Mountaine shall become
120 To mee a sacred Altar, and a Tombe
To famous *Alcon :* heere, as Dayes, Months, Yeares
Do circling glide, I sacrifice will teares,
Heere spend my remnant Tyme, exil'd from Mirth
Till Death in end turne Monarch of my Earth.

114 NO. thou wert come, but chang'd to dust   124 NO. Till Death
at last

125   Sheepheards on *Forth*, and yee by *Doven* Rockes
    Which use to sing and sport, and keep your Flockes,
    Pay Tribute heere of Teares ; yee never had
    To aggravate your Moanes a cause more sad ;
    And to their sorrowes hither bring your Mandes
130 Charged with sweetest flowres, and with pure Handes,
    (Faire nymphes) the blushing *Hyacinth* and Rose
    Spred on the Place his Relicts doth enclose ;
    Weave Garlands to his Memorie, and put
    Over his Hearse a Verse in Cypresse cut :
135 " Vertue did die, Goodnesse but harme did give
    After the noble *Alcon* left to live,
    Friendship an Earth-quake suffer'd ; loosing Him,
    Loves brightest Constellation turned Dim."

[125] NO. and you   [132] NO. do enclose   [136] NO. *Alcon* ceas'd to live

Madrigals, etc.

First printed in the *Poems* (1614?),
and subsequently suppressed
by Drummond.

Madrigals, etc.

[i]

Clorus.

SWanne *which so sweetly sings,*
By Aska's Bancks, and pitifully plaines,
That old Meander *neuer heard such Straines,*
Eternall Fame, thou to thy Countrie brings :
5 *And now our* Calidon
Is by thy Songs made a new Helicon.
Her Mountaines, Woods, and Springs,
While Mountaines, Woods, Springs be, shall sound thy
        Praise,
And though fierce Boreas *oft made pale her Bayes,*
10 *And kill those* Mirtills *with enraged Breath,*
Which should thy Browes enwreath ;
    Her Floods haue Pearles, Seas Amber doe send foorth,
    Her Heauen hath golden Starres to crowne thy Woorth.

I. ¹⁰ O. *these*

[ii]

Son.

A Ye me, and am I now the Man whose Muse
In happier Times was wont to laugh at Loue
And those who suffred that blind Boy abuse
The noble Gifts were giuen them from aboue ?
5 What Metamorphose strange is this I proue ?
My selfe now scarse I finde my selfe to be,
And thinkes no Fable Circes Tyrannie,
And all the Tales are told of changed Ioue,
Vertue hath faire with her Philosophie
10 My Mind vnto a better Course to moue,
Reason may chide her full, and oft reproue
Affections Power, but what is that to me
Who euer thinkes, and neuer thinkes on Ought
But that bright Cherubine that thralles my Thought.

[iii]

MAD.

TRees happier farre then I,
Which haue the Grace to heaue your Heads so hie,
And ouer-looke those Plaines :
Grow till your Branches kisse that lofty Skie
5 Which her (sweet Her) containes.
There make her know mine endlesse Loue, and Paines,
And how these Teares which from mine Eyes doe fall,
Helpt you to rise so Tall :
Her tell, as once I for her sake lou'd Breath,
10 So for her sake I now court lingring Death.

II. ¹ NO. and I am now [In the Oxford copy of D and in that at
Haigh Hall, and I am now is corrected in ink to and am I now This
makes a question mark at the end of the fourth line necessary.] ⁹ NO.
Vertue hath taught with ¹⁰ O. My Mind into ¹¹ O. chide her fill
¹⁴ NO. which thralls

III. ² In the Oxford copy of D, " Head " is corrected to " Heads "
The Haigh Hall copy of D has " Head " ⁵ NO. (sweet selfe) ⁸ O.
Help you ⁹ NO. Tell her

[iv]

To Sleepe.

HOw comes it Sleepe, that thou
Euen kisses me affords
Of her (deare her) so farre who's absent now ?
How did I heare those Words,
5 Which Rockes might moue, and moue the Pines to bow ?
Aye mee before halfe Daye
Why didst thou steale away ?
Returne, I thine for euer will remaine,
And onlie bring with thee that Guest againe.

[v]

An Almanacke.

THis strange Ecclipse one sayes
Strange Wonders doth fortell,
But yee whose Wyfes excell,
And loue to count their Praise,
5 Shut all your gates, your Hedges Plant with Thornes,
The Sunne menac'd the World this Time with Hornes.

IV. ⁹ NO. *If thou wilt bring*
V. ³ NO. *But you* ⁶ NO. *The Sun did threat*

[vi]

A Chaine of Gold.

ARe not those Lockes of Gold
Sufficient Chaines the wildest Harts to hold ?
Is not that Yuorie Hand
A Diamantine Band,
5 Most sure to keepe the most vntamed Minde,
But yee must others finde ?
O yes : why is that Golden One then borne
Thus free in Chaines (perhaps) Loues Chaines to scorne.

[vii]

EPITAPH.

THE Bawd of Iustice, he who Lawes controll'd,
And made them fawne, and frowne as he got gold,
That Proteus of our State, whose Hart and Mouth
Were farther distant than is North from South,
5 That Cormorant who made himselfe so grosse
On Peoples Ruine, and the Princes Losse,
Is gone to . and though he here did euill,
He meanes below to prooue an honest Deuill.

VI. ⁷ NO. *then worne*
VII. ⁷ NO. *Is gone to Hell*   ⁸ NO. *He there perchance may prove
an honest devill.*

[viii]

A TRANSLATION.

FIerce Robbers were of old
  Exild the Champian Ground,
From Hamlets chas'd, in Citties kill'd or bound,
And onely Woods, Caues, Mountaines, did them hold :
5 But now (when all is sold)
Woods, Mountaines, Caues, to good Men be refudge,
And doe the Guiltlesse lodge,
And cled in Purple Gownes
The greatest Theeues command within the Townes.

[ix]

COme Citizens erect to Death an Alter,
  That sau'd to you Axe, Fuell, Timber, Halter.

[x]

Proteus of Marble.

THis is no worke of Stone,
  Though breathlesse, cold it seeme and sense hath none,
But that false God which keepes
The monstruous people of the raging Deepes :
5 Now that he doth not change his Shape this while,
Is 't not thus constant more you to beguile ?

VIII. [8] NO. *clad*
IX. [2] NO. *Who keeps you from Axe*
X. [2] NO. *Though it seems breathlesse, cold, and sense hath none*
[6] D has " *It's not* "—which can hardly be right—, and no question mark
at the end of the line.

[xi]

The Statue of *VENVS* sleeping.

P^{*Assenger vexe not thy Minde*}
  To make mee mine Eyes vnfold,
For when thou them doest behold,
Thine perhaps they will make blinde.

[xii]

LAVRA to PETRARCH.

I Rather loue a Youth and childish Rime,
  Then thee whose Verse and Head be wise through time.

[xiii]

A Louers Prayer.

N^{*Eare to a Christall Spring,*}
  With Thirst and Heat opprest,
Narcissa *faire doth rest,*
Trees pleasant Trees which those green plaines forth bring
5 *Now interlace your trembling Tops aboue*
And make a Canopie vnto my Loue,
So in Heauens highest House when Sunne *appeares,*
Aurora *may you cherish with her Teares.*

        XI. ³ NO. *For if thou shouldst them behold*
        XII. ² NOP. *Than thee*

[xiv]

For Dorvs.

WHy Nais *stand yee nice*
   Like to a well wrought Stone,
When Dorus *would you kisse ?*
Denie him not that blisse,
5 *He's but a Childe (old Men be Children twice)*
And euen a Toothlesse one :
And when his Lips yours touch in that delight
Yee need not feare he will those Cherries bite.

[xv]

Loue vagabonding.

SWeet Nymphes *if as yee straye*
   Yee finde the froth-borne Goddesse of the Sea,
All blubbred, pale, vndone,
Who seekes her giddie Sone,
5 *That litle God of Loue,*
Whose golden shafts your chastest Bosomes proue :
Who leauing all the Heauens hath runne away :
If shee to him him findes will ought impart
Her tell he Nightlie lodgeth in my Heart.

XIV. ⁴ O. *bless*
XV. ⁶ N, *and the Haigh Hall copy of* D, *have "chastests"* ⁸ NO. *If
ought to him that finds him she'll impart*

[xvi]

Phræne.

Aonian *Sisters helpe my* Phrẹnes *Praise to tell,*
Phrẹne *hart of my hart with whom the Graces dwel,*
For I surcharged am so sore that I not know
What first to praise of her, her Brest, or Necke of Snow,
5 *Her Cheeks with Roses spred, or her two Sun-like Eies,*
Her Teeth of brightest Pearle, her Lips where Svveetnes *lies :*
But those do praise themselues, being to all Eyes set forth,
That Muses *yee need not to say ought of their Worth,*
Then her white sistring Papes essaye for to make knowne,
10 *But her white sistring Papes through smallest Vail are showne,*
Yet Shee *hath some thing else more worthie then the rest*
Not seene, goe sing of that farre beneath her Brest
Whichmounts like fair Parnasse, *where Pegasse wel doth run :*
Here Phræne *stay'd my* Muse *ere shee had well begun.*

XVI. *In P, this piece is entitled "* Nisa's praise *"*
  [1] P. Ye sisters muses help by Nisa's praise to tell   [2] P. Nisa heart
of my heart where all the Graces dwell   [3] P. For I o'ercharged am
so sore that I know not   [4] P. praise of her her hair or milkie throt
[6] P. of finest pearles   [7] P. But these so praise themselves   [9] P.
Then her alabaster paps seeke ye for to make known   NO. *Then*
[N. *Than*] *her white swelling paps*   [10] P. But her alabaster paps
through smallest crape are shown.   NO. *But her white swelling paps*
[11] P. else praiseworthier   NO. *than the rest.*   [12] P. Vnseene go tell of
that which lies beneath her breast   NO. *of that which lies beneath* [*In
the Oxford copy of* D, *"* farre *" is inserted before "* farre,*" in Drummond's
hand.*]   [13] P. Mounting   NO. *And mounts*   [14] P. Here Nysa

[xvii]

Desired Death.

DEare Life while as I touch
　These Corrall Ports of blisse,
Which still themselues do kisse,
And sweetly me inuite to do as much,
5 All panting in my Lips,
My Life my Heart doth leaue,
No sense my Senses haue,
And inward Powers doe find a strange Ecclipse,
This Death so heauenly well
10 Doth so me please, that I
Would neuer longer seeke in sense to dwell,
If that euen thus I only could but die.

[xviii]

Phœbe.

IF for to be alone and all the Night to wander
　Maids can proue chast, then chast is Phœbe without
　　slander.

Ansvver.

FOol still to be alone, all Night in Heauen to wander,
　Wold make the wanton chast, then she's chast without
　　slander.

XVII. [1] NO. *while I do touch* [2] O. *of Bless* [4] *The Haigh Hall copy of D has a full stop at the end of this line.* [6] NO. *My Heart my Life doth leaue*
XVIII. [2] P. *Maids can be chaste then chaste is Diane* [4] P. *Can make the wanton chaste then Dianes chaste but slander.* [*In the Haigh Hall copy of D, the full stop after " slander " is omitted.*]

Commendatory Verses.

Reprinted from the Original Works
to which they were prefixed.
1614-1635.

Commendatory Verses.

i.

To Sʳ W. A.

[Prefixed to " DOOMES-DAY," by Sir William Alexander.
Edinburgh, 1614, 4to.]

L Ike *Sophocles* (the hearers in a trance)
　With *Crimson Cothurne* on a stately Stage
If thou march forth (where all with pompe doth glance)
To mone the *Monarches* of the Worlds first Age ;
5 Or if, like *Phœbus*, thou thy Selfe aduance,
All bright with *sacred Flames*, known by Heauēs Badge,
To make a *Day*, of Dayes which scornes the Rage,
Whilst when they end it, what should come doth
　　Scance ;
Thy *Phœnix-Muse* still wing'd with *Wonders* flies,
10 Praise of our *Brookes*, Staine to old *Pindus Springs*,
And who thee follow would, scarce with their Eyes
Can reach the *Spheare* where thou most sweetlie sings.
　Though string'd with *Starres* Heauēs *Orpheus Harpe*
　　enrolle,
　More worthy Thine to blaze about the Pole.

WILLIAM DRVMMOND.

ii.

To the Author.

Sonnet.

[Prefixed to " The famous Historye of PENARDO AND LAISSA,"
by Patrik Gordon.   Dort, 1615, 8vo.]

COme forth, *Laissa*, spred thy lockes of Gold,
Show thy cheekes roses in their virgine Prime,
And though no gĕmes the decke which Indies hold,
Yeild not vnto the fairest of thy tyme.
5 No ceruse brought farre farre beyond the seas,
Noe poisone lyke Cinabre Paints thy face,
Let them haue that whose natiue hues displeas,
Thow graceth nakednesse, it doth the grace.
Thy Syre no pyick-purse is of others witt,
10 Those Jewellis be his oune which the adorne ;
And though thow after greatter ones be borne,
Thou mayst be bold euen midst the first to sitt,
    For whilst fair Iuliett, or the farie quene
    Doe liue with theirs, thy beautie shall be seene.

M. William Drommond.

iii.

ON THE DEATH OF GODEFRID VANDER HAGEN.

[Prefixed to G. Vander Hagen, "MISCELLANEA POEMATA."
Middelburgi, 1619, 4to.]

SCarce I four Lusters had enjoyed Breath,
When my Lifes Threid was cut by cruel Death ;
Few were my Yeares, so were my Sorrowes all,
Long Dayes haue Drammes of sweet, but Pounds of Gall ;
5 And yet the fruites which my faire Spring did giue,
Proue some may longer breath, not longer liue.
That craggie Path which doth to Vertue lead,
With steps of Honor I did stronglie tread ;
I made sweet Layes, and into Notes diuyne
10 Out-sung *Apollo* and the *Muses* nyne.
Forths sweetest Swannets did extolle my Verse,
Forths sweetest Swannets now weepe o're my Hearse,
    For which I pardone Fates my date of Yeares ;
    Kings may haue vaster Tombes, not dearer Teares.

W. Drvmmond.

iv.

Of my Lord of *Galloway* his learned Commentary on the Reuelation.

[Prefixed to " PATHMOS ; OR A COMMENTARY ON THE
REVELATION OF SAINT IOHN," by William Cowper,
Bishop of Galloway.   London, 1619, 4to.]

T*O this admir'd Discouerer giue place,*
  Yee who first tam'd the Sea, the Windes outranne,
And match'd the Dayes bright Coach-man in your race,
Americus, Columbus, Magellan.

5 *It is most true that your ingenious care*
  And well-spent paines another world brought forth,
For Beasts, Birds, Trees, for Gemmes and Metals rare,
Yet all being earth, was but of earthly worth.

Hee a more precious World to vs descryes,
10 *Rich in more Treasure then both Indes containe,*
Faire in more beauty then mans witte can faine,
Whose Sunne not sets, whose people neuer dies.
  Earth shuld your Brows deck with stil-verdant Bayes,
  But Heauens crowne his with Stars immortall rayes.

Master *William Drumond* of
Hawthorn-denne.

V.

ON THE BOOKE.

[Prefixed to " HEPTAMERON, THE SEVEN DAYES," &c., by
A. Symson.   Sainct Andrews, 1621, 8vo.]

GOD *binding with hid* Tendons *this great* ALL,
Did make a LVTE *which had all parts it giuen ;*
This LVTES *round* Bellie *was the azur'd Heauen,*
The Rose *those Lights which Hee did there install ;*

5   *The* Basses *were the Earth and Ocean,*
The Treble *shrill the Aire ; the other* Strings
The vnlike Bodies were of mixed things :
And then His Hand to breake sweete Notes began.

Those loftie Concords did so farre rebound,
10   *That Floods, Rocks, Meadows, Forrests, did them heare,*
Birds, Fishes, Beasts, danc'd to their siluer sound ;
Onlie to them Man had a deafned Eare :
    Now him to rouse from sleepe so deepe and long,
    God wak'ned hath the Eccho *of this Song.*

W. D.

vi.

On These Lockes.

[Prefixed to " SAMSONS SEAVEN LOCKES OF HAIRE,"
by A. Symson, Sainct Andrewes. 1621, 8vo.]

Lockes, *Ornament of Angels, Diademes*
Which the triumphing Quires aboue doe crowne ;
Rich Curles of Bountie, Pinnions of Renowne,
Of that immortall Sunne immortall Beames ;

5 Lockes, *sacred* Lockes, *no, adamantine Chaines,*
Which doe shut vp and firme together binde
Both that Contentment which in Life wee finde,
And Blisse which with vnbodied Soules remaines ;

Faire Locks, *all* Locks *compar'd to you (though gold)*
10 *Are* Comets-Locks, *portending Harme and Wrath,*
Or bauld Occasions-Locke, *that none can holde,*
Or Absaloms, *which worke the Wearers death.*

If hencefoorth Beautie e're my Minde subdue,
It shall (deare Locks) *be for what shines in you.*

W. D.

vii.

PARAINETICON.

[Prefixed to " PALLAS ARMATA, OR MILITARIE INSTRUCTIONS for the Learned," by Sir Thomas Kellie. Edinburgh, 1627, 4to.]

P*Oore* Rhene, *and canst Thou see*
 Thy Natiues *Gore Thy Christall Curles deface,*
 Thy Nymphes *so bright which bee,*
 Halfe-Blackamores embrace,
5 *And (dull'd with Grapes) yet not resente Thy Case ?*
Fallen are Thy Anadeames,
 O of such goodlie Cities Famous Flood !
 Dimm'd bee Thy Beauties Beames,
 And with Thy Spoyles and Blood
10 *Hell is made rich, prowd the Iberian Blood.*
 And You, faire Europes *Queen,*
 Which hast with Lillies deckt your purple Seate,
 Can you see those haue beene
 Sterne Cometes to Your State,
15 *On Neighboures Wracke to grow so hugelie great ?*
Looke how much Iber *gaines,*
 By as much lessened is Your flowrie Throne ;
 O doe not take such paines
 On Bartholomewes *alone,*
20 *But seeke to reacquire your* Pampelone.
Braue People, which endwell
 The happiest Ile that Neptunes *armes embrace ;*
 World, which doth yet excell
 In what first Worlds did grace,
25 *Doe neuer to base seruitude giue Place :*
Marshalle your Wits and Armes,
 Your Courage whett with Pittie and Disdaine,
 Your deeme your Allies Harmes ;
 All lose or re-obtaine,
30 *And either Palme or fatall Cypresse gaine.*

To this Great Spirits Frame
    If moulded were All Mindes, all Endeuoures,
    Could Worth *thus All inflame,*
    Then not this Ile were Ours
35   *Alone, but all betweene Sunnes golden Bowres.*

W. DRVMMOND.

viii.

OF THE BOOKE.

[Prefixed to " THE TRVE CRVCIFIXE FOR TRUE
CATHOLICKES," by Sir William Moore.   Edinburgh, 1629, 8vo.]

YOu that with awfull eyes and sad regards,
    Gazing on Masts of Ships crost with their yards ;
Or when yee see a *Microcosme* to swim,
At eury stroake the *Crucifixe* doe limne
5 In your Braines Table ; or when smaller things,
As pyed Butter-flyes, and Birds their wings
Doe raise a *Crosse*, streight on your knees doe fall
And worship ; you, that eurye painted wall,
Grac't with some antik face, some *Godling* make,
10 And practise whoordome for the *Crosses* sake
With *Bread, stone, mettall* ;   Read these sacred *Layes*,
And (*Proselytes*) proclaime the *Authors* praise :
Such *Fame* your *Transformation* shall him giue,
With *Homers* Euer that his *Name* shall liue.

W. D.
Of Hawthorn-denne.

ix.

[Subjoined to " A FVNERALL SERMON, Preached at the buriall of
Lady Iane Maitlane, daughter to the Right Noble Earle, Iohn
Earle of Lauderdail."   Edinburgh, 1633, 4to.]

THe flowre of virgins in her prime of years
  By ruthlesse *destinies* is ta'ne away,
And rap'd from earth, poore earth, before this day
Which ne're was rightly nam'd a vale of tears.

5 *Beautie* to heauen is fled, sweet *modestie*
No more appears ; she whose harmonious sounds
Did rauish sense, and charm mindes deepest wounds,
Embalm'd with many a tear now low doth lie.

Fair hopes evanish'd are ; she should have grac'd
10 A princes marriage-bed, but (lo !) in heauen
Blest paramours to her were to be giuen ;
She liu'd an angel, now is with them plac'd.

Vertue was but a name abstractly trim'd,
Interpreting what she was in effect,
15 A shadow from her frame, which did reflect
A portrait by her excellencies lim'd.

Thou whom free-will or chance hath hither brought,
And readst, here lies a branch of *Metlands* stem,
And *Seatons* offspring, know that either name
20 Designes all worth yet reach'd by humane thought.
  Tombs (elsewhere) rise, life to their guests to giue,
  Those ashes can frail monuments make liue.

                              M. W. Drumond.

IX. 9. NO. now vanish'd are   13 NO. Vertue is   21 NO. use Life
22 NO. These

x.

Of Persons Varieties.

[Prefixed to " VARIETIES," &c., by David Person of Loghlands.
London, 1635, 4to.]

THe Lawyer here may learne Divinity,
　　The Diuine Lawes, or faire Astrology,
The Dammaret respectiuely to fight,
The Duellist to court a Mistresse right ;
5 Such who their name take from the Rosie-Crosse,
May here by Time learne to repaire their losse :
All learne may somewhat, if they be not fooles ;
Arts quicklier here are lesson'd than in Schooles.

xi.

Distich, of the same.

THis Booke a World is ; here if errours be,
　　The like (nay worse) in the great world we see.

William Drummond,
Of *Hathorn-den*.

Posthumous Poems.

I.

First published in Phillips' edition (1656),
and now corrected according to the
Manuscripts.

Posthumous Poems.

I.

i.

WHat course of life should wretched Mortalles take ?
In courtes hard questiones large contention make ;
Care dwelles in houses, labour in the feild,
Tumultuous seas affrighting dangeres yeild.
5 In foraine landes thou neuer canst be blest,
If rich thou art in feare, if poore distrest.
In wedlock frequent discontentmentes swell,
Vnmaried persones as in desertes dwell.
How many troubles are with children borne ?
10 Yet hee that wants them countes himself forlorne.
Young men are wanton and of wisdome voyd,
Gray haires are cold, vnfit to be imployd.
Who would not one of those two offeres choose :
Not to be borne ; or breath with speed to loose ?

I. In NO, this poem is entitled " A Translation Of S. *John Scot* his
verses beginning *Quod vitæ sectabor iter.*"
² NO. In Books ¹³ NO. Who would not one of those two offers
try ¹⁴ NO. Not to be borne: or, being borne, to dye ? [*The reading
adopted by NO in ll.* ¹³ *and* ¹⁴ *appears in* P *as a correction by the side
of the original reading, but in a later hand, which is certainly not that
of Drummond.*]

173

ii.

All good hath left this age, all trackes of shame,
Mercie is banished and pittye dead,
Justice from whence it came to heauen is fled,
Relligion maim'd is thought an idle Name.
5 Faith to distrust and malice hath giuen place,
Enuie with poysond teeth hath freindship torne,
Renowned knowledge lurkes, despisd, a scorne,
Now it is euill all euill not to embrace.
There is no life saue vnder seruile Bandes,
10 To make Desert a Vassall to their crimes
Ambition with Auarice ioyne Handes ;
O euer-shamefull, O most shamelesse Tymes !
    Saue that Sunnes light wee see, of good heare tell,
    This Earth wee courte so much were verye Hell.

iii.

Doth then the world goe thus, doth all thus moue ?
Is this the Justice which on Earth wee find ?
Is this that firme decree which all doth bind ?
Are these your influences Powers aboue ?
5 Those soules which Vices moodye Mistes most blind,
Blind Fortune blindlie most their friend doth proue :
And they who Thee (poore Idole) Vertue loue
Plye like a feather toss'd by storme and wind.
Ah ! (if a Prouidence doth swaye this all ?)
10 Why should best Mindes groane vnder most distresse,
Or why should pryde Humilitie turne Thrall,
And injuryes the Innocent oppresse ?
    Heauens hinder, stope this fate, or grante a Tyme
    When Good maye haue as well as Bad their prime.

II. ⁷ NO. Renowned Knowledge is a despis'd scorne   ⁸ NO.
Now evill 'tis ¹³ NO. here tell ¹⁴ O. court too much
    III. ⁸ O. Fly like ¹¹ NO. make thrall

iv.

A Replye.

Who do in good delight
That souueraine Iustice euer doth rewarde,
And though sometyme it smyte,
Yet it doth them reguard ;
5 For euen amidst their Griefe
They find a strong reliefe :
And Death it selfe can worke them no despight.
Againe in euill who ioye
And doe in it grow old,
10 In midst of Mirth are charg'd with sinnes annoye,
Which is in conscience scrolld ;
And when their lifes fraile thread is cut by Tyme,
They punishment find equall to each cryme.

v.

Beauties Frailtye.

Looke how the maying Rose
At sulphures azure fumes,
In a short space her crimsin blush doth lose,
And all amaz'd a pallid whit assumes :
5 So Tyme our best consumes,
Makes youth and Beautie passe,
And what was pryde turnes horrour in our Glasse.

V. This piece has no title in NO.
1 NO. Look how in *May* the Rose

vi.

To a swallow, building neare the statue of Medea.

Fond Prognèe, chattering wretch,
That is Medea, there
Wilt thou thy yonglinges hatch ?
Will shee keep thyne, her own who could not spare ?
5 Learne from her franticke face
To seeke some fitter place.
What other mayst thou hope for, what desire,
Saue Stygian spelles, woundes, poison, iron, fire ?

vii.

Venus armed.

As to trye new alarmes,
In Ioues great Court aboue
The wanton Queene of Loue
Of sleeping Mars put on the horrid armes.
5 Her gazing in a glasse
To see what thing shee was,
To mocke and scoffe the blew-eyed maide did moue.
Who said, sweet Queene thus should yee haue been dight
When Vulcan tooke you napping with your knight.

VII. ¹ NO. To practice new alarmes   ⁵ NO. Where gazing

viii.

The Boares head.

Amidst a pleasant greene
Which sunne did seldome see,
Where play'd Anchises with the Cyprian Queene,
The Head of a wild boare hang on a Tree :
5 And driuen by zephyres breath
Did fall, and wound the louelye youth beneath,
On whom yet scarce appeares
So much of bloud as Venus eyes shed teares.
But euer as shee wept her Antheme was,
10 Change, cruell change, alas !
My Adon, whilst thou liud, was by thee slaine,
Now dead this louer must thou kill againe !

ix.

To an Owle.

Ascalaphus tell mee,
So may nights courtaine long tyme couer Thee,
So yuie euer maye
From irksome light keep chamber thyne and bed,
5 And in moones liurey cled
So mayst thou scorne the Quiristeres of Daye :
When plaining thou dost staye
Neare to the sacred window of my deare,
Dost euer thou her heare
10 To wake, and steale swift houres from drowsye sleep ?
And when shee wakes, doth ere a stollen sigh creep
Into thy listning Eare ?
If that deafe God doth yet her carelesse keep,
In lowder notes My Grief with thyne expresse,
15 Till by thy shrickes shee thinke on my distresse.

IX. ⁴ NO. keep thy Chamber and Bed

x.

Daphne.

Now Daphnès armes did grow
In slender Branches, and her braided haire
Which like gold waues did flow
In leauie Twigs was stretched in the aire;
5 The grace of either foot
Transform'd was to a root,
A tender Barke enwrapes her Bodye faire.
Hee who did cause her ill
Sor-wailing stood, and from his blubb'red eyne
10 Did showres of teares vpon the rine distill
Which watred thus did bude and turne more greene.
O deep Dispaire ! o Hart-appalling Griefe !
When that doth woe encrease should bring reliefe.

xi.

The Beare of loue.

In woodes and desart Boundes
A beast abroad doth roame,
So louing sweetnesse and the honnyecombe
That it of Beas contemptes alarmes and woundes :
5 I by like pleasure led
To proue what heauens did place
Of sweet on your faire face,
Whilst therewith I am fed,
Rest carelesse (Bear of loue) of hellish smart
10 And how those eyes afflicte and wound my hart.

X. In NO, this piece is entitled " *Daphnis.*"
¹ NO. Now *Daphnis*   ⁴ NO. were stretched   ¹⁰ NO. rind
XI.   ⁴ NO. It doth despise the armes of Bees and wounds

xii.

Galateas Sonnets.

[A.]

Joas in vaine thou brings thy rimes and songs
Of th' old Thebaine deck't with the withered flowres ;
In vaine thou tells the faire Europas wrongs,
And Hers whom Joue deceau'd with golden showres.
5 I thinke not loue ore thee his wings hath spred,
Or if that passion hath thy soule opprest,
Its onlie for some Grecian Mistresse dead,
Of such old sighs thou doth discharge thy brest.
How can true loue with fables hold a place ?
10 Thou who thy loue with fables hath enamll'd,
Thy loues a fable and thy part dissembled,
Thou doth but court my grace more to disgrace :
    I can not thinke thou art tane with my lookes ;
    Thou did but learne thy loue in louers books.

XII. [A.] In NO, this and the next four sonnets are entitled
" *Five Sonnets for* Galatea."
    ¹ NO. *Strephone* in vaine   ² NO. Deckt with grave *Pindars* old and
withered flow'rs ³ NO. In vaine thou count'st   ⁴ NO. And her
⁵ NO. Thou hast slept never under Mirtles shed   ⁷ NO. It is but for
some   ¹⁰ NO. Thou who with fables doth set fo: h thy love   ¹¹ NO.
Thy love a pretty fable needs must prove   ¹² NO. Thou suest for
grace, in scorne more to disgrace   ¹³ NO. I cannot thinke thou wert
charm'd by my looks   ¹⁴ NO. O no, thou learn'dst thy love

[B.]

No more with sugred speach infect my eares,
Tell me no more how that yee pine in Anguish,
And when yee sleepe no more saye that yee languish,
And in delight no more tell yee spend teares.
5 Haue I such owlie eies that they not see
How such are made braine-sicke be Appollo,
Who foolish boaste the Muses doe them follow?
Though in loues lyuery yet no louers be.
If wee poore soules a fauor but them show,
10 That straight with wondring pens abroad is blazed,
They raise their Name our fame to ouerthrow,
Our vice is noted whilst their wits are praised :
     In silent thoughts who can not secrets couer,
     He may well saye, but not well be a louer.

XII. [B.] [1] NO. No more with Candid words infect [3] NO.
When sound ye sleep: no more [4] NO. No more in sweet despite
say you spend teares [5] NO. Who hath such hollow eyes as not to see
[6] NO. How those that are haire-brain'd boast of *Apollo* [7] NO. And
bold give out the Muses do them follow [8] NO. Though in loves Library
no Lover's he [O. be] [9] NO. soules least favour [10] NO. That straight
in wanton Lines abroad [11] NO. Their name doth soar [O. Their Names
do soar] on our fames overthrow [12] NO. Mark'd is our lightnesse
whilst [13] NO. can no secret [14] NO. He may, say we, but not well,
be a Lover.

[C.]

Yee who with curious words and Dedals art,
Frame laberinthes our Beautie to surprise,
Telling strange cassills forged in the skies,
And tails of Cupids bow, and Cupids dart ;
5 Well, how so ere yee acte your faigned smart,
Molesting quiet eares with tragicke cries,
When yee accuse our chastities best part,
Called Crueltie, yee seeme not halfe too wise.
Euen yee your selues estime it worthie praise,
10 Beauties best guard, that Dragon which doth keepe
Th' Hesperian fruit, and which in you doth raise
That Delian wit which other wayes should sleepe :
  To cruell Nymphes your lines doe fame afford,
  Of many pitifull scarce halfe a word.

XII. [C.] ¹ NO. Ye who with curious numbers, sweetest art
² NO. Frame *Dedall* Nets our beauty ³ NO. Castles builded ⁵ NO.
Well howsoever ⁷ NO. When you ⁸ NO. Nam'd cruelty ⁹ NO.
Yea, ye yourselves it deem most worthy praise ¹¹ NO. *Hesperian*
fruit, the spur in you does raise ¹² NO. wit that otherwaies may
sleep ¹⁴ NO. Of [N *has the misprint* Oft] many pittifull, not one
poore word

[D.]

If it be loue to wish that all the Night
Wee spend in sad regreats with waking eies,
And when the sunne enpurples ali the skies
To liue in languish, spoiled of all delight ?
5 If it be loue to wish that Reasons light
In our wake Minds by passion darkened be,
Till Heauen and Earth do scorne our miserie,
Whilst blindfold led wee nere doe ought aright ?
If it be loue to wish our chastetie
10 May subiect be vnto a basse desire,
And that our harts heale a more cruell fire
Then that Athenian in his Bull did frie ?
    Then sure yee loue ; but causers of such woes
    No louers be to loue, but hatefull foes.

XII. [D.] [1] NO. If it be love to wake out all the night   [2] NO. And watchfull eyes drive out in dewie moanes [3] NO. And when the Sun brings to the world his light [4] NO. To waste the Day in teares and bitter groanes [5] NO. If it be love to dim weake reasons beame [6] NO. With clouds of strange desire, and make the mind [7] NO. In hellish agonies a heav'n to dreame [8] NO. Still seeking Comforts where but griefs we find [9] NO. If it be love to staine with wanton thought [10] NO. A spotlesse chastity, and make it try   [11] NO. More furious flames than his whose cunning wrought [12] NO. That brazen Bull where he intomb'd did fry [13] NO. Then sure is Love the causer of such woes [14] NO. Be ye our Lovers, or our mortall foes

[E.]

And would yee then shake off loues golden chaine,
With which yee saye 'tis freedome to be bound,
And cruell heale of loue the noble wound,
That yee so soone Hopes blysse seeke to obtaine?
5 All things beneath pale Cynthias changing Round
Ore which our Grande dame Nature here doth raigne,
What they desire, when they in end haue found,
Into decadence fall and slacke remaine :
The herbes behold which in the meades doe grow,
10 Till to hight they come but then decaye,
The ocean waues tumultuoslie which flow
Till they embrace the banks, then rune awaye :
   So is't with loue : that thou may loue me still,
   O no ! thinke not, I'll yeld vnto thy will.

XII. [E.] ¹ NO. And would you ² NO. With which it is best
freedome ³ NO. And Cruell do ye [O. you] seek to heale the Wound
⁴ NO. Of Love, which hath such sweet and pleasant paine ⁵ NO.
All that is subject unto natures raigne ⁶ NO. In Skies above, or on
this lower round ⁷ NO. When it is long and far sought, end hath
found ⁸ NO. Doth in *Decadens* fall and ⁹ NO. Behold the Moon
how gay her face doth grow ¹⁰ NO. Till she kisse all the Sun, then
doth decay ¹¹ NO. See how the Seas tumultuously do flow ¹² NO.
Till they embrace lov'd bankes, then post away [*In* P, loued bankes
they kisse *is written in above* they embrace the banks, *in Drummond's
hand.*] ¹³ NO. So is't with love, unlesse you love me still ¹⁴ NO. O
do not thinke Ile yeeld unto your will.

xiii.

On the Death of a Margarite.

In shelles and gold pearles are not keept alone,
A Margarite here lies beneath a stone ;
A Margarite that did excell in worth
All those rich Gemmes the Indies both bring forth ;
5 Who had shee liu'd when good was lou'd of men
Had made the Graces foure the Muses ten,
And forc'd those happye tymes her dayes that claim'd
To be from her the age of pearle still nam'd.
Shee was the rarest jewell of her kynd,
10 Gract with more beautye than shee left behind,
All Goodnesse Vertue Wonder, and could cheare
The sadest Minds : Now Nature, knowing heere
    How Things but showen, then hiden, ar loud best,
    This Margaret shrin'd in this marble chest.

xiv.

Nor Amaranthes nor Roses doe bequeath
Vnto this Herse, but Tamariskes and Vine,
For that same thirst though dead yet doth him pine,
Which made him so carowse whilst hee drew breath.

xv.

Epitaph.

Heer S—— lyes, most bitter gall,
Who whilst hee liud spoke euill of all,
Onlye of God the Arrant Sot
Nought said, but that hee knew him not.

XIII. In NO, this piece is entitled "*An Epitaph of one named Margaret.*"

⁴ NO. both send forth ⁸ NO. From her to be ¹⁰ NO. with more lustre ¹¹ NO. vertue, Bounty ¹⁴ N. 'shrin'd

XV. In NO, this piece is entitled "Aretinus *Epitaph.*"

¹ NO. Here *Aretinus* lies most bitter [O. bitter] gall

xvi.

The oister.

With open shells in seas, on heauenly due
A shining oister lushiouslie doth feed,
And then the Birth of that ætheriall seed
Shows, when conceau'd, if skies lookt darke or blew :
5 So doe my thoughts (celestiall twins) of you,
At whose aspect they first beginne & breed,
When they are borne to light demonstrat true,
If yee then smyld, or lowr'd in murning weed.
Pearles then are framd orient, faire in forme,
10 In their conception if the heauens looke cleare ;
But if it thunder, or menace a storme,
They sadlie darke and wannish doe appeare :
Right so my thoughts are, so my notes do change,
Sweet if yee smyle, & hoarse if yee looke strange.

xvii.

All Changeth.

The angrye winds not ay
Doe cuffe the roring deep,
And though Heauens often weep
Yet doe they smyle for joy when com'd is May,
5 Frosts doe not euer kill the pleasant flowres,
And loue hath sweets when gone are all the sowres.
This said a shepheard closing in his armes
His Deare, who blusht to feele loues new alarmes.

XVI. In NO, this sonnet is entitled "*Comparison of his thoughts to Pearls.*"
⁴ NO. if Skies looke   ⁷ NO. When they came forth to light   ⁹ NO. Pearles then are orient fram'd, and faire in   ¹⁰ NO. If heavens in their conceptions do looke cleare   ¹¹ NO. But if they thunder, or do threat a storme   ¹² NO. darke and cloudy   [*In* P, swarthye *is written in above* wannish *in Drummond's hand.*]   ¹³ NO. thoughts and so my notes
XVII. ⁴ NO. for joy when comes dismay

xviii.

Silenus to King Midas.

The greatest Gift that from their loftie Thrones
The all-gouerning powers to men can giue
Is that hee neuer breath, or breathing once
A suckling end his dayes, and leaue to liue :
5 For then hee neither knowes the woe nor joy
Of life, nor feares the stigian lakes annoy.

xix.

To his amorous Thoughts.

Sweet wanton thought which art of Beautye borne,
And which on Beautye feedst & sweet Desire,
Who like the Butterflye dost endlesse turne
About that flame that all so much admire ;
5 That heauenlye face which doth outblush the Morne,
Those yuoryd hands, those Threeds of golden wyre,
Thou still surroundest, yet darst not aspire
To vew Mynds beautyes which the rest adorne.
Sure thou dost well that place not to come neare,
10 Nor see the maiestye of that faire court ;
For if thow sawst the vertues ther resort,
The pure intelligence that moues that spheare,
    Like soules departed to the Ioyes aboue,
    Backe neuer wouldst thou come, nor thence remoue.

XVIII. ³ NO. to man
XIX. ² NO. And who on beauty feedst, and ³ NO. Like taper
flee, still circling, and still turne ⁵ NO. That heavenly faire, which
⁶ NO. Those Ivory hands ⁸ NO *omit this verse.* ¹¹ NO. saw'st what
wonders there resort [*In* P, wonders *is written in above* vertues *in
Drummond's hand.*] ¹² NO *have the misprint* poore *for* pure ¹³ NO.
Like soules ascending to ¹⁴ NO. wouldst thou turne
    To this poem O *adds the following verses :*
      What can we hope for more ? what more enjoy ?
      Since fairest Things thus soonest have their End,
      And as on Bodies Shadows do attend,
      Soon all our Bliss is followed with Annoy.
      Yet she's not Dead, she Lives where she did Love,
      Her Memory on Earth, her Soul above.

XX.

Verses of the late Earl of Pembroke

I.

The doubtfull Feares of change so fright my mynd,
Though raised to the highest ioy in loue,
As in this slipperye state more Griefe I find
Than they who neuer such a Blisse did proue,
5   But fed with lingring Hopes of future Gaine
Dreame not what 'tis to doubte a loosers paine.

II.

Desire a safer Harbour is than feare,
And not to rise lesse Danger than to fall ;
The want of jewells wee farre better beare
10 Than so possest, at once to loose them all :
    Vnsatisfied Hopes Tyme may repaire
    When ruyn'd Faith must finish in despaire.

III.

Alas ! yee looke but vp the Hill on mee,
Which showes to you a faire and smooth Ascent,
15 The precipice behind yee can not see,
    On which high Fortunes are too pronelie bent :
    If there I slippe what former Ioy or Blisse
    Can heale the Bruisse of such a fall as this ?

E. P.

XX. In NO, these stanzas are erroneously entitled " *Verses on
the late* William *Earle of* Pembrook."
   2 O. raised in   6 N. to doubt a Lovers paine

xxi.

A Replye.

I.

Who loue enjoyes, and placed hath his Minde
Where fairer Vertues fairest Beautyes grace,
Then in himselfe such store of worth doth finde,
That hee deserues to hold so good a place :
5   To chilling Feares how can hee be set forth ?
    Who feares, condemnes his owne, doubtes otheres
    worth.

II.

Desire, as flames of zeale, Feares, Horrors, meets,
They rise who shake of falling neuer prou'd.
Who is so daintye, satiate with sweets,
10 To murmure when the bancket is remou'd ?
    The fairest Hopes Tyme in the Budde destroyes,
    When sweet are Memories of ruyn'd Ioyes.

III.

It is no Hill but Heauen where yee remaine,
And whom Desert aduanced hath so hie
15 To reach the Guerdon of his burning paine,
Must not repine to fall, and falling die :
    His Hopes are crown'd ; what years of tedious breath
    Can them compare with such a happy Death ?

W. D.

XXI. ³ N. Than ⁶ NO. Whose feares condemne his own, doubts
others worth ? ⁷ NO. Feare ⁸ NO. They rise who fall of falling

xxii.

A Translation.

1.

Ah ! silly Soule, what wilt thou say
When he whom earth and Heavens obey
Comes Man to judge in the last Day ?

2.

When He a reason askes, why Grace
5 And Goodnesse thou wouldst not embrace,
But steps of Vanity didst trace ?

3.

That Day of Terrour, Vengeance, Ire,
Now to prevent thou should'st desire,
And to thy God in haste retire.

4.

10 With watry Eyes, and Sigh-swollen Heart,
O beg, beg in his Love a part,
Whilst Conscience with remorse doth smart.

5.

That dreaded Day of wrath and shame
In flames shall turne this Worlds huge Frame,
15 As sacred Prophets do proclaime.

6.

O ! with what Griefe shall Earthlings grone,
When that great Judge set on his Throne,
Examines strictly every One.

XXII. These verses are not in P.

7.

Shrill-sounding Trumpets through the Aire
20 Shall from dark Sepulchres each where
Force wretched Mortalls to appeare.

8.

Nature and Death amaz'd remaine
To find their dead arise againe,
And Processe with their Judge maintaine.

9.

25 Display'd then open Books shall lye
Which all those secret crimes descry,
For which the guilty World must dye.

10.

The Judge enthron'd (whom Bribes not gaine)
The closest crimes appeare shall plaine,
30 And none unpunished remaine.

11.

O who then pitty shall poor me !
Or who mine Advocate shall be ?
When scarce the justest passe shall free.

12.

All wholly holy dreadfull King,
35 Who freely life to thine dost bring,
Of Mercy save me Mercies spring.

13.

Then (sweet Jesu) call to mind
How of thy Paines I was the End,
And favour let me that day find.

14.

40 In search of me Thou full of paine
 Did'st sweat bloud, Death on Crosse sustaine,
 Let not these suff'rings be in vaine.

15.

 Thou supreame Judge, most just and wise,
 Purge me from guilt which on me lies
45 Before that day of thine Assize.

16.

Charg'd with remorse (loe) here I grone,
Sin makes my face a blush take on ;
Ah ! spare me prostrate at thy Throne.

17.

Who *Mary Magdalen* didst spare,
50 And lend'st the Thiefe on Crosse thine Eare,
 Shewest me fair hopes I should not feare.

18.

My prayers imperfect are and weake,
But worthy of thy grace them make,
And save me from Hells burning Lake.

19.

55 On that great Day at thy right hand
 Grant I amongst thy Sheep may stand,
 Sequestred from the Goatish Band.

---

  [42] N. Let not these suff'rages [51] O. Shew me

20.

When that the Reprobates are all
To everlasting flames made thrall,
60 O to thy Chosen (Lord) me call!

21.

That I one of thy Company,
With those whom thou dost justifie,
May live blest in Eternity.

xxiii.

To the Memory of [John, Earl of Lauderdale.]

[A.]

Of those rare worthyes which adorn'd our North
And shin'd like constellationes, Thou alone
Remained last (great Maitland) chargd with worth,
Second on Vertues Theater to none :
5 But finding all eccentricke in our Tymes,
Relligione in superstition turn'd,
Justice silenc'd, renuersed or enurn'd,
Truth faith and charitie reputed crymes :
The young Men destinat'd by sword to fall
10 And Trophèes of their countryes spoiles to reare,
Strange lawes the ag'd and prudent to appall,
And force sad yokes of Tyrannie to beare,
And for nor great nor vertuous Mindes a Roome,
Disdaining life thou shrunke into thy Tombe.

XXIII. [A.] In N, the three following epitaphs are entitled
" *Vpon* John *Earle of* Laderdale *his Death.*"
[1] NO. who adorn'd [3] NO. Remain'dst [4] NO. Second in [6] NO.
Religion into [7] NO. Justice silenc'd, exiled, or inurn'd [9] NO.
destinate [12] NO. And forc'd [14] N. Disdaining life, thou shouldst
(*sic !*) into thy Tombe O. Disdaining Life, thou shroud'st in thee thy
Tomb

[B.]

When Misdeuotione all-where shall haue place,
And loftie oratours in Thundring Termes
Shall moue you (people) to arise in armes
And churches hallowed policie deface :
5 When yee shall but one generall sepulcher
(As Auerröes did one generall soule)
On high on low, on good on bad confer,
And your dull predecessours Rites controule ;
Ah ! spare this Monument ; Great Guestes it keepes,
10 Three graue justiciares whom true worth did raise ;
The Muses Darlinges whose losse Phœbus weepes,
Mankynds delight, the Glorie of their Dayes.
More wee would saye, but feare and stand in aw
To turne Idolators and breake your law.

[C.]

Doe not repine (blest soule) that vulgare wittes
Doe make thy worth the matter of their verse,
No high-straind Muse our tymes and sorrowes fittes
And wee doe sigh, not sing, to crown thy Herse.
5 The wisest Prince e're manag'd Brittaines state
Did not disdaine in numberes cleare and braue
The vertues of thy syre to celebrate,
And fixe a rich Memoriall ou'r his Graue.
Thou didst deserue no lesse, and heere in iet,
10 Gold, Brasse, Touch, Porpherie, the Parian stone,
That by a princes hand no lines are set
For Thee ; the cause is now this land hath none :
Such giant moodes our paritie forth bringes,
Wee all will nothing be or all be kinges.

XXIII. [B.] ¹ NO. misdevotion every where shall take place
⁵ NO. When you ¹² NO. Best mens delight
XXIII. [C.] ¹ NO. that humble wits ⁸ NO. on his Grave ¹⁰ NO.
Gold, Touch, Brasse, Porphyrie, or *Parian* stone

xxiv.

To the Memorie of the excellent ladye Isabell, Countesse of Lawderdale.

Fond wight, who dreamest of Greatnesse, Glorie, State,
And worlds of pleasures, Honoures dost deuise,
Awake, learne how that heere thou art nor great,
Nor glorious ; by this Monument turne wise.

5 One it enshrineth, sprung of auncient stemme,
And (if that Bloud Nobilitie can make)
From which some kinges haue not disdaind to take
Their prowd Descent, a rare & matchless gemme.

A Beautie too heere by it is embrac't,
10 Than which no blooming Rose was more refind,
Nor Mornings blush more radiant neuer shind,
Ah ! too too like to Morne and Rose in last.

It holdes her who in wits ascendant farre
Did Tymes and sex transcend, to whom the Heauen
15 More vertues than to all this age had giuen,
For Vertue Meteore turnd when shee a starre.

Faire Mirth, sweet Conuersation, Modestie,
And what those kings of numberes did conceaue
By Muses Nyne or Graces more than Three,
20 Lye closd within the compasse of this Graue.
    Thus death all earthlye gloryes doth confound,
    Loe, what of worth a litle Dust doth bound !

XXIV. 9 N. A Beauty here it holds by full assurance   O. A Beauty
here it holds, alas too fast   11 NO. radiant ever   12 NO. at last   14 NO.
Did Yeares   19 N. moe than   22 NO. Loe ! how much Worth

XXV.

Far from these Bankes exiled be all Joyes,
Contentments, Pleasures, Musick (cares reliefe)
Tears, Sighs, Plaints, Horrours, Frightments, sad Annoies
Invest these Mountaines, fill all Hearts with Griefe.

5 Here Nightingals and Turtles, vent your moanes ;
Amphrisian Shepheard here come feed thy Flockes,
And read thy *Hyacinth* amidst our Groanes,
Plaine Eccho thy *Narcissus* from our Rocks.

Lost have our Meads their Beauty, Hills their Gemms,
10 Our Brooks their Christall, Groves their pleasant shade,
The fairest Flow'r of all our Anademms
Death cropped hath, the *Lesbia* chaste is dead.

Thus sigh'd the Tyne, then shrunke beneath his Urne,
And Meads, Brooks, Rivers, Hills about did mourne.

XXV. This piece is not in P.
6 NO. Flocke

xxvi.

Like to the Gardens Eye, the Flower of Flow'rs
With purple Pompe that dazle doth the Sight ;
Or as among the lesser Gems of Night,
The Usher of the Planet of the Houres :
5 Sweet Maid, thou shinedst on this World of ours,
Of all Perfections having trac'd the hight,
Thine outward frame was faire, faire inward Powers,
A Saphire Lanthorne, and an incense light.
Hence, the enamour'd Heaven as too too good
10 On Earths all-thorny soyle long to abide,
Transplanted to their Fields so rare a Bud,
Where from thy Sun no cloud thee now can hide.
  Earth moan'd her losse, and wish'd she had the grace
  Not to have known, or known thee longer space.

xxvii.

Madrigal.

Hard Laws of mortall Life !
To which made Thrales, we come without consent
Like Tapers lighted to be early spent,
Our Griefes are alwaies rife,
5 When joyes but halting march, and swiftly fly
Like shadows in the Eye :
The shadow doth not yeeld unto the Sun,
But Joyes and Life do waste even when begun.

XXVI. This piece is not in P.
[11] O. Translated to their Fields
XXVII. This piece is not in P.

xxviii.

On the death of a nobleman in Scotland, buried at Aithen.

Aithen, thy Pearly Coronet let fall ;
Clad in sad Robes, upon thy Temples set,
The weeping Cypresse, or the sable Jet.

Mourne this thy Nurslings losse, a losse which all
5 *Apollos* quire bemoanes, which many yeares
Cannot repaire, nor Influence of Spheares.

Ah ! when shalt thou find Shepheard like to him,
Who made thy Bankes more famous by his worth,
Then all those Gems thy Rocks and Streams send forth ?

10 His splendor others Glow-worm light did dim,
Sprung of an ancient and a vertuous Race,
He Vertue more than many did embrace.

He fram'd to mildnesse thy halfe-barbarous swaines,
The Good-mans refuge, of the bad the fright,
15 Unparaleld in friendship, worlds Delight,

For Hospitality along thy Plaines
Far-fam'd, a Patron, and a Patterne faire,
Of Piety, the Muses chiefe repaire.

Most debonaire, in Courtesie supreame,
20 Lov'd of the meane, and honour'd by the Great,
Ne're dasht by Fortune, nor cast down by Fate,
To present, and to after Times a Theame.

Aithen, thy Teares poure on this silent Grave,
And drop them in thy Alabaster cave,
25 And *Niobes* Imagery become ;
And when thou hast distilled here a Tombe,
Enchace in it thy Pearls, and let it beare,
Aithens best Gem and honour shrin'd lies here.

XXVIII. This piece is not in P.

xxix.

Epitaph.

Fame, Register of Tyme,
Write in thy scrowles, that I,
A wisdome louer, and sweet poesie,
Was croped in my Prime,
5 And ripe in worth, though scarce in yeares, did die.

xxx.

Justice, Truth, Peace, and Hospitalitie,
Friendship, and Loue, being resolued to dye
In these lewd tymes, haue chosen heere to haue
With just, true, pious, kynd DALYELL their graue ;
5 Hee them cherish'd so long, so much did grace,
That they than this would choose no dearer place.

XXIX. [3] NO. Of Wisdome [5] NO. though green in yeares, did dye
XXX. [4] NO. With just true pious — their grave [5] NO. Them
cherish'd he so much [6] NO. That they on Earth would choose none
other Place

xxxi.

When Death to deck his Trophees stopt thy breath,
Rare Ornament and Glory of these Parts :
All with moist Eyes might say, and ruthfull hearts,
That things immortall vassal'd were to Death.

5 What Good, in Parts on many shar'd we see
From Nature, gracious Heaven, or Fortune flow,
To make a Master-Piece of worth below,
Heaven, Nature, Fortune, gave in grosse to Thee.

In Honour, Bounty, Rich, in Valour, Wit,
10 In Courtesie, Borne of an ancient Race,
With Bayes in war, with Olives crown'd in Peace,
Match'd great, with Off-spring for great Actions fit.

No Rust of Times, nor Change, thy Vertue wan,
With Times to change, when Truth, Faith, Love decay'd,
15 In this new Age (like Fate) thou fixed stay'd
Of the first World an all-substantiall Man.

As earst this Kingdome given was to thy Syre,
The Prince his Daughter trusted to thy Care,
And well the credit of a Gem so rare
20 Thy loyalty and merit did require.

Yeares cannot wrong thy Worth, that now appeares
By others set as Diamonds among Pearles,
A Queens deare Foster, Father to three Earles,
Enough on Earth to triumph are o're yeares.

25 Life a Sea-voyage is, Death is the Haven,
And fraught with honour there thou hast arriv'd,
Which Thousands seeking have on Rocks been driven,
That Good adornes thy Grave, which with thee liv'd :

For a fraile Life which here thou didst enjoy,
30 Thou now a lasting hast freed of Annoy.

XXXI. This piece is not in P.
1 N has the *misprint* stop *for* stopt

xxxii.

Within the Closure of this Narrow Grave
Lye all those Graces a Good-wife could have :
But on this Marble they shall not be read,
For then the Living envy would the Dead.

xxxiii.

The daughter of a king, of princelye partes,
In Beautie eminent, in Vertues cheife,
Load-starre of loue and load-stone of all Hartes,
Her freindes and Husbandes onlie Joy, now Griefe,
5 Enclosed lyes within this narrow Graue,
Whose Paragone no Tymes, no Climates haue.

XXXII. This piece is not in P.
XXXIII. ⁵ NO. Is here pent up within a Marble Frame ⁶ NO.
Whose Paralell no Times, no Climates claime

xxxiv.

Verses fraile Records are to keep a Name,
Or raise from Dust Men to a Life of Fame,
The sport and spoyle of Ignorance ; but far
More fraile the Frames of Touch and Marble are,
5 Which envy, Avarice, Time e're long confound,
Or mis-devotion equalls with the Ground.
Vertue alone doth last, frees man from Death,
And, though despis'd and scorned here beneath,
Stands grav'n in Angels Diamantine Rolles,
10 And blazed in the Courts above the Poles.
Thou wast faire Vertues Temple, they did dwell,
And live ador'd in thee, nought did excell
But what thou either didst possesse or love,
The Graces Darling, and the maids of *Jove*,
15 Courted by Fame for Bounties which the Heaven
Gave thee in great, which if in Parcels given
To many, such we happy sure might call,
How happy then wast thou who enjoyedst them all ?
A whiter Soule ne're body did invest,
20 And now (sequestred) cannot be but blest,
Inrob'd in Glory, 'midst those Hierarchies
Of that immortall People of the Skies,
Bright Saints and Angels, there from cares made free
Nought doth becloud thy soveraign Good from Thee.
25 Thou smil'st at Earths Confusions and Jars,
And how for *Centaures* Children we wage wars :
Like honey Flies, whose rage whole swarmes consumes
Till Dust thrown on them makes them vaile their
    plumes.
Thy friends to thee a Monument would raise,
30 And limne thy Vertues ; but dull griefe thy Praise
Breakes in the Entrance, and our Taske proves vaine,
What duty writes that woe blots out againe :
Yet Love a Pyramid of Sighs thee reares,
And doth embaulme thee with Fare-wells and Teares.

XXXIV. This piece is not in P.

XXXV.

Rose.

Though Marble, Porphyry, and mourning Touch—
May praise these spoiles, yet can they not too much ;
For Beauty last, and   this Stone doth close,
Once Earths Delight, Heavens care, a purest Rose.
5 And (Reader) shouldst thou but let fall a Teare
Upon it, other flow'rs shall here appeare,
Sad Violets and Hyacinths which grow
With markes of griefe : a publike losse to show.

XXXVI.

Relenting Eye, which daignest to this Stone
To lend a look, behold, here be laid one,
The Living and the Dead interr'd, for Dead
The Turtle in its Mate is ; and she fled
5 From Earth, her   choos'd this Place of Griefe
To bound   Thoughts, a small and sad Reliefe.
His is this Monument, for hers no Art
Could frame, a Pyramide rais'd of his Heart.

XXXVII.

Instead of Epitaphs and airy praise
This Monument a Lady chaste did raise
To her Lords living fame, and after Death
Her Body doth unto this Place bequeath,
5 To rest with his, till Gods shrill Trumpet sound,
Though time her Life, no time her love could bound.

XXXV–XXXVII. These pieces are not in P.
XXXVI. ² N *reads* here he laid one—*which is obviously an error for*
here be laid one   O. here laid in one   ⁷ O. He is this Monument

Posthumous Poems.

II.

First published in the edition of 1711,
and now corrected according to
the Manuscripts.

Posthumous Poems.

II.

i.

THe scottish kirke the English church doe name,
The english church the Scotes a kirke doe call ;
Kirke and not church, church and not kirke, O shame !
Your kappa turne in chi, or perishe all :
5 Assemblies meet, post Bishopes to the court ;
If these two Nationes fight, its strangeres sport.

I. ⁶ O. 'tis Strangers sport

ii.

Against the king, sir, now why would yee fight ?
Forsooth because hee made mee not a knight.
And yee my lordes, why arme yee against Charles ?
Because of lordes hee would not make us Earles.
5 Earles, why lead you forth these angrye bandes ?
Because wee will not quite the churches landes.
Most hollye church-Men, what is your intent ?
The king our stipendes largelie did augment.
Commones, to tumult thus how are yee driuen ?
10 Our priestes say fighting is the way to Heauen.
Are these iust cause of Warre, good Bretheren, grante ?
Him Plunder ! hee nere swore our couenant.
   Giue me a thousand couenants, I'll subscriue
Them all, and more, if more yee can contriue
15 Of rage and malice ; and let eurye one
Blake treason beare, not bare Rebellione.
I'll not be mockt, hist, plunder'd, banisht hence
For more yeeres standing for a . . . prince.
The castells all are taken, and his crown,
20 The sword and sceptre, ensignes of Renown,
With the lieutenant fame did so extoll,
And all led captiues to the Capitoll ;
I'll not die Martire for any mortall thing,
It's enough to be confessour for a king.
25 Will this you giue contentment, honest Men ?
I haue written Rebelles, pox vpon the pen !

II. In P, ll. ¹³⁻²⁶ constitute a separate piece.
  ² O. he dubb'd me not   ³ O. why arm ye 'gainst King *Charles* ?
⁵ O. these Warlike Bands ?   ⁹ O. why are You driven ?   ¹⁰ O. Priests
us persuade it is the Way to Heaven   ¹¹ O. good people   ¹² O. Hoe !
Plunder ! Thou ne're   ¹⁹ O. His Castles   ²⁰ O. His Sword   ²¹ O.
With that   ²² O. And Captives carried to   ²⁴ O. 'Tis enough   ²⁶ O.
I've

iii.

The King a *Negative Voice* most justly hath,
Since the *Kirk* hath found out a *Negative Faith.*

iv.

In parlament one voted for the king,
The crowd did murmur hee might for it smart;
His voice again being heard, was no such thing,
For that which was mistaken was a fart.

v.

Bold Scotes, at Bannochburne yee killd your king,
Then did in parlament approue the fact;
And would yee Charles to such a non-plus bring,
To authorize Rebellion by an act?
5   Well, what yee craue, who knowes but granted maye be?
But if hee do it, cause swadle him for a Babye.

vi.

A Replye.

Swadl'd is the Babye, and almost two yeeres
(His swadling tyme) did neither crye nor sturre,
But star'd, smyld, did lye still, void of all feares,
And sleept, though barked at by eurye curre:
5   Yea, had not wakt, if Leslea, that hoarse Nurce,
Had not him hardlie rock't; old wyues him curse!

vii.

The king nor Bond nor oath had him to follow
Of all his subiects; they were giuen to Thee,
Leslea. Who is the greatest? By Apollo,
The Emprour thou, some palsgraue scarce seemd hee.
5 Could thou throw lordes as wee doe bishopes down,
Small distance were between thee and a crown.

III. This piece is not in P.
V. ⁶ O. But if he do't
VII. ¹ O. nor Band, nor Host   ⁴ O. scarce seems he   ⁵ O. Could'st
thou pull Lordes

viii.

On Pime.

When Pime last night descended into Hell,
Ere hee his coupes of Lethè did carouse,
What place is this (said hee) I pray mee tell ?
To whom a Diuell : This is the lower howse.

ix.

The Statue of Alcides.

Flora vpon a tyme
Naked Alcides statue did behold,
And with delight admird each arme and lime :
Onlie one fault (shee said) could be of it told ;
5 For by right symmetrye
The craftsman had him wrongd,
To such talle iointes a taller club belongd.
The club hung by his thigh :
To which the statuary angrie did replye,
10 Faire Nymphe, in auncient dayes your holes by farre,
Were not so hudglye vast as now they are.

x.

Great lyes they preach who tell the church cannot err,
Lesse lyes, who tell the king's not head of her ;
Great lyes, who saye we may shed bretherens blood,
Lesse lyes, who tell dombe bishopes are not good ;
5 Great lyes they preach, saye we for Religion fight,
Lesse lyes who saye the king does nothing right ;
Great lyes & less lyes, fooles will saye heere I
Playe on Mens nailes.   Who sayes so doth not lie.

VIII. In O, this piece has no title.
[1] O. When lately *Pim*   [2] O. E're he the Cups of Lethe   [3] O. What
Place that was, he called loud to tell.
IX. [3] O. admired each amorous Limb   [4] O. of't told   [8] O. hang
[9] O *omits* angrie   [10] O. your . . . by far
X. [1] O. *Great Lyes* they tell, preach our Church   [2] O. *Less Lies*,
who say   [3] O. *Great Lyes*, who cry we may shed others Blood   [4] O.
who swear   [5] O. they preach, say we for God   [6] O. who guess   [7] O.
Great Lyes and less *Lyes* all our Aims descry   [8] O. To Pulpits some,
to Camp the rest apply.

xi.

Most royall sir, heere I doe you beseech
Who art a lyon, to heare a lyons speech ;
A Miracle ; for since the dayes of Æsope
Till ours no lyon yet his voice dard hoise up
5 To such a Majestie.   Then, king of Men,
The king of Beastes speakes to thee from his Den ;
A fountaine now.   That lyon which was lead
By Androclus through Rome had not a head
More rationale than this, bred in this Nation,
10 Who in your presence warbleth his oration ;
For though hee heere enclosed be in plaster,
When hee was free hee was the Townes Shole Master.
Then like a Thisbè let mee not affraye
You when from Ninus Tombe shee ranne away.
15 This well yee see is not that Arethusa
The Nymphe of Sicily, no !   Men may carowse a
Health of plump Lyçus noblest Grapes
From these faire conduites, and turne drunke like apes.
This sacred spring I keep as did that Dragon
20 Hesperian apples.   And now Sir, a plague on
This poore Town if heere yee be not Well come ;
But who can question this, when euen a Well come
Is, euen the gate.   I would say more ;
But words now failing, dare not, least I rore.

XI. In O, this piece is entitled " *A Speech at the King's Entry into
the Town of* Linlithgow, *pronounced by Mr.* James Wiseman, *School-
Master there, inclosed in a Plaister made in the Figure of a Lyon.*"
   [1] O. Thrice Royal   [4] O. No Lyon till those times his Voice dar'd
raise up   [7-10] *are wanting in* O.   [11] O. Who, tho' he now inclosed be
in Plaister   [12] O. When he was free was *Lithgow's* wise School-master
[13-24] *are wanting in* O.

xii.

The country Maid.

A country Maid amazon-like did ryde,
To sit more sure with legge on either syde ;
Her Mother who her spyed, sayd that ere long
Shee might due pennance suffer for that wrong ;
5 For when tyme should more yeeres on her bestow,
That Horses haire between her thighes would grow.
Scarce winter twice was come, as was her told,
When shee found all to frizell there with gold,
Which first her made affraid, then turnd her sicke,
10 And keept her in her bed almost a weeke.
At last her mother calls, who scarce for laughter
Could heare the pleasant storie of her daughter ;
But that this thought no longer should her vex
Shee said that barded thus was all the sex ;
15 And to proue true that now shee did not scorne,
Reueald to her the gate where shee was borne.
The girle, that seeing, cryed, now freed of paine,
Ah ! Mother, yee haue ridden on the maine.

XII. This piece has no title in O.
⁴ O. She should just   ⁵ O. should on her   ⁹ O. Which first made
her   ¹⁰ O. And forc'd her keep her Bed   ¹³ O. But that this Frenzy
should no more her vex   ¹⁴ O. She swore thus bearded were their
weaker sex   ¹⁵ O. Which when deny'd, think not (said she) I scorn
¹⁶ O. Behold the place (poor Fool) where thou was born   ¹⁷ O. now
void of

xiii.

Gods iudgments seldome vse to cease, vnlesse
The sinnes which them procurd men doe confesse.
Our cryes are Baalles priestes, our fasting vaine,
Our prayers not heard, nor answered vs againe :
5 Till periurye, wrong, rebellion, be confest,
Thinke not on peace, nor to be fred of pest.

xiv.

The King gives yearly to his Senate Gold
Who can deny but Justice then is sold !

xv.

Epitaph.

Heere Rixus lies, a Nouice in the lawes,
Who plaines Hee came to Hell without a cause.

XIV. This piece is not in P.

xvi.

Translation of the death of a sparrow, out of Passerat.

Ah ! if yee aske (my friendes) why this salt shower
My blubbered eyes vpon this paper power,
Dead is my sparrow ; he whom I did traine,
And turnd so toward, by a cat is slaine.
5 Skipping no more now shall hee on me attend.
Light displeaseth : would my dayes could end !
Ill heare no more him chirpe forth prettye layes ;
Haue I not cause to curse my wretched dayes ?
A Dedalus hee was to snatch a flye,
10 Nor wrath nor wildnesse men in him could spye ;
If to assault his taile that any dard,
He pinchd their fingers, and against them warrd :
Then might bee seene the crest shake vp & down,
Which fixed was vpon his litle crown ;
15 Like Hectores, Troyes strong bulwarke, when in ire
Hee ragd to set the Grecian fleet on fire.
But ah, alas ! a cat this pray espyes,
Then with a traitrous leap did it surprise.
Vndoubtedlie this bird was killd by treason,
20 Or otherwise should of that feind had reason.
So Achilles thus by Phrigian heard was slaine,
And stout Camilla fell by Aruns vaine :
So that false horse which Pallas raisd gainst Troy,

XVI. In O, this piece is entitled " PHYLLIS *On the Death of her Sparrow.*"
    3 O. Gone is my Sparrow   5 O. No more with trembling Wings shall he attend   6 O. His watchfull Mistress. Would my Life could end !   7 O. No more shall I him hear chirp pretty Lays   8 O. to loath my tedious days ?   9 O. to catch a Fly   10 O. Nor Wrath, nor Rancour Men   11 O. To touch or wrong his Tail, if any dar'd   13 O. Then might that Crest be seen shake   14 O. was unto   18 O. Then with a Leap did thus our Joys surprise   20 O. Or otherways had of that Fiend   21 O. Thus was *Achilles* by weak *Paris* slain

Priame & that faire cittye did destroy.
25 Thou now, whose heart is swelled with this vaine glorye,
Shalt not liue long to count thy honours storye.
If any knowledge bideth after death
In sprites of Birdes whose bodyes haue no breath,
My dearlings sprit sal know in lower place,
30 The vangeance falling on the cattish race.
For neuer chat nor catling I sal find,
But mawe they shall in Plutos palace blind.
Ye who with panted pens & bodies light
Doe dint the aire, turne hadervart your flight,
35 To my sad teares apply these notes of yours,
Vnto this Idol bring a Harvest of flours ;
Let him accepte from vs, as most deuine,
Sabean incense, milke, food, suetest vine ;
And on a stone these vords let some engraue :
40 The litle Body of a sparrow braue
In a foul gloutonous chats vombe closd remaines,
Vhose ghost now graceth the Elysian plaines.

24 O. King *Priame* and that City   25 O. is big with this frail **Glory**
26 O. long to tell   27 O. resteth after Death   28 O. In Ghosts
of Birds, when they have left to breath   29 O. My Darling's Ghost
32 O. But mew shall they in   33 O. gawdy Wings   34 O. hitherwards
35 O. comply these Notes   36 O. an harv'st   39 O. And on a Stone
let us these Words   40 O. *Pilgrim, the Body of a Sparrow brave*   41 O.
In a fierce gluttonous Cat's Womb

xvii.

Saint Peter, after the denying his master.

Like to the solitarie pelican,
The shadie groues I hant & Deserts wyld,
Amongst woods Burgesses, from sight of Man,
From earths delights, from myne owne selfe exild.
5 But that remorse which with my falle beganne,
Relenteth not, nor is by change beguild,
But rules my soule, and like a famishd chyld
Renewes its cryes, though Nurse doe what shee can.
Looke how the shricking Bird that courtes the Night
10 In ruind walles doth lurke, & gloomie place :
Of Sunne, of Moone, of Starres, I shune the light,
Not knowing where to stray, what to embrace :
 How to Heauens lights should I lift these of myne,
 Since I denyed him who made them shine ?

XVII. In O, this sonnet is entitled " Peter, *after the Denial of his Master.*"
 ⁴ O. Delight ⁵ *In* P, sinne *is written in above* falle *in Drummond's hand.* ⁶ O. nor is by Change turn'd mild ⁷ O. But rents my Soul ⁸ O. Nurse does ¹⁰ O. Wall ¹² O. where to stay ¹⁴ O. Sith [*In* P, denyed thee *is written in alongside* denyed him *in Drummond's hand.*]

xviii.

The woefull Marie midst a blubbred band
Of weeping virgines, neare vnto the Tree
Where God Death sufferd, Man from Death to free,
Like to a plaintfull Nightingale did stand,
5   That sees her younglings reft before her eies
And hath nought else to guarde them but her cries.

Loue thither had her brought, and misbeliefe
Of that report which charg'd her mind with feares,
But now her eies more wretched than her eares
10 Bare witnesse (ah ! too true) of feared griefe :
Her doubtes make certaine, and her Hopes destroy,
Abandoning her soule to blacke annoy.

Long fixing downecast eies on earth, at last
Shee longing did them raise (O torturing sight !)
15 To view what they did shune, their sole delight,
Embrued in his owne bloud, and naked plac't
To sinefull eies, naked saue that blake vaile
Which Heauen him shrouded with, that did bewaile.

It was not pittie, paine, griefe, did possesse
20 The Mother, but an agonie more strange ;
When shee him thus beheld, her hue did change,
Her life (as if shee bled his bloud) turnd less :
Shee sought to plaine, but woe did words deny,
And griefe her suffred onlye sigh, O my,

XVIII. In O, these stanzas are entitled " *On the Virgin.*"
⁴ *In* P, wailing *is written in above* plaintfull *in Drummond's hand.*
⁵ *In* P, Which *is written in above* That *in Drummond's hand.*   ⁸ O.
Of these sad News, which charg'd her Mind to Fears [*In* P, these
strange newes which filled her all with *is written in above* that report
which charg'd her mind with *in Drummond's hand.*]   ⁹ O. then her
Tears   ¹¹ *In* P, made *is written in above* make *and* did *above* and *in
Drummond's hand.*   ¹³ O. down-cast Eyes [*In* P, lights *is written
in above* eies *in Drummond's hand.*]   ²¹ O. Cheek's Roses in pale
Lillies straight did change   ²² O. Her Sp'rits   ²³ O. When she him
saw, Wo did all Words deny [*In* P, would haue plaind *is written in
above* sought to plaine, *in Drummond's hand.*]   ²⁴ O. her only suffer'd

25 O my deare Lord and Sone !   Then shee began :
　Immortall birth ! though of a mortall borne,
　Eternall Bontie which doth heauen adorne,
　Without a Mother, God ; a father, Man :
　　Ah ! what hast thou deserud, what hast thou done,
30 　Thus to be vs'd ? Wooe 's mee, my sone, my sone !

　How blamed 's thy face, the glorie of this All !
　How dim'd thyne eyes, loade-starres to Paradise !
　Who, as thou now wert trim'd a sacrifice,
　Who did thy temples with this crown impale ?
35 　Who raisd thee, whom so oft the angelles serud,
　　Betwext those theeues who that foul Death deserud ?

　Was it for this I bred thee in my wombe,
　My armes a cradle made thee to repose,
　My milke thee fed, as morning dewe the Rose ?
40 Did I thee keep till this sad time should come,
　　That wretched Men should naile thee to a Tree,
　　And I a witnesse of thy panges must bee ?

　It is not long, the way o'respred with flowres,
　With shoutes to ecchoing Heauen and Montaines rold,
45 Since (as in triumph) I thee did behold
　With royall pompe aproch proud Sions Towres :
　　Loe, what a change ! who did thee then embrace,
　　Now at thee shake their heads, inconstant race !

　Eternall Father ! from whose piercing eie
50 Hide nought is found that in this All is found,
　Daigne to vouschafe a looke vpon this Round,
　This Round, the stage of a sad Tragedie :
　　Looke but if thy deare pledge thou heere canst know,
　　On an vnhappie Tree a shamefull show.

30 O. Thus to be treat ?   **31** O. Who bruis'd thy Face, the glory
32 O. Who Eyes engor'd, Load-Stars   **33** O. Who, as thou were a
trimmed Sacrifice   **34** O. Did with that cruel Crown thy Brows impale?
36 *In* P, *which is written in above* who *in Drummond's hand.*   **37** O. Thou
bred wast in my Womb ?   **38** O. Mine Arms a Cradle serv'd Thee to
Repose ?   **43** O. bestrow'd [*In* P, bestrawd *is written in above*
o'respred *in Drummond's hand.*]   **46** O. In Royal   **50** O. that in this
All is form'd   **51** O. unto this Round

55 Ah ! looke if this be hee almightie King,
 Ere that Heauen spangled was with starres of gold,
 Ere World a center had it to vphold,
 Whom from eternitie thou forth didst bring.
     With vertue, forme and light, who did adorne
60   Heauens radiant Globes, see where he hangs a scorne.

 Did all my prayers serue for this ?   Is this
 The promise that celestiall herault made
 At Nazareth, when ah ! to mee he said
 I happy was, and from thee did mee blisse ?
65   How am I blist ?   No, most vnhappy I
 Of all the Mothers vnderneath the skie.

 How true and of choysd oracles the choice
 Was that, blist Hebrew, whose deare eies in peace
 Sweet Death did close, ere they saw this disgrace,
70 Whenas thou saidst with more than angelles voice,
     The son should (Malice sign) be set apart,
     Then that a sword should pierce the mothers hart !

 But whither dost thou goe, life of my soule ?
 O stay while that I may goe with thee ;
75 And do I liue thee languishing to see,
 And can not griefe fraile lawes of life controule ?
     Griefe, if thou canst not, come cruel squadrons, kill
     The Mother, spare the sonne, he knowes no ill ;

 Hee knowes no ill ; those pangs, fierce men, are due
80 To mee and all the world, saue him alone ;
 But now he doth not heare my bitter mone ;
 Too late I crye, too late I plaintes renew ;
     Pale are his lips, downe doth his head decline,
     Dim turn those eies once wont so bright to shine.

---

⁵⁶ O. Before Heavens spangled were with   ⁶⁰ O. Skie's radiant   [*In*
P, Towres *is written in above* Globes, *in Drummond's hand.*]   ⁶¹ *In* P,
tend to *is written in above* serue for *in Drummond's hand.*   ⁶³ O. At
Nazareth, when full of Joy he said   ⁶⁴ O. bless   ⁶⁷ O. of choise Oracles
⁶⁹ O. Mild Death   ⁷⁰ O. When he fore-spake with   ⁷⁴ O. O stay a little
till I dye with Thee   ⁷⁷ O. If Grief prove weak come   ⁷⁹ *In* P, base
is written in above fierce *in Drummond's hand.*

85 The Heauens which in their orbes still constant moue,
That guiltie they may not seeme of this crime,
Benighted haue the golden eie of Time.
And thou, base Earth, all this thou didst approue,
  Vnmoud, this suffrest done upon thy face!
90   Earth trembled then, and shee did hold her peace.

xix.

A Character of the Anti-Couenanter, or Malignant.

Would yee know these royall knaues
Of free Men would turne vs slaues ;
Who our Vnion doe defame
With Rebellions Wicked Name ?
5 Read these Verses, and yee il spring them,
Then on Gibbetes straight cause hing them.
They complaine of sinne and follye,
In these tymes so passing hollye
They their substance will not giue,
10 Libertines that we maye liue ;
Hold that people too too wantom,
Vnder an old king dare cantom.
They neglecte our circular Tables,
Scorne our actes and lawes as fables,
15 Of our battales talke but meeklye,
With sermones foure content them weeklye,
Sweare King Charles is neither Papist,
Armenian, Lutherian, Atheist ;
But that in his Chamber-Prayers,
20 Which are pour'd 'midst Sighs and Tears,

⁸⁵ O. in their Mansions constant move ⁸⁶ O. That they may not
seem guilty of ⁸⁸ O. Ungrateful Earth, canst thou such Shame approve
⁸⁹ O. And seem unmov'd this done upon thy face ?
XIX. Verses ¹⁹⁻⁷² are not in P.
¹¹ O. Hold those Subjects ¹³ O. Neglect they do our ¹⁶ O. With
four Sermons pleas'd are weekly ¹⁸ O. or Atheist

To avert God's fearful Wrath,
Threatning us with Blood and Death,
Persuade they would the Multitude,
This King too holy is and good.
25 They avouch we'll weep and groan
When Hundred Kings we serve for one,
That each Shire but Blood affords
To serve the Ambition of young Lords,
Whose Debts ere now had been redoubled,
30 If the State had not been troubled.
Slow they are our Oath to swear,
Slower for it Arms to bear ;
They do Concord love and Peace,
Would our Enemies embrace,
35 Turn Men Proselytes by the Word,
Not by Musket, Pike, and Sword.
They Swear that for Religion's Sake
We may not massacre, burn, sack ;
That the Beginning of these Pleas
40 Sprang from the ill-sped ABC's ;
For Servants that it is not well
Against their Masters to Rebel ;
That that Devotion is but slight
Doth force men first to swear, then fight ;
45 That our Confession is indeed
Not the *Apostolick CREED*,
Which of Negations we contrive,
Which *Turk* and *Jew* may both subscrive ;
That Monies should Men's Daughters marry,
50 They on frantick War miscarry,
Whilst dear the Souldiers they pay,
At last who will snatch all away,
And as Times turn worse and worse,
Catechise us by the Purse ;
55 That Debts are paid with bold stern Looks,
That Merchants pray on their Compt-books ;
That Justice, dumb and sullen, frowns

To see in Croslets hang'd her Gowns ;
That Preachers ordinary Theme
60 Is 'gainst Monarchy to declaim ;
That since Leagues we began to swear,
Vices did ne're so black appear ;
Oppression, Blood-shed, ne're more rife,
Foul Jars between the Man and Wife ;
65 Religion so contemn'd was never,
Whilst all are raging in a Fever.
They tell by Devils and some sad Chance
That that detestable League of *France*,
Which cost so many Thousand Lives,
70 And Two Kings by Religious Knives,
Is amongst us, though few descry ;
Though they speak Truth, yet say they Lye.
Hee that sayes that night is night,
That halting folk walk not vpright,
75 That the owles into the spring
Doe not nightingalles outsing ;
That the seas wee can not plough,
Plant strawberryes in the raine-bow ;
That waking men doe not sound sleep,
80 That the fox keepes not the sheep ;
That alls not gold doth gold appeare,
Belieue him not although hee sweere.
To such syrenes stope your eare,
Their societyes forbeare.
85 Tossed you may be like a waue,
Veritye may you deceaue ;
True fools they may make of you ;
Hate them worse than Turke or Jew.
Were it not a dangerous Thing,
90 Should yee againe obey the king,
Lordes losse should souueraigntie,

73 O. He who   74 O. That criple Folk   77 O. we may not   78 O.
Ropes make of the rainy Bow   79 O. That the Foxes keep not Sheep
80 O. That Men waking do not sleep   85 O. Ye may be tossed   87 O.
Just Fools   88 O. Then hate them   90 O. Should we

Souldiours haste backe to Germanie,
Justice should in your Townes remaine,
Poore Men possesse their own againe,
95 Brought out of Hell that word of plunder
More terrible than diuell & Thunder,
Should with the Couenant flye away,
And charitye amongst vs stay?
When yee find those lying fellowes,
100 Take & flowere with them the Gallowes ;
On otheres yee maye too laye hold,
In purse or chestes if they haue Gold.
Who wise or rich are in the Nation,
Malignants are by protestation.
105 Peace and plentie should vs nurish,
True religion with vs flourish.

XX.

Song of Passerat.

Amintas, Daphnè.

D. Shephard loueth thow me vell ?
A. So vel that I cannot tell.
D. Like to vhat, good shephard, say ?
A. Like to the, faire, cruell May.
5 D. Ah ! how strange thy vords I find !
But yet satisfie my mind ;
Shephard vithout flatterie,

---

93 O. in our Towns   96 O. Devil or Thunder   98 *In O, the two last
lines of the poem, with the variant* 'mongst us *for* with us *in the second
line, are placed here.*   99 O. When you find these   101 O. you may
102 O. Chest

XX. In O, this piece is entitled " A Pastoral Song. *Phyllis and
Damon.*"

1 O. Shepheard dost thou love me well ?   2 O. weak Words [*In
P, Better than poor words can tell is written in above* So vel that I
cannot tell *in Drummond's hand.*]   5 O. O how strange these Words I
find   6 O. Yet to satisfy my Mind   7 O. Shepheard without mocking
me

Beares thow any loue to me,
Like to vhat, good shephard, say ?
10 A. Like to the, faire, cruell May.
    D. Better answer had it beene
       To say, I loue thee as mine eine.
    A. Voe is me, I loue them not,
       For be them loue entress got,
15   At the time they did behold
       Thy sueet face & haire of gold.
    D. Like to vhat, good shephard, say ?
    A. Like to thee, faire cruell May.
    D. But, deare shephard, speake more plaine,
20   And I sal not aske againe ;
       For to end this gentle stryff
       Doth thow loue me as thy lyff ?
    A. No, for it doth eb & flow
       Vith contrare teeds of grief & voe ;
25   And now I thruch loues strange force
       A man am not, but a dead corse.
    D. Like to vhat, good shephard, say ?
    A. Like to thee, faire, cruel May.
    D. This like to thee, O leaue, I pray,
30   And as my selfe, good shephard, say.
    A. Alas ! I do not loue my selff,
       For I me split on beuties shelff.
    D. Like to vhat, good shephard, say ?
    A. Like to the, faire, cruel May.

[8] O. Have I any Love for thee   [12] O. To say thou lov'd me as thine Eyne   [13] O. Wo is me, these I love not   [14] O. entrance   [15] O. At that Time   [16] O. and Locks of Gold   [19] O. Once, (dear Shepheard) speak more plain   [21] O. Say, to end   [23] O. No, for it is turn'd a Slave   [24] O. To sad Annoys, and what I have   [25] O. Of Life by Love's stronger Force   [26] O. Is reft, and I'm but a dead Cors   [29] O. Learn I pray this, like to thee   [30] O. And say I love as I do me   [32] O. For I'm split

xxi.

The Kirrimorians *and* Forfarians *met at* Muirmoss,
The Kirrimorians *beat the* Forfarians *back to the Cross.*
Sutors ye are, and Sutors ye'll be ;
F——s upon Forfar, Kirrimuir *bears the Gree.*

xxii.

Of all these Rebelles raisd against the king
It's my strange hap not one whole man to bring :
From diuerse parishes yet diuerse men ;
But all in halfes and quarteres : Great king, then,
5 In halfes and quarteres sith they come gainst Thee,
In halfes and quarteres send them back to mee.

XXI. This piece is taken from the introductory memoir to the folio edition (O), where it is attributed to Drummond. It does not appear in P.

XXII. This piece is also found in the introductory memoir to the folio edition (O), but appears in P.

[1] O. *Of all these Forces*   [5] O. *if they come*   [6] O *has the alternative :* " *In Legs and Arms send thou them back to me.*"

Posthumous Poems.

III.

Reprinted from the Transactions of
the Society of Antiquaries of Scotland,
and now revised according to
the Manuscripts.

Posthumous Poems.

III.

i.

D. A. Johnstones Eden-Bourgh.

INstall'd on Hills, her Head neare starrye bowres
Shines Eden-Bourgh, prowd of protecting powers.
Justice defendes her Heart ; Religion East
With temple decketh ; Mars with towres doth guard
 the West ;
5 Fresh Nymphes and Ceres seruing, waite vpon her,
And Thetis (tributarie) doth her honour.
The sea doth Venice shake, Rome Tiber beates,
Whilst shee but scornes her Vassall Watteres Threates.
For scepteres no where standes a Town more fitt,
10 Nor place where Town Worlds Queene may fairer sitt.

SONNETS.

ii.

To the honorable Author, S[IR] J[OHN] SK[ENE].

All lawes but cob-webes are, but none such right
Had to this title as these lawes of ours,
Ere that they were from their cimerian Bowres
By thy ingenious labours brought to light.
5 Our statutes senslesse statues did remaine,
Till thou (a new Prometheus) gaue them breath,
Or like ag'd Æsons bodye courb'd to death,
When thou young bloud infus'd in eurye veine.
Thrice-happye Ghosts ! which after-worlds shall wow,
10 That first tam'd barbarisme by your swords,
Then knew to keepe it fast in nets of words,
Hindring what men not suffer would to doe ;
　　To Joue the making of the World is due,
　　But that it turnes not chaos, is to you.

iii.

O Tymes, o Heauen that still in motion art,
And by your course confound vs mortall wights !
O flying Dayes ! o euer-gliding Nights,
Which passe more nimble than wind or archers dart !
5 Now I my selfe accuse, excuse your part,
For hee who fixd your farr-off shining lights,
You motion gaue, and did to mee impart
A Mind to marke and to preuent your slights.
Lifes web yee still weaue out, still (foole) I stay,
10 Malgrè my iust Resolues, on mortall things.
Ah ! as the Bird surprisd in subtile springs,
That beates with wing but cannot flye away,
　　So struggle I, and faine would change my case,
　　But this is not of Nature, but of grace.

II. ⁹ *In* P, must *is written in above* shall *in Drummond's hand.*

iv.

Rise to my soule, bright Sunne of Grace, o rise !
Make mee the vigour of thy Beames to proue,
Dissolue this chilling frost which on mee lies,
That makes mee lesse than looke-warme in thy loue :
5 Grant mee a beamling of thy light aboue
To know my foot-steps, in these Tymes, too wise ;
O ! guyde my course & let mee no mor moue
On wings of sense, where wandring pleasure flyes.
I haue gone wrong & erred, but ah, alas !
10 What can I else doe in this dungeon darke ?
My foes strong are, & I a fragil glasse,
Houres charged with cares consume my lifes small sparke ;
  Yet, of thy goodnesse, if I grace obtaine,
  My life shall be no lose, my death great gaine.

v.

First in the orient raign'd th' assyrian kings,
To those the sacred persian prince succeeds,
Then he by whom the world sore-wounded bleeds,
Earths crowne to Greece with bloodie blade he brings ;
5 Then Grece to Rome the Raines of state resignes :
Thus from the mightie Monarche of the Meeds
To the west world successiuelie proceeds
That great and fatall period of all things ;
Whilst wearied now with broyles and long alarmes,
10 Earths maiestie her diademe layes downe
Before the feet of the vnconquered crowne,
And throws her selfe (great Monarch) in thy armes.
  Here shall she staye, fates haue ordained so,
  Nor has she where nor further for to goe.

vi.

Sonnet before a poëme of *Irene*.

Mourne not (faire Grece) the ruine of thy kings,
Thy temples raz'd, thy forts with flames deuour'd,
Thy championes slaine, thy virgines pure deflowred,
Nor all those greifes which sterne Bellona brings :
5 But murne (faire Grece) mourne that that sacred band
Which made thee once so famous by their songs,
Forct by outrageous fate, haue left thy land,
And left thee scarce a voice to plaine thy wrongs ;
Murne that those climates which to thee appeare
10 Beyond both Phọbus and his sisteres wayes,
To saue thy deedes from death must lend thee layes,
And such as from Museus thou didst heare ;
   For now Irene hath attaind such fame,
   That Heros Ghost doth weep to heare her name.

vii.

I feare to me such fortune be assignd
As was to thee, who did so well deserue,
Braue HAKERSTOWNE, euen suffred here to sterue
Amidst basse minded freinds, nor true, nor kind.
5 Why were the fates and furies thus combind,
Such worths for such disasters to reserue ?
Yet all those euills neuer made the suerue
From what became a well resolued mind ;
For swelling Greatnesse neuer made the smyle,
10 Dispising Greatnesse in extreames of want ;
O happy thrice whom no distresse could dant !
Yet thou exclaimed, ô Time ! ô Age ! ô Isle !
   Where flatterers, fooles, baudes, fidlers, are rewarded,
   Whilst Vertue sterues vnpittied, vnregarded.

viii.

Sonnet qu'un poet[e] Italien fit pour vn bracelet
de cheveux qui lui auoit estè donnè
par sa maistresse.

O chiome, parte de la treccia d' oro
Di cui fè amor il laccio, oue fui colto
Qual semplice augelletto, e da qual sciolto
Non spero esser mai piu, si pria non moro ;
5 Io vi bacio, io vi stringo, io vi amo e adoro,
Perche adombrasti gìa quel sacro volto
Che a quanti in terra sono il pregio ha tolto,
Ne lascia senza inuidia il diuin choro :
A voi dirò gli affanni, e i pensier miei,
10 Poi che lungi è mia donna, e parlar seco
Mi nega aspra fortuna, e gli empi diei.
Lasso ! guarda se amor mi fa ben cieco,
Quando cercar di scioglierme io dovrei,
La rete porto e le catene meco.

ix.

In the same sort of rime.

O haire, sueet haire, part of the tresse of gold
Of vich loue makes his nets vher vretchet I
Like simple bird vas taine, and vhile I die
Hopelesse I hope your faire knots sal me hold ;
5 Yow to embrasse, kisse, and adore I'm bold,
Because ye schadow did that sacred face,
Staine to al mortals, vich from starrie place
Hath jalous made these vho in spheares ar rold :
To yow I'l tel my thochts & invard paines
10 Since sche by cruel Heauens now absent is,
And cursed Fortune me from her detaines.
Alas ! bear vitnesse how my reason is
Made blind be loue, vhile as his nets and chaines
I beare about vhen I should seeke my blisse.

x.

In frier sort of rime.

O haire, faire haire, some of the goldin threeds
Of vich loue veues the nets that passion breeds,
Vher me like sillie bird he doth retaine,
And onlie death can make me free againe ;
5 Ah I yow loue, embrasse, kisse, and adore,
For that ye schadow did that face before ;
That face so ful of beautie, grace, and loue,
That it hath jalous made Heauens quier aboue :
To yow I'l tel my secret thochts and grief
10 Since sche, deare sche, can graunt me no reliefe.
Vhile me from her, foul traitour, absence binds,
Vitnesse, sueet haire, vith me, how loue me blinds ;
For vhen I should seeke vhat his force restraines,
I foolish beare about his nets and chaines.

xi.

Paraphrasticalie translated.

Haire, suet haire, tuitchet by Midas hand
In curling knots, of vich loue makes his nets,
Vho vhen ye loosest hang me fastest band
To her, vorlds lilie among violets ;
5 Deare fatall present, kissing I adore yow,
Because of late ye shade gaue to these roses
That this earths beautie in ther red encloses ;
I saw vhile ye them hid thay did decore yow :
I'l plaine my voes to yow, I'l tel my thocht,
10 Alas ! since I am absent from my juel,
By vayvard fortune and the heauens more cruel.
Vitnesse be ye vhat loue in me hath vrocht,
In steed to seeke th' end of my mortall paines,
I take delyt to veare his goldin chaines.

xii.

Bembo in his Rime. 2 Son.

Si come suol, poi che 'l verno aspro e rio
Parte, e da loco a le stagion migliori,
Vscir col giorno la ceruetta fuori
Del suo dolce boschetto almo natio ;
5 Et hor' super vn colle, hor longo vn rio,
Lontana de le case è da pastori
Gir secura pascendo herbette e fiori,
Ovunque più la porta il suo desio ;
Ne teme di saetta o d' altro inganno,
10 Se non quando e colta in mezo il fianco,
Da buon arcier che di nascosto scocchi :
Cosi senza temer futuro affanno
Moss' io, donna, quel dì che bei vostr' occhi
Mempiagar, lasso ! tuto 'l lato manco.

xiii.

In the same sort of Rime.

As the yong faune, vhen vinters gone avay
Vnto a sueter saison granting place,
More vanton growne by smyles of heuens faire face,
Leauith the silent voods at breake of day,
5 And now on hils, and now by brookes doth pray
On tender flowres, secure and solitar,
Far from all cabans, and vher shephards are ;
Vher his desir him guides his foote doth stray,
He fearith not the dart nor other armes
10 Til he be schoot in to the noblest part
By cuning archer, vho in dark bush lyes :
So innocent, not fearing comming harmes,
Vandering vas I that day vhen your faire eies,
Vorld-killing schafts, gaue deaths vounds to my hart.

xiv.

In rime more frie.

As the yong stag, vhen vinter hids his face
Giuing vnto a better season place,
At breake of day comes furth vanton and faire,
Leauing the quiet voods, his suet repaire,
5 Now on the hils, now by the riuers sides,
He leaps, he runs, and vher his foote him guides,
Both sure and solitaire, prayes on suet flowrs,
Far fra al shephards and their helmish bours ;
He doth not feare the net nor murthering dart,
10 Til that, pour beast, a schaft be in his hart,
Of on quho pitilesse in embush laye :
So innocent vandring that fatall daye
Vas I, alas ! vhen vith a heauenlie eie,
Ye gaue the blowe vher of I needs must die.

xv.

Paraphrasticalie translated.

As the yong hart, when sunne with goldin beames
Progressith in the first post of the skie,
Turning old vinters snowie haire in streames,
Leauith the voods vher he vas vont to lie,
5 Vher his desir him leads the hills among,
He runes, he feades, the cruking brookes along,
Emprison'd onlie with heauens canopie ;
Vanton he cares not ocht that dolour brings,
Hungry he spares not flowres vith names of kings ;
10 He thinkes al far, vho can him fol espie,
Til bloudie bullet part his chefest part :
In my yong spring, alas ! so vandred I,
Vhen cruel sche sent out from iettie eie
The deadlie schaft of vich I bleding smart.

MADRIGALS.

xvi.

On the image of Lucrece.

Wise Hand, which wiselie wroght
That dying Dame who first did banish kings,
Thy light & shadow brings
In doubt the wondring thought,
5   If it a substance be or faignet show,
That doth so liuelie smart.
The colours stroue for to haue made her liue,
Wer not thy hart said No,
That fear'd perchance the wound so should her griue :
10   Yet in the fatall blow
She seemes to speake, nay speakes with Tarquins hart ;
But death her stays, surprising her best part.

xvii.

Neroes image.

A cunning hand it was
Of this hard rocke did frame
That monster of all ages, mankinds shame,
Ferce Nero, hells disgrace :
5   Of wit, sence, pitie void,
Did he not liuing, marble hard surpasse,
His mother, master, countrie, all destroyed ?
Not altring his first case,
A stone he was when set vpon a throne,
10 And now a stone he is, although throwne downe.

XVI. [12] P *reads, as an alternative*—If death her stayd not, killing
her best part.

xviii.

Amphion of marble.

This Amphion, Phidias frame,
Though sencelesse it apeare,
Doth liue, and is the same
Did Thebes towres vpreare ;
5   And if his harpe he tuitche not to your eare,
No wonder, his harmonious sounds alone
Wauld you amaze, & change him selfe in stone.

xix.

Of a Be.

Ingenious was that Bee
In lip that wound which made,
And kind to others, though vnkind to thee ;
For by a iust exchange,
5   On that most liulie red
It giues to those reuenge,
Whom that delitious, plump, and rosie part,
All pittilesse (perhaps) now wounds the hart.

xx.

Of Chloris.

Forth from greene Thetis Bowers
The morne arose ; her face
A wreath of rayes did grace,
Her haire raind pearles, her hand & lap dropt flowres.
5   Led by the pleasant sight
Of those so rich and odoriferous showres,
Each shepheard thither came, & nimphes bright :
Entrancd they stood ; I did to Chloris turne,
And saw in her more grace than [in] the Morne.

xxi.

Chloris enamoured.

Amintas, now at last
Thou art reuengd of all my rigor past ;
The scorning of the, softnesse of thy hart,
Thy longings, causefull teares,
5 Doe double griefe each day to mee impart.
I am not what I was,
And in my Miseries I thyne doe glasse ;
Ah ! now in perfect yeares,
E'r Reason could my coming harmes descrie,
10 Made loues fond Taper flie,
I burne mee thinkes in sweet & fragrant flame :
Aske mee noe more : Tongue hide thy Mistres shame.

xxii.

Regrat.

In this Worlds raging sea
Where many Sillas barke,
Where many Syrens are,
Saue, and not cast away,
5 Hee onlye saues his barge
With too much ware who doth it not o'recharge ;
Or when huge stormes arise,
And waues menace the skies,
Giues what he got with no deploring show,
10 And doth againe in seas his burthen throw.

xxiii.

A sigh.

Sigh, stollen from her sweet brest,
What doth that marble hart ?
Smartes it indeed, and feales not others smart,
Grieues it, yet thinkes that others grieued ieast ?
5   Loue or despight, which forct thee thence to part
Sweet harbinger, say from what vncouth guest ?
Sure thou from loue must come,
Who sighd to see there drest his marble Tombe.

xxiv.

Stollen pleasure.

My sweet did sweetlie sleep,
And on her rosie face
Stood teares of pearle which Beauties selfe did
    weepe ;
I (wond'ring at her grace)
5   Did all amazd remaine,
When loue said, foole, can lookes thy wishes crowne ?
Time past comes not againe.
Then did I mee bow downe,
And kissing her faire brest, lips, cheekes, & eies,
10 Prou'd heere on earth the ioye of Paradise.

xxv.

Of a Kisse.

Lips, double port of loue,
Of joy tell all the arte,
Tell all the sweetnesse lies
In earthlie paradise,
5   Sith happy now yee proue
What blisse
A kisse
Of sweetest Nais can bring to the hart.
Tell how your former joyes
10   Haue beene but sad annoyes :
This, onlye this, doth ease a long felt smart,
This, onlye this, doth life to loue impart.
Endymion, I no more
Enuie thy happye state,
15   Nor his who had the fate
Rauisht to be and huggd on Ganges shore :
Enuie nor yet doe I
Adon, nor Joues cup-bearer in the skie.
Deare crimson folds, more sweetnesse yee doe beare
20   Than Hybla Tops or Gardenes of Madere.
Sweet, sweetning Midases, your force is such,
That eurye thing turnes sweet which yee doe touch.

xxvi.

A Locke desired.

I neuer long'd for gold ;
But since I did thy dangling haire behold,
Ah ! then, then was it first
That I prou'd Midas thrist ;
5   And what both Inde and rich Pactolus hold
Can not my flames allay,
For onlie yee, faire Treseresse, this may,
Would yee but giue a locke to helpe my want,
Of that which prodigall to winds yee grant.

xxvii.

Persuasive dissuading.

Show mee not lockes of Gold,
Nor blushing Roses of that virgine face,
Nor of thy well-made leg and foote the Grace ;
Let me no more behold
5   Soule-charming smyles nor lightnings of thyne eye,
For they (deare life) but serue to make mee dye.
Yes, show them all, and more ; vnpine thy brest,
Let me see liuing snow
Where straw-berries doe grow ;
10   Show that delitious feild
Which lillies still doth yeeld,
Of Venus babe the Nest :
Smyle, blush, sigh, chide, vse thousand other charmes ;
Mee kill, so that I fall betweene thyne armes.

xxviii.

Prometheus am I,
    The Heauens my ladyes eye,
From which I stealing fire,
Find since a vulture on my hart to tyre.

xxix.

Non vltra.

When Idmon saw the eyne
Of Anthea his loue,
Who yet, said he, such blazing starres hath seene,
Saue in the heauens aboue ?
5   She thus to heare her praise
Blusht, and more faire became.
For nought (said he) thy cheekes that Morne do raise
For my hart can not burne with greater flame.

XXIX. [8] *In* P, feale a *is written in above* burne with *in Drummond's hand.*

xxx.

Fragment.

Now Phœbus vhept his horse vith al his might,
Thinking to take Aurora in her flight ;
But sche, vho heares the trampling of his steeds,
Gins suiftlie gallop thruch heauens rosie meeds.
5 The more he runs, the more he cums her neare ;
The lesse her sped, sche finds the more her feare.
At last his coursiers angry to be torne,
Her tooke ; sche vith a blush died al the morne.
Tethis, agast to spie her greens made red,
10 All drousie rose furth of her corral bed,
Thinking the Nights faire Queen suld thole sume harmes,
Sche saw poor Tithons vyff in Phœbus armes.

xxxi.

Fragment.

It Autumne vas, and cheereful chantecleare
Had varn'd the vorld tuise that the day drew neare ;
The three parts of the night almost var spent,
Vhen I poure vretch, vith loue & fortune rent,
5 Began my eies to close, & suetest sleep,
Charming my sence, al ouer me did creep,
But scars vith Lethè drops & rod of gold
Had he me made a piece of breathing mold . . .

EPIGRAMS, &c.

Verses written long since concerning these present
   tymes, made at random, *a las roguerias de ses
   amicos :* Skeltonicall verses, or dogrel rimes.

xxxii.

The king good subiectes can not saue : then tell
Which is the best, to obeye or to rebell ?

xxxiii.

Happie to be, trulye is in some schoole-
Maisteres Booke, be either king or foole.
How happie then are they, if such men bee,
Whom both great fooles and kinges the world doth see.

xxxiv.

When Charles was yong, to walke straight and vpright,
In Bootes of lead thralld were his legges, though Rockes ;
Now old, not walking euen vnto their sight,
His countrye lordes haue put him in their stokes.

xxxv.

The parlament lordes haue sitten twice fiue weekes,
Yet will not leaue their stooles, knit vp their breekes ;
Winter is come, dysenteryes preuaile :
Rise, fooles, and with this paper wype your taile.

xxxvi.

The parlament the first of June will sit,
Some saye, but is the yeere of God to it?
Fourtie: no, rather make it fourtie one,
And one to fourtie, but yee then haue none.

xxxvii.

Zanzummines they obeye the king doe sweare,
And yet against King Charles in armes appeare.
What king doe yee obeye, Zamzummines, tell,
The king of Beane, or the blake prince of Walles?

xxxviii.

Behold (O Scots!) the reueryes of your King;
Those hee makes Lordes who should on gibbetes hing.

xxxix.

S. Andrew, why does thou giue up thy Schooles,
And Bedleme turne, and parlament house of fooles?

PAR.

Old dotard (Pasquill) thou mistaketh it,
Montrose confined vs here to learn some wit.

xl.

Epitaph of a Judge.

Peace, Passenger, heere sleepeth vnder ground
A Judge in ending causes most profou. 1;
Thocht not long since he was laid in this place,
It's lustres ten since he corrupted was.

xli.

Bishopes are like the turnores, most men say;
Though now cryed down, they'll vp some other day.

XXXVIII. ¹ P *has the alternative*—Britannes, admire the extra-
vagancyes of our King.

xlii.

When discord in a Towne the Toxan ringes,
Then all the rascalls turne vnto vs Kinges.

xliii.

A prouerbe.

To singe as was of old, is but a scorne,
The kings chaffe is better than others corne ;
Kelso can tell his chaffe away did fly,
Yet had no wind : Benedicite !
5 The corne unmowed on Duns-Law strong did shine,
Lesley, could thou haue shorne, it might beene thyne.

xliv.

The creed.

Q. How is the Creed thus stollen from vs away ?
A. The ten Commandements gone, it could not stay.
Q. Then haue wee no Commandements ? o wonder !
A. Yes, wee haue one for all : goe fight & plunder.

xlv.

On Marye Kings pest.

Turne, citezenes, to God ; repent, repent,
And praye your beadlam frenzies may relent :
Thinke not Rebellion a trifling thing,
This plague doth fight for Marye & the king.

xlvi.

Heere couered lies vith earth, vithout a tombe,
Vhose onlie praise is, that he died at Rome.

xlvii.

A prouerbe.

God neuer had a Church but there, Men say,
The Diuell a chapell hath raised by some wyles.
I doubted of this saw, till on a day
I Westward spied great Edinbroughs Saint Gyles.

xlviii.

Flyting no reason hath, for at this tyme,
It doth not stand with reason, but in ryme.
That none saue thus should flyte, had wee a law,
What rest had wee ? how would wyves stand in aw,
5 And learne the art of ryming ! Then how well
Would this and all good flyting pamphlets sell !

xlix.

On Pomponatius.

Trade softlie, passenger, vpon this stone,
For heere enclosed stayes,
Debarrd of Mercies Rayes,
A Soule, whose Bodye swore it had not one.

l.

On the isle of Rhe.

Charles, would yee quaile your foes, haue better lucke ;
Send forth some Drakes, and keep at home the Ducke.

li.

Epitaph.

Sancher whom this earth scarce could containe,
Hauing seene Italie, France, and Spaine,
To finish his travelles, a spectacle rare,
Was bound towards Heauen, but dyed in the aire.

lii.

An image to the pilgrime.

To worship mee, why come ye, Fooles, abroad ?
For artizans made me a demi-god.

liii.

Rames ay runne backward when they would aduance ;
Who knowes if Ramsay may find such a chance,
By playing the stiff Puritane, to weare
A Bishopes rocket yet another yeare.

liv.

Momus, with venom'd tooth, why wouldst thou teare
Our Muses and turne Mores those virgines faire ?
Nor citizen nor manners doe they brand,
Nor of the Town ought, saue where it doth stand.
5 I curst (I doe confesse) some nastye Mire,
And lake, deem'd poison by all Pęanes Quire :
Endwellares safe, I hartlie wisht the Towne
Turn'd in one Rock, and still wish 't o're-throwne.
Else-where a nobler Town might raised bee,
10 For skie, aire, sweeter, and in boundes more free ;
Yet there to dwell no shame is, nor be borne ;
Pearles dwell in oysteres, Roses grow on Thorne.
His Rome when Cęsare purposed to make new,
Himselfe straight fire-brandes on their Rafteres threw.
15 If in these wishes ought deserueth blame,
A Caledonian king first wisht the same.
My Muse (perhaps) too bold is, but farre farre
From tartnesse brest, from gall her paperes are.

lv.

On a glasse sent to his best beloued.

Oft ye me aske vhome my sweet faire can be ?
Looke in this christal and ye sal her see ;
At least some schade of her it vil impart,
For sche no trew glasse hath excep my hart.
5   Ah, that my brest var made of christal faire
That she might see her liulie portrat there !

lvi.

Sextain.

With elegies, sad songs, and murning layes,
Quhill Craig his Kala wald to pitie moue,
Poore braine-sicke man ! he spends his dearest dayes ;
Such sillie rime can not make women loue.
5   Morice quho sight of neuer saw a booke
With a rude stanza this faire Virgine tooke.

lvii.

Encomiastike verses before a book entitled *Follies*.

At ease I red your Worke, and am right sorrye
It came not forth before *Encomium Morie*,
Or in the dayes when good king James the first
Carowsd the Horses spring to quench his thirst ;
5 I durst haue giuen my Thombe and layed a wager
Thy Name had grac't the chronicle of Jhon Maior.
Had thou liu'd in the dayes of great Augustus,
(Hence, vulgare dotards, hence, vnlesse yee trust vs)
Thy Workes (with geese) had kept the Capitole,
10 And thou for euer been a happy soule,
Thy statue had been raisd neare Claudianus,
And thou in court liu'd equall with Sejanus.
Cornelius Tacitus is no such Poet,
Nor Liuie ; I'll say more ere that I goe yet.
15 Let all that heare doe weare celestiall bonnetes
Lyke thyne (they cannot write four-squared sonnetes)
Which shine like to that Mummye brought from Venice,
Or like the french kings relicks at Saint Denis.
It is a matter of regrate and pittie
20 Thou art not read into that famous citie
Of Constantine, for then the Turckes and Tartares
Had drunke with vs, and like to ours worne gartares ;
And the strange Muphetees and hard Mameluckes
Had cut their beardes, and got by hart thy Bookes.
25 If any them detract, though hee were Xenaphon,
Thou shalt haue such reuenge as ere was tane of one,
From this our coast vnto the Wall of China,
Where Maides weare narrow shoes ; thou hast been a
Man for enuie, though such forsooth was Horace,
30 Yet thou no lesse dost write than hee, and soare ass
As farre in this our tongue as any Latines,
Though some doe reade their verse, that ware fine satines ;
Romes latest wonder, great Torquato Tasso,
Writing, to thee were a pecorious asse, hoe !
35 Now, to conclude, the nine Castalian lasses
Their Maidenheades thee sell for fannes and glasses.

EPITAPHS.

lviii.

To the Memorie of his much louing and beloued Master, M. F. R.

No Wonder now if Mistes beclowde our Day,
Sith now our earth lakes her celestiall RAY ;
And Phœbus murnes his preest, and all his quire,
In sables wrapt, weep out their sacred fire ;
5 Far well of latin Muses greatest praise,
Whither thou red graue proses or did raise
Delight and wonder by a numbrous straine ;
Fare well Quintilian once more dead againe ;
With ancient Plautus, Martiall combined,
10 Maro and Tullie, here in one enshrined.
Bright RAY of learning which so cleare didst streame,
Fare well Soule which so many soules did frame.
  Many Olympiades about shall come,
  Ere Earth like thee another can entombe.

LVIII. ² *In* P, late *is written in above* now *in Drummond's hand.*

lix.

D. O. M. S.

What was mortall of THOMAS DALYELL of Binnes lyeth
here.   Hee was descended of the auncient race of the L⁵.
of Dalyell now deseruedlye aduanced to be Earles of
Carnewath.   His integritie and worth made him an vn-
remoued Justice of Peace, and . . . . . yeeres Sherife in the
Countie of Linlythgow.   Hee lefte, successoures of his
vertues and fortunes, a Sonne renowned by the warres,
and a Daughter marryed to William Drummond of
Reckertown.   After 69 yeeres pilgrimage heere on Earth,
hee was remoued to the repose of Heauen, the 10 of
Februarye 1642.

Justice Truth, Peace, and Hospitalitie,
Friendship and Loue, being resolued to dye
In these lewd Tymes haue chosen heere to haue
With just, true, pious, kynd DALYELL their Graue ;
5 Hee Them cherish'd so long, so much did grace,
That they than this would choose no dearer place.

T. Filius manibus charissimi patris parentauit.

lx.

Epitaph.

If Monumentes were lasting wee would raise
A fairer frame to thy desertes & praise ;
But Auarice or Misdeuotiones Rage
These tumbling down, or brought to nought by age,
5 Twice making man to dye, This Marble beares
An Embleme of affection & our teares.

lxi.

To the Memorie of the vertuous Gentlewoman RACHELL
LINDSAY, Daughter of Sir Hierosme Lyndsay, Principall King
of Armes, and Wyfe to Lieutenant Colonell Barnad Lindsay,
who dyed the . . day of May, the yeere 1645, after shee
had liued . . . . yeeres.

The Daughter of a king, of princelye partes,
In Beautie eminent, in Vertues cheife,
Load-starre of loue, and load-stone of all Hartes,
Her freindes and Husbandes onlie Joy, now Griefe,
5 Enclosed lyes within this narrow Graue,
Whose Paragone no Tymes, no Climates haue.

Maritus mœrens posuit.

lxii.

To the Memorie of . . .

As nought for splendour can with sunne compare
For beautie, sweetnesse, modestie, ingyne,
So shee alone vnparagon'd did shyne,
And angelles did with her in graces share.

5 Though few heere were her dayes, a span her life,
Yet hath Shee long tyme liud, performing all
Those actiones which the oldest doe befall,
Pure, fruitfull, modest, Virgine, Mother, Wife.

For this (perhaps) the fates her dayes did close,
10 Her deeming old ; perfection doth not last,
When courser thinges scarce course of tyme can waste ;
Yeeres liues the worthlesse bramble, few dayes the Rose.

Vnhappye Autumne, Spoyler of the flowres,
Discheueler of Meades and fragrant plaines,
15 Now shall those Monethes which thy date containes,
No more from Heuens be nam'd, but Eyes salt showres.

lxiii.

To the Memorie of the worthye ladye, the ladye Craigmillare.

This Marble needes no teares, let these be powr'd
For such whom Earths dull bowelles haue emboured
In chyld-head or in youth, and lefte to liue
By some sad chance fierce planetes did contriue.
5 Eight lustres, twice full reckened, did make Thee
All this lifes happinesse to know ; and wee
Who saw thee in thy winter (as men flowres
Shrunke in their stemmes, or Iliums faire towres
Hidde in their rubbidge) could not but admire
10 The casket spoyled, the Jewell so intiere ;
For neither judgment, memorye, nor sence
In thee was blasted, till all fled from hence
To thy great Maker ; Earth vnto earth must,
Man in his best estate is but best Dust.
15 Now euen though buryed yet thow canst not dye,
But happye liust in thy faire progenie
To out-date Tyme, and neuer passe away.
Till Angelles raise thee from thy Bed of claye,
And blist againe with these heere loud thow meet,
20 Rest in fames Temple and this winding sheet :
Content thou liu'd heere, happye though not great,
And dyed with the kingdome and the state.

lxiv.

D. O. M. S.

What was mortall of W. RAMSAY lieth heere. Hee was
the Sonne of John Ramsay, L. of Edington, Brother to the
right honorable William, the first earle of Dalhousye, a
linage of all vertues in peace and valour in warre, renowned
by all tymes, and second to none ; a youth ingenuous, of
faire hopes, a mild sweet disposition, pleasant aspect,
countenance ; his Kinreds delight and joy, now their
greatest displeasure and sorrow ; hauing left this transi-
torye Stage of cares, when hee but scarce appeared vpon
it, in his tender nonage.

      So falles by Northern blast a Virgine rose,
      At halfe that doth her bashfull bosome close ;
      So a sweet flowrish languishing decayes
      That late did blush when kist by Phoebus rayes.
5   Though vntymelie cropp'd, leaue to bemoan his fate,
      Hee dyed with our Monarchie and State.

His Mother out of that care and loue she caryed to him,
to continue heere his memorie (some space) raised this
Monument, Anno 1649, mense . . .

      Immortale decus superis.

LXIV. ⁷ *In* P, from *is written in above* out of *in Drummond's hand.*

Posthumous Poems.

IV.

From the Hawthornden Manuscripts.
Not published in any former edition.

Posthumous Poems.

IV.

ECLOGUES.

i.

Eclogue.

Damon and Moeris by a christal spring
Vher a greene sicamour did make a schade,
And fairest floures the banckes all couering,
Theer oft to stay the vandring Nymphes had made,
5   Vhile voods musicians from the trees aboue
    On eurye branche did varble furth ther loue,

On grassie bed all tyrd them selues did lay
To schune suns heat and passe the tedious houres
Delyting now to see theer lambkins play
10 Then to veaue garlands for theer paramours.
    Damon tormentet vas with Amarillis
    And Moeris brunt in loue of farest Phillis.

Phillis the louliest lasse that flockes ere fed
By Tanais siluer streames, vhos heaunlie eie
15 In chaines of gold this shephard captiue led,
    Or he knew vhat vas loue or libertie.
    Sweet Amarillis far aboue the rest
    Of Askloua maids estimed the best.

In curious knotes vhile thay theer vorke adorne,
20 Mixing pyed dezies with sad violets,
Vhit lilies with that flour vhich like the morne
Doth blush and beautie to the garland sets,
　　Damon, vhom loue and voes had sore dismaid,
　　Thus gan to say or Loue thus for him said.

25 Faire Tanais Nymphes & ye Nymphes of the voods
Vhich usse in schadie groues to dance and sing,
Ye Montaine sisters sisters of the floods
On softest sand vhich oft ar carroling,
　　Heere bring your flours and this garland make faire
30 　　To set vpon my Phillis amber haire.

Do not disdaine to be a schade, sweet flours,
To fairest tresses vnder vhich doth grow
The rose and lilie far excelling yours,
The red cinabre and the milke vhit snow.
35 　About her temples vhen I sal yow place
　　Them you can not (sweet flowres) they shall yow grace.

Suouft vinged archers & ye sea-borne queene,
In Mirrhas child if yee tooke ere delight,
If ere vith flames your hart hath touched beene,
40 Enambushd lie you by this red & vhit,
　　That vhen her lockes this coronet anademe sal part,
　　A hundred cupids may steal to her hart.

Her hart then coldest Alpine yce more cold,
Mor hard yet precious as the diamond,
45 The noblest conquest that vith dart of gold
Loue euer made since he culd shoot or vound.
　　But he that fort not darring to essay
　　Contents you vith her eies & ther doth play.

Nou Ceres tuise hath cut her yellow lockes,
50 The swellow tuise the spring about hath brocht,
Tuise hath ve vaind the yonglins of our flockes
Since I alas vas forc't, & al for naught,
    Be cruel her to cry, veep & complaine
    Vnto this montaine, forrest, riuer, plaine.

55 My flockes sem'd partneres of ther masters voe :
The Bell-bearer the troupes that vsd to lead
His vsuall feading places did forgoe,
And lothing three-leu'd grasse hold vp his head ;
    The valkes, the groues which I did hant of yore
60   My fate and Phillis hardnesse seemd deplore.

The goate-foote syluans vnder schadie trees
Did solemnize the accents of my plent
Vith grones, the vatrie Nymphes with veeping eies
And vide spred lockes I oft haue seen lament.
65   Among the rest a Nymphe sueet, vanton, gay,
    Rising aboue the streames thus hard I say.

Phillis sueet honor of these suetest voods,
Vert thou but pitiful as thow art faire,
The vorthiest gem of al our Tanais floods ;
70 But as in beautie so in hardness rare
    To al these graces that so do grace the ;
    Ah, learne to loue, & no mor cruel be !

The flowres, the gemmes, the mettales, all behold,
The lambes, the doues, the gold spangl'd bremes in
    streames,
75 Al thes be vorkes of loue ; the Tygresse bold
Made mild by loue her in-bred furie teames ;
    In heauen, earth, aire, since all vhere loue we see,
    O, learne to loue, and no more cruel be !

In toilesome paines to vast our virgin yeares
80 And louelesse liue, is not to liue but breath ;
Loue is the tree vhich most contentment beares,
Vhose fruits euen makes vs liue beyond our death ;
  Sweet loue did make thy Mother bring forth thee ;
  Ah, learne to loue, and no more cruel be !

85 Earths best perfections doth but last short time,
Riche Aprils treasure pleaseth much the eie,
But as it grows it passeth in its prime.
Thinke, & vel thinke, thy beautie thus must dye ;
  Vhen vith van face thow sal loke in thy glasse
90   Then sal thow sigh : vould I had lou'd, alas !

Looke but to Cloris louing lou'd againe,
How glad, how merrillie, sche spends each daye,
Like cherful vine vhom chaste elme doth sustaine,
Vhile her sweet yonglings doe about her play ;
95   Vhen thow the vant sal find of such a grace
  Then sal thow sigh : vould I had lou'd, alas !

But vho is Damon vhom thow suld disdaine :
The heauens on him some gifts hath euen let fal ;
Gay is hee ; vealth his cabane doth containe ;
100 He loues the much, & that is more then al.
  If crueltie thy loue in him deface
  Then sal thow say : that I had lou'd, alas !

Flora him lou'd, if ere in clearest brooke
Narcissus like thy face thow did admire,
105 As faire as thow, yet Flora he forsooke
Vith al her gifts, & foole did the desire.
  If he his thochts againe on Flora place
  Then sal thow sigh : vould I had lou'd, alas !

This said the Nymphe, & ther vith al sche sanke
110 The clearest streame beneath, vho al dismaid
At her depart come playning to the banke,
And on his face a hundred frownes bevrayed.
 I lay as on vhom some strange dreame makes vake,
 Then homvard to my cabane did me take.

115 The floods sal backvard to ther fontaines rune,
The spring shall vant its floures, the pleasant floures
On barren rockes sal grow depriu'd of sune,
The sune sal leaue the heuens tuelue shining boures ;
 Heuens vithout starres sal be, starres cease to moue,
120 Ere euer I my Phillis leaue to loue.

Pant my hart doth vhen I thinke on that day,
That fatal day, vhen sche vith looshung haire
And vhitest petticot in new borne may,
To gather floures did to our meeds repaire,
125 Vhile I did rest beneath an ancient oke,
 Caring for nocht but how to fead my flocke.

I saw her rune and as sche ran me thocht
The feilds about did smyle ; beside the streames
Then sat schee down, vhere sune to kisse her sought ;
130 But schee with vaile eclipsd his vanton beames.
 I hard her breath few vords, vith loue & feare
 To vhich vinds, mountaines, voods, did leane their eare.

Deceu'd perchance vith that most liulie hew,
A bee did hurt her lip that mad her veep,
135 And moisten cheeke & chin with sweetest due,
Vhich semed to fal, but Cupid did it keep ;
 For vhen rebellious harts ganstands his dart
 He steeps it in these teares, & then thay smart.

Vithal sche rose, & in vatrie floods glasse
140 Angerlie mild the litil vound to looke,
Her selff sche drest, but Kala coming vas
Vho made her stay, & so her mande sche tooke,
   Of golden vonderes to make poore the Mead,
   Vhile on her face my hungry eyes did feed.

145 At sight of her plump lips blush did the rose,
To see her vaines the violets grew paile,
The Marigold her precious leaues did close,
Amazd to find her haire so farre preuaile ;
   The lilies in her hand apeard not vhit.
150   Thus dazel'd vas my sight vith sueet delight.

Ourchargd at last sche to her village vent,
Leauing a thousand diuerse thoughts in mee
Like ciuill foes tumultuouslie which vent
All their best strenhtes till all enuasseld be.
155   Then tyrd vith vo I laid me in my bed,
   Vher al the Nyt the Hyacynthe I red.

Vhat vonder her sueet eies culd me beguile
Vhich kendle desire then vhen thay vtter breath,
And euen vhen sche vald froune yet seme to smile,
160 Life promising vhen most thay threaten death !
   For these faire tuines I rather stil be sad
   Then by an others loue euen be made glad.

I. 145 *In* P, red *is written in above* plump *in Drummond's hand.*

ii.

Eclogue.

Syrenus.   Montanus.

Sy. Vhile dayes bright coachman makes our schadows
   schort,
  And panting rests him in his halff dayes course,
  Vhile gladder shephards giue them selues to sport,
  Let vs deare Montane rest vs by this source,
5   Vher ve may stanche our thrist vith coldest
    streames,
   And vnder schade be fred of Phebus beames.

M. Content am I ; but since Syluanus left
  This earthlie round I neuer like that spring,
  The vearie place from me my ioyes hath reft,
10 Vhen I behold vher he vas vont to sing,
   Syluane vell knowne, the honor of our voods,
   Vho made the rocks to heare & stayed the floods.

Sy. Bevaile not Syluane, since he is releu'd
  Of flesclie bonds and these our mortal toiles,
15 Vith sad misfortunes now he is not grieuet.
  This earth is framd for deaths triumphing spoiles ;
   The pleasant leaues, the suetest floures decayes,
   And fairest things doth last the fewest dayes.

M. Th'enuyous heauens, befor the course of time
20 Stole the from earth for to enrich theer spheares,
  Vhile scars thow flourish't in thy youthful prime,
  Filling our harts vith voe, our eies vith teares.
   Syren, for these deare dayes that heer thow spent,
   Stay not my grief but help me to lament.

25 *Sy.* If floods of teares from the elysian plaine
    Culd call a happie gost, if sights culd giue
    A sparke of lyff, then Phillis schoures of raine
    And lasting grones might make him yet to liue.
      Yet in remembrance of this orphane place,
30   And her Il murne, Il sing vith the a space.

  M. A streame of teares, poore riuer christalline,
    Len these mine eies ; so may along thy banks
    Sueet roses, lilies, & the columbine,
    In pleasant flourish keep theer statlie ranks,
35   To vash Syluanus Tombe, that of my sorrow
      The floods, the hils, the mids, a part may borrow.

  Sy. Len me the voice that Boreas hath the giuen,
    Stracht reachet pin, vhen he his blows redoubles ;
    So may thy loftie head mont vp to heauen,
40   & neare heareefter feare his angry troubles,
      That my sad accents may surpasse the skies,
      & make heuens echoes answer to my cries.

  M. Forests since your best darling now is gone,
    Vho your darke schadows suetnet vith his layes,
45   Teache al your nightingales at once to grone,
    Cut your greene lockes, let fal your palmes & bayes,
      Let not a mirtil tree be in yow found,
      But eurie vher vith cypress sad abound.

  Sy. Faire Midows from vhose tender bosome springs
50   The vhite Narcissus, Venus deare delight,
    The Hyacinth, & others vho var kings
    And ladies faire vhen thay enioyd this light,
      In mourning blake your princely coulours die,
      Bow downe your heads, vhile sighing zephires flee.

55 *M.* Vhat now is left vnto this plane but veeping ?
This litil flood that sometime did inuite
Our vearied bodies to sueet rest and sleeping,
Vith his soft murmur semes to vaile our plight,
 Telling the rocks, the banks, vheer ere he goes,
60 & the vyde ocean, our remedlesse voes.

Sy. As Philomela sight vpon a tree,
Me thocht (for vhat thinks not a troublet mynd ?)
Vith her old grieues, amids her harmonie,
Syluanus death, our losse, sche oft combind,
65 Vherto tuo vidow turtles lent theer eares,
 Syne planed that Nature had not giuen them teares.

M. The earth althocht cold vinter kil her flowres,
And al her beautie eurie vher deface,
Vhen Phebus turnes into his hoter boures,
70 Made ful of lyff smiles vith her former grace ;
 But so soone as, alas, mans giuen to death,
 No sunne againe doth euer make him breath.

Sy. The Moone that sadlie cheers the gloomie night,
Vhen sche in deaths blake armes a vhile remaines,
75 New borne doth soone recev her siluer light
And queenlike glances or the silent plaines ;
 The stars sunke in the vest again doth rise ;
 But man, forgot, in vglie horror lies.

M. Ah souueraine poures, vhen ye did first deuise
80 To make poore man, vhy brak ye not the molde ?
Vith fleschie maskes vhy did ye sprits disguyse ?
Caussing a glasse so foole that liquor hold,
 Vith cryes & paine him bringing to the light,
 Happie t'haue sleepe in a eternal night.

85 *Sy.* Happie t'haue sleepe in a eternal night
    & neuer interrup that silent rest,
    He felt no voes if he had no delight,
    He did not know vhat's euil, of nocht vhat's best ;
      If he vsd not th'vnperfyt piece of reason,
90   He feard not voes to come at eurie season.

M. If that I var againe for to be framd,
    & that the heuens vald freelie to me giue
    Vhat of the things below I suld be made,
    A hart, a doue, I rather choose to liue,
95   Then be a man, my losses stil lamenting,
      Tost first with passion, then vith sore repenting.

Sy. If I var one of yow my sille lambes,
    I suld not beene oprest vith th'vncuth caire
    That mankind hath, nor felt the cruel flames
100   Of Phillis eies, nor knowne vhat vas despaire :
      Sueet harmlesse flocke, vhen as ye stray alone,
      Ar ye affraid of Styx or Phlegeton ?

M. The mids ar not embled vith so manie floures,
    So many hews heuens doth neuer borrow,
105   So many drops hath not the april schoures,
    As ve poore vretchet men hath vorlds of sorrow :
      For these, o glorious gifts of noble skies,
      Vith bitter teares ye fillet hath our eies.

Sy. Vith bitter teares ye fillet hath our eies,
110   And fostreth vith beguiling hope our mind
    Vith promist good that doth vs stil intice :
    Lo, seeke ve ve vot not vhat, and so mad blind
      Ve follow lies and change to taste of ioyes,
      But hauing changd ve find but new annoyes.

115 *M.* If lies bred ioyes and vertue bring voe,
    Fals thochts be ful of comfort, trewth of sadnesse,
    Velcome braue lies of that I neuer know!
    Vnhappie trewth to take from me my gladnesse ;
      For thocht ve veep our voes ve cannot mend them,
120   & ve may end our selues befor ve end them.

SONNETS AND MISCELLANEOUS PIECES.

iii.

In S^r. P. d. R.

Great Paragon, of Poets richest Pearle,
Beneath the artick circles statlie pole
Abut quoes point the sphears of knouledge role,
The magnes of al mynds, ear-charming Mearle ;
5 The perfumd cabinet quher muses duel,
Enameling neu-found skyes vith starres of gold,
Quher Pallas vith the free-borne queens enrold,
And beutie, stryffs it selff for to excel.
Farre-virthier Orpheus then they quho suel
10 Vith sacred Pegasus azure streames,
Or he quho brocht from Heauen the fyrie beames :
Mor fit for Phœbus Bay then Phebus sel.
  Thy perfyt praises if the vorld vold vrit
  Must haue againe thy selff for to end it.

iv.

Faire cruel Siluia since thow scornes my teares,
And ouerlookes my cares vith carelesse eie ;
Since my requests in loue offends thy eares,
Hensefoorth I vowe to hold my pace in thee and die.
5 But vhile I hold my pace thes things sal crie :
The brookes sal murmure, & the vinds complaine ;
The hils, the dails, the deserts vher I lie,
Vith Echoes of my plents sal prech my paine.
Yet put the case thay silent vald remaine ;
10 Imagine brookes & vinds vald hold theer pace,
Suppone hils, dailes, and deserts vald disdaine
T'acquant thy deaff disdaines vith my disgrace ;
   Yet vhile thay dombe, thow deaff, to me sal proue,
   My death sal speake and let the know my loue.

v.

Great Queene whom to the liberall Heauens propine
All what their force or influence can impart ;
Whose Vertues rare, whose Beauties braue but art
Makes thee aboue thy sacred sex to shine.
5 Resembling much those Goddesses diuine ;
The thundrers Bride for thy heroicke hart,
Cytheręa for proportion of each part,
Joues braine-born gyrle for judgment and ingyne.
But now I feare my flatrie flows to farre ;
10 Three Goddesses in one are rarelie seene,
Nor can a goddesse be vngrate—you are.
What rests then but, a Woman, and a Queene :
   A Woman in vnconstancie and change,
   A Queene because so statlie & so strange.

vi.

De Porcheres, on the eies of Madame la Marquise de Monceaux, vret this sonnet.

Ce ne sont pas des yeux, ce sont plustost de dieux :
Ils ont dessus les rois la puissance absoluë.
Dieux, non, ce sont des cieux : ils ont la couleur bluë,
Et le mouuement prompt comme celuy des cieux.
5 Cieux, non, mais deux soleils clairement radieux,
Dont les rayons brillans nous offusquent la veuë.
Soleils, non, mais esclairs de puissance incognuë,
Des foudres de l'Amour signes presagieux,
Car s'ils estoient des dieux, feroient ils tant de mal ?
10 Si des cieux, ils auroient leur mouuement esgal.
Deux soleils ne se peut : le soleil est vnique.
Esclairs, non, car ceux-cy durent trop et trop clairs.
Toutefois ie les nomme a fin que ie m'explique,
Des yeux, des dieux, des cieux, des soleils, des esclairs.

Thus englished.

Wer these thine eies, or lightnings from aboue,
Vhose glistring glances dazel'd so my sight ?
I tooke them to be lightnings send from Joue
To threten that theer thunder bolt vald light.
5 But lightnings culd not lest so long so bright.
Thay rather semed for to be suns, vhose rayes
Promou'd to the Meridian of theer might,
Did change my noisome nights in joyful dayes.
But euen in that theer nomber them bevrayes
10 Suns ar thay not : the vorld endures but one.
Theer force, theer figure, & theer coulour sayes
That thay ar heuens ; but heuens on earth ar none.
    Be vhat thay vil, theer poure in force agrees :
    The heauns, the sune, the lightnings, and her eies.

vii.

Ah! eyes, deare eyes, how could the Heuens consent
To giue to you occasion of those teares ?
Brest, sugred Brest that Globes of Beautie beares,
With sighes why should yee swell—with teares be sprent ?
5 Hair, that in spight of griefe art excellent,
What haue you done ?   That hand you wronglie teares ;
Voice, through deare portes of pearle and rubies sent,
Why should yee moane ?   mor fit to tune heauens
        spheares.
Foule Grief, the scourge of life, from heauen exild,
10 Child of Mishap, the Hells extreame disgrace,
Brother to paine, Mans weaknesse, forster child,
How did thou mount to so diuine a place ?
        Yet Grief, come there, so stranglie she thee furmes,
        That thou seemst Joy, while shee thus sweetlie murnes.

viii.

To my Ladye Mary Wroath.

For beautye onlye, armd with outward grace,
I scorne to yeeld, to conquerre, or to striue ;
Let shallow thoughtes that can no deeper dyue,
As fits their weaknesse, rest vpon a face.
5 But when rare partes a heunlye shape confines,
Scarce reacht by thoughtes, not subiect to the sight,
Yet but the lanterne of a greater light,
Wher worth accomplisht crownd with glorie shines,
Then when bright vertue raignes in beautyes throne,
10 And doth the hart by spirituall magick moue,
Whilst reasone leads though passiones follow loue,
Lothd may hee be that likes not such a one.
        If it not lou'd so braue a mynd thus shown,
        I hated had the basenesse of myne own.

ix.

Our faults thy wrath deserued haue, alas !
And thou must craue iust count of eurye deed ;
But if our faults their punishment doe passe,
Thy Goodnesse farre our errors doth exceed.
5 All, all crye mercye, chargd with grief & teares,
A iust remorse orthrowing wylier powers ;
Reason can not effect in many yeeres
What thy great wisdome can in few short howres.
Passed ills wee see the present murne,
10 Stand fearfull & amazd of what should come,
Euen those hidden fires eternaly that burne ;
For wretched life deserueth such a doome.
    But loue to vs a ray send from thy face,
    And after open wyde the Gates of Grace.

x.

Or the vinged boy my thochts to the made thral,
When babie-like I knew not vhat vas loue,
My vit embrasing al my vit could proue,
At others lacing, fearing not my fal,
5 Vith two faire eies vher Cupids mother smyld,
Thow oft inuited me to venter boldlie,
As if my sad lookes spake minds langage coldlie,
Til vith thes gleames in end I vas beguild.
But free thow kneust I vas no more mine awne,
10 Charmed in thes circles vher I forc'st remaine ;
Churlish thow doth thy vonted smyles retaine,
And, voe is me ! giues oft a cruel frowne.
    Alas ! if loue in lookes hath made such change,
    Vnkind I loue the not but yet am strange.

IX. ⁶ *In* P, subdewing *is written in above* orthrowing *in Drummond's hand.*

xi.

Essay out of the Italien.

Melpomene in Athenes neuer song
More sueter accents, nor a more sad dittie,
Nor neare made harts bleed vith a greater pitie,
Vhere Tyber playes his floury banks along,
5 Then vhen she veeping daigned by Forth to sing,
Forth vhere thy heuenlie suannet loues to dwel,
Forth that may claime the name of that faire vel
Vhich Horses haue from flintie rocke mad spring.
But Medwaye, Seuern, Tames vil not consent.
10 To Monarks fals if y'il not giue such praise,
Yet grant at least to them, in sueet sad layes
Vho help faire Sions virgins, to lament.
　　And if these trumpets yeilds not schrillest sounds,
　　Forth boasts of him vho song the Turquish vounds.

xii.

To Anne, the french Queen, new come from
Spaine, and applyable to Marye of England,
meeting the King at Douer.

En fin la voyci, nous voyons ces beaux yeux,
    L'amour de la terre et des cieux,
Dont nostre Mars, en son choix bienheureux,
    Est si fort amoureux.
5 Le ciel n'a iamais ioint à tant de beautè
    Vn si douce Maiestè,
Qui dans le cœur inspire, tour à tour,
    Le respect et l'amour.
En fin la voyci, nos vœux sont accomplis,
10   Nos esprits d'aise remplis ;
Puisse en tous deux, par vn heureux destin,
    Viure vn amour sans fin !

At length heere shee is : wee haue got those bright eyes.
More shine now our earth than the skyes !
And our Mars, happye in his high desire,
Is all flame by this fire.

5 The spheeres in so heunlye face neuer fixed
High state with so meeke graces mixed,
Which in all harts about it round inspires
True respect & chast fires.

At length both are met : our designes crowned are ;
10 Each soule in the ioy hath a share ;
May in both brestes this Isle of Vnion giue
Onlye one hart to liue !

xiii.

Fragment.

Like vnto her nothing can be namd :
The mold is broke vherin dear sche vas framd.
Vho may of her rare beautie count ich part,
And all these gifts heauen doth to her impart,
5 On Affricke shores the sand that ebs & flows,
The skalie flockes that vith old Proteus goes,
He sur may count, and al these vaues that meet
To vashe the Mauritanian Atlas feet—
Her curlet haire, faire threeds of finest gold,
10 In nets & curious knots mens harts to hold,
Her forhead large & euen of vhich the lilies
Do borrow beautie & the daffadilies,
Faire ebaine bows aboue her heunlie eies,
Vher tratrous loue in silent ambush lies,
15 Vell framd her nose, her cheekes vith purest red,
Cinabre like, most dantelie ar spred,
Prettie & schort her eares, vith heunlie smiles
Her visage schind that sadest eies beguiles,
To orient perles her teeth do nothing yeild,
20 Nor lips to coral, or of gueles a feild ;
Juno vith maiestie, & faire aurore,
Vith blush & fingers did this sueet decore ;
The Graces gaue theer smiles & did reioice
To heare her sing vith Phebus heaunlie voice,
25 Pallas gaue vit, the vertews gaue theer part :
Liuing the heauen thay loget in her hart.

xiv.

Fragment.

A faire, a sueet, a pleasant heunlie creature
Lycoris vas—the miracle of Nature :
Her haire more faire then gold of Tagus streames
Or his that cheeres the vorld vith golden beames,
5 Her suetest mouth & lips that halff shee closes
Did nothing yeild to corral & fresh roses,
Her brow more vhite, more beautiful & gay
Then is a day but clouds in mids of May,
Vnder the vhich tuo equal planets glancing
10 Cast flames of loue, for loue theer stil is dancing ;
Vhile jurie, vith a dantiest purple spred,
Of her faire cheks resembld the fairest red ;
Her nek semd framd by some most curious master,
Most vhite, most smoth, a piece of alabaster ;
15 Vpon her brest two aples round did grow,
Vith tops of strawberries more vhite then snow :
So far in grace sche did excell each other
That Cupid vald haue taine her for his mother.

xv.

To my ladye Mary Wroath.

Who can (great lady) but adore thy name
To which the sacred band are bound to bow.
Of men your vncle first, of woemen yow,
Both grace this age, & it to both giues fame.

5 Your spacious thoughts with choice inuentiones free,
Show passiones power, affectiones seuerall straines ;
And yet one sort, and that most rare remaines,
Not told by you, but to be proud by me.

No face at all could haue my hart subdued,
10 Though beautyes Sune in the Meridian shind ;
Yet by the glorye lightning from a mynd,
I am her captiue whom I neuer knew.

Sprightes wanting bodyes are not barrd from loue,
But feele, not tuching ; see, though wanting eyes ;
15 Aboue grosse senses reach true vertue flyes,
And doth by sympathye effectuall proue.

Then wonder not to see this flame burst forth,
Nor blame mee not who dare presume so much ;
I honor but the best, and hold you such ;
20 None can deserue & I discerne your worth.

In spight of fortune though you should disdaine,
I can enjoy this fauour fate assignes ;
Your speaking portrait drawn with liuing lines,
A greater good than louers vse to gaine.

25 My loue may (as begune) last without sight,
And by degrees contemplatiuly grow ;
Yet from affection curious thoughtes most flow :
I long to know whence comes so great a light,

And wish to see (since so your spright excelles)
30   The Paradise where such an Angell dwelles.

xvi.

Sur les œuures poetiques de Guillaume Alexandre, Sieur De Menstre.

Menstre, Mignon de Pinde, astre des escossois,
Le premier entre nous qu'osa toucher le bois
Du docte Delien, faisant le monde entendre
Les bourdons de ton luth, cõme vn autre Terpandre ;
5 Esprit des bons esprits, qu'a charmè par ta vois
La dure Mort et fait reuiure les grands rois,
A bon droict maintenant, qu'on peut nõmer Monarque,
Puisque par ton sçauoir il ont vaincu les Parques,
Ces rois qui te doyuent autant de lauriers
10 Que leurs bras ont dontè des peuples guerriers.
Tout ce n'estoit assez : au comble de ta gloire,
Tu ensignas l'amour aux filles de Memoire ;
Le Pau deuint honteux, Seine cacha son chef
A peine le monstrant au soleil derechef ;
15 Les Charites dansent, Amour ses traits redore
Et aueugle s'estonne, voyant ta belle Aurore.
Dedans ta bouche naisse vne manne de miel,
Tousiours ton nom Douen alle bruant au ciel,
Tousiours sois tu aimè d'Apollon et ton prince,
20 Fils aisnè de Pallas, l'honneur de ta prouince !

MADRIGALS AND EPIGRAMS.

xvii.

Loue once thy lawes
I did rebellious blame,
When they did cause
My chastest hart to flame
5 With fruitlesse vaine desire
Of her, who scorneth both thy dartes & fire.
But now (iust Loue)
Thee and thy lawes I free,
And doe reproue
10 My selfe, since plaine I see
The best but worthye is
To couuet, not enjoye such blisse.

xviii.

Of Anthea.

When Hylas saw the eyne
Of Anthea his loue,
Who e're (said hee) such burning lampes hath seene,
Vnlesse in Heauen aboue ?
5 Shee at his sillie praise
With blush more faire became.
In vaine (said hee) cheekes [in] skies that Morne do raise,
For my hart can not feele a greater flame.

xix.

In ashe her lies the wanton God of loue,
By her whom for I die.
For longtyme hauing hee
Bent all his powres her marble hart to moue,
5 In spight of dart of gold
And torch of heunlye fire
That neere would know desire,
Nay what is strange mor harder grew & cold,
Hee dowbting if the flame vnquencht remand the same,
10 Wherwith hee heuen & earth did burne of old,
Proud on him selfe his brandones force,
Which, ere hee wist, consumd his litle corse.

xx.

On a lamp.

Faithfull and loued light
That silent sees our thefts,
Be glad at the sweet sound of kisses sweet.
Oh! doe not dye! but if thou lou'st to die,
5 Dye amidst our delight
When languish both our brests.
So, thou mayst dye at ease ;
For lamps to mee, no starres, are her faire eyes.

xxi.

Amarillis to her dog Perlin.

Faire Perlin doe not barke,
Poore foole dost thou not know
My louer, my desire?
If thou dost turne my fow,
5 Who to mee shall be true?
Thou neare shall after any kisses haue.
Ist not enough all day
That thou do with mee stay?
Giue place to night, and like her silent bee,
10 Lulld with the noyse that kisses make to thee.

xxii.

This Monument vnder
Doth lie the wonder
Of that faire brest which Loue dar'd neuer tuch.
His courage kill'd him ; but was it not much
5 A flea should bold and naked without armes
Of Loueres wronged thus reuenge the harmes?
Amantes proprio aere
Militi bene merenti posuere.

XXI. [10] *In* P, sound *is written in above* noyse *in Drummond's hand.*

xxiii.

The Gods haue heard my vowes;
Fond Lyce those faire Browes
Wont scorne with such disdaine
My Loue, my teares, my paine.

5 But now those springtide Roses
Are turned to winter poses,
To Rue & tyme & sage,
Fitting that shriueled age.

Now, youthes with hote desire,
10 See, see, that flamelesse fire,
Which earst your hartes so burned,
Quicke into ashes turned!

xxiv.

On the lut of Margarite.

The harmonie vherto the heauens doe dance,
Keeping to curious notes a suoft cadance,
Nor al Joues quiristers ar not so suet
As is the voice & lut of Margarite.
5 If angry vith his sheares he had vndoone thee,
Her onlie voice vald serue againe to tune thee;
If he phlegrean squadrons vald bring vnder,
Her lut vald combat better then his thunder.

xxv.

If it be trew that Echo doth remaine
Mong hardest rockes, alas
Calling so oft for Grace
To her hard hart, vhy anser'st not againe ?
5 Vhile vinds and tempests blow
The Echoes silent ar,
And neuer answer : sounds are sent to far.
So, troublet vith thy stormes of loue and voe,
Or distant then vhen most thy griefe doth flow,
10 Sche doth no answer giue.
Yet this thow may beleaue
That silence ofter is aye then no.

xxvi.

Idas to schune sunnes beames
Did soume in cristal flood.
Perchance, like faire Aurore,
At Ganges bankes Phillis came to the schore.
5 He lookt vher as sche stood,
And stracht did burne amidst these coldest streames.

xxvii.

O most perfidious face
That hauing lost thy loue
Dost yet retaine thy wonted hew & grace !
Thy smyling eyes said
5 Thy splendour should be gone,
Thy cheekes faire roses fade
And furrowed be with wrinkles shown,
Ere thy affection any whit decay,
Which now is cold & dead.
10 Now, Tyme, haste, make her old :
In siluer turne her lockes, her face like gold.

XXVII. 10 *In* P, poste *is written in above* haste *in Drummond's hand.*

xxviii.

Epitaph.

Heere lyes a Docter who with droges and pelfe
Could not corrupte Death, but dyed himselfe.

xxix.

Epitaph.

Heer lyes a cooke who went to buye ylles,
But met death in the Market who turned vp his heeles.

xxx.

That which preserueth cherries, peares and plumes
Can not preserue the liuer, lights and lungs.

xxxi.

A lady in her prime to whom was giuen
As much perfection as could flow from Heauen,
Who, had shee liud when good was loud of men,
Had made the Graces fiue, the Muses ten.

xxxii.

Strange is his end, his death most rare and od,
Who made his god his gold, his gold his god.

xxxiii.

Killd by ingratitude heere blest within doth rest :
To marye or not to marye which is best.

xxxiv.

Epitaphe on a Cooke.

Heere lyes a sowre and angry cooke,
A miser, wretched man ;
Who liued in smoke, & dyed in smoke,
Besides his frying pan.

xxxv.

On a noble man who died at a counsel table.

Vntymlie Death that neither wouldst conferre,
Discourse nor parley with our great Treasurer,
Had thou beene as hee was or one of his tribe,
Thou wouldst haue spar'd his life & tane a Bribe.
5 Hee who so long with gold & subtil wit,
Had iniurd strong law & almost conquerd it,
Hee who could lenthen causes and was able
To sterue a suiter at the counsel Table,
At lenth not hauing euidents to show,
10 Was faine (Good lord) to take's Death.   It was so.

xxxvi.

Mops gaue his fath to Anne and Helen, yet doth ow :
Quho sayes good Mopsus hath no fath he lies, for he
    hath tuo.

xxxvii.

Tom moneyless his agnus dei hath sold,
For he had rather vant his God then gold.

xxxviii.

To build a tombe Jhone doth him daylie paine ;
For suth he fears his father rise againe.

xxxix.

Ye veep as if your husbands death yow griuit ;
Ye onlie veep the old man so long liuit.

xl.

Hear lyeth Jean that some tyme vas a maid ;
But quhen that vas, it cannot vel be said.

xli.

Paule vent to Toune to saue him selfe from horning ;
Scarse vas he gone, vhen Kite him hornd that morning.

xlii.

On the poems of ——.

Thocht poets skil her vant, thinke it no crime,
For he knows nocht of poesie but rime.

xliii.

Zoilus eies in glasse did see them selues looke euen :
That each of them micht gree, then both did pray to
heauen.

xliv.

A foolish change made vretchet Chremes dead :
His hairs gat gold, and they left him but lead.

xlv.

Jeane cal not your husband hart vhen ye him kis :
The harts doo losse ther hornes, but he keeps euer his.

xlvi.

Thocht louers lie borne by the streame of yuth,
Yet vhen thay say ther dames no mortal creatures
Can be, but something els, sure they say truth :
Vomen adord in feinds do change ther natures.

xlvii.

Into the sea al cornards Thomas vist,
But his faire vyff to suyme bad him learne first.

xlviii.

Chremes did hing him selff vpon a tree
Because the price of Ceres fruits did alter ;
His seruant ran and cut the rope, but he,
Com'd to him selff, socht monnoye for the halter.

xlix.

Be reasons good Jhon him a christian proueth :
H'il drinke strong vine, & flesh of suine vel loueth.

l.

Vhy byeth old Chremes land so near his death ?
Like loueth like : he halfe earth liketh earth.

li.

Charles the IX of France.

Vhy vomets Charles so much blood from his brest ?
The bloud he dranke he culd not vel dygest.

lii.

Out of Passerat.

Vho cuckhold is & tries it not,
A honest man he is God vot ;
Vho vell it sees yet vil not see,
A vise subtile man is hee ;
5 Vho searcheth if his head be hornd,
At best is vorthie to be scornd.

liii.

Samarias Motheres when to Death they steru'd
Did make a couenant their sonnes to eate ;
The first (poor foole) aduanced hers for meate,
The other, pitifull, hid and preseru'd :
5 Comparisones are odious, therefore I
To Britannes kingdome will not this applye.

liv.

Two Bittes of Noses may make on tall nose.
Philip on Nose-bit had, Leslea another ;
Leslea a goodlye piece to make of those
Determinates to ioyne the two together ;
5 But when Philps nose should but haue been his pray,
He tooke his head : lords was not that foule playe ?

lv.

Epitaph.

Truth hatred breedes.
Who lyes beneath this stone
Thou shalt not know,
Yet know hee's not alone :
5 About him staye some findes for his euill deedes.
Let him who reedes
In haste this place foregoe.

lvi.

Discontented Phillis.

Blacke are my thoughts as is my Husbands haire,
My fortune ill-proportiond like his face,
My Mind wantes joyes, his countenance all grace,
His wit is lead, Myne heauye is with care :
5 In things so great since so conforme wee be,
Who then can say but that wee well agree.

lvii.

Vindiciae against the Com̄ones for B. C.

Some are that thinke it no way can agree
A Bishop good good Minister can bee,
Nay, that no more be in one man these can
Than to be honest and a Puritan.
5 How farre they runne astray and strangelie erre,
This Man showes, Man good, Bishop, Minister.
Onlie one fault hee had, for he did proue
Too meeke for this world, too too much a doue.
Hence Harmelesse liu'd hee and exposd to wronges,
10 And now lyes murthered by injurious tongues.
Such which talke still of Relligion,
Yet hold it best in practike to haue none,
Who deeme men like to him to be great euills,
May God to preach to them raise vp some else.

lviii.

Heere lye the Bones of a gentle horse
Who liuing vsed to carrye the corse
Of an insolent preacher. O had the asse
Of Balaam him carryed, he had told what hee was !
5 Now courteous readeres tell so, if yee can,
Is the Epitaph of the horse or of the Man ?

Poems

of

Doubtful Authenticity.

Poems

of

Doubtful Authenticity.

I.

VIL: DRUMMONDS LINES ONE THE BISCHOPES: 14 APPRYLL 1638.

Doe all pens slumber still, darr not one tray
In tumbling lynes to lett some pasquill fly ?
Each houer a Satyre creuith to display
The secretts of this Tragick Comick play.
5 If Loue should let me vrett, I think you'd see
The Perenies and Alpes cum skipe to me,
And lauch them selues assunder ; If I'd trace
The hurly-burly of stait bussines,
And to the vorld abused once bot tell
10 The Legend of Ignatian Matchiuell,
That old bold smouking Monster, and the pryde
Of thesse vsurping prælats that darr ryde
Vpone Authority, and Looke so gay
As If (goodmen) they ought (forsuith) to suay
15 Church, stait, and all : plague one that damned crew
Of such Hells black-mouth'd houndes ; its of a New
That Roman pandars boldly dar'd to vo

I. From Manuscript 19.3.8, in the Advocates' Library, Edinburgh, in the handwriting of Sir James Balfour, Lyon King of Arms.
  9 MS. *reads* abſñed *after* vorld   16 MS. *reads* as (If goodmen)
17 MS. *reads* ov.   *Probably the right reading is* vo = wo = woo.

Nay, straine a gentle king thesse things to doo,
That Moue the French, Italian, & Spaine,
20 In a luxurious and insulting straine
To sing te Deum, causse they houpe to see
The Glorie of the popeisch prelacie
Raissed aboue his Royall throne apaice,
To Droune his miner Light vith prouder face.
25 Thesse hounds they haue ingaged him one the stage
Of Sharpe-eyed Europe, nay, ther's not a page
Bot thinks he may laugh freily quhen he sees
Kings Buffons acte, and Bischopes Tragedies.
Should aney dauly with the lyons paw,
30 Then knou a distance, Se[r]pents stand in aw.
Naye, pray you Heauens, once lend me bot your thunder,
Ile crusch and teare thesse sordid slaues assunder,
And leuell with the dust ther Altars horne,
With the lascivious organs, pieties scorne ;
35 Or lett me be as king, then of their skine
Ile causse dresse lether and fyne Marikin,
To couer coatches (quher they wount to ryde)
And valk in bootes and shoes made of ther hyde,
Vhipe them at neighbour princes courts to show,
40 That No Nouations Scotts zeall can allow.
I sacrefisse vold such presumtious slaues
To my deir people, beat to dust the knaues,
Then of the pouder of ther bons to dray
The hare and pereuige to the popes lackay.
45 I noblie should resent and take to heart
Thesse pedants pryde that make poore Brittane smart,
Confound the church, the stait, and all the nation
With appish fooleries and abomination,
Leaues churches desolate, and stopes the mouth
50 Of faithfull vatchmen quho dare preach bot treuth ;
Incendiary fyrebrands, whosse proud wordes
Drope blood, and sounds the clattring Noysse of Suordis.
Had I bot halffe the spyte of Galloway Tom,

43 MS. Then if

That Roman snakie viper, I'd fall from
55 Discreitter lynes, and rube ther itching eare
With Spanish Nouells : bot I will forbeare.
Becausse my foster and my amorous quill
Is not yet hard, proud pasquills to distill,
I doe intreat that droll Johne de Koell
60 To sting them with satyres hatcht in hell ;
Each doge chyde thesse tabacco breathed deuyns,
Each pen dairt volums of acutest lynes,
And print the shame of that blacke troupe profaine
In liuid vords, with a Tartarian straine.
65 Since I a Louer am, and know not how
To lim a Satyre in halffe hyddeous hew,
Lyke to polypragmatick Macheuell,
In pleasant flame (not stryffe) I loue to duell.
    Bot nou to Paris back I goe to tell
70   Some neues to plotting Riceleu : fair you well.

II.

FOR THE KINGE.

Seinge.

From such a face quhois excellence
May captiuate my souerainges sense,
And make him, Phœbus lyk, his throne
Reseinge to some young Phaeton
5 Quhosse skilles and unluckey hand
May proue the Ruine of this Land,
Vnlesse Grate Ioue, doune from the skayes
Beholding our calamities,
Strick with his hand that can not er
10 The proud vsurping character,
And cur, tho' Phœbus er, our voe :
From such a Face as may work so,
    Quhersoeuer he has his being,
    Blis my souerainge & his seing.

II. From Manuscript 19.3.8, in the Advocates' Library, Edinburgh, in the handwriting of Sir James Balfour, Lyon King of Arms.
    In O, the title is " The Five Senses."
    5 O. unstayed Hand [MS. *reads* unstuckey]   6 O. of the Land
7 O. from the Sky 8 O. Beholding Earth's Calamity 10 O. usurping
Charioter 11 O. (tho' *Phœbus* grieve) our Wo 12 O. as can work so
13 O. thou hast a Being

Heiringe.

15 From Jests profaine and flatring toungues,
From Baudie tailles, from beastly songes,
From after-supper suites that feir
A parliament & byes it deir ;
From Spanisch tretties that may wound
20 Our countries peace, our Gospell sound ;
From Ioues fals freinds that wald intyss
My souerainge from heauens paradize ;
From profeitts such as Achabes wer,
Quhosse flattring smouthes my souerainges eare,
25   With fanceis more nor hes maker feiring ;
Bliss My soueraing & his heiring.

Taistinge.

From all fruittes that are forbiddin,
Such for wich old Eue was chiddin ;
From Bread of Labowrers, Suyet & toyle,
30 From the poore widowes mythe & oyle ;
From the canditis poysoned baittes
Of Jesuitts and the desaittes,
Italian sallets, & Romisse d[r]ogis,
The milk of Babells proud houris duggis ;
35 From Blood of Innocents oftin vrongit
From thair estaits thats from them throngit ;
From Wyne that may disturbe the braine,
And from the dangerous figges of Spaine ;
  At all banquetts & al feasting,
40   Bliss my soueraing and his taisting.

[16] O. Tales and beastly Songs   [18] O. A Parliament or Council's Ear
[20] O. the Gospel's Sound   [21] O. From Job's   [24] O. Whose Flatterings
sooth   [25] O. His Frowns more than his Maker's fearing   [27] O. From
all Fruit that is forbidden   [29] O. Labours   [30] O. Meal and Oyl   [31] O.
From Blood of Innocents oft wrangled   [32] O. From their Estates, and
from that's strangled   [33] O. From the candid poyson'd Baits   [34] O.
Of *Jesuites* and their Deceits   [MS. *repeats* of *after* milk]   [35] O.
Italian Sallads, Romish Drugs   [36] O. The Milk of *Babel's* proud Whore's
Dugs   [37] O. that can destroy

Smellinge.

Quher Myrre and Incence are often throwen
One Altars built to gods unknowen,
O lett my soueraing neuer smell
Such damd perfumes ; thy'r fitt for hell.
45 Lett no such sent his nossethirles staine,
From smells that poyson may the braine,
Heauens still preserue him.   Nixt I craue
Thow will be pleassed, Grate God, to saue
My soueraing from a Ganemed
50 Quhosse hoourische breath hath pouer to lead
His Maiestie such way he list ;
O neuer lett such lippes be kist ;
From any breath so far excelling
Bliss my soueraing & his smelling.

Feillinge.

55 From prick of Conscience, such a stinge
As kills the soule, Heauens blisse my king ;
From such a brybe as may withdraw
His thoughts from Equitie and Law ;
From such a smouth and bardles chine
60 As may prouocke or tempt to sin ;
From such a hand quhosse palme may
My soueraing leid out from the way ;
From things pollutit and wncleine,
From all thats beastly and obschene ;
65 From quhat may set his soule one reilling,
Bliss my soueraing & his feillinge.

In O, the lines entitled " Feeling " precede those entitled " Smelling."
[41] O. Where Myrrh and Frankincense is thrown   [42] O. The Altar's
built   [43] O. never dwell   [44] O. Perfumes are fit   [46] O. poyson can
[48] O. Thou wilt   [51] O. His Excellence which Way it list   [52] O. O let such
Lips be never kist   [53] O. From a Breath   [56] O. As stays the Soul   [58] O.
Equity or Law   [61] O. whose moist Palm may   [62] O. lead out of the
Way.   [64] O. From all Things beastly   [65] O. From that may set his
Soul a reeling.

Epiloge.

And nou, grate God, I humbley pray
That thow may take the selue away,
That keipis my soueraings Eiyes from woing
70 The thing that may be his vndooing.
And lett him heir, good God, the soundis
As weill of men as of hes houndis.
Giue him a taist, and truly too
Of quhat hes subiects undergo.
75 Giue him all feilling of ther wois,
Then sune no doubt his royall noisse
Will quickly smell thesse Rascalls furthe,
Quhosse blacke deids haue ecclipsit his worth ;
Then found syne scurgit for ther offences,
80 Heauens blisse my soueraign and his senses.

In O, the title is not " Epiloge," but " The Abstract," and there are
the sub-titles " Seeing," " Hearing " (over ll. 71-2), " Taste " (over ll.
73-4), " Feeling & Smelling."
67 O. just God   68 O. That thou wilt take the Slime away   69 O.
from seeing   70 O. The Things that will be our Undoing   71 O. then
let him   75 O. Give him a   76 O. And then no doubt   79 O. They
found and scourg'd

III.

HYMNS.

———

i.

Hymn.

Him whom the Earth, the Sea, and Sky
Worship, adore, and magnify,
And doth this threefold Engine steer,
Mary's pure Closet now doth bear.

5 Whom Sun and Moon, and Creatures all,
Serving at Times, obey his Call ;
Pouring from Heaven his Sacred Grace,
I' th' Virgin's Bowels hath ta'ne Place.

Mother most blest by such a Dower,
10 Whose Maker, Lord of highest Power,
Who this wide World in Hand contains,
In thy Womb's Ark himselfe restrains.

Blest by a Message from Heaven brought,
Fertile with Holy Ghost full fraught ;
15 Of Nations the desired King,
Within thy Sacred Womb doth spring.

Lord, may Thy Glory still endure,
Who born wast of a Virgin pure ;
The Father's and the Sp'rit's of Love,
20 Which endless Worlds may not remove.

III. Reprinted from the folio edition of Drummond's *Works* (1711).

ii.

An Evening Hymn.

Maker of all, we Thee intreat,
Before the joyful Light descend,
That Thou with wonted Mercy great
Us as our Keeper would'st defend.

5 Let idle Dreams be far away,
And vain Illusions of the Night ;
Repress our Foe, least that he may
Our Bodies to foul Lust incite.

Let this, O Father, granted be,
10 Through our dear Saviour's boundless Merit,
Who doth for ever Live with Thee,
Together with the holy Spirit.

iii.

Complaint of the Blessed Virgin.

The Mother stood with Grief confounded,
Near the Cross ; her Tears abounded
   While her dear Son hanged was,
Through whose Soul, her Sighs forth venting,
5 Sadly mourning and lamenting,
   Sharpest Points of Swords did pass.
O how sad and how distress'd,
Was the Mother ever-bless'd,
   Who God's only Son forth-brought :
10 She in Grief and Woes did languish,
Quaking to behold what Anguish
   To her noble Son was wrought.

iv.

Hymn upon the Nativity.

Christ, whose Redemption all doth free,
Son of the Father, who alone
Before the World began to be,
Didst spring from Him by Means unknown;

5 Thou his clear Brightness, thou his Light,
Thou everlasting Hope of all,
Observe the Prayers which in Thy Sight
Thy Servants through the World let fall.

O dearest Saviour, bear in Mind
10 That of our Body Thou a Child
Didst whilom take the natural Kind,
Born of the Virgin undefil'd.

This much the present Day makes known,
Passing the Circuit of the Year,
15 That thou from thy high Father's Throne
The World's sole Safety didst appear.

The highest Heaven, the Earth, and Seas,
And all that is within them found,
Because he sent Thee us to ease,
20 With mirthful Songs his Praise resound.

We also who redeemed are
With Thy pure Blood from sinful State,
For this thy Birth-Day will prepare
New Hymns this Feast to celebrate.

25 Glory, O Lord, be given to Thee
Whom the unspotted Virgin bore,
And Glory to Thee, Father, be,
And th' holy Ghost for ever more.

v.

Hymn upon the Innocents.

Hail, you sweet Babes, that are the Flowers,
Whom (when you Life begin to taste,)
The Enemy of Christ devours,
As Whirlwinds down the Roses cast.

5 First Sacrifice to Christ you went,
Of offer'd Lambs a tender Sort ;
With Palms and Crowns you Innocent
Before the sacred Altar sport.

vi.

Dedication of a Church.

Jerusalem, that place Divine,
The Vision of sweet Peace is nam'd,
In Heaven her glorious Turrets shine,
Her Walls of living Stones are fram'd,
5   While Angels guard her on each Side,
Fit Company for such a Bride.
She deckt in new Attire from Heaven,
Her Wedding-Chamber now descends,
Prepar'd in Marriage to be given
10 To Christ, on whom her Joy depends.
   Her Walls wherewith she is inclos'd,
   And Streets are of pure Gold compos'd.
The Gates adorn'd with Pearls most bright
The Way to hidden Glory show ;
15 And thither by the blessed Might
Of Faith in Jesus's Merits go
   All these who are on Earth distrest,
   Because they have Christ's Name profest.
These Stones the Work-men dress and beat,
20 Before they throughly Polisht are,
Then each is in his proper Seat
Establisht by the Builder's Care,
   In this fair Frame to stand for ever,
   So joyn'd that them no Force can sever.
25 To God, who sits in highest Seat,
Glory and Power given be,
To *Father, Son,* and *Paraclete,*
Who reign in equal Dignity ;
   Whose boundless Power we still adore,
30   And sing their Praise for ever-more.

vii.

Hymn.

Jesv, our Prayers with Mildness hear,
Who art the Crown which Virgins decks,
Whom a pure Maid did breed and bear,
The sole Example of her Sex.

5 Thou feeding there where Lillies spring,
While round about the Virgins dance,
Thy Spouse dost to Glory bring,
And them with high Rewards advance.

The Virgins follow in thy Ways
10 Whithersoever thou dost go,
They trace thy Steps with Songs of Praise,
And in sweet Hymns thy Glory show.

Cause thy protecting Grace, we pray,
In all our Senses to abound,
15 Keeping from them all harms which may
Our Souls with foul Corruption wound.

Praise, Honour, Strength, and Glory great
To *God*, the *Father*, and the *Son*,
And to the *holy Paraclete*,
20 While Time lasts, and when Time is done.

viii.

Hymn.

Benign Creator of the Stars,
Eternal Light of faithful Eyes,
Christ, whose Redemption none debars,
Do not our humble Prayers despise :

5 Who for the state of Mankind griev'd,
That it by Death destroy'd should be,
Hast the diseased World reliev'd,
And given the Guilty Remedy.

When th' Evening of the World drew near,
10 Thou as a Bridegroom deign'st to come
Out of thy Wedding-Chamber dear,
Thy Virgin Mother's purest Womb.

To the strong Force of whose high Reign
All Knees are bow'd with Gesture low,
15 Creatures which Heaven or Earth contain,
With Rev'rence their Subjection show.

O holy Lord, we thee desire,
Whom we expect to judge all Faults,
Preserve us, as the Times require,
20 From our deceitful Foes Assaults.

Praise, Honour, Strength, and Glory great
To God, the Father, and the Son,
And to the holy Paraclete,
Whilst Time lasts, and when Time is done.

ix.

Hymn for Sunday.

O blest Creator of the Light,
Who bringing forth the Light of Days
With the first Work of Splendor bright,
The World didst to Beginning raise ;

5 Who Morn with Evening joyn'd in one,
Commandedst should be call'd the Day ;
The foul Confusion now is gone,
O hear us when with Tears we Pray ;

Lest that the Mind with Fears full fraught,
10 Should lose best Life's Eternal Gains,
While it hath no Immortal Thought,
But is inwrapt in sinful Chains.

O may it beat the inmost Sky,
And the Reward of Life possess ;
15 May we from hurtful Actions fly,
And purge away all Wickedness.

Dear Father, grant what we intreat,
And only Son who like Power hast,
Together with the *Paraclete,*
20 Reigning whilst Times and Ages last.

X.

Hymn for Monday.

Great Maker of the Heavens wide,
Who, least Things mixt should all confound,
The Floods and Waters didst divide,
And didst appoint the Heavens their bound ;

5 Ordering where heavenly Things shall stay,
Where Streams shall run on earthly Soyl,
That Waters may the Flames allay,
Least they the Globe of Earth should spoil ;

Sweet Lord, into our Minds infuse
10 The Gift of everlasting Grace,
That no old Faults which we did use
May with new Frauds our Souls deface.

May our true Faith obtain the Light,
And such clear Beams our Hearts possess
15 That it vain Things may banish quite,
And that no Falshood it oppress.

Dear Father, grant what we intreat, *etc.*

xi.

Hymn for Tuesday.

Great Maker of Man's earthly Realm,
Who didst the Ground from Waters take,
Which did the troubled Land o'rewhelm,
And it unmoveable didst make,

5 That there young Plants might fitly spring,
While it with golden Flowers attir'd
Might forth ripe Fruit in Plenty bring,
And yield sweet Fruit by all desir'd;

With fragrant Greenness of thy Grace,
10 Our blasted Souls of Wounds release,
That tears foul Sins away may chase,
And in the Mind bad Motions cease:

May it obey thy heavenly Voice,
And never drawing near to Ill,
15 T' abound in Goodness may rejoyce,
And may no mortal sin fulfil.

Dear Father, *etc.*

xii.

Hymn for Wednesday.

O holy God of heavenly Frame,
Who mak'st the Pole's high Center bright,
And paint'st the same with shining Flames,
Adorning it with beauteous Light ;

5 Who framing on the fourth of Days
The fiery Chariot of the Sun,
Appoint'st the Moon her changing Rays,
And Orbs in which the Planets run,

That Thou might'st by a certain bound,
10 'Twixt Night and Day Division make,
And that some sure Sign might be found
To shew when Months Beginning take ;

Men's Hearts with lightsome Splendor bless,
Wipe from their minds polluting spots,
15 Dissolve the Bond of Guiltiness,
Throw down the Heaps of sinful Blots.

Dear Father, *etc.*

xiii.

Hymn for Thursday.

O God, whose Forces far extend,
Who Creatures which from Waters spring
Back to the Flood dost partly send,
And up to th' Air dost partly bring ;

5 Some in the Waters deeply div'd,
Some playing in the Heavens above,
That Natures from one Stock deriv'd
May thus to several Dwellings move ;

Upon thy Servants Grace bestow,
10 Whose Souls thy bloody Waters clear,
That they no sinful Falls may know,
Nor heavy Grief of Death may bear ;

That Sin no Soul opprest may thrall,
That none be lifted high with Pride,
15 That Minds cast downward do not fall,
Nor raised up may backward slide.

Dear Father, *etc.*

xiv.

Hymn for Friday.

God, from whose Work Mankind did spring,
Who all in Rule dost only keep,
Bidding the dry Land forth to bring
All kind of Beasts which on it creep ;

5 Who hast made subject to Man's Hand
Great Bodies of each mighty Thing,
That taking Life from thy Command,
They might in Order serve their King ;

From us thy Servants (Lord) expel
10 Those Errors which Uncleanness breeds,
Which either in our Manners dwell,
Or mix themselves among our Deeds.

Give the Rewards of joyful Life,
The plenteous Gifts of Grace encrease,
15 Dissolve the cruel Bonds of Strife,
Knit fast the happy League of Peace.

Dear Father, *etc.*

XV.

Hymn for Saturday.

O Trinity, O blessed Light,
O Unity, most principal!
The fiery Sun now leaves our Sight,
Cause in our Hearts thy Beams to fall.

5 Let us with Songs of Praise divine,
At Morn and Evening Thee implore,
And let our Glory bow'd to Thine,
Thee glorify for ever-more.

To God the Father Glory great,
10 *And Glory to his only Son,*
And to the holy Paraclete,
Both now and still while Ages run.

xvi.

Upon the Sundays in Lent.

Hymn.

O merciful Creator, hear
Our Prayers to Thee devoutly bent,
Which we pour forth with many a Tear
In this most holy Fast of *Lent*.

5 Thou mildest Searcher of each Heart,
Who know'st the weakness of our Strength,
To us forgiving Grace impart,
Since we return to Thee at length.

Much have we sinned to our Shame,
10 But spare us who our Sins confess;
And for the Glory of thy Name,
To our sick Souls afford Redress.

Grant that the Flesh may be so pin'd
By Means of outward Abstinence,
15 As that the sober watchful Mind
May fast from Spots of all Offence.

Grant this, O blessed Trinity,
Pure Unity, to this incline,
That the Effects of Fasts may be
20 A grateful Recompence for Thine.

xvii.

On the Ascension Day.

O *Jesu*, who our Souls dost save,
On whom our Love and Hopes depend,
God, from whom all Things Being have,
Man, when the World drew to an end ;

5 What Clemency Thee vanquisht so,
Upon Thee our foul Crimes to take,
And cruel Death to undergo,
That Thou from Death us free might make ?

Let thine own Goodness to Thee bend,
10 That thou our Sins may'st put to Flight ;
Spare us, and as our Wishes tend,
O satisfy us with Thy Sight.

May'st Thou our joyful Pleasures be,
Who shall be our expected Gain,
15 And let our Glory be in Thee,
While any Ages shall remain.

xviii.

Hymn for Whitsunday.

Creator, Holy Ghost, descend,
Visit our Minds with thy bright Flame,
And thy celestial Grace extend,
To fill the Hearts which Thou didst frame :

5 Who *Paraclete* art said to be,
Gift which the highest God bestows,
Fountain of Life, Fire, Charity,
Oyntment whence Ghostly Blessing flows.

Thy seven-fold Grace Thou down dost send,
10 Of God's right Hand Thou finger art,
Thou by the Father promised
Unto our Mouths dost Speech impart.

In our dull Senses kindle Light ;
Infuse thy Love into our Hearts,
15 Reforming with perpetual Light
Th' Infirmities of fleshly Parts.

Far from our Dwelling drive our Foe,
And quickly Peace unto us bring ;
Be thou our Guide, before to go,
20 That we may shun each hurtful Thing.

Be pleased to instruct our Mind,
To know the Father and the Son,
The Spirit who them both dost bind,
Let us believe while Ages run.

25 To God the Father Glory great,
And to the Son who from the dead
Arose, and to the *Paraclete*,
Beyond all Time imagined.

xix.

On the Transfiguration of our Lord, the Sixth of August ; A Hymn.

All you that seek Christ, let your Sight
Up to the Height directed be,
For there you may the Sign most bright
Of everlasting Glory see.

5 A radiant Light we there behold,
Endless, unbounded, lofty, high ;
Than Heaven or that rude Heap moie old,
Wherein the World confus'd did lye.

The Gentiles this great Prince embrace ;
10 The Jews obey this King's Command,
Promis'd to *Abraham* and his race
A Blessing while the World shall stand.

By Mouths of Prophets free from Lyes,
Who seal the Witness which they bear,
15 His Father bidding testifies
That we should Him believe and hear.

Glory, O Lord, be given to Thee,
Who hast appear'd upon this Day ;
And glory to the Father be,
20 And to the Holy Ghost for ay.

XX.

On the Feast of St. Michael the Arch-Angel.

To Thee, O Christ, Thy Father's Light,
Life, Vertue, which our Heart inspires,
In Presence of thine Angels bright,
We sing with Voice and with Desires :
5 Our selves we mutually invite
To Melody with answering Quires.
With Reverence we these Souldiers praise,
Who near the heavenly Throne abide,
And chiefly him whom God doth raise
10 His strong Celestial Host to guide,
Michael, who by his Power dismays,
And beateth down the Devils pride.

Breviuſcula, & *Compendiuſcula,* **Tellatio;**
D E
Storia memorabili Fechtæ mervelabilis
Quæ fuit
Inter *Muckreillios,* & *Horsboyos,* atque *Ladaos,* &c.
In hoc Libellulo, cujus Inſcriptio Famoſa hæc eſt,

POLEMO-MEDINIA
I N T E R
Vitarvam & Nebernam,

Placidè & Jocosê tractatur.

EDINBURGI,
Re-printat 1684.

II

PLATE 12.—FACSIMILE OF TITLE-PAGE.

Page 310

IV.

POLEMO-MIDDINIA

INTER

VITARVAM

ET

NEBERNAM.

NYmphæ quæ colitis highissima monta *Fifæa*,
Seu vos *Pittenwema* tenent seu *Crelia* crofta,
Sive *Anstræa* domus, ubi nat haddocus in undis,
Codlineusque ingens, & fleucca & sketta pererrant
5 Per costam, et scopulis lobster mony-footus in udis
Creepat, & in mediis ludit whitenius undis ;
Et vos skipperii, soliti qui per mare breddum
Valde procul lanchare foris, iterumque redire,
Linquite scellatas bottas shippasque picatas,
10 Whistlantesque simul fechtam memorate bloodæam,
Fechtam terribilem, quam marvellaverit omnis
Banda Deum, & Nympharum Cockelshelleatarum,
Maia ubi sheepifeda atque ubi solgoosifera *Bassa*
Suellant in pelago, cum Sol boottatus *Edenum*
15 Postabat radiis madidis & shouribus atris.
Quo viso, ad fechtæ noisam cecidere volucres,

IV. Reprinted from the edition of 1684, collated with the edition
of 1691, and with an earlier undated edition.
5 Q. in undis 7 QR. solitis qui 8 RS. foras 11 S. marvellaverat
12 QS. Cockelshelearum 13 QS *omit* ubi *before* Solgoossifera

Ad terram cecidere grues, plish plashque dedere
Sol-goosi in pelago prope littora *Bruntiliana* ;
Sea-sutor obstupuit, summique in margine saxi
20 Scartavit prælustre caput, wingasque flapavit ;
Quodque magis, alte volitans heronius ipse
Ingeminans clig clag shyttavit in undis.
Namque in principio (storiam tellabimus omnem)
Muckrellium ingentem turbam *Vitarva* per agros
25 *Nebernæ* marchare fecit, & dixit ad illos :
Ite hodie armati greppis, dryvate caballos
Crofta per & agros *Nebernæ*, transque fenestras :
Quod si forte ipsa *Neberna* venerit extra,
Warrantabo omnes, & vos bene defendebo.
30 Hic aderant *Geordie Akinhedius*, & little *Johnus*,
Et *Jamie Richæus*, & stout *Michæl Hendersonus*,
Qui jolly tryppas ante alios dansare solebat,
Et bobbare bene, & lassas kissare bonæas ;
Duncan Oliphantus valde stalvartus, & ejus
35 Filius eldestus joly boyus, atque *Oldmoudus*,
Qui pleugham longo gaddo dryvare solebat,
Et *Rob Gib* wantonus homo, atque *Oliver Hutchin*,
Et plouky-fac'd *Wattie Strang*, atq; inkne'd *Alshinder Atkin*,
Et *Willie Dick* heavi-arstus homo, pigerrimus omnium,
40 Valde lethus pugnare, sed hunc Corn-greivus heros
Nout-headdum vocavit, & illum forcit ad arma.
In super hic aderant *Tom Tailor* & *Tom Nicolsonus*,
Et *Tamie Gilchristus*, & fool *Jockie Robinsonus*,
Andrew Alshinderus, & *Jamie Thomsonus*, & alter
45 (Heu pudet, ignoro nomen) slaveri-beardus homo,

[17] QR. Ad noisam cecidere [18] QS. Sol-goosæ [19] S. Seasurer [21] S. altre volitans [23] S. à principio [27] QS. Nebernæ per crofta, atque ipsas ante fenestras [30] QR. & *Rob Nicolsonus* [32] Q. Qui Jolly tryppans ante alias dansare solebat S. Qui gillatis pulchris ante alias dansare solebat R. ante alias [35] QR. Jelly-boyus [39] *After this verse* S *inserts the following :* Qui tulit in pileo magnum rubrumque favorem [42] S. *Tom Taylor*, & *Hen Watsonus* 44 S. & *Jamy Tomsonus*, & unus. *After this verse* S *inserts the following verses :* Norland-bornus homo valde Anticovenanter, | Nomine *Gordonus*, valde blackmoudus, & alter

Qui pottas dightabat, & assam jecerat extra.
Denique præ reliquis *Geordium* affatur, & inquit,
Geordie, mi formanne, inter stoutissimus omnes,
Huc ades, & crooksaddeliis, heghemisque, creilisque,
50 Brechimmisque simul cunctos armato jumentos ;
Amblentemque meam naiggam, fattumque magistri
Curserem, & reliquos trottantes simul averos,
In cartis yockato omnes, extrahito muckam
Crofta per & agros *Nebernæ* transque fenestras,
55 Quod si forte ipsa *Neberna* contra loquatur,
In sidis tu pone manus, et dicito, *fart, jade.*
Nec mora, formannus cunctos flankavit averos,
Workmannosque ad workam omnes vocavit, & illi
Extemplo cartas bene fillavere gigantes :
60 Whistlavere viri, workhorsosque ordine swieros
Drivavere omnes, donec iterumque iterumque
Fartavere omnes, & sic turba horrida mustrat,
Haud aliter quam si cum multis *Spinola* trouppis
Proudus ad *Ostendam* marchasset fortiter urbem.
65 Interea ipse ante alios piperlaius heros
Præcedens, magnam gestans cum burdine pyppam,
Incipit *Harlæi* cunctis sonare Batellum.
Tunc *Neberna* furens, foras ipsa egressa vidensque
Muck-creilleos transire viam, valde angria facta,
70 Haud tulit affrontam tantam, verum, agmine facto
Convocat extemplo horsboyos atque ladæos,
Jackmannum, hyremannos, pleughdryv'sters atq; pleugh-
        mannos,
Tumblentesque simul ricoso ex kitchine boyos,
Hunc qui gruelias scivit bene lickere plettas,

---

[46] QS. dightavit S. assas [47] Q. Denique pro reliquis [49] S. Huc ades
& crooksadelos, hemmesque, crelesque [50] S. Brechemmesque simul
omnes bindato jumentis [52] S. sumito averos [54] S. Crofta per &
riggas, atque ipsas ante fenestras [55] S. *Nebernæ*, & aliquid sin ipsa
contra loquatur [58] S. omnes vocavit [60] QR. workhorsque [61] S.
Drivavere foras [64] QR. merchasse [65] S. Interea ante alios Dux
piperlarius heros [68] S. furens, yettam ipsa egressa vidensque [69] S.
Muck-cartas [74] R. lingere QS. Hunc qui dirtiferas tersit cum
dishclouty dishas

75 Hunc qui dirtiferas tersit cum dishcloute dishas ;
Et saltpannifumos, & widebricatos fisheros,
Hellæosque etiam salteros eduxit ab antris
Coalheughos nigri grinnantes more divelli ;
Life-guardamque sibi sævas vocat improba lassas
80 *Magæam* magis doctam milkare cowæas,
Et doctam sweeppare fleuras, & sternere beddas,
Quæque novit spinare, & longas ducere threedas ;
Nansæam claves bene quæ keepaverat omnes,
Yellantemque *Elpen*, & longo bardo *Anapellam*,
85 Fartantemque simul *Gyllam*, gliedamque *Ketæam*
Egregie indutam blacco caput suttie clutto,
*Mammæam*que etiam vetulam, quæ sciverat aptè
Infantum teneras blande oscularier arsas,
Quæque lanam cardare solet olifingria *Beattie*.
90 Tum vero hungræos ventres *Neberna* gruelis
Farsit, & guttas rasuinibus implet amaris,
Postea newbarmæ ingentem dedit omnibus haustum :
Staggravere omnes, grandesque ad sidera riftos
Barmifumi attollunt, & sic ad prælia marchant.
95 Nec mora, marchavit foras longo ordine turma,
Ipsa prior *Neberna* suis stout facta ribauldis,
Roustæam manibus gestans furibunda goulæam,
Tandem muckcreilios vocat ad pellmellia fleidos.
Ite, ait, uglei felloēs, si quis modo posthac
100 Muckifer has nostras tentet crossare fenestras,
Juro ego quod ejus longum extrahabo thrapellum,
Et totam rivabo faciem, luggasque gulæo hoc
Ex capite cuttabo ferox, totumque videbo
Heart-blooddum fluere in terram. Sic verba finivit.
105 Obstupuit *Vitarva* diu dirtfleyda, sed inde
Couragium accipiens, muckcreilleos ordine cunctos
Middini in medio faciem turnare coegit.

[75] QS. Hunc qui gruelias scivit bene lickere plettas   [76] QR. & wide-
bricate fishartos   [77] R. satyros   [78] QR. Coalheugheis   S. girnantes
[84] S. lango-berdamque *Anapellam*   [87] S. simul vetulam   [89] S. greasy-
fingria   [92] QR *omit this verse.*   [93] S. riftas   [95] R. turmis   [98] QR.
Tantem   [100] Q. tentent   [101] Juro quod ego   [102] R. Et ejus scartabo
faciem   [104] QR. & sic

O qualem primo fleuram gustasses in ipso
Batalli onsetto ! pugnat muckcreillius heros
110 Fortiter, & muckam per posteriora cadentem
In creillis shoollare ardet : sic dirta volavit.
O qualis feire fairie fuit, si forte vidisses
Pypantes arsas, & flavo sanguine breickas
Dripantes, hominumque heartas ad prælia fantas !
115 O qualis hurlie burlie fuit ! namque alteri nemo
Ne vel foot-breddum yerdæ yeeldare volebat :
Stout erant ambo quidem, valdeque hard-hearta caterva.
Tum vero è medio mukdryv'ster prosilit unus,
Gallantæus homo, & greppam minatur in ipsam
120 Nebernam, quoniam misere scaldaverat omnes,
Dirtavitque totam petticottam gutture thicko,
Perlineasque ejus skirtas, silkamque gownæam,
Vasquineamque rubram mucksherdo begariavit.
Sed tamen ille fuit valde faint-heartus, & ivit
125 Valde procul, metuens shottum woundumque pro-
fundum ;
At non valde procul fuerat revengda, sed illum
Extemplo Gyllæa ferox invasit, & ejus
In faciem girnavit atrox, & tigrida facta,
Bublentem grippans bardum, sic dixit ad illum :
130 Vade domum, filthæe nequam, aut te interficiabo.
Tum cum gerculeo magnum fecit Gilliwyppum,
Ingentemque manu sherdam levavit, & omnem
Gallenteÿ hominis gash-beardum besmiriavit.
Sume tibi hoc (inquit) sneezing valde operativum
135 Pro præmio, swingere, tuo. Tum denique fleido
Ingentem Gilliwamphra dedit, validamque nevellam,
Ingeminatque iterum, donec bis fecerit ignem
Ambobus fugere ex oculis : sic Gylla triumphat.
Obstupuit bumbasedus homo, backumque repente

111 S. In crelibus 112 QS. O quale hoc hurly burly fuit 115 QS. O
qualis fery faire fuit 122 R. ejus strippas 123 S. mucksherda 124 S. Et
tunc 125 S. shottam 126 S. Sed nec valde procul fuerat revengia in
illum 127 S. invadit 129 S. berdam 131 S. Tunc 133 S. gashbeardam
136 Q. ravellam

140 Turnavit veluti nasus bloodasset, & *O fy!*
Ter quater exclamat, & O quam sæpe nizavit!
Disjuniumque omnem evomuit valde hungrius homo
Lausavitque supra & infra, miserabile visu,
Et luggas necko imponens, sic cucurrit absens,
145 Non audens gimpare iterum, ne worsa tulisset.
Hæc *Vitarva* videns, yellavit turpia verba,
Et *fy, fy!* exclamat, prope nunc victoria losta est.
Elatisque hippis magno cum murmure fartum
Barytonum emisit, veluti *Monsmegga* cracasset:
150 Tum vero quaccare hostes, flightamque repente
Sumpserunt, retrospexit *Jackmannus,* & ipse
Sheepheadus metuit sonitumque ictumque buleti.
Quod si King Spanius, *Philippus* nomine, septem
Consimiles hisce habuisset forte canones
155 Batterare *Sluissam, Sluissam* dingasset in assam;
Aut si tot magnus *Ludovicus* forte dedisset
Ingentes fartas ad mœnia *Montalbana,*
Ipsam continuo tounam dingasset in yerdam.
Exit Corngreivus, wracco omnia tendere videns,
160 Consiliumque meum si non accipitis, inquit,
Formosas scartabo facies, & vos wirriabo.
Sed needlo per seustram broddatus, inque privatas
Partes stobbatus, greittans, lookansque grivatè,
Barlafumle clamat, & dixit, *O Deus, O God!*
165 Quid multis? Sic fraya fuit, sic guisa peracta est,
Una nec interea spillata est droppa cruoris.

---

[140] QR. turpavit S. & *O God* [142] S. Desjuniumque omne [143] S. mirabile visu [146] S. Hæc *Neberna* videns QR. Tunc Vitarva videns [147] S *inserts here the following verse:* Nec mora, terribilem fillavit dira Canonem [148] S. fartam [149] Barytonam [150] S. quackarunt [151] QR. Sumere Jackmannum tremens respexit, & illum [152] QR. Sheipheaddum metuens [154] S. Hisce consimiles [155] QR. Batterasse [156] QR. Aut si septem tales *Ludovicus* forte dedidet [161] S. Pulchras scartabo facies [165] QR. Quid multos?

V.

TO THE READER.

No cankring Envy, Malice, nor Despite
Stirr'd vp these men so eagerly to flyte,
But generous Emulation ; so in Playes
Best actors flyte and raile, and thousand wayes
5 Delight the itching Eare ; So wanton Curres
Walk'd with the gingling of a Courteours spurres,
Barke all the night, and never seeke to bite :
Such bravery these verses mov'd to write,
Would all that now doe flyte would flyte like those,
10 And Lawes were made that none durst flyte in prose ;
How calme were then the world ? perhaps this Law
Might make some madding wives to stand in aw,
And not in filthy Prose out-roare their men :
But read these Roundelayes to them till then.
15 Flyting no reason hath, and at this tyme
Heere it not stands by Reason, but by Ryme ;
Anger t'asswage, make Melancholy lesse,
This flyting first was wrote, now tholes the Presse.
  Who will not rest content with this Epistle,
20   Let him sit downe and flyt, or stand or whistle.

V. Reprinted from the second edition (the first is lost) of *The
| Flyting | Betwixt | Montgomery | And | Polwart. | Edinburgh, |
Printed by the Heires of Andro Hart, 1629.*

NOTES.

Y

NOTES.

FLOWRES OF SION.

Sonnet i, p. 5, l. 8. *Caul(e)* : " a spider's web " ; now obsolete. Derived apparently from O.F. *cale* (cf. Fr. *calotte*), a kind of " small cap," or headdress. In the sixteenth century the word is also used in the sense of " net," " network." Probably the development of meaning from " cap " to " web " is " cap," " open-work cap," " net," " web."

Sonnet iii, p. 7. This sonnet opens on the same note as one of Molza's (*Delle Rime Scelte di Diversi Avtori*, vol. i. p. 105, Venetia, 1586).

l. 12. *restes* : " remains." Cf. note to l. 5 of Sextain ii, vol. i. p. 199.

Sonnet iv, p. 7. The opening lines are suggested by Sonnet c of Petrarch's *Rime* :

> Non d' atra e tempestosa onda marina
> Fuggio in porto già mai stanco nocchiero,
> Com' io dal fosco e torbido pensiero
> Fuggo ove 'l gran desio mi sprona e 'nchina, etc.

Sonnet vi, p. 8. Translated from the following sonnet by Marino (*Rime*, 1602, pt. i. p. 178) :

> Se di questo volume ampio le carte,
> Che mondo ha nome, e 'n cui chiaro si legge
> Del' Autor, che 'l compose, e che 'l corregge
> L' alto sauer, la prouidentia, e l' arte,

331

Volgesse altri con studio : a parte a parte
La 'nfinita bontà, l' eterna legge
Impareria di lui, che tutto regge,
Quasi ascose dottrine in lor consparte.
Ma l' huom de' fregi suoi purpurei, e d' oro,
Qual semplice fanciul, che nulla intende,
S' arresta sol nel publico lauoro.
E de le note sue non ben comprende
Gli occulti sensi : e de' secreti loro
(Vaneggiante, ch' egli è) cura non prende.

Doubtless Drummond had also in mind the following lines
of Sonnet xi of *Astrophel and Stella* :

For like a child, that some fair book doth find,
With gilded leaves or coloured vellum plays ;
Or, at the most, on some fair picture stays :
But never heeds the fruit of writer's mind.

Compare likewise *Arcadia* (p. 112) :

So have I seen trim books in velvet dight,
With golden leaves, and painted babery
Of silly boys, please unacquainted sight.

Sonnet vii, p. 9. Lines 9-14 allude to the old belief
that the ancient oracles ceased with the birth of Christ.

Sonnet ix, p. 11. Translated from the following sonnet
by Marino (*Rime,* 1602, pt. i. p. 190) :

Felice notte, ond' a noi nasce il giorno,
Di cui mai più sereno altro non fue,
Che fra gli horrori, e sotto l' ombre tue
Copri quel Sol, ch' al' altro Sol fa scorno.
Felici uoi, che 'n pouero soggiorno,
Pigro asinello, e mansueto bue,
Al pargoletto Dio le membra sue
State a scaldar co' dolci fiati intorno.
Felici uoi, degnate a tanti honori,
Aride herbette, e rustica capanna,
Ch' aprir vedete a mezzo 'l Verno i fiori.
Così diceano a suon di rozza canna
Innanzi al gran bambin chini i pastori,
E sudò l' elce, e 'l pin nettare, e manna.

ll. 9 and 12. *spred* : *Reed* : an incorrect rhyme [ɛ̄ ? : ī],
according to the normal English pronunciation of the time.
Cf. *feed* : *Bed* (ii. p. 34, ll. 40 and 42).

Sonnet xii, p. 12. Suggested by one of Desportes'
" sonnets spirituels " (*Œuvres,* ed. Michiels, p. 508) :

De foy, d'espoir, d'amour et de douleur comblée,
  Celle que les pécheurs doivent tous imiter,
  O Seigneur ! vint ce jour à tes piés se jetter,
  Peu craignant le mespris de toute une assemblée.
Ses yeux, sources de feu, d'où l'Amour à l'emblée
  Souloit dedans les cœurs tant de traits blueter,
  Changez en source d'eau, ne font que dégouter
  L'amertume et l'ennuy de son âme troublée.
De ses pleurs, ô Seigneur ! tes piés elle arrosa,
  Les parfuma d'odeurs, les seicha, les baisa
  De sa nouvelle amour monstrant la véhémence.
O bien-heureuse femme ! ô Dieu tousjours clément !
  O pleur ! ô cœur heureux ! qui n'eut pas seulement
  Pardon de son erreur, mais en eut récompense.

Sonnet xiii, p. 13. Again translated from a sonnet by
Marino (*Rime,* pt. i. p. 200) :

Cangia contrada, e 'n procurar diletto
  Altronde, unqua non hebbi altro ch' affanno,
  Volgendo in signoria d' empio Tiranno
  I dolci imperi del paterno affetto.
Di ricche mense, e piume, e d' aureo tetto,
  D' accorti serui in uece (ahi duolo, ahi danno)
  Questi, ch' io guardo, hor compagnia mi fanno,
  È son' herbe il mio cibo, e sassi il letto.
Hor, che la dura fame, e 'l giogo io sento,
  Torno Padre e Signor : tua pietà grande
  Scusi le colpe, ond' io mi lagno, e pento.
Così la 'ue gran quercia i rami spande
  Pensaua il garzon folle : e 'l sozzo armento
  Vdia da presso ruminar le ghiande.

Sonnet xiv, p. 13. Luigi Groto, who was on
Drummond's shelves, has a sonnet on the same theme,
beginning, " Pelicano diuin, da' col tuo sangue," which
however has no resemblance in particulars with that of
Drummond.

I. An Hymne of the Passion, p. 14. A rendering of Sannazaro's Lamentation on the dead body of the world's Redeemer (*Opere*, Padova, 1723, p. 405):

> Se mai per meraviglia alzando il viso
>> Al chiaro ciel, pensasti, o cieca gente,
>> A quel vero Signor del Paradiso :
> E se vedendo il Sol dall' Oriente
>> Venir di rai vestito, e poi la notte
>> Tutta di lumi accesa, e tutta ardente :
> Se i fiumi uscir dalle profonde grotte,
>> Ed in sue leggi star ristretto il mare ;
>> Nè quelle udiste mai transgresse, o rotte ;
> Se ciò vi fu cagion di contemplare
>> Quei che 'n questa terrena immagin nostra
>> Nostro stato mortal volse esaltare :
> Volgete gli occhi in qua ; ch' or vi dimostra
>> Non quella forma, oimè, non quel colore
>> Che fingean forse i sensi in mente vostra.
> Piangete il grande esizial dolore ;
>> Piangete l' aspra morte, e 'l crudo affanno,
>> Se spirto di pietà vi punge il core.
> Per liberarvi dall' antiquo inganno
>> Pende, come vedete, al duro legno ;
>> E per salvarvi dal perpetuo danno.
> Inudita pietà, mirabil pegno ;
>> Donar la propria vita, offrir il sangue,
>> Per cui sol di vederla non fu degno !
> Vedete, egri mortali, il volto esangue,
>> Le chiome lacerate, e 'l capo basso,
>> Qual rosa che calcata in terra langue.
> Piangi, inferma Natura, piangi, lasso
>> Mondo, piangi, alto ciel, piangete, venti,
>> Piangi tu, cor, se non sei duro sasso :
> Queste man che composer gli elementi,
>> E fermar l' ampia terra in su gli abissi,
>> Volser per te soffrir tanti tormenti.
> Per te volser in croce esser affissi
>> Questi piè, che solean premer le stelle :
>> Per te 'l tuo Redentor dal ciel partissi, etc.

This is Drummond's sole attempt in the metre (*terza rima*) of the original.

l. 37. *trade* = " tread." This seems to be a spelling of *tread* meant to indicate the pronunciation of the period [træd]. Cf. vol. ii. xlix, li, p. 245.

l. 59. *ordures*: " filth," " dirt "; now archaic. Fr. *ordure*.

Sonnet xvi, p. 17. Compare this sonnet on the two rhyme-words *life* and *death* with the similar one in Du Bellay's *L'Olive* (*Œuvres poétiques*, ed. Chamard, i. p. 119):

> Dieu, qui changeant avec' obscure mort
> Ta bienheureuse & immortelle vie,
> Fus aux pecheurs prodigue de ta vie,
> Pour les tirer de l'eternelle mort :
> Celle pitié coupable de ta mort
> Guide les paz de ma facheuse vie,
> Tant que par toy à plus joyeuse vie
> Je soy' conduit du travail de la mort.
> N'avise point, ô Seigneur ! que ma vie
> Se soit noyée aux ondes de la mort,
> Qui me distrait d'une si doulce vie.
> Oste la palme à cet' injuste mort,
> Qui ja s'en va superbe de ma vie,
> Et morte soit tousjours pour moy la mort.

II. An Hymne of the Resurrection, p. 18, l. 32. *lackeyes* : this appears to be a spelling for the dissyllabic archaic form *lackĕs*, which Drummond uses to suit the exigencies of the metre.

ll. 37-38. *East : Nest* : the usual pronunciation of *east* was [ēst], but the pronunciation [ɛst] is also quoted by contemporary grammarians. Cf. *West : East* (ii. p. 59, ll. 317-318).

l. 59. *loosed* : the past tense in Scots of the verb to *lose*, of which the present in Scots is *losse* (cf. vol. ii. p. 46, l. 311).

l. 95. *wanning* : " turning wan," from *wan*, " to become pale."

l. 105. *ammell* : " enamel " ; O.F. *amal, *amail, *esmail* ; Fr. *émail*. Now obsolete and replaced by the compound *enamel*.

l. 137. *sex* : the form " *sex* " is still used in Lothian and Fife by the side of *sax*. Drummond uses *six* and *sex* indifferently.

III. An Hymne of the Ascension, p. 22, l. 26. *viue* : " bright," " clear " ; in that sense a Scotticism.

ll. 38 and 40. *were* : *are* : to obtain a correct rhyme it is necessary to pronounce *were* as [war], according to a common Mid.-Scots tendency to broaden the *e* to an *a* before *r* or *n*. Cf. note to l. 163 of Song i, vol. i. p. 175.

l. 85. *Prest* : a Scots form of *priest* [prēst] used for the sake of rhyme (cf. "*preest*," vol. ii. p. 249, l. 3). The normal English pronunciation of the word in Drummond's day was, as now [prīst].

l. 95. *entheate* : " divinely inspired " ; Greek ἔνθεος.

Sonnet xvii, p. 26. A close translation of one of Marino's sonnets, with an undoubted improvement in the closing lines (*Rime*, pt. i. p. 176) :

Sotto caliginose ombre profonde
Di luce inaccessibile sepolti
Tra nembi di silentio oscuri, e folti,
L' eterna Mente i suoi secreti asconde.
E s' altri spia per queste nebbie immonde
I suoi giudici in nero velo auolti,
Gli humani ingegni temerari, e stolti,
Col lampo abbaglia, e col suo tuon confonde.
O inuisibil Sol, ch' a noi ti celi
Dentro l' abisso luminoso, e fosco,
E de' tuoi propri rai te stesso ueli ;
Argo mi fai, dou' io son cieco e losco,
Nela mia notte il tuo splendor riueli,
Quanto t' intendo men, più ti conosco.

l. 3. *ebane* : a sixteenth-seventeenth-century form of *ebon*, *ebony*.

l. 11. *proper Rayes* : " own " rays. Cf. vol. ii. p. 101, l. 1109.

Sonnet xix, p. 28, ll. 2-4. *Isle* : *tyle* : the spelling " *tyle* " for *toile* is no doubt meant to satisfy the eye, but

would not be a correct rhyme even in Drummond's day ;
the value of the rhyme-vowels in the two words " *isle*,"
" *tyle* " was then probably [ei : əi].

l. 7. *marish* : " marsh " ; obsolete, except poetically
and dialectally. The origin of this form (M.E. has more
commonly *mareis, mares* ; O.F. *marais, mareis,* Fr.
marais) is somewhat obscure ; it may represent the
occasional O.F. *maresche.*

l. 11. *turne* : " return." Cf. vol. i. Son. ix, ll. 1 and 5,
p. 61.

Madrigal IV. p. 28.   Borrowed from a madrigal by
Valerio Belli, an obscure Italian poet of the end of the
sixteenth century (*Madrigali dell' eccellentissimo Sig.
Valerio Belli*, Venetia, 1599, p. 43) :

> Questo mondo è vna caccia, è cacciatrice
>   La Morte vincitrice :
> I veltri suoi rapaci
> Sono cure mordaci,
> E morbi, e mal, da cui cacciati siamo :
> E se talhor fuggiamo,
> Vecchiezza sua compagna,
> Ci prende ne la ragna.

The Italian original is found in vol. viii. of the Hawthornden MSS., copied out in Drummond's hand.

Sonnet xxi, p. 29, ll. 1-2.

> *As are those Apples, pleasant to the Eye,*
> *But full of Smoke within* . . . —

a reference to the " apples of Sodom " or Dead Sea fruit,
supposed to grow near the shores of the Dead Sea, and
described by Josephus (*The Jewish History*, bk. iv. ch.
viii.) as of fair appearance externally, but dissolving, when
grasped, into smoke and ashes. This, needless to say, is
a traveller's tale, supposed by some to refer to the fruit
of the Solanum Sodomeum, a kind of apple allied to the
tomato. To Josephus is also due the absurd statement
that the destroyed towns of Sodom and Gomorrah lie

under the Dead Sea. The site of the cities was probably
not far from the Dead Sea, but has not been ascertained.

Sonnet xxiii, p. 31. Compare this sonnet with one on
the same theme in Marino's " Rime boscherecce " (*Rime,*
1602, pt. i. p. 70) :

> O rossignol, che 'n sì soaue stile
> Vaghe rime mi detti : ò se talhora
> Quando è pigra a tornar, chiami l' Aurora,
> O se dal verde tuo saluti Aprile :
> Certo, poiche 'l tuo tremulo sottile
> Cantar sì mi diletta, e m' innamora,
> O del ciel chiudi in te Musa canora,
> O se' tu fra gli Amori il più gentile.
> Che sciôr sì dolce infatigabil canto
> Senza spirto diuin non ben sapresti
> Lieue, e picciola piuma, e nata al pianto.
> Ma qual può mortal penna i tuoi celesti
> Pregi agguagliar ? la mia non giunge a tanto,
> S' al' ingegno, a la man le tue non presti.

Sonnet xxiv, p. 31. A paraphrase of a sonnet by
Guglia (*Delle Rime Scelte di Diversi Avtori,* Venetia, 1586,
vol. i. p. 259) :

> Come, s' auien, che città degna e pura,
> Di scelerata man, stuol aspro & empio ;
> Sia fatta graue e doloroso scempio ;
> Nel sangue immersa, al foco accesa e oscura :
> Non puo far sì l' iniqua sorte e dura,
> Ch' vn simulacro ornato, vn' arco, vn Tempio
> Non resti intiero, e con eterno esempio,
> Entro l' afflitte e tenebrose mura.
> Cosi dopo tant' aspri oltraggi, e indegni,
> Onta a le stelle, auuolto a l' altro velo
> Il cor candido serbo, altero e raro.
> E tal forma i pensier di gloria degni,
> Che uiurà, spero, eterno al caldo, al gielo,
> Malgrado al mondo, a morte, al tempo auaro.

ll. 13-14.

> *From this so high transcending Rapture springes,*
> *That I, all else defac'd, not enuie Kinges.*

The fountain-head of this couplet is no doubt the closing lines of Shakespeare's thirty-ninth sonnet :

> For thy sweet love remember'd such wealth brings
> That then I scorn to change my state with kings.

Sonnet xxvi, p. 32, l. 8. *deniz'd* = " denizened " : " naturalized "—as in Sonnet xv of *Astrophel and Stella* :

> With newborn sighs and denizened wit do sing.

IV. An Hymne of True Happinesse, p. 33, l. 11. *hang* : " hung." Cf. note to l. 110, Song i, vol. i. p. 173.

l. 91. *well* : " welfare."

V. An Hymne of the Fairest Faire, p. 37. This may be called an amplification of Ronsard's " Hymne de l'Eternité " (*Œuvres*, ed. Marty-Laveaux, iv. p. 159), whole passages being little more than translation. The following lines of the original, corresponding to lines 13-56 of Drummond's hymn, will show how closely he adapts his model :

> Donne moy s'il te plaist, immense Eternité,
> Pouuoir de celebrer ta grande Deité.
>
> Afin que ma chanson soit viue autant de iours,
> Qu'eternelle tu vis sans voir finir ton cours.
>
> Tout au plus haut du Ciel dans vn throne doré
> Tu te sieds en l'habit d'vn manteau coloré
> De pourpre rayé d'or, passant toute lumiere
> Autant que ta splendeur sur toutes est premiere :
> Et là tenant au poing vn grand Sceptre aimantin,
> Tu etablis tes loix au seuere Destin,
> Qu'il n'ose outrepasser, & que luy-mesme engraue
> Fermes au front du Ciel : car il est ton esclaue,
> Ordonnant dessous toy les neuf temples voutez
> Qui dedans & dehors cernent de tous costez,
> Sans rien laisser ailleurs, tous les membres du monde
> Qui gist dessous tes pieds, comme vne boule ronde.
> A ton dextre costé la Ieunesse se tient,
> Ieunesse au chef crespu, de qui la tresse vient
> Par flots iusqu'aux talons d'vne enlasseure entorse,
> Enflant son estomac de vigueur et de force.

Ceste belle Ieunesse au teint vermeil & franc,
D'vne boucle d'azur ceinte desur le flanc,
Dans vn vase doré te donne de la destre
A boire du Nectar, afin de te faire estre
Tousiours saine & disposte, & afin que ton front
Ne soit iamais ridé comme les nostres sont.
Elle de l'autre main vigoreuse Déesse
Repousse l'estomac de la triste Vieillesse,
Et la banist du Ciel à coups de poing, afin
Que le Ciel ne vieillisse & qu'il ne prenne fin.
A ton autre costé la Puissance eternelle
Se tient debout plantée, armée à la mammelle
D'vn corselet graué qui luy couure le sein,
Branlant de nuict & iour une espée en la main,
Pour fidele garder les bords de ton Empire,
Ton regne & ta richesse, afin que rien n'empire
Par la fuite des ans, & pour donner la mort
A quiconque voudroit ramener le Discord,
Discord ton ennemy, qui ses forces assemble
Pour faire mutiner les Elemens ensemble
A la perte du Monde & de ton doux repos,
Et voudroit, s'il pouuoit, r'engendrer le Chaos.
Mais tout incontinent que cest ennemy brasse
Trahison contre toy, la Vertu le menasse,
L'eternelle Vertu, & le chasse en Enfer
Garroté pieds et mains de cent chaisnes de fer.

l. 12. *Sarcells* : " pinions " ; a term in falconry.

ll. 49-50. *would* : *old* : a correct rhyme, the value of
the rhyme vowel in each case being [oʷ].

l. 96. *Gelsemine* : " jasmine " ; Ital. *gelsomino*.

ll. 149-162. The well-known similar passage in Pope's
Essay on Criticism is obviously modelled on these lines of
Drummond.

l. 184. *doth* : " dost." Cf. note to l. 1 of Son. liii,
vol. i. p. 205.

ll. 195-200.

Starres, Hoste of Heauen, yee Firmaments bright Flowrs,
Cleare Lampes which ouer-hang this Stage of ours,
Yee turne not there to decke the Weeds of Night,
Nor Pageant-like to please the vulgare Sight,

Great Causes sure yee must bring great Effectes,
But who can descant right your graue Aspects ?

This passage affords an excellent example of the imitative habits of Drummond's muse. In it is embodied the substance of Sonnet xxvi of *Astrophel and Stella,* as the following quotation will show :

> Though dusky wits dare scorn astrology,
> And fools can think those lamps of purest light—
> Whose number, ways, greatness, eternity,
> Promising wonders, wonder do invite—
> To have for no cause birthright in the sky,
> But for to spangle the black weeds of Night,
> Or for some brawl, which in that chamber high
> They should still dance to please a gazer's sight.
> For me, I do Nature unidle know,
> And know great causes great effects procure,
> And know those bodies high reign on the low.

The subtle way in which the Laird of Hawthornden wove the choice flowers of his favourite English model into the texture of his own verse has, as far as we are aware, no exact parallel in English literature, but in France and in Germany the same methods, roughly speaking, were employed by two poets almost contemporary with Drummond—Mathurin Régnier and Martin Opitz. That Opitz's poems frequently come near being a mere tessellation from Ronsard is well known. More recently M. Joseph Vianey, in his admirable study on Mathurin Régnier (Paris, 1896), has demonstrated that the French satirist made use of a somewhat similar method of conveyance (less clumsily than Opitz, and more after the fashion of Drummond), not only from his favourite poet Ronsard, but also from the pages of Jodelle, Baïf, Belleau, and Desportes.

l. 256. *Asterismes of Glasse* : an " asterism " is an appearance of light in the shape of a six-rayed star, seen in some crystals, as in star sapphire.

l. 264. *disualu'd* : " not of equal value." Usually the word means " to treat as of no value."

l. 271. *No Snake did met her Meads* : "*met*" is a Scots p.p. of *mete*, "to measure." Here in the sense of to "traverse" (a certain distance, a tract of country), to "travel over."

VI. A Prayer for Mankinde, p. 47, l. 14. *Doe thou reuenge* : "if thou take revenge."

l. 18. *destaind* = "distained" : "defiled."

l. 46. *guishing* : in *Vrania* Drummond uses the normal form "gushing" in the same poem. Cf. Mid. Dutch *guysen*.

VII. The Shadow of the Iudgement, p. 50. This unfinished poem, the longest of Drummond's single compositions, is replete with reminiscences of Ronsard's "Hymne de la Justice" (*Œuvres*, iv. p. 203), although the resemblance in particulars is slight, except perhaps in the complaint of Justice to the King of Ages. The Day of Judgment was a theme that lent itself readily to the indicting of verse in the manner and spirit of Du Bartas, and of Sylvester his English imitator. Indeed, the passage (ll. 215-266) describing the three Furies—War, Famine, and Pestilence—is obviously modelled on the corresponding lines of the French original. The fact that King James had translated this portion of Du Bartas' *Sepmaine* in his *Poeticall Exercises* (1591) may have served as an additional inducement to Drummond to produce a fresh version of one of his favourite passages.

l. 24. *Brawle* : a kind of dance ; Fr. *branle*.

l. 41. *clip* : "embrace." Cf. vol. i. xxv, l. 1, p. 110.

l. 46. *beganne . . . deplore* : Drummond rarely uses *begin* without *to* before the infinitive following, though he does so frequently in the case of *seem*.

l. 82. *vent* : "publish."

l. 87. *neither World* : "*neither*" is an occasional form of *nether* found in the sixteenth and seventeenth centuries, and now obsolete.

l. 122. *execute*: "executed." Cf. note to l. 8 of lxxx, vol. i. p. 242.

l. 175. *Hæmus*: a lofty range of mountains, separating Thrace and Moesia.

Athos: the mountainous peninsula, also called Acte, which projects from Chalcidice in Macedonia. At its extremity it rises to the height of 6349 feet.

l. 189. *More* = "Moor": "black."

l. 199. *yce-sheekle*: "icicle." The O.E. type *is-gicel* (for which is actually found *ises gicel*) is from *is* (ice) + *gicel* (= ickle = icicle). The development would be approximately *is-gicel* [īsjikl] > [iššikl]. For [sj] > [š] cf. the modern pronunciation of *sure* [šū° '] from an earlier [sjūr]. In English the second element has retained an independent stress only in some corrupt dialect forms ; but the word was sometimes pronounced as a compound in the seventeenth century.

l. 224. *trilles*: "trickles" ; now obsolete.

l. 234. *none end*: cf. note to l. 3, Mad. i, vol. i. p. 226.

l. 238. *Lane*: "lean" ; probably a spelling meant to indicate a dialectal pronunciation of the time [læn].

snarl'd haire: "tangled" hair. *Snarl* in that sense is now chiefly confined to the dialects, and to the United States.

l. 252. *banded*: "marked with bands" or "stripes."

l. 271. *Great Quinzai*: cf. note to l. 111 of *Forth Feasting*, vol. i. p. 246.

Susanias pride: Susiana, or Elam, of which the capital was Susa, the same as the Biblical Shushan, a town of Persia, and one of the most important cities of the old world. From the time of Darius I. Susa was the chief residence of the Achaemenian kings. It had been the centre of the old monarchy of Elam, and had undergone many vicissitudes before it fell into the hands of the Persians. The site of the ancient Susa lies in the plain, between the courses of the Kerkha (the ancient Choaspes) and the Dizful, one of the affluents of the Pasitigris.

l. 273. *Parthenopè* : a name given to Naples by Virgil and Ovid, because Naples was founded by the Chalcidians of Cumae, on the site of an ancient place called Parthenope, after the Siren of that name.

l. 274. *Euripus* : a narrow channel between Boeotia and the island of Euboea, notorious for its treacherous changing currents.

l. 286. *topsiturnie* : a modification, suggested by *turn*, of *topsyturvy*, found in the sixteenth and seventeenth centuries by the side of *topsyturvy*. The editors of the Maitland Club edition and Ward have amended without any justification the reading of the original into " *topsyturvy.*"

l. 319. *eight* : the ordinal is not infrequently identical with the cardinal form in the sixteenth century, and much later in dialects, including Scots.

l. 320. *chopes* : " changes."

l. 326. *propine* : " to present," " give," " bestow " ; Gk. προπίνειν, " to drink to another," also " to give freely." Much used in Middle Scots.

l. 424. *mustereth into humane Shapes* : " reveals itself in human form." For this use of *muster* cf. note to l. 220 of Song ii, vol. i. p. 215.

l. 428. *Electar* : " amber " ; Greek ἤλεκτρον.

l. 452. *Collin* : " a small hill " ; Fr. *colline*. Obsolete and rare, used in the seventeenth century, in the form " *colline*," by Evelyn (1641) also, in his *Diary*, i. 291 : " A nobly well-wall'd, wooded, and watered park, full of fine collines and ponds."

A CYPRESSE GROVE.

Drummond's imitative proclivities are just as apparent in his prose essay as in his verse. Our researches have revealed the fact that he is most indebted to Montaigne's *Essais*, Pierre Charron's *De la Sagesse*, and to Innocenzio

Ringhieri's *Dialoghi della vita et della morte* (Bologna, 1550), of which he possessed a French translation by J. Louveau (Lyon, 1557). Though the phraseology is not very similar, Drummond's philosophic meditation on Death is closely related to that of Ringhieri. The latter is a debate between Life and Death, in which Life claims that existence in this world is the height of man's happiness, and accuses Death of cutting short that happiness. Life enumerates the joys of living, the beauty of the universe, family ties and affections, etc. Death on the other hand maintains that he is a beneficent being who opens the only path by which man can enter into more lasting joys—the joys of Immortality. He describes the calamities of the world, shows how the life of man is but a journey of tribulation from the very beginning. In the end, he convinces Life that Immortality belongs to man, and can only be attained through death, and that Life and Death need not therefore be enemies.

l. 6. *by onelie Conceptions*: *only* in the sense of " mere " or " sole " is now obsolete.

ll. 19-35. Ringhieri introduces the subject in much the same way :

" J'estimoys estre maintenant comme j'ay de coustume aux Isles tresheureuses de fortune, ou pour dire mieux au cueur de toute la nature cachée : mais si je ne suis deceue je croy que je suis pour ce point je ne scay comment entre tombeaux et sepultures, ce qui ne m'advint jamais certainement si quelques songes ou imaginations vaines ne me sont apparues en quelque maniere estrange. Mais comment cela se peust il fayre si ce sommeil et la mort qui sont liez ensemble d'estroitte parenté ne vindrent jamais en ma cognaissance, vray est que je l'ay entendu souvente-fois nommer à mes parens pour une chose plaisante, les autres l'estiment hydeuse," etc.

ll. 45-52. Compare Ringhieri :

" Si tu scavois comment je me moque en moy mesmes avec ces ombres icy de ce que les gens prisent tant ceste vie mortelle et ne font aucune estime de la celeste et plus excellente vie, disans avec ce philosophe que je suis la derniere chose des espouvantables et terribles."

l. 66. *Monethes* : during the sixteenth and seventeenth centuries the spelling *moneth* was almost universal.

ll. 105-113. Compare Charron's *De la Sagesse* (Paris, 1674), book ii. chap xi. :

"Cette grande assistance des parens & amis apporte mille incommoditez, presse & estouffe le mourant : on luy tourmente l'vn les oreilles, l'autre les yeux, l'autre la bouche ; les cris & les plaintes si elles sont vrayes serrent le cœur, si feintes & masquées font dépit."

l. 113. *auerre* : " verify," " confirm " ; now obsolete.

ll. 115-136. Compare Charron's *De la Sagesse* (*ibid.* pp. 404 and 406) :

"Car c'est vne piece de l'ordre de l'vniuers, & de la vie du monde. Voulez-vous qu'on ruïne ce monde, & qu'on en fasse vn tout nouueau pour vous ? La mort tient vn tres-grand rang en la police, & grande republique de ce monde : & est de tres-grande vtilité, pour la succession & durée des œuures de nature : la defaillance d'vne vie est passage à mille autres : *sic verum summa nouatur.* Et non seulement c'est vne piece de ce grand tout, mais de ton estre particulier, non moins essentielle, que le viure, que le naistre : en fuyant de mourir tu te fuis toy-mesme : ton estre est egalement party en ces deux, la vie & la mort ; c'est la condition de ta creation. Si tu te fasches de mourir, il ne falloit pas naistre, l'on ne vient point en ce monde à autre marché que pour en sortir, qui se fasche d'en sortir, n'y deuoit pas entrer. Le premier iour de ta naissance t'oblige & t'achemine à mourir comme à viure.

Nascentes morimur finisque ab origine pendet.

. . . Tiercement c'est vne chose raisonnable & juste, que de mourir ; c'est raison d'arriuer au lieu, où l'on ne cesse d'aller, si l'on n'y craint d'arriuer, il ne faut pas cheminer, mais s'arrester ou rebrousser chemin, ce que l'on ne peut. C'est raison que tu fasse place aux autres, puisque les autres te l'ont fait : si vous avez fait vostre profit de la vie, vous estes repû & satisfait, allez vous-en, comme celuy qui appelé en vn banquet a pris sa refection. Si vous n'en auez sceu user & qu'elle vous soit inutile, que vous chaut-il de la perdre ? à quoy faire la voulez vous encore ? C'est vne debte qu'il faut payer, c'est vn depost qu'il faut rendre à toute heure, qu'il est redemandé. . . . C'est contre raison donc de regimber contre la mort, puis que par là vous vous acquittez de tant, & vous vous déchargez d'vn grand conte. C'est chose generale & commune à tous de mourir, pourquoy t'en fasche-tu ? veux-tu auoir vn privilege nouueau & non encores veu, & estre seul hors du sort commun de tous ? Pourquoy crains-tu d'aller où tout le monde va, ou tant de millions sont desia, & où tant de millions te suiuront : la mort est également certaine à tous."

l. 118. *grudge at* : " grumble at," " complain about." Cf. l. 300 below.

l. 130. *lose* : " loss " ; a Scots form.

l. 145. *swipt* : past participle of the Scots verb *swipe*, " to sweep."

ll. 160-161. *now looking blacke, than pale and wanne* : the adverb *then* is often found in Middle Scots in the form " *than*."

ll. 175-180. Compare Montaigne, *Essais*, bk. i. ch. xix. :

" Mais nature nous y force. 'Sortez,' dit-elle, 'de ce monde comme vous y estes entrez. Le mesme passage que vous fites de la mort à la vie, sans passion et sans frayeur, refaites le de la vie à la mort.' "

ll. 189-196. Compare Montaigne, *Essais* (*ibid.*) :

" Parquoy c'est pareille folie de pleurer de ce que d'icy à cent ans nous ne vivrons pas que de pleurer de ce que nous ne vivions pas il y a cent ans."

The pages in which man's weakness and nothingness are set forth evidently owe a great deal to Montaigne's " Apologie de Raimond Sebond " (*Essais*, bk. ii. ch. xii.). In some passages such as the following (ll. 225-236) Drummond departs very little from his model :

" . . . Ce furieux monstre, à tant de bras et à tant de teste c'est touiours l'homme, foible, calamiteux et miserable ; ce n'est qu'une fourmilliere esmeue et eschauffee ;

It nigrum campis agmen :

un souffle de vent contraire, le croassement d'un vol de corbeaux, le fauls pas d'un cheval, le passage fortuit d'un aigle, un songe, une voix, un signe, une brouee matiniere, suffisent à le renverser et porter par terre. Donnez luy seulement d'un rayon de soleil par le visage, le voilà fondu et esvanouï ; qu'on lui esvente seulement un peu de poulsiere aux yeulx, comme aux mouches à miel de nostre poëte."

l. 231. The first edition (1623) has *there mistereth* (from the verb *mister*, now obsolete ; O.F. *mestier*, "need "), which is equivalent to "*there needeth*," the reading of the second edition (1630), but which Drummond probably abandoned as being almost exclusively a Scots word.

ll. 237-245. Compare Ringhieri :

"Je ne te parle point à combien d'infirmités est subjecte ceste miserable creature, qui viennent à retomber en l'Âme, et combien lui fault de médecines lesquelles nonobstant qu'elles soyent innombrables si est ce qu'elles sont cause de mauvaises qualitez, et plusieurs maux nouveaux."

l. 253. *tapist* : "hidden," "concealed." *Tapised* or *tapist* is the past participle of the verb *tapis, tapish*, which is now obsolete or archaic. Fr. *(se) tapir, tapiss-*. It is archaically used by Scott in *Peveril*, xxxiii. : "your father . . . is only tappiced in some corner."

l. 267. *happelie* = "haply" : "by chance," "perchance"; now obsolete.

l. 286. *Euripe* : cf. note to l. 274 of "The Shadow of the Iudgement," vol. ii. p. 344.

ll. 286-307. Compare Charron, *De la Sagesse*, bk. i. ch. iv. :

"Premierement au desir, l'homme ne peut asseoir son contentement en aucune chose, & par desir mesme & imagination. Il est hors de nostre puissance de choisir ce qu'il nous faut : quoy que nous ayons desiré, & qu'il nous aduienne ; il ne nous satisfait point, & allons beants apres les choses inconnuës & à venir, d'autant que les presentes ne nous saoulent point, & estimons plus les absentes. Que l'on baille à l'homme la carte blanche ; que l'on le mette à mesme de choisir, tailler & prescrire, il est hors de sa puissance de le faire tellement, qu'il ne s'en dédise bientost, en quoy il ne trouue à redire, & ne vueille adjouster, oster, ou changer ; il desire ce qu'il ne scauroit dire. Au bout du compte rien ne le contente, il se fasche & s'ennuye de soy-mesme."

l. 295. *launce* : to "launch"; now obsolete. O.F.

lancier, Fr. *lancer.* The form *launch* is from the N.E. Old French form *lanchier.*

l. 344. *towseth* : cf. note to l. 183 of *Forth Feasting,* vol. i. p. 247.

l. 350. *Magnes* : an obsolete form of *magnet.*

In his general conception of the futility of human knowledge Drummond again follows Montaigne closely ; in some passages he borrows his very words :

ll. 352-354. Compare Montaigne, *Essais,* bk. ii. ch. xii. :

"Sont ce pas des songes de l'humaine vanité, de faire de la lune une terre celeste ? y songer des montaignes, des vallées, comme Anaxagoras ? y planter des habitations et demeures humaines, et y dresser des colonies pour nostre commodité, comme faict Platon et Plutarque ? et de nostre terre, en faire un astre esclairant et lumineux ? "

ll. 375-376. *Prodigalls mis-spend them, Wretches mis-keepe them* : the word *wretch,* in the sense of " miser," " niggard," appears to be peculiar to Scots.

ll. 384-387. Compare Charron, *De la Sagesse,* bk. ii. ch. xi. :

"La vie se mesure par la fin, pourueu qu'elle en soit belle, tout le reste à sa proportion : la quantité ne sert de rien pour la rendre plus ou moins heureuse, non plus que la grandeur ne rend pas le cercle plus rond que le petit ; la figure y fait tout."

l. 389. *ensueth* : " followeth " ; now obsolete in that sense.

ll. 392-395. Compare Montaigne, *Essais,* bk. ii. ch. xii. :

"Quant à la beauté du corps, avant passer oultre, il me fauldroit sçavoir si nous sommes d'accord de sa description. Il est vraysemblable que nous ne scavons gueres que c'est que beauté en nature et en general, puisque à l'humaine et nostre beauté nous donnons tant de formes diverses, de laquelle, s'il y avoit quelque description naturelle, nous la recognoistrions en commun, comme la chaleur du feu."

l. 400. *preuenting* : " anticipating." Cf. note to l. 11 of iv, vol. i. p. 161.

ll. 436-450. Compare Ringhieri :

"Pour te manifester un beau secret qui te devroit beaucoup consoler et adoucir l'amertume que tu as conclue, il fault que tu saches que ton empire ne serait pas de telle varieté, beauté et ornement comme il est, si je ne t'enseignoye à le renouveler toujours comme aguisant le fer à ma pierre, le voyant corrompre par moy en tant de sortes ; en quoy on peult comprendre ton industrie et tes forces invincibles : tellement qu'en deux ou trois siecles seulement tu aurais avec nature donné vie a tout humaine generation, qui eust esté conduite à la vieillesse laide et odieuse par le moyen du temps soudain qui corrompt et gaste toutes choses avec ses plaies venimeuses.   On ne verroyt autre chose par les cités et villages que corps languissans, malades, courbez, membres tremblans, poils chenutz, visages palles et ridez, sens d'enfance, et plaintes de cest aage ennuyeus et plein de beaucoup de facheries ou elle t'honnore a present avec sy belle et merveilleuse diversité de choses, combien que les complexions soyent variables, les visages, les membres, et toutes les figures de corps, les moyens, les œuvres, les vertus, les conditions et fortunes . . . tout ce que je trouve de vif et sec en ce tien plaisan jardin et nouveau pré florissant avec la trop grande abondance de tous aages, je le viens à reduire à convenable perfection pour la plus grande felicité et bonne grace."

l. 445. *courbing* : " bending," " bowing " ; Fr. *courber*. In Modern English the form is *curb*, but *curb* has lost the meaning of " to bend."

l. 468. *crasie* = " crazy " : " diseased," " sickly " ; now obsolete.

l. 471. *euill complexioned* : " with a bad (bodily) constitution."

l. 477. *artere* : an obsolete form of *artery*.

l. 489. *Weeke* : there seem to have been at least two forms of the word in M.E. (*wicke* and *weke*).   The form *weeke* used here by Drummond, and also by Spenser (*Faerie Queene*, II. x. 30), represents the second form.

l. 492. *witnesse* : " attest," " show " ; now obsolete.

l. 496. *No otherwise* : " not " otherwise.   This use of *no* is found in M.E., and in the sixteenth and seventeenth centuries, but is now confined to Scots.

ll. 508-515. Compare Montaigne, *Essais*, bk. i. ch. xix. :

"J'y ay a escient meslé quelque peu d'amertume pour vous empescher, voyant la commodité de son usage, de l'embrasser trop avidement et indiscretement."

See also Charron, *De la Sagesse*, bk. ii. ch. xi. p. 399.

ll. 519-526. Compare Charron, *De la Sagesse*, bk. ii. ch. xi. p. 399 :

"Celuy-là vit vrayement libre, qui ne craint point la mort : au contraire le viure est seruir, si la liberté de mourir en est à dire. La mort est le seul appuy de nostre liberté, commune & prompte recepte à tous maux : c'est donc estre bien miserable (& ainsi le sont presque tous) qui trouble la vie par le soin & crainte de la mort, & la mort par le soin de la vie."

ll. 540-543. Compare Montaigne, *Essais*, bk. i. ch. xix. :

"Tu as passé les termes accoustumez de vivre ; et qu'il soit ainsi, conte de tes cognoissans combien il en est mort avant ton aage plus qu'il n'en y a qui l'ayent atteint."

ll. 543-548. Compare Montaigne, *Essais* (*ibid.*) :

"Et si vous avez vescu un jour, vous avez tout veu : un jour est égal a tous jours. Il n'y a point d'autre lumiere ny d'autre nuict. Ce soleil, cette lune, ces estoilles, cette disposition, c'est celle mesme que vos ayeuls ont jouye et qui entretiendra vos arriere-nepveuz."

ll. 552-555. Compare Montaigne, *Essais* (*ibid.*) :

"Le plus et le moins en la nostre, si nous la comparons à l'eternité ou encores à la durée des montaignes, des rivieres, des estoilles, des arbres et mesmes d'aucuns animaux, n'est pas moins ridicule."

ll. 558-562. Compare Montaigne, *Essais* (*ibid.*) :

"Mais quoy ! les jeunes et les vieux y pensent aussi peu les uns que les autres. Et n'est homme si decrepite, tant qu'il voit Mathusalem devant, qui ne pense avoir encore vingt ans dans le corps."

l. 559. *one of Platos yeares* : the Platonic year, also called " great " or " perfect " year, was the name given to a great cycle of years, at the end of which it was supposed that the celestial bodies will be found in the same place they were in at their creation. The Platonic year was supposed to be equal to twenty-five thousand Julian years.

ll. 580-587. Compare Ringhieri :

". . . le temps de la vie n'est autre chose qu'une course perpetuelle à la mort, tout aussi qu'ung torment, par le vanissment et la continuelle volée des siecles, et n'est permis à aucun de demourer, ou s'en aller plus tard : mais également chacun est emporté. Et celuy qui ha vescu plus brefve espace de la vie, n'ha point plutost acomply ses jours, que celuy qui s'en est allé plus tard : veu que chacun est rauy d'un égal moment : et s'il semble qu'il y ayt quelque difference c'est, que l'ung ha prins le chemin plus long, et l'autre plus court ; car celuy qui passe plus longu'espace de temps, ne va pas plus tard, mais acomplist plus de voyage. . . ."

l. 585. *rubbige* : an obsolete form of *rubbish*.

l. 592. *let* : "hindrance." Cf. note to l. 4, lxxvi, vol. i. p. 241.

l. 608. *concreded* = concredit : "entrust."

l. 623. *Papers* : "literature."

l. 626. *import* : "imply," "indicate" ; now obsolete.

l. 633. *Pleasants* : "clowns," "jesters" ; now obsolete.

l. 656. *Siracusianes Spheare* : the sphere of Archimedes.

l. 681. *auouch* : "avow," "acknowledge" ; now obsolete. O.F. *avochier*.

l. 683. *Pismire* : an "ant" ; now obsolete except dialectally. From *piss* + *mire* (an "ant" ; M.E. *mire*) ; from the urinous smell of an ant-hill.

l. 696. *imagine mee* : "mee" is a case of the so-called "ethic" dative. Cf. Mätzner, *Grammatik* (3rd edit.), ii. 227, and W. Franz, *Shakespeare-Grammatik*, 1900, p. 121.

l. 704. *that Grot in Pausilipo* : Pausilippo or Posilippo, a mountain to the S.W. of the city of Naples, advancing into the sea opposite the island of Nisida. The famous grotto of Pausilippo is a tunnel cut through the tufa rock, 2316 feet in length, 22 feet broad, and 87 feet high. Over its entrance is the tomb of Virgil, situated in a vineyard amid tufa rocks, and hung round with ivy and other creeping plants.

l. 715. *backward*: "reluctant," "bashful."

l. 727. *leas* = "lees": "protection," "shelter"; rarely used in the plural as here, and now chiefly applied to the side (of a ship, the land, etc.) that is turned away from the wind.

l. 737. *improue*: "disprove"; now obsolete.

l. 744. *descant of*: "make remarks" or "observations upon"; now rare and followed by *on* or *upon*. Cf. Kingsley, *Alt. Locke*, vi.: "He ran on descanting coarsely on beauties."

ll. 745-749. Compare Ringhieri:

"Or quelle chose peult on trouver plus belle que l'ame Immortelle ornée de si grande beauté, car si on la pouvoyt une foys veoyr des yeux corporels ou la comprendre par aucun sens, elle embraseroyt les cueurs de merveilleuses amours de sa divinité."

l. 765. *apt*: "fit," "prepared" (of persons); now archaic.

l. 766. *amated*: "dismayed," "confounded"; O.F. *amater*, or *amatir*, from O.F. *mat*, "dejected," "downcast." The verb *amate* had grown obsolete before 1700, but is used archaically by Lytton and Keats.

l. 774. *Mirrouer*: Middle Scots has the French form *mirroir*, of which *mirrouer* is another spelling, indicating the French pronunciation of the time.

parcell: "particle," like the French word *parcelle* from which it is derived. It is now archaic.

l. 795. *destained*: "defiled." Cf. note to l. 18, vi, vol. ii. p. 342.

l. 834. *let*: "hinder"; now obsolete.

l. 942. Perhaps an allusion to Henry, Prince of Wales.

l. 966. *Peiser*: "poiser," "weigher."

l. 968. *abused*: "cheated," "deceived"; now obsolete, but preserved in the negative *disabuse*.

ll. 970-976. Compare Montaigne, *Essais*, bk. i. ch. xix. :

"La mort est origine d'une autre vie : ainsi pleurasmes nous et ainsi nous cousta - il d'entrer en cette-cy, ainsi despouillasmes nous de nostre ancien voile en y entrant."

ll. 995-1021. Compare Ringhieri :

"Tu est trop vaine, et ces tiens hommes sont trop ingénieux à s'abuser eux mesmes, si vostre desir et l'esperance s'arreste aux choses sensibles et aux sentimens, mais si l'Ame raisonnable vient à la consideration du vray homme interieur, laissant l'escorce caduque . . . tu verras que . . . pour luy se tournent les cieux, avec si grand temperament, et semble quasi, que les estoilles et le soleil qui engendrent, illuminent et conservent toutes choses en sa faveur, ont esté ainsi faitz vertueux et admirables, seulement pour lui monstrer qu'il descend d'une haute source et divin commencement, et se glorifient d'estre contemplés de luy comme vray adorateur de vrays dieux, et maistre general de la Terre et de la mer. De la vient que tout se reduit et se rend a luy comme à sa reigle et chef, cest a dire le vray : l'homme est un grand miracle de nature si on le considere bien. . . . Tout est en luy, comme en sa fin, et luy est en Dieu (qui est chose merveilleuse)."

l. 1011. *Trunchman.* Ward commits a startling error concerning the word "*trunchman.*" In a note he says : "*Trunchman* : perhaps one who holds the truncheon as a symbol of command." The word "*interpreter*" with which "*trunchman*" is immediately conjoined in Drummond's text ought to have shown Ward that we are here in presence of the French word *trucheman* (or *truchement*, to use the modern spelling admitted by the Academy), of Arabic origin, meaning an "interpreter," and found in sixteenth-seventeenth century English and Scots. One naturally recalls Molière's "Où est le truchement, pour lui dire qui vous êtes ? " (*B. Gent.* v. 4).

ll. 1013-1021. Ward points out that this is borrowed from the *Heptaplus* of Pico della Mirandola, Lib. v. :

"Est autem hæc diversitas inter Deum et hominem, quod Deus in se omnia continet, uti omnium principium, homo autem in se omnia continet uti omnium medium, quo sit ut in Deo sint omnia meliore nota quam in seipsis, in homine inferiora nobiliori sint conditione, superiora autem degenerent. . . .

Homini mancipantur terrestria, homini favent cœlestia, quia et cœlestium et terrestrium vinculum et nodus est ; nec possunt utraque hæc non habere cum eo pacem, si modo ipse secum pacem habuerit, qui illorum in seipso pacem et fœdera sancit."

ll. 1015-1021 recall another passage in Ringhieri :

" De deux contraires et diverses natures Dieu veult unir cest animal prodigieux qui est l'homme, avec un heureux accord pour mieux manifester sa puissance, affin qu'il fust comme ung neud et moyen de choses inferieures et divines."

l. 1042. *pore-blind Moles* : the origin of the first element of this word, which in the sixteenth to seventeenth centuries was variously represented as *pore*, *poor*, *pour*, may be the O.F. intensive *pur-*, *pour-* (*per*) ; but if the sense of totally blind which appears in the oldest example of the word (1297) was the original one, it had come before the beginning of the fifteenth century to mean something less than blind, and was soon written as one word.

l. 1050. *rander* = " render." Cf. note to l. 163 of Song i, vol. i. p. 175.

l. 1078. *Orient* : " shining," " radiant."

l. 1182. *Spagericke* : " chemist " ; a follower of the chemistry of Paracelsus.

On the Report of the Death of the Author, p. 105. These strophes by Sir William Alexander, as well as the sonnet following, belong to the year 1620, and refer to Drummond's long and serious illness in that year.

l. 16. *tosse* : " agitate," " disturb " ; now obsolete.

To S. W. A., p. 106. This very graceful sonnet of Drummond to Sir William Alexander appears in the Hawthornden MSS. (vol. x. p. 10) in the following form, with many interesting variants :

DAMON TO ALEXIS.

Though I haue twice beene at the gates of Death
And twice escapd those Portes that euer murne,
This but a respit is, a Pawse of breath,
For I by Signes find I shall soone returne.

Amidst thy heauen-borne cares and courtlye Toyles
Alexis when thou shalt heare wandring fame
Tell Death hath triumphd o're my mortall spoyles
And that I am on earth but a sad name ;
If thou ere heldst mee deare ? by all our loue,
By eurye soft discourse soulecharming verse,
I coniure thee, and by the mayds of Joue,
To wryte this sad remembrance on my herse,
   Her Damon lyes whose songs did sometyme grace
   The murmuring Eske, may Roses decke this Place.

l. 2. *shoote* [šūt] : a sixteenth-century form of the p.p. of *shut*.

l. 5. *Amidst thy sacred Cares, and courtlie Toyles* : the words " *sacred Cares* " are an allusion to the translation of the Psalms, undertaken by King James, in collaboration with Alexander, and published at Oxford in 1631, under the heading, *The Psalmes of King David : Translated by King James*.

To the Memorie of . . . Iane Countesse of Perth, p. 107. This lady was the wife of Drummond's patron and clan-chief, John Drummond, Earl of Perth. As this sonnet already appears in the first edition of *Flowres of Sion* (1623), she must have died before that date.

To the obsequies of . . . Iames, etc., p. 108, l. 2. *That King, Whose Brest Ægeria did inflame* : according to the Roman legend, Egeria, goddess of fountains, was the consort and counsellor of King Numa, who used to meet her in a grotto in the precincts of the Camenae.

THE ENTERTAINMENT OF
KING CHARLES.

ll. 11-12. Πτερωτὸν στρατόπεδον : " the winged camp." It is doubtful, however, if Edinburgh is the place referred to by Ptolemy.

l. 15. *Castra Puellarum*: Edinburgh Castle. The name "Maiden Castle" was given to the castle of Edinburgh from a very remote period. Father Hay asserts that the castle derived this appellation from the nuns who had their dwelling there (*Lib. Cartarum Sanctæ Crucis*, p. xxii, Edinb. 1841). Others, with more probability, think that it received the name of "Maiden" from its impregnable position on the rock.

l. 19. *Cardan* (Ital. *Cardano*; Latinised *Cardanus*), a celebrated mathematician, physician, naturalist and philosopher, born at Pavia in 1501. He professed mathematics at Milan, and subsequently became professor of medicine at Pavia, and later at Bologna. In 1571 he went to Rome, where he died, September 2, 1576, just after having completed his remarkable autobiography, *De Propria Vita*. It may be mentioned that in 1552 he visited Scotland, on the invitation of Archbishop Hamilton, and succeeded in curing the primate of a long-standing asthma, which had defied the efforts of the most famous physicians. His two best works, containing a summary of his ideas on physics and metaphysics, are *De Subtilitate Rerum* and *De Rerum Varietate*. Drummond possessed a copy of the latter work.

l. 25. *Lithus*: Leith water.

l. 43. *seeded*: "sown with seed"; "studded."

l. 49. *Vltra Sauromatas*: the meaning is that superstition was banished beyond the regions of the Sarmatians, or Sauromatae as they were also called in antiquity, a name somewhat vaguely applied to a savage and nomadic race who spoke the same language as the Scythians, and who roamed over the wide plains of eastern Europe from the Vistula and the Danube to the Volga and Caucasus.

l. 91. *then* = "than" throughout *The Entertainment*. This is a common usage in the sixteenth century, and occasionally in the early seventeenth century; but by about 1700 the conjunction was differentiated from the adverb as *than*.

l. 145. *shew* : a Scots and northern dialect preterite of *show*.

l. 150. *S.P.Q.E.P.* = Senatus Populusque Edinburgensis posuerunt.

l. 156. *Abacke* : "abacus," a level tablet on the capital of a column, supporting the entablature.

l. 164. *flourishes* : "florid decorations."

l. 183. *Panisques* : cf. note to l. 371 of *Forth Feasting*, vol. i. p. 248.

l. 197. *Sedullius*, an Irish-Scot grammarian of the ninth century, who must not be confused with his more famous namesake Coelius Sedulius, the Christian poet of the first half of the fifth century, whose fame rests mainly upon a long poem, *Carmen Paschale*, based on the four gospels.

John Duns (1265 or 1275–1308), one of the foremost of the schoolmen, born probably at Duns in Berwickshire, though Down (Dunum) in Ulster, and Dunstane in Northumberland, have also claimed him as their own. He became professor of philosophy in the University of Paris in the early years of the fourteenth century, and there won for himself the distinctive title, by which he is generally known, of " Doctor Subtilis," for his wonderful display of dialectical ingenuity in the defence of the doctrine of the Immaculate Conception.

ll. 197–198. *William Elphinstone* (1431–1514), bishop of Aberdeen, and founder of Aberdeen University. Elphinstone was at once the foremost churchman and statesman of his time in Scotland.

l. 198. *Hector Boece* (or, more properly, Boyis), a distinguished Scottish historian, born about 1465 at Dundee, died in 1536. After having completed his studies at the University of Paris, he was invited by Bishop Elphinstone to preside over the University newly founded by that prelate at Aberdeen. Boece's principal work, published at Paris in 1526, is his *Scotorum Historia ab illius Gentis origine*. It was translated into Scots by Bellenden at the command of James V.

John Major, or Mair, schoolman and historian, was born near North Berwick, Haddingtonshire, about 1470, and died in 1550. He taught at Paris, Glasgow, and Aberdeen. At Glasgow he had as one of his pupils John Knox, and at St. Andrews George Buchanan, who accused him of teaching the art of sophistry rather than dialectics. His best known work is his combined history of England and Scotland, which is said to be still of real value as a record of facts, and by reason of the author's independent judgment. Though admirable for his sturdiness and independence of character, John Major was a reactionary, and the acknowledged champion of mediaevalism in his day against the new light of the Renaissance.

l. 199. *Gawain* or *Gavin Douglas* (? 1474–1522), bishop of Dunkeld, the famous early Scottish poet. His principal works are *The Palice of Honour* and *King Hart* (both allegories after the fashion of the time), and a translation of the *Aeneid* with prologues. This last work, finished most likely in 1531, is the first version of a Latin classic published in Britain.

Sir David Lindsay (1490–1555), one of the best, and long the most popular of the older Scottish poets. For fully two centuries Lindsay was the poet of the Scottish people, and at one time his writings were in nearly every household in Scotland. This extraordinary vogue is explained not only by the fact that they were of local interest, but perhaps still more by reason of Lindsay's good sense and complete mastery of the popular speech. Their poetical value, however, is not great. The chief of them are *The Dreme, The Satyre of the Thrie Estaitis*, and *The Historie of Squyer Meldrum*.

l. 203. *purle* : thread or cord made of twisted gold or silver wire, used for bordering and embroidering.

l. 212. *Queene Anna* : Anne of Denmark (1574–1619), who in 1589 married James VI. of Scotland, the future James I. of England.

ll. 247-248. *Thy life was kept*, etc. : these two lines are repeated, with a slight variation, from *Forth Feasting* (ll. 117-118).

l. 275. *sad Damasse* : " dark-coloured damask." *Sad* (cf. l. 250 above) in the sense of " dark " is now obsolete. Cf. *Faerie Queene*, i. xii. 5 : " Arayd in antique robes downe to the grownd, And sad habiliments." *Damasse* is a Scots form of *damask*, a rich silk fabric woven with elaborate designs and figures, often with a variety of colours.

l. 276. *Frenzend* : *frenze* is a Middle Scots form of *to fringe* (M.E. *frenge*).

l. 277. *Gourd* : in heraldry, a representation of the fruit (a kind of pumpkin) of that name.

ll. 287-288. *in others hands* : *other* is used elliptically in Scots, where English requires *each other*.

I. p. 118, l. 36. *rampant* : " rearing " or " standing with the fore-paws in the air."

l. 41. *Quinzaye* : cf. note to l. 111 of *Forth Feasting*, vol. i. p. 246.

l. 53. *shed* = " shade " ; an obsolete Scots form of the word.

ll. 53-60. These lines recall the following passage in the fourth of Buchanan's *Sylvæ* :

> Illa pharetratis est propria gloria Scotis,
> Cingere venatu saltus, superare natando
> Flumina, ferre famem, contemnere frigora et æstus ;
> Nec fossa et muris patriam, sed Marte tueri,
> Et spreta incolumem vita defendere famam.

l. 57. *wastest Lakes* = " vastest lakes." The printers of the time seem to have confused *waste* and *vast*. Cf. vol. ii. p. 128, l. 31.

l. 100. *Orion* : cf. note to l. 201 of *Forth Feasting*, vol. i. p. 247.

II. p. 127, l. 6. *the Maying rose* : " the May rose." The word " *Maying* " in this sense is not recorded in dictionaries, but its use by Drummond is confirmed by its repetition in vol. ii. v. l. I, p. 175. Ward, following Phillips, reads "*morning rose*," for which there is no authority.

l. 28. *Azymuth*: an arc of the heavens extending from the zenith to the horizon which it cuts at right angles. The word is derived from Arabic *as* (= *al*) + *sumūt* = "the" + "direction."

III. p. 128, l. 7. *The old Leucadian Syth-bearing Sire*: the "*Syth-bearing Sire*" is Saturn, who in later times was identified with the Greek god Kronos. The epithet "*Leucadian*," however, is not applicable to Saturn, but to Apollo, who had a famous temple on the promontory of Leucas or Leucadia.

IV. p. 129, l. 8. *tunder*: "tinder"; a Scots form, also found in the English northern dialects and in Lincolnshire. M.E. and Mod. E. *tinder* regularly represent O.E. *tynder*; the form *tunder* (also found in M.E.) is probably from O.N. *tundr*, "tinder."

l. 25. *Supercheries*: Fr. *supercherie*; "deceit," "fraud."

l. 26. *beagling*: "spying." The verb *beagle*, which is not registered in the N.E.D., evidently means "scent out," "hunt out," "spy," and is derived from *beagle*, a small variety of hound.

l. 29. *Paranymph*. This word can mean "best man," or "bridesmaid." From the latter is easily derived that of "effeminate man," which seems to be intended here.

l. 53. *Beyond Alcides Pillars*: the pillars of Heracles or Hercules, Calpe and Abyla, on the two sides of the straits of Gibraltar, set up by Hercules, in memory of his arrival, when seeking the oxen of the giant Geryones.

Heracles was surnamed "Alcides," on account of his strength (ἀλκή).

VII. p. 132, l. I. *The Acidalian Queene*: Venus. On this epithet of Venus cf. note to l. 32 of Song i, vol. i. p. 171.

VIII. p. 132, l. 6. *Tiphone* : according to Hesiod, the youngest son of Gaea by Tartarus. He was regarded as the symbol of the fire and smoke in the interior of the earth, and of their destructive forces.

l. 13. *Typhis* : "mariner." Typhis was the helmsman of the ship Argo.

ll. 13-14. *lost* : *coast* : probably a correct rhyme, the value of the rhyme-vowel being [ō].

IX. p. 133, l. 18. *Garamants* : the inhabitants of the ancient Phazania, or Fezzan as it is now called, a province of North Africa, to the south of Tripoli.

TO THE EXEQUIES, Etc.

This elegy was the last of Drummond's poems to appear during his lifetime. It was written on the occasion of the death of Sir Anthony Alexander, the second son of his old friend Sir William Alexander. Sir Anthony died in London on the 17th September 1637; his body was brought by sea to Scotland, and interred in the church at Stirling. Drummond's pastoral elegy was issued in Edinburgh early in the following year, as a separate publication. The piece does not bear his name; but it has always been included among his works and is undoubtedly his, as any one acquainted with Drummond's style will readily grant.

The Scottish poet's lament on the death of young Alexander is an adaptation, in condensed form, of a Latin pastoral elegy, entitled *Alcon*, by Baldassar Castiglione, the famous author of *Il Cortegiano*. Castiglione's reputation to-day rests mainly on his *Courtier*; but in the sixteenth century he ranked high among the Neo-Latin poets, as long as Latin continued, as it did till early in the seventeenth century, to vie with the vernacular for the expression of poetic thought. He was especially admired for his elegiac efforts, and of these none seems to have aroused more attention than his *Alcon* (on the death of a long-cherished friend snatched away by illness in the prime of youth), chiefly because, in spite of the unmistakable artificiality of the *genre*, the truth of sorrow occasionally bursts through the trammels of bucolic romance, and reaches the free heights of natural feeling. Critics of authority are agreed that Castiglione's lament formed part of Milton's reading preparatory to the composition of *Lycidas*. A few general reminiscences, however, is all that Milton's immortal monody may owe to Castiglione. It is possible also that a few faint traces of Drummond's dirge are discernible in *Lycidas*, though any similarity is perhaps best explained by the fact that the two English poets had recourse to the same model. Drummond's pastoral elegy, on the other hand, follows step by step the general outline of *Alcon*, and in several passages descends to frank adaptation.

The two compositions open on identical notes, except that Drummond expresses himself in slightly different words, and omits some twenty lines of Castiglione which follow on those quoted (*Carmina quinque Poetarum*, Venice, 1549, p. 149) :

> Ereptum fatis primo sub flore juventae
> Alconem nemorum decus, et solatia amantum,
> Quem toties fauni, et Dryades sensere canentem,
> Quem toties Pan est, toties miratus Apollo,
> Flebant pastores ; ante omnes carus Iolas
> Tristia perfundens lacrimis manantibus ora,
> Crudeles superos, crudeliaque astra vocabat.

In the next passage the resemblance becomes closer, but this time Drummond expands the original somewhat :

> Alcon deliciæ musarum, et Apollinis, Alcon
> Pars animæ, cordis pars Alcon maxima nostri,
> Et dolor, his lacrimas oculis habiture perennes,
> Quis Deus, aut quis te casus miser abstulit ? ergo
> Optima quæque rapit duri inclementia fati ?
> Ergo bonis tantum est aliquod male numen amicum ?

Non metit ante diem lactentes messor aristas,
Immatura rudis non carpit poma colonus ;
At fera te ante diem mors nigro immersit Averno,
Injecitque manus rapidas crescentibus annis.

The fields, lakes, rivers, and forests lament the loss of
the dear departed friend. Why is Destiny so cruel ?
The grass, though cut down, sprouts from the stem,
and the setting sun will again visit the earth, and rise
when he has laved his face in the western seas. But
Death is unrelenting ; to the winds are cast the sad
shepherd's vows and entreaties :

Heu miserande puer, tecum solatia ruris,
Tecum amor, et Charites periere, et gaudia nostra ;
Arboribus cecidere comæ, spoliataque honore est
Silva suo ; solitasque negat pastoribus umbras ;
Prata suum amisere decus, morientibus herbis
Arida ; sunt sicci fontes, et flumina sicca.
Infœcunda carent promissis frugibus arva :
Et mala crescentes rubigo exedit aristas.
Squallor tristis habet pecudes, pecudumque magistros,
Impastus stabulis sævit lupus ; ubere raptos
Dilaniatque ferus miseris cum matribus agnos ;
Perque canes prædam impavidus pastoribus aufert ;
Nil nisi triste sonant et silvæ, et pascua, et amnes,
Et liquidi fontes, tua tristia funera flerunt
Et liquidi fontes, et silvæ, et pascua et amnes.
Heu miserande puer, tangunt tua funera Divos.
Per nemora agricolæ flentes videre Napeas,
Panaque, Silvanumque, et capripedes Satyricos.
Sed neque jam lacrimis, aut questu fata moventur
Impia, nec nostras audit mors surda querelas.
Vomeribus succisa suis moriuntur in arvis
Gramina ; deinde iterum viridi de cespite surgunt,
Rupta semel non deinde annectunt stamina Parcæ.
Aspice, decendens jam Sol declivis Olympo
Occidit, et moriens accendit sidera cœlo ;
Sed tamen occiduo cum laverit æquore currus,
Idem iterum terras orienti luce reviset.
Aut ubi nigra semel duræ nos flumina mortis
Lavere, et clausa est immitis janua regni,
Nulla unquam ad superos ducit via ; lumina somnus

Urget perpetuus, tenebrisque involvit amaris ;
Tunc lacrimæ incassum, tunc irrita vota, precesque
Funduntur, fert vota Notus, lacrimasque precesque.

Then follows a passage of twelve lines in Drummond, absent in Castiglione, which celebrates the virtues of the dead shepherd. The two poets next recall the happy days spent by the two fellow-swains, heedless of care, in amorous play :

Heu miserande puer fatis surrepte malignis,
Non ego te posthac pastorum astante corona
Victorem aspiciam volucri certare sagitta ;
Aut jaculo, aut dura socios superare palæstra ;
Non tecum posthac molli resupinus in umbra
Effugiam longos æstivo tempore Soles ;
Non tua vicinos mulcebit fistula montes,
Docta nec umbrosæ resonabunt carmina valles :
Non tua corticibus toties inscripta Lycoris,
Atque ignis Galatea meus nos jam simul ambos
Audierunt ambæ nostros cantare furores.

This part of the narrative is elaborated at greater length in Castiglione's version. Iolas continues his lament in an outburst of passionate sorrow. " Like brothers," he exclaims, " we lived our lives till now from infancy : heat and cold, days and nights, we bore ; our herds were reared with toil and care together. We lived one common life. Why, then, when thou must die, am I still left to live ? Alas ! in evil hour the wrath of Heaven withdrew me from my native land, nor suffered me to close thy lids with a friend's hands ! Happy Leucippus to whom Alcon with failing breath declared his last commands, and whom, the last rites performed, a kindly fate called away to the nether shades to share sweet Alcon's company."

These (twenty-five) verses are omitted by Drummond, who replaces them by eight others which condense and generalise the contents of the original in somewhat pedestrian style. But the inventive powers of the Scottish poet are soon exhausted ; with wonted docility he once more seeks his model's guiding hand. The imitation is never servile; and most readers will not grudge their admiration for what is on the whole a skilful and tasteful exercise in paraphrase :

Quin etiam sortis duræ, ignarusque malorum
Vana mihi incassum fingebam somnia demens.
Hæc ego rura colam celeberrima, tum meus Alcon
Huc veniet linquens colles, et inhospita saxa,
Infectasque undas, et pabula dira veneno ;
Molliaque inviset prata hæc, fluviosque salubres.
Occurram longe, et venientem primus amicum
Agnoscam, primus caris complexibus ora
Impediam, excutient hilares nova gaudia fletus,
Sic tandem optato læti sermone fruemur ;
Aerumnasque graves, olim et transacta vicissim
Damna referre simul, rursusque audire juvabit,
Tum veteres sensim fando repetemus amores,
Delitiasque inter pastorum, et dulcia ruris
Ocia, securæ peragemus tempora vitæ.
Hæc amat arva Ceres, juga Bacchus, pascua Apollo,
Ipsa Pales herbas pecori, lac sufficit agnis ;
Montibus his passim teneræ assuevere Napeæ
Sæpe feras agitare, et sæpe agitare choreas ;
Hic redolens sacros primævæ gentis honores.
Perluit antiquas Tyberis decora alta ruinas ;
Hic umbræ nemorum, hic fontes, hic frigida Tempe ;
Formosum hic pastor Corydon cantavit Alexin.
Ergo ades ô dilecte puer : te pascua, et amnes
Expectant ; tibi jam contexunt florea serta,
Adventuque tuo testantur gaudia Nymphæ ;
Summittitque novos tellus tibi Dædala flores.
Hæc ego fingebam miser, ah spe ductus inani,
Nescius omne nefas morti fatisque licere.

In a trance, Idmon calls up the image of Alcon. With outstretched arms he advances to embrace the friend whom he imagines to be still alive, but in his stead he clasps a coffin.

This passage has no parallel in Castiglione. However. the poetic stream of the two elegies soon meets again :

At postquam frustrata leves abiere per auras
Vota mea, et vivos Alconis cernere vultus

Non licuit, vivasque audire et reddere voces,

. . . . . .

Ipse meis manibus ripa hac Anienis inanem
Constituam tumulum, nostri solatia luctus,
Atque addam pia thura focis, manesque ciebo.

Both compositions close with an admonition to the
nymphs and shepherds to bewail the beloved youth, reft
from their midst by fate malign. Garlands they shall
weave to his memory, and flowers scatter on his tomb :

Vos mecum ô pueri bene olentes spargite flores,
Narcissum, atque rosas, et suave rubentem Hyacinthum,
Atque umbras hedera lauroque inducite opacas,
Nec desint casiæ, permixtaque cinnama amomo,
Excitet ut dulces aspirans ventus odores.
Nos Alcon dilexit multum, et dignus amari
Ipse fuit nobis, et tali dignus honore.
Interea violas intertexent Amaranthis,
Et tumulo spargent flores, et serta Napeæ,
Et tumulo mœstæ inscribent miserabile carmen.
" Alconem postquam rapuerunt impia fata,
Collacrimant duri montes, et consitus atra est
Nocte dies, sunt candida nigra, et dulcia amara."

l. 62. *tedious* : " wearisome," " irksome " ; obsolete
in that sense, except in certain dialects.

l. 100. *Pales* : cf. note to l. 225 of *Forth Feasting*,
vol. i. p. 247.

l. 132. *Relicts* : cf. note to lxxx, l. 4, vol. i. p. 242.

MADRIGALS, Etc.

I. Clorus, p. 149. On this piece see Notes, vol. i.
p. 157.

II. Sonnet, p. 150, l. 7. *thinkes* : cf. note to l. 16 of
Sextain i, vol. i. p. 180.

l. 9. *hath faire* : this expression, which we have been

unable to trace in any dictionary, appears to be equivalent to the French *avoir beau*.

IV. To Sleepe, p. 151. Suggested by the following sonnet of Bembo (*Rime*, In Venetia, MDXL., p. 28) :

> Sogno ; che dolcemente m' hai furato
> A morte, & del mio mal posto in oblio ;
> Da qual porta del ciel cortese & pio
> Scendesti a rallegrar un dolorato ?
> Qual angel hai la su di me spiato ;
> Che si mouesti al gran bisogno mio ?
> Scampo a lo stato faticoso & rio
> Altro che 'n te non ho lasso trouato.
> Beato se', ch' altrui beato fai :
> Se non ch' usi troppo ale al dipartire ;
> E 'n poca hora mi toi quel, che mi dai.
> Almen ritorna : & già che 'l camin sai,
> Fammi talhor di quel piacer sentire ;
> Che senza te non spero sentir mai.

VI. A Chaine of Gold, p. 152. Compare the following madrigal by Marino (*Rime*, 1602, pt. ii. p. 114) :

> Che noue arti son queste ?
> Per catenarmi il core,
> Vai catenato Amore ?
> Che uale altra catena,
> Oue la bianca man, l' aurato crine
> Mille ne tesse, e più tenaci, e fine ?
> Così per premio di mia lunga pena
> Con queste braccia un dì dato mi sia
> Di far catena a la catena mia.

VII. Epitaph, p. 152, l. 5. *grosse* : " big," " fat," " coarse."

VIII. A Translation, p. 153. We have not succeeded in discovering the original of this piece.

l. 2. *Exild the Champian Ground* : the adjective " *champian* " (or *champion*), of which the modern equivalent is *champaign*, means " pertaining to the open unenclosed country," " the open land."

XI. The Statue of Venus sleeping, p. 154. See vol. i. xlii, p. 117.

XIV. For Dorvs, p. 155. Suggested by a madrigal of Marino (*Rime,* 1602, pt. ii. p. 40), entitled " Scherzo sopra il canto d 'un vecchio sdentato." To the toothless old man his mistress replies :

> Che, se mi baci, i baci
> Temer non deggio almen, che sien mordaci.

There is a shorter version of this trifle in the Hawthorn-den MSS. :

> Why Nais ar yow nice
> Old Dorus for to kiss ?
> The oldest ar most wise :
> Denie him not that bliss ;
> Although his lips be cold and want delight,
> Y'ar sure he shall not your soft cherrie bite.

l. 1. *nice* : " timid," " shy." Cf. note to l. 186 of Song i, vol. i. p. 176.

XV. Loue vagabonding, p. 155, l. 3. *blubbred* : cf. note to l. 9 of Sonnet i, vol. i. p. 207.

l. 6. The Haigh Hall copy of the advance issue of the *Poems,* as well as Phillips, read "*chastests Bosomes,*" which is an instance of a curious Middle Scots usage, according to which many adjectives and pronouns took a plural form when in agreement with a plural noun. The usage appears to have been a literary mannerism unknown to the spoken dialect. Cf. G. Gregory Smith, *Specimens of Middle Scots,* Introd. p. xxxii.

XVI. Phræne, p. 156, l. 9. *sistring* : " having a relationship comparable in some way to that of sisters." Drummond uses the word again, with the same value as in the present line, in one of his " Familiar Epistles " (*Works,* 1711, p. 140) : " The Roman was almost naked from the Waste upwards discovering the sistering Apples of her Breast." Cf. also Shakespeare, *A Lover's Complaint*, ll. 1-2 :

> From off a hill whose concaue Wombe reworded
> A plaintfull story from a sistring vale.

COMMENDATORY VERSES.

I. To Sr. W. A., p. 161. *Doomsday*, on which Sir William Alexander had been engaged for many years, and which he intended to be his greatest work, was first published in 1614 by Andro Hart of Edinburgh. In its original form it consists of four books, in eight-line rhyming stanzas, which were ultimately extended to twelve books in Alexander's collected poetical works, published in 1637, under the title of *Recreations with the Muses*. Each book, called "The First Hour," "The Second Hour," etc., describes one of the hours of the Day of Judgment. Although it can hardly be denied that *Doomsday* wearies the reader by reason of its monotonous length, this is a fault which it shares with not a few other longer poems of the religious kind. It contains, nevertheless, several passages of considerable merit, as these two stanzas may perhaps serve to illustrate :

> The stately Heauens which glory doth array,
> Are mirrours of God's admirable might ;
> There, whence forth spreads the night, forth springs the day,
> He fix'd the fountaines of this temporall light,
> Where stately stars enstall'd, some stand, some stray,
> All sparks of his great power (though small yet bright).
> By what none utter can, no, not conceiue
> All of his greatnesse, shadowes may perceiue.

> What glorious lights through christall lanternes glance,
> (As alwaies burning with their Maker's loue)
> Spheares keepe one musicke, they one measure dance,
> Like influence below, like course aboue,

And all by order led, not drawne by chance,
With majestie (as still in triumph) moue.
And (liberall of their store) seeme shouting thus ;
"Looke up all soules, and gaze on God through us."

Alexander's *Doomsday* was manifestly written to emulate the famous *Sepmaine* of the French Huguenot poet Du Bartas, at a time when these long-winded epics were in vogue, and won for Alexander a great, if only transient, reputation.

Another version of this sonnet, differing considerably from the present one, and interesting because it contains several Scotticisms, figures in vol. ix. of the Hawthornden MSS. :

Whidder braue sprit like Sophocles thow pranse
With crimson cothurne on a statlie stage
That glistring lamps and gazing eies makes glance,
Wailing the Monarches of the worlds first age ;
Or Phœbus-like thow doth thy selff aduance,
With dazeling Diamonds decke, and heaunlie sage
To make a day that sal not feare the rage
Of Times ay whirling wheeles, nor fates nor chance ;
               ^{on}
Phœnix with wings of wonder stil thow flies,
Praise of our Brooks, staine to old Pindus springs.
Thes who the follow wauld, scars with theer eies
Aproche the spheare wheer thow most suetlie sings :
  Thocht Fame mong stars did Orpheus lyre enrolle,
  Thine worthier is to blase about the pole.

ll. 1-4 allude to Alexander's *Monarchicke Tragedies—Darius, Crœsus, The Alexandrian Tragedy,* and *Julius Cæsar.* On these tragedies see vol. ii. p. 394.

ll. 6-7. *Badge: Rage:* probably a correct rhyme, according to the pronunciation of the time, the value of the rhyme-vowel in each case being [a, or a fronted].

l. 8. *Scance:* "scan," "scrutinize." Chiefly Scots in the middle period.

II. To the Author, p. 162. The author in question is one Patrick Gordon, who flourished between 1614 and 1650. In 1614 he published *Neptunus Britannicus*

Corydonis, a Latin poem deploring the death of Prince Henry. The next year he issued two long narrative poems in heroic verse, of which one was *The famous Historye of Penardo and Laissa*. Neither have any literary value.

l. 9. *Thy Syre no pyick-purse is of others witt;* recalls the following line of Sir Philip Sidney (*Ast. and Stella*, Son. lxxiv, l. 8) :

I am no pick-purse of another's wit.

III. On the Death of Godefrid Vander Hagen, p. 163. Little is known of Godfried van der Hagen, except that he was born at Middelburg towards the end of the sixteenth century ; and that in 1617 he was a student at the University of St. Andrews.

IV. Of my Lord of Galloway . . ., p. 164. William Cowper or Couper (1568–1619) was born in Edinburgh, the son of a merchant tailor. He graduated at St. Andrews in 1583. After having been admitted minister of Bothkennar in Stirlingshire, and afterwards of Perth (1595), he was promoted to the bishopric of Galloway (1612), and was also appointed dean of the Chapel Royal. His religious writings are a good deal superior to most of the similar productions of the time, and include, among others, *The Anatomy of a Christian Man* (1611), *Good News from Canaan* (1613), *A Mirror of Mercy* (1614), etc. His complete works appeared in 1623.

V. On the Booke, p. 165. The person to whom this and the following sonnet are addressed by Drummond is Archibald Simson (1564 ?–1628), a Scottish divine, born at Dunbar, probably in 1564. He took a prominent part, on the side of the Presbyterians, in the conflict between church and state. As a writer, he composed a congratulatory poem in praise of James VI. for *The Muses' Welcome*, apart from the two productions to which are prefixed these commendatory verses. Several of his works remain in manuscript in the Advocates' Library.

l. 4. *Rose* : a knot or ornamental device in the sound-hole or the table of certain stringed instruments of the guitar type.

VII. Paraineticon, p. 167. Sir Thomas Kellie's book is a kind of manual on the exercise of infantry. It also contains an exhortation to the reader in which the author calls upon his countrymen to take up arms in aid of Elizabeth, Queen of Bohemia, sister of Charles I. Drummond's stanzas were evoked by this exhortation, or "*paraineticon,*" of Kellie's.

l. 20. Drummond suggests that though part of the Kingdom of Navarre was acquired by the French in 1589, they would do well, instead of spending their time in massacres like that of St. Bartholomew, to endeavour to regain the whole of the ancient kingdom of Navarre, together with Pampeluna, its ancient capital.

VIII. Of the Booke, p. 168. Sir William Moore, or more properly Mure (1594–1657), of Rowallan, was perhaps the most accomplished poet on the Covenanting side, in which connection it may be mentioned that his mother was a sister of Alexander Montgomerie. *The True Crucifixe for True Catholickes*, in more than 3200 lines, consists in great part of an attack on the Roman Catholics. His best work is undoubtedly his version, in verse also, of the story of Dido and Aeneas (1614), which shows considerable mastery of his craft. His works were published in 1898 by the Scottish Text Society.

IX. p. 169. The young lady mourned in these lines was the daughter of John Maitland, first Earl of Lauderdale. She was born on the 1st of October 1612, and died on the 8th of December 1631. Her mother was Lady Isabel Seyton or Seaton (cf. l. 19), the sister of Lady Sophia Seyton, the wife of Sir David Lindsay, Lord Balcarres.

X. Of Persons Varieties, p. 170. David Person's *Varieties* treats of many topics, among others of alchemy. For this reason it is that Drummond (l. 5) recommends the book to the Rosicrucians, who were much addicted to that black art.

l. 8. *lesson'd* : " taught."

POSTHUMOUS POEMS.

I.

Of the posthumous poems printed for the first time in Phillips's edition, two are wrongly attributed by him to Drummond, and have therefore been omitted in the present edition. They are Daniel's well-known sonnet to Sleep (*Delia*, li), and a hymn, beginning " Saviour of mankind, Man Emanuel," by George Sandys, which may be found in his *Relation of a Journey begun An. Dom. 1610* (London, 1615).

I. p. 173. This piece appears, as already pointed out, in Phillips's edition of the *Poems*, with the title " A Translation of S. John Scot his verses, beginning : Quod vitæ sectabor iter." The original is obviously the well-known epigram attributed to Posidippus (*Anth. Pal.* ii. 71). Sir John Scott's elegy, printed in *Delitiæ Poetarum Scotorum* (ii. pp. 482-483), is a free paraphrase of the same epigram, extending the ten verses of Greek to thirty-eight of Latin, so that Phillips's rubric can hardly be a true indication of Drummond's source. Drummond's immediate model was not Sir John Scott's version, but one by Ronsard (*Œuvres*, ii. p. 57), as an examination of the phraseology clearly shows :

> Quel train de vie est-il bon que ie suiue,
> À fin, Muret, qu'heureusement ie viue ?
> Aux Cours des Rois regne l'ambition,
> Les Senateurs sont pleins de passion :
> Les maisons sont de mille soucis pleines,
> Le labourage est tout rempli de peines,
> Le matelot familier du labeur
> Dessus les eaux pallit tousiours de peur.

Celuy qui erre en vn païs estrange,
S'il a du bien, il craint qu'on ne le mange :
L'indigence est vne extreme douleur.
Le mariage est comblé de malheur,
Et si lon vit sans estre en mariage,
Seul & desert il faut vser son âge :
Auoir enfans, n'auoir enfans aussi
Donne tousiours domestique souci.
La ieunesse est peu sage & mal-habile,
La vieillesse est languissante & debile,
Ayant tousiours la mort deuant les yeux.
Donque, Muret, ie croy qu'il vaudroit mieux
L'vn de ces deux, ou bien iamais de n'estre,
Ou de mourir si tost qu'on vient de naistre.

The epigram of Posidippus is prettily translated by Philip Ayres (1638–1712) (Saintsbury, *Minor Poets of the Caroline Period*, ii. 343). The reply by Metrodorus, asserting the contrary in every particular, is translated in the *Arte of English Poesie* (bk. iii. ch. 19), attributed to Puttenham, and also by Philip Ayres.

III. p. 174. Translated, with a variation in the concluding lines, from Sannazaro (*Opere volgari*, Padova, 1723, p. 342) :

Così dunque va 'l mondo, o fere stelle ?
    Così giustizia il ciel governa e regge ?
    Quest' è 'l decreto de l' immota legge ?
    Queste son l' influenzie eterne, e belle ?
L' anime ch' a virtù son più ribelle,
    Fortuna esalta ognor tra le sue gregge ;
    E quelle, per che 'l vizio si corregge,
    Suggette espone a venti, ed a procelle.
Or non devria la rara alma beltade,
    Li divini costumi, e 'l sacro ingegno,
    Alzar costei sovr' ogni umana sorte ?
Destino il vieta ; e tu perverso, indegno
    Mondo, il consenti.   Ahi cieca nostra etade !
    Ahi menti de' mortali oblique e torte !

ll. 7-8.
And they who Thee (poore Idole) Vertue loue
Plye like a feather toss'd by storme and wind.

The editors of the *Works* (1711) replace " *plye* " by " *fly*."
Plye, however, is the correct reading, and is here used in
the nautical sense of " to beat up against the wind."

V. Beauties Frailtye, p. 175. In the Hawthornden
MSS. (vol. x. p. 152) one reads, under the heading " Jodel
in Dido," the following lines from the French poet
Jodelle's tragedy *Didon* :

              . . . beaux teints
Qui tout ainsi qu'on voit la fumee azuree
Du soulphre, reblanchir la Rose coloree,
De moment en moment par l'extresme douleur.
Change avec un effroy sa rosine couleur.

These lines are obviously Drummond's source. This is
proved by various rough copies in the Hawthornden
MSS., with numerous erasures and emendations, which
show how Drummond gradually transformed the material
of the French poet into a neat madrigal.

   l. 1. *maying Rose* : " May rose." Cf. note to l. 6 of
ii, vol. ii. p. 360.

VI. To a swallow . . ., p. 176. Translated from a
madrigal by Mauritio Moro (*I Tre Giardini de' Madrigali*,
Venetia, 1602, pt. iii. p. 125) :

Garrula Rondinella,
   Quest' è Medea crudele, e ancor nol vedi ?
   Se l' empia ai figli suoi fu fiera, e fella,
   Che farà a' tuoi c' ha in seno ?
   Sciocca, da lei che chiedi ?
   Foco, ferro, ò veleno ?
   Mira al tuo scampo, mira,
   Ch' il suo petto crudele auampa d' ira.

VII. Venus armed, p. 176. Adapted from another
madrigal of Mauritio Moro's (*ibid.* p. 134) :

Cinte le spalle hauea,
   E de l' arme di Marte ornato il petto,
La bella Citherea :
Onde Pallade ciò prese a diletto,

E disse : o vaga Dea
Fu d' huopo l' arme, allhora,
Ch' aprl i furti d' Amor, chi 'l Mondo infiora, etc.

Doubtless Drummond had also read the following Latin epigram by Sannazaro (*Opera Omnia, Latine Scripta*, Venetiis, 1570, p. 93) :

Induerat thoraca humeris, galeamque decoro
Aptarat capiti, Marte jubente, Venus.
Nil opus his, Sol, Diva, inquit : sumenda fuerunt,
Cum uos ferratæ circuiere plagæ.

l. 9. *When Vulcan tooke you napping with your knight* : Vulcan was the husband of Venus, and the "*knight*" is Mars, who was notorious for his amours with Venus.

VIII. The Boares head, p. 177, l. 3. *Where play'd Anchises with the Cyprian Queene* : the "*Cyprian Queene*" is Aphrodite or Venus, who fell in love with Anchises, by whom she became the mother of Aeneas.

l. 4. *hang* : see note to l. 110, Song i, vol. i. p. 173.

IX. To an Owle, p. 177, l. 1. *Ascalaphus* : son of Acheron and Gorgyra. When Pluto gave Persephone permission to return to the upper world, provided she had eaten nothing, Ascalaphus declared that she had eaten part of a pomegranate. Persephone in revenge changed him into an owl, by sprinkling him with water from the river Phlegethon (Ovid, *Metam.* v. 8-9).

X. Daphnè, p. 178. Transformed from a sonnet by Garcilaso (*Obras*, Madrid, 1911, p. 220) :

A Dafne ya los brazos le crecían,
Y en luengos ramos vueltos se mostraban ;
En verdes hojas vi que se tornaban
Los cabellos que al oro escurecían.
De áspera corteza se cubrían,
Los tiernos membros, que aún bullendo estaban ;
Los blancos pies en tierra se hincaban,
Y en torcidas raíces se volvían.
Aquel que fué la causa de tal daño,
Á fuerza de llorar, crecer hacía
Este árbol que con lágrimas regaba.

¡ Oh miserable estado, oh mal tamaño !
¡ Que con lloralla cresca cada día
La causa y la razón por que lloraba !

XII. Galateas Sonnets, A. p. 179. This sonnet, and
the next, should be read in connection with Sonnets iii and
xv of *Astrophel and Stella*, and with the following passage
in Sidney's *Apologie for Poetrie*: "But truely many of
such writings as come vnder the banner of vnresistable
loue, if I were a Mistres, would neuer perswade mee they
were in loue ; so coldely they apply fiery speeches, as men
that had rather red Louers writings, and so caught vp
certain swelling phrases."

l. 2. *th' old Thebaine*: Pindar, the greatest of the
Greek lyric poets, born about 522 B.C. at Cynoscephalae,
near Thebes.

l. 3. *In vaine thou tells the faire Europas wrongs*: according to the legend, the beauty of Europa charmed Zeus,
who assumed the form of a bull and mingled with the herd
as Europa and her maidens were sporting on the sea-shore.
Encouraged by the tameness of the animal, Europa
ventured to get on his back ; whereupon the god rushed
into the sea and carried her over to Crete.

XII. B. p. 180, l. 6. *be* = " by " ; the Scots form. Cf.
vol. ii. p. 222, l. 14 ; p. 231, ix, l. 13 ; p. 259, l. 53, etc.

XII. C. p. 181, l. 10. *that Dragon*: the dragon Ladon
who watched over the golden apples of the Hesperides.

l. 12. *Delian wit*: pertaining to Apollo of Delos, who
in course of time grew to be regarded as the god of song
and poetry.

XII. D. p. 182. This is a common type with the
Continental sonneteers. Probably Drummond's model
was the following sonnet by Desportes (*Œuvres*, ed.
Michiels, p. 25) :

Si c'est aimer que porter bas la vue,
Que parler bas, que soupirer souvant,
Que s'égarer solitaire en rêvant,
Brûlé d'un feu qui point ne diminue ;

Si c'est aimer que de peindre en la nue,
 Semer sur l'eau, jetter ses cris au vant,
 Chercher la nuict par le soleil levant,
 Et le soleil quant la nuict est venue ;
Si c'est aimer que de ne s'aimer pas,
 Haïr sa vie, embrasser son trespas,
 Tous les amours sont campez en mon ame ;
Mais nonobstant, si me puis-je louer
 Qu'il n'est prison, ny torture, ny flame,
 Qui mes desirs me sçeust faire avouer.

l. 6. *wake* = " weak " : a Scots form. Cf. the rhyme *weake* : *lake* (vol. ii. p. 191, l. 52), and the note to l. 7 of Song i, vol. i. p. 210.

l. 12. *Then that Athenian in his Bull did frie* : cf. note to ll. 1-2 of Son. liv, vol. i. p. 206.

XIV. p. 184. A note by Drummond, printed in *Archaeologia Scotica* (vol. iv. p. 79), contains a different version of this epitaph :-

GUAZZO HATH THIS EPITAPH ON A DRUNCKARD.

Nè le Rose, nè Amaranthi, ma qui presso,
 Di me versate vino, che da sete,
 Son così in morte, come in vita oppresso.

Which is,

Nor Roses to my tomb, nor Lillies giue,
 But nappye Aile, or Bacchus strongest Wine ;
 For that same thirst, doth yet euen dead mee pine,
 Which made me so carowse when I did liue.

The Hawthornden MSS. (vol. x. p. 166) also contain a third version, differing slightly from the two others :

OUT OF THE ITALIAN.

Nor roses to my tombe nor lilies giue,
 But suetest grapes & Bacchus finest vine,
 For that same thrist, though dead, yet doth me pine,
 Which mad me so carouse while I did liue.

XV. Epitaph, p. 184. An adaptation by Drummond of the well-known epitaph on Aretino, erroneously supposed to have been engraved on his tomb in the church of Saint Luke's at Venice :

Condit Aretini Cineres lapis iste sepultos,
Mortales atro qui sale perfricuit.
Intactus Deus est illi, causamque rogatus
Hanc dedit, ille, inquit, non mihi notus erat.

Or in the Italian :

Qui giace l' Aretin amaro tosco
Del sem' human, la cui lingua trafisse
Et vivi & morti : d' Iddio mal non disse,
El si scusò, co 'l dir, io no 'l conosco.

And still more briefly :

Qui giace l' Aretin, Poëta Tosco,
Che d' ognun disse malo che di Dio,
Scusandosi col dir : io no 'l conosco.

XVIII. Silenus to King Midas, p. 186. Compare the following passage from the first book of Cicero's *Tusculanae Quaestiones* :

" Affertur etiam de Sileno fabella quaedam ; qui cum a Mida captus esset, hoc ei muneris pro sua missione dedisse scribitur : docuisse regem, non nasci homini longe optimum esse ; proximum autem, quam primum mori."

XX. Verses of the late Earl of Pembroke, p. 187. Following the mistake of Phillips, who entitles these stanzas " Verses *on* (instead of *of*, as in the manuscripts) the late William, Earl of Pembroke," recent editors of Drummond's poems, including Ward, have been at a loss to identify the author, in spite of the signature " E. P." The writer of the poem is William Herbert, third Earl of Pembroke (1580–1630), nephew on his mother's side to Sir Philip Sidney. To him and his brother Philip the First Folio Shakespeare was dedicated.

XXII. A Translation, p. 189. A translation of the *Dies Irae*, with the exception of the first four stanzas.

l. 24. *Processe* : " action," " law-suit."

XXIII. To the Memory of . . ., p. 192. These three sonnets were written to the memory of John Maitland, first Earl of Lauderdale. He died on the 20th of January 1645, and was buried at the church at Haddington. He was a statesman of great reputation for ability and literary culture. Though he finally sided with the Covenanters, and was chosen in 1644 President of the Covenanting Scottish Parliament, Drummond hints that he was by no means an enthusiastic supporter of the party to which he belonged. The " *three graue justiciars* " alluded to in the second sonnet were Lauderdale, his father, and grandfather. In the third of these sonnets (ll. 5-8) Drummond makes special mention of the fact that James I., who had been a great admirer of the father of the deceased Earl, namely Sir John Maitland, first Lord Maitland of Thirlstane, Chancellor of Scotland, had on that nobleman's death (Oct. 1595) honoured him with an epitaph written with his own royal hand, and engraved on Sir John's monument in Haddington church.

XXIII. A. p. 192, l. 7. *renuersed* : " overturned," " overthrown " ; now obsolete. Fr. *renverser*.

enurn'd : obsolete variant of " inurned " : " to place in an urn " ; " to entomb," " to bury."

XXIV. To the Memorie of . . ., p. 194. In memory of Isabel Seyton or Seaton, wife of John Maitland, first Earl of Lauderdale, and mother of Lady Jane Maitland. She died in November 1638.

l. 12. *last* : " continuation," " duration " ; now rare.

XXVI. p. 196. In memory of Lady Jane Maitland, daughter of John, Earl of Lauderdale. She died, in the prime of her youth, in December 1631, and was buried at Haddington. A touching poem by Drummond (see vol. ii. p. 169) was subjoined, with about fourscore other pieces, in Latin and English, by different friends of the Maitland family, to her funeral sermon, published in 1633.

XXX. p. 198. See vol. ii. lix, p. 250, for a more complete version of this piece.

XXXI. p. 199. Ward has proved that the subject of this epitaph is Alexander, seventh Lord Livingston and first Earl of Linlithgow, who died in April 1622. Drummond alludes to the fact that to Livingston was committed the care of the infant Princess Elizabeth, who became Queen of Bohemia in 1619. The "*three earls*" were his son Alexander, who succeeded him as Earl of Linlithgow, and his two sons-in-law, the Earls of Eglinton and Wigton.

l. 8. *in grosse* : " on a large scale," " in large quantities " ; now obsolete. Fr. *en gros*.

ll. 13-14.

> *No Rust of Times, nor Change, thy Vertue wan,*
> *With Times to change, when Truth, Faith, Love decay'd.*

We interpret "*wan*" as being the old preterite (still used dialectally) of *win*, and the meaning would be, " No Rust of Times . . . conquered, *i.e.* compelled, thy Vertue to change with Times," etc.

XXXIII. p. 200. The full version of this piece from the Hawthornden MSS. (vol. x. p. 85) is given by Laing (*Archaeologia Scotica*, iv. p. 114). Cf. vol. ii. lxi, p. 251.

XXXIV. p. 201, l. 16. *in great* : " in large quantities," " wholesale." Cf. Fr. *en grand*, Ger. *im Grossen*.

XXXV.-XXXVII. p. 202. These three epitaphs are printed, in Phillips's edition, with the title " Rose," as if they referred to one person. They have, however, no connection. The third refers to James Drummond, first Earl of Perth, who died in December 1611, and was buried in Seton Chapel. Though we are told (l. 6) that no time could bound his wife's love, that lady married Francis Stuart, Earl of Bothwell, less than three years after her husband's demise.

POSTHUMOUS POEMS

II

Of the posthumous poems printed for the first time in the folio edition of Drummond's collected works, one has been omitted as not belonging to Drummond—the " Elegy on Gustavus Adolphus," written by Henry King, Bishop of Chichester. We have also relegated the various pieces included in the folio edition under the rubric " The five Senses," to the " Poems of Doubtful Authenticity," for reasons there stated.

I. p. 205. A reference probably to the General Assembly which met at Glasgow on the 21st of November 1638.

II. p. 206. The following passage in Masson's *Drummond of Hawthornden* (pp. 301-302) is the best commentary on this epigram : " The reference . . . is to the taking of Dalkeith Palace on Sunday the 2nd of March, 1639, by a band of a thousand armed Covenanters, led by the Earls of Rothes, Home, and Lothian, and Lords Yester, St. Clair, and Balmerino. Edinburgh Castle had been seized the day before, and other castles and places of strength were being seized about the same time in other parts of Scotland ; but this taking of Dalkeith Palace was particularly impressive from the fact that the keeper who surrendered it was Traquair himself, ' that lieutenant fame did so extol,' and who was now the king's chief minister in Scotland, and also from the fact that among the spoil taken from the Palace were the Scottish regalia, or as the annalist Balfour calls them, ' the royal ensigns of the kingdom, crown, sword, and sceptre.' They were conveyed the same night to Edinburgh Castle—' the Capitol,' as Drummond calls it—and deposited there with great ceremony. After that, Drummond means to say, what could a man do ? Was one to stand out longer, and be mocked, hissed, plundered, and perhaps banished, for a —— Prince (does the blank cover some disrespectful epithet ?) whose own chief minister had succumbed, and who could not save even his own regalia ?

" The inference is that Drummond did stand out no longer, but did, in the last week of March, or early in April, subscribe the Covenant, whether in his own parish of Lasswade, or elsewhere within the bounds of the Dalkeith Presbytery, or more publicly in Edinburgh."

III. p. 207. An allusion possibly to the Marquis of Hamilton's unsuccessful attempt to veto the proceedings of the Glasgow Assembly in the King's name.

V. and **VI.** p. 207. The " *Rebellion* " referred to in line 4 of the first of these epigrams is probably the Edinburgh riot of 1637. In the second epigram the reference is probably to the first Bishops' War, nearly two years later. Lesley is of course Field-Marshal Lesley, the Scottish commander-in-chief, who is the subject of the next epigram.

VIII. p. 208. John Pym, the famous parliamentarian, died on the 8th of December 1643.

IX. p. 208. A French original of this piece figures in the Hawthornden MSS.

XI. p. 209, l. 4. *hoise up* : " hoist up." Cf. note to l. 6, iv, vol. i. p. 161.

ll. 13-14.

> *Then like a Thisbè let mee not affraye*
> *You when from Ninus Tombe shee ranne away—*

Thisbe was a beautiful Babylonian maiden, beloved by Pyramus. On one occasion they agreed to meet at night near the tomb of Ninus. Thisbe arrived there first, and while she was waiting for Pyramus, she perceived a lioness, which had just torn to pieces an ox, and took to flight. While running away she lost her veil, which the beast tore and befouled with blood. Pyramus on arriving found the veil, and killed himself in despair at the supposed murder of his beloved. When Thisbe returning from her flight found his corpse she also killed herself with his sword (Ovid, *Metam.* iv. 1).

l. 15. *This well yee see is not that Arethusa* : the nymph Arethusa, one of the Nereids, pursued by the river-god Alpheus, implored the assistance of Diana or Artemis, who changed her into the fountain of Arethusa in the island of Ortygia at Syracuse in Sicily (Ovid, *Metam.* v. 8).

l. 17. *Lyęus* : Lyaeus, or the " care-dispeller," was one of the appellations of Dionysus, the god of wine.

XII. The country Maid, p. 210, l. 14. *barded* : " bearded." The form *berd* of the verb *beard* is found in the sixteenth century, and under the influence of *r* was often pronounced and written *bard*, particularly in Scots.

XIII. p. 211. In the last line Drummond is probably alluding to the plague which raged in Scotland throughout the year 1645.

XVI. Translation of the death of a sparrow . . ., p. 212. The original in Passerat (*Poésies françaises*, ed. Blanchemain, i. p. 56) runs as follows :

> Demandez vous, Amis, d'où viennent tant de larmes
> Que me voyez rouler sur ces funebres carmes ?
> Mon Passereau est mort, qui fut si bien appris :
> Hélas ! c'est faict de luy, vne Chate l'a pris.
> Ie ne le verray plus en sautelant me suiure :
> Or' le iour me deplaist, or' ie suis las de viure.
> Plus donc ie ne l'orray chanter son pilleri ?
> Et n'ay-ie pas raison d'en estre bien marri ?
> Il estoit passé maistre à croquer vne mousche :
> Il n'estoit point gourmand, cholere ny farousche,
> Si on ne l'attaquoit pour sa queue outrager :
> Lors il pinçoit les doigts, ardent à se vanger.
> Adonc vous l'eussiez veu crouller la rouge creste
> Attachée au sommet de sa petite teste,
> Tel que l'on veit Hector, mur de ses citoyens,
> Dedans les Grecques naufs lancer les feux Troyens.
> Toutesfois vne Chate, espiant ceste proye,
> D'vn sault, à gueule bée, engloutit nostre ioye.

Le pauuret, pour certain, fut pris en trahison,
Autrement de la Chate il eust eu sa raison.
Le pasteur Phrygien ainsi vainquit Achille,
Et le vain Geneuois la vaillante Camille.
Ainsi le grand cheual que Pallas charpenta
Contre le vieil Priam des soldats enfanta.
Toy qui en as le cœur enflé de vaine gloire,
Bien peu te durera l'honneur de ta victoire.
Si quelque sentiment reste apres le trespas
Aux espris des oiseaux qui trebuschent là bas.
L'ame de mon mignon se sentira vengée
Sur le sang ennemy de la Chate enragée.
Ie ne rencontreray ny Chate ny Chaton
Que ie n'enuoye apres miauler chez Pluton.
Vous qui volez par l'air entendans les nouuelles
De ceste digne mort, tournez icy vos ælles;
Venez, piteux oiseaux, accompagner mes pleurs,
Portons à son idole vne moisson de fleurs.
Qu'il reçoiue de nous vne agreable offrande
De vin doux & de laict, d'encens & de viande:
Puis engrauons ces mots sur son vuide tombeau:
Passant, le petit corps d'vn gentil Passereau
Gist au ventre goulu d'vne Chate inhumaine,
Aux champs Elysiens son Ombre se proumeine.

l. 4. *toward*: "not froward"; "docile," "ready to do or to learn."

l. 22. *And stout Camilla fell by Aruns vaine*: Camilla, daughter of King Metabus, was one of the swift-footed servants of Diana. She assisted Turnus against Aeneas, and after slaying many Trojans was at length killed by Aruns.

l. 29. *sal know*: the Scots form *sal* for *shall*, still used in Mod. Scots, is the usual form in Drummond's manuscript poems. In the same way he uses *suld* for *should*. Cf. vol. ii. p. 222, l. 20; p. 231, ix, l. 4; p. 241, xxx, l. 11; p. 247, lv, l. 2, etc.

l. 31. *chat*: "cat"; apparently simply a carry over from Passerat's French. Wright (*English Dialect Dictionary*) registers the form *chat*, but only for Devonshire.

l. 34. *hadervart*: Mid. Scots form of "hitherward."

XVIII. p. 215.   Imitated from a Canzone of Marino entitled " Stabat Mater dolorosa " (*Rime*, 1602, pt. ii. 179). The imitation, however, is never servile, as the following passages, in which Drummond comes nearest to his model, will show.

ll. 1-5. *The woefull Marie midst a blubbred band*, etc. Compare Marino :

> . . . . . .
>
> Sconsolata Maria
> Qual tortorella uedoua, languia.
>
> Staua l' addolorata
> Al duro tronco appresso,
> A par del tronco stesso
> Immobile, insensata :
> In piè reggeala Amore,
> E sosteneala in uita il suo dolore.

ll. 13-18. *Long fixing downecast eies on earth, at last*, etc. Compare Marino :

> Tutta struggeasi in pianto
> Mirando (ahi scempio crudo)
> Lo 'nsanguinato ignudo,
> Ignudo, se non quanto
> D' un negro uelo ombroso
> Cinto l' hauea d' intorno il Ciel pietoso.

ll. 24-34. *And griefe her suffred onlye sigh, O my*, etc. Compare Marino :

> . . . . . .
>
> E pianse, e disse, O mio :
> Ma l' interruppe il pianto, e non finio.
>
> O mio (poscia riprese)
> Figlio, de la paterna
> Bellezza imago eterna,
> Chi costà ti sospese ?
> Chi t' ha sì concio ? o quale
> (Tua no) sì graue fu colpa mortale ?
>
> Chi d' atro sangue ha tinto
> Quegli occhi (oimè) quel uiso
> Specchi di Paradiso ?

> Chi quelle chiome ha cinto
> Di duri aghi pungenti,
> Già coronate in Ciel di stelle ardenti ?

ll. 37-60. *Was it for this I bred thee in my wombe,* etc.
Compare Marino :

> Te dunque in sen portai,
> Te lieta in fasce auinsi,
> Te dolce in braccio strinsi,
> Te di latte cibai,
> Sol perchè stratio e scempio
> Fesse di te sì crudo il popol' empio ?
>
> Già ti uid' io di fiori
> Ornato, e d' altri fregi
> Fra' peregrini Regi
> Nel' antro, e fra' pastori :
> Hor' hai su questo monte,
> Pendente fra duo rei, bestemmie, & onte.
>
> Di sete aspra, & amara
> Oimè, ueggio languirti,
> Nè pur mi lice offrirti
> Pria, che 'n te Morte auara
> Lo strale ultimo scocchi,
> Qual dele poppe già, l' urne degli occhi.
>
> Gli occhi uolgi, & assisa
> Padre eterno del Cielo
> In quel lacero uelo :
> Mira in che strania guisa,
> Pende dal crudo legno,
> Riconosci (se sai) l' amato pegno.
>
> Pon mente, se son quelle
> Le man, quelle le piante,
> Quelle le luci sante,
> Ond' hebber già le stelle
> Forma, uirtute, e raggi,
> Fatte hor segni al' ingiurie, & a gli oltraggi.

In the latter part of the poem the Italian original is
considerably condensed.

ll. 61-78.

> *Did all my prayers serue for this ?   Is this*
> *The promise that celestiall herault made,* etc.

Compare Marino :

> Son queste (ahi lassa) sono
> Le tue promesse queste,
> Messaggiero celeste ?
> Già non son' io non sono
> Fra l' altre benedetta,
> Ma sour' ogni altra misera, e negletta.

> . . . .

> Quanto del uecchio hebreo,
> Che chiuse i lumi in pace,
> Fu l' oracol uerace :
> Ch' un giorno acerbo e reo
> Deuea madre e figliuolo
> L' uno uccider' il ferro, e l' altra il duolo.

> Figlio, indugia il morire,
> Ritien lo spirto ancora
> Tanto che teco i' mora :
> Che 'n sì graue martire
> Di cor, d' anima priua,
> Com' esser può, che senza uita i' viua ?

> Pur se 'l mio graue affanno
> Non è sì graue, e forte,
> Che basti a darmi morte ;
> Voi pronte al' altrui danno
> Crudelissime squadre,
> Che non ferir col figlio anco la madre ?

ll. 85-90. *The Heauens which in their orbes still constant moue,* etc. Compare Marino :

> Per non mirarlo, serra
> Il Ciel gli occhi sereni.
> Ma tu come il sostieni
> Ingratissima Terra ?
> Qui Christo estinto giacque,
> E la terra si scosse, & ella tacque.

l. 16. *Embrued* = " imbrued " : " stained," " dyed " (especially with blood).

l. 31. *blamed* : " pale," " blanched." We can find no record in any dictionary of the verb *blame* in that sense, though such a verb would be naturally derived from Fr.

blémir (also *blesmir, blaimir* in O.F.), " to render livid or pale." It may be noted that the verb *blemish*, which is derived from *blemiss-*, the extended stem of *blémir*, is occasionally found in the sixteenth century with the meaning that *blame* has here.

l. 33. *wert* = " wast " : *wert* for *wast* prevailed in literature during the seventeenth and eighteenth centuries, and has been used by many writers of the nineteenth century, but chiefly in poetry, or in sustained prose.

l. 67. *choysd* : past participle of the Scots *choise* (Fr. *choisir*), " to choose."

XIX. p. 218. **A Character of the Anti-Couenanter, or Malignant.** This lampoon, turned ironically by Drummond against himself, is modelled, both as regards matter and form, on some biting verses which Passerat composed for the *Satire Ménippée*. The opening lines of the original (ed. M. C. Read, p. 220) are quoted in illustration :

> Pour connoistre les Politiques,
> Adherents, Fauteurs d'Heretiques;
> Tant soient-ils cachez et couvers,
> Il ne faut que lire ces vers.
>   Qui se plaint du temps et des hommes,
> En ce siecle d'or où nous sommes ;
> Qui ne veut donner tout le sien,
> À ceste cause il ne vaut rien.

l. 5. *spring* : " to start," or " cause to rise " (like game).

l. 6. *hing* : " hang." Cf. note to l. 110 of Song i, vol. i. p. 173.

l. 12. *cantom* = " canton" : properly to " subdivide into cantons " or " districts " ; to " subdivide," to " sever," to " secede."

l. 25. *avouch* : " affirm." Cf. note to l. 681 of *A Cypresse Grove*, vol. ii. p. 352.

l. 58. *Croslets* = " corslets." The metathesis of *r* is characteristic of Scots and of the northern dialects. Cf. *thrist* (vol. ii. xxvi, p. 239, l. 4), *brunt* (vol. ii. p. 257, l. 12), etc.

l. 100. *flowere* : " adorn," " decorate " ; now obsolete.

XX. Song of Passerat, p. 221.   The original in
Passerat (*Poésies françaises*, ed. Blanchemain, i. p. 141)
runs as follows :

Elle.	Pastoureau, m'aimes-tu bien ?
Lui.	Je t'aime, Dieu sçait combien
Elle.	Comme quoi ?
Lui.	Comme toi,
	Ma rebelle
	Pastourelle.
Elle.	En rien ne m'a contenté
	Ce propos trop affetté,
	Pastoureau, sans moquerie
	M'aimes-tu ? di, ie te prie
	Comme quoi ?
Lui.	Comme toi,
	Ma rebelle
	Pastourelle.
Elle.	Tu m'eusses répondu mieus,
	Je t'aime comme mes yeux.
Lui.	Trop de haine ie leur porte :
	Car ils ont ouuert la porte
	Aux peines que i'ay receu,
	Des lors que ie t'apperçeu :
	Quand ma liberté fut prise
	De ton œil qui me maistrise.
Elle.	Comme quoi ?
Lui.	Comme toi,
	Ma rebelle
	Pastourelle.
Elle.	Pastoureau, parle autrement
	Et me di tout rondement,
	M'aimes-tu comme ta vie ?
Lui.	Non, car elle est asseruie
	A cent & cent mille ennuis,
	Dont aimer ie ne la puis,
	N'estant plus qu'vn corps sans ame
	Pour trop cherir vne dame.
Elle.	Comme quoi ?
Lui.	Comme toi
	Ma rebelle
	Pastourelle.

Elle. Laisse là ce Comme toi :
　　　　Dis, ie t'aime comme moi.
Lui. Je ne m'aime pas moy-mesmes.
Elle. Di moy doncques, si tu m'aimes,
　　　　　　　Comme quoi ?
Lui. Comme toi,
　　　　Ma rebelle
　　　　Pastourelle.

It is interesting to note that this pretty song was also imitated by the German poet G. R. Weckherlin (1584–1653). His model, however, cannot have been Drummond, as is generally supposed, for Drummond's poem was not published till 1711, in the folio edition of his *Works*.

. l. 14. *Entress* : "entrance" ; found in the sixteenth and seventeenth centuries, chiefly in Scots.

l. 25. *thruch* : Scots for *through*. Cf. the forms *thochts* (ix, l. 9, vol. ii. p. 231), *vrocht* (xi, l. 12, vol. ii. p. 232), *ocht* (xv, l. 8, vol. ii. p. 234), *brocht* (i, l. 50, vol. ii. p. 259), *nocht* (ii, l. 88, vol. ii. p. 266), etc.

XXI. p. 223. These lines are explained in the introductory memoir prefixed to the folio edition of 1711 :

"In the year 1645, when the Plague was raging in Scotland, our Author came accidentally to Forfar, but was not allowed to enter any House, or to get Lodging in the Town, tho' it was very late : He went some Two Miles farther to Kirrimuir, where he was well received and kindly entertained. Being informed, that the Towns of Forfar and Kirrimuir had a Contest, about a Piece of Ground, call'd The Muirmoss, he wrote a Letter to the Provost of Forfar, to be communicated to the Town-Council in Haste. It was imagined this Letter came from the Estates, who were then sitting at St. Andrew's : So the common Council was called with all Expedition, and the Minister sent for, to Pray for Direction and Assistance in Answering the Letter, which was opened in a solemn

Manner. It contained the following Lines." Next follow the lines in question.

l. 4. *Kirrimuir bears the Gree* : Kirrimuir " bears away the palm " ; " takes the highest honours." This use of the word *gree* (O.F. *gree*), especially in the phrase " bear, take, win the gree," is almost confined to Scots in the middle period, and is now exclusively dialectal, particularly Scots and Northumbrian.

XXII. p. 223. Relates to the first Bishops' War, May and June 1639. Here again the memoir prefixed to the folio edition is the best commentary : " He was a great Cavalier, and much addicted to the King's Party ; yet was forced to send Men to the Army which fought against the King : And, his Estate lying in three different Shires, he had not Occasion to send one intire Man, but Halfs and Quarters, and such like Fractions : Upon which he wrote *ex tempore* the following Verses to his Majesty." Next follow the verses in question.

POSTHUMOUS POEMS.

III.

I. D. A. Johnstones Eden-Bourgh, p. 227. A rendering from the Latin of Arthur Johnston, Physician to King Charles (1587–1641), a native of Aberdeenshire. In his day he enjoyed a great reputation as a writer of Latin verse. Many of his poems are included in the *Delitiæ Poetarum Scotorum* (Amsterdam, 1637), and his complete Latin works were collected and printed in 1642, at the instigation of Sir John Scott of Scotstarvet, under the title *Arturi Johnstoni, Scoti, Medici Regii, Poemata Omnia, Middelb. Zeland, ex officina Mouleriana*, 1642. His Latin address to Edinburgh is as follows :

> Collibus assurgens geminis, caput inserit astris,
>   Et tutelares cernit Edina deos.

Sceptra thronique pedem firmant et regia ad ortum,
    Solis ad occasum Mars tegit arce caput ;
Claro mille animos exercet Phœbus ab Austro,
    Ad Boream Pallas dædala mille manus.
Templa tenent vicina deæ Pietasque Themisque,
    Enthea qua puro pectore vita salit :
Ancillatricem Cererem, Nymphasque ministras,
    Et vectigalem despicit inde Thetin.
Romuleam Tibris, Venetam mare territat urbem,
    Quas regit undarum ridet Edina minas.
Crede mihi, nusquam vel sceptris aptior urbs est,
    Vel rerum domina dignior urbe locus.
Verum ut sint multis istæc communia, soli
    Privus et insignis hic tibi cedit honos :
Nemo unquam nisi scurra levis, vel tressis agaso,
    Est ausus famam contemerare tuam.

II. To the honorable Author, S. J. Sk., p. 228.
This sonnet was probably addressed to Sir John Skene of
Curriehill, Clerk Register, on the publication in 1609 of
his translation of the *Regiam Majestatem. The Auld
Lawes and Constitutions of Scotland.*

l. 3. *cimerian Bowres* : the Cimmerii are a mythical
people mentioned by Homer, who dwelt in the farthest
west on the ocean, enveloped in constant mists and
darkness.

l. 7. *Or like ag'd Æsons bodye* : Aeson, son of Cretheus,
king of Iolcos in Thessaly, was deposed by his half-brother
Pelias and killed while his son Jason was away on the
Argonautic expedition. According to Ovid Aeson lived to
an old age, survived the return of the Argonauts, and was
made young again by Medea (*Metam.* vii. 2).

courb'd : on this form see note to l. 445 of *A Cypresse
Grove,* vol. ii. p. 350.

III. p. 228, l. 10. *Malgrè* : on the form *malgré* cf. note
to l. 14 of Son. xxiv, vol. i. p. 188.

V. p. 229. This sonnet was evidently written in
allusion to *The Monarchicke Tragedies* by Sir William
Alexander, Earl of Stirling, consisting of *Darius* (1603),

Crœsus (1604), *The Alexandrian Tragedy* (1605), *Julius Cæsar* (1607), to the latter of which he added those that had preceded, and reissued all four under the title of *The Monarchicke Tragedies.* All these tragedies are in rhyme, and though containing some passages of stately verse, they are absolutely devoid of any dramatic action, resembling in that particular the contemporary French classical tragedies by which they were no doubt inspired.

VI. Sonnet before a poëme of Irene, p. 230. We have not succeeded, any more than Laing, in ascertaining on what poem this sonnet was written.

VII. p. 230. The person referred to in this sonnet appears to be Colonel James Halkerston, about whom very little is known for certain, except that he contributed some Latin epigrams to the *Deliticæ Poetarum Scotorum.*

VIII.–XV. pp. 231-234. Drummond found the two Italian sonnets in question, with three different translations varying in literalness, in the *Recherches de la France* of Estienne Pasquier (bk. vii. ch. 8). An absolute proof that we are here in presence of the Scottish poet's source is afforded by the fact that in the Hawthornden MSS. the first of the Italian sonnets is entitled by Drummond " Sonnet qu'un Poet Italien fit pour vn bracelet de cheveux qui lui avoit estè donnè par sa maistresse "— which are the very words used by Pasquier himself to introduce the Italian poet's composition. The first of these Italian sonnets (" O chiome, parte de la treccia d' oro "), of which the author is not mentioned by Pasquier, and whom Ward failed to identify, is by Antonio Tebaldeo (*Opere d'Amore di Messer Antonio Tebaldeo*, Venezia, 1550, No. 106), one of the poets of the Quattrocento.

XI. p. 232, l. 1. *tuitchet* = " twitched," from *twitch*, " to draw tightly together," " to tie in a knot." Cf. Milton, *Lycidas* 192, " twitched his mantle blew."

l. 8. *decore*: " adorn." Cf. note to l. 11, Song ii vol. i. p. 194.

XIII. p. 233, l. 7. *cabans* : on *caban* see note to l. 96, Song i, vol. i. p. 210.

l. 10. *schoot* : a Scots form [šŏt] of the p.p. of *shoot*.

XIV. p. 234, l. 8. *fra* : Scots for " from."

helmish bours : the word *helmish* is not recorded in any dictionary, as far as we are aware. The *N.E.D.* notes that the word *helm* ("helmet," properly "covering") was used in O.E., as it is now in parts of Scotland and in the northern English counties, for the " crown " or " top " of anything, and more especially for the " leafy top of a tree." The conjunction of " *helmish* " with " *bours* " shows that this is here the meaning, and that *helmish* is equivalent to " leafy and thick."

l. 9. *murthering* : "murdering." Cf. note, l. 14, Son. xliv, vol. i. p. 201.

l. 11. *on* = " one."

quho = " who." The early English guttural initial *hw*, *wh*, are represented in Mid. Scots by *quh*, *qwh*. There are several examples of this spelling in Drummond's manuscript poems.

embush = ambush ; O.F. *embusche*. This form, alongside *ambush*, is found during the second half of the sixteenth century and the early seventeenth century.

XV. p. 234, l. 6. *cruking* = " crooking " : " bending," " meandering."

XVI. On the image of Lucrece, p. 235, l. 2. *That dying Dame who first did banish kings* : the rape of Lucretia, the wife of L. Tarquinius Collatinus, led to the dethronement and banishment of Tarquinius Superbus, and the establishment of the republic.

l. 9. Laing reads " *give* " as the last word of this verse—which gives no satisfactory meaning. The manuscript has clearly " *griue*," i.e. " grieve."

XVII. Neroes image, p. 235. Translated from the following madrigal by Marino (*Rime*, 1602, pt. ii. p. 146) :

Fu dotta mano, che finse
   In sì viua scoltura
   Del superbo Neron l' empia figura.
   Nè già meglio il potea
   Per pareggiar Natura,
   L' Arte formar, che 'n fredda pietra, e dura :
   Ch' ancor quando viuea,
   E la patria, e la madre arse, & estinse,
   Di senno, di pietà, di senso casso,
   Altro non fu, ch' vn duro, e freddo sasso.

XVIII. Amphion of marble, p. 236. Again from a
madrigal by Marino (*Rime*, 1602, pt. ii. p. 147), but with a
modification in the theme :

      Non è di vita priuo,
         Non è di spirto casso,
         Quest' Anfion di sasso,
         Anzi sì viue, e spira,
         Che, se 'l plettro mouesse insù la lira,
         Quand' ei non fusse viuo,
         La sua stessa armonia
         Auiuar lo poria.

   l. 5. *tuitche* : *tuitch* or *twitch* : a Scots form of *to
touch*.

XIX. Of a Be, p. 236. Suggested by, and condensed
from, a madrigal of Guarini (*Rime*, 1598, p. 94), entitled
" Baciate Labra " :

      Punto da vn' ape, a cui
         Rubaua il mele il pargoletto Amore,
         Quel rubato licore
         Tutto pien d' ira, e di vendetta pose
         Su le labra di rose
         A la mia Donna, e disse, in voi si serbe
         Memoria non mai spenta
         De le soaui mie rapine acerbe ;
         E chi vi bacia senta
         De l' ape ch' io prouai dolce, e crudele
         L' ago nel core, e ne la bocca il mele.

XXII. Regrat, p. 237. Transmuted, as the title helps to indicate, from a sonnet of Desportes (*Œuvres*, ed. Michiels, p. 190) :

> Ceux que trop d'avarice, ou trop peu de sagesse,
>   Dans un foible vaisseau fait sur mer voyager,
>   Et qui cherchent la mort au rivage estranger,
>   Poinds d'un sale desir qui n'a jamais de cesse,
> Si le juste courroux de Neptune les presse,
>   Et qu'ils perdent l'espoir par l'effroy du danger,
>   Chacun à qui mieux mieux pour la nef décharger,
>   Jette au milieu des eaux sa plus chere richesse.
> Moi qui d'un beau desir me sentoy enflammer,
>   Je m'embarquay joyeux sur l'amoureuse mer,
>   Qui de flots et de vents aussi tost fut couverte ;
> Pour décharger ma nef, j'ay franchement jetté
>   Tout ce qui m'estoit cher, l'ame et la liberté,
>   Et n'ay point de regret d'avoir fait cette perte.

The form *Regrat(e)* in the title (cf. lvii, l. 19, p. 248) is a Mid. Scots form of *regret*.

l. 2. *Where many Sillas barke* : Scylla is represented in mythology as a fearful monster dwelling on the rock of that name between Italy and Sicily, who barked like a dog, and had twelve feet and six long necks and heads, each of which contained three rows of sharp teeth.

XXIII. A sigh, p. 238. Borrowed from the following madrigal by Marino (*Rime*, 1602, pt. ii. p. 77) :

> Sospir, che del bel petto
>   Di Madonna esci fore,
>   Dimmi, che fa quel core ?
>   Serba l' antico affetto ?
>   O pur messo se' tu di nouo amore ?
>   Deh no, più tosto sia
>   Sospirata da lei la morte mia.

l. 4. *ieast* : an Elizabethan form of *jest*.

XXIV. Stollen pleasure, p. 238. From the following madrigal by Tasso (*Rime*, Venice, 1608, pt. ii. p. 215) :

Dolcemente dormiva la mia Clori,
 E 'ntorno al suo bel volto
 Givan scherzando i pargoletti Amori
 Mirav' io da me tolto
 Con gran diletto lei,
 Quando dirmi sentì, Stolto, che fai ?
 Tempo perduto non s' acquista mai.
 Allor' io mi chinai così pian piano,
 E baciandole il viso
 Trovai quanta dolcezza ha il paradiso.

XXV. Of a Kisse, p. 239, l. 21. *Sweet, sweetning Midases*, etc. : on the story of King Midas see note to l. 1 of Son. xlviii, vol. i. p. 203.

XXVI. A Locke desired, p. 239, l. 4. *thrist* = " thirst." On the frequency in Scots of the metathesis of *r* see note to l. 58, xix, vol. ii. p. 390.

l. 7. *faire Treseresse* : possessor of fine tresses.

XXIX. Non vltra, p. 240, ll. 1-2. *Idmon* and *Anthea* are imaginary names.

XXX. Fragment, p. 241, l. 4. *Gins* : " begins." *Gin*, now obsolete or archaic, is an apheetic form of *begin*.

l. 11. *thole* : " endure," " suffer " ; now obsolete, except in Scots and certain northern dialects.

XXXI. Fragment, p. 241. A faithful rendering of a passage from one of Passerat's elegies (*Poésies françaises*, ed. Blanchemain, ii. p. 88). Evidently a juvenile exercise :

Nous estions en Autonne ; & ià l'oiseau cresté
Qui annonce le iour, deus fois auoit chanté :
Les trois parts de la nuit estoient quasi passées :
Quand las & trauaillé d'amoureuses pensées,
Ie receu le sommeil, qui coullant gracieus
Fit cesser les ennuis de mon cœur soucieus.
A grand' peine auoit-il mes paupieres fermées
De sa baguette d'or, & de liqueurs charmées
Arrousé mon cerueau. . . .

XXXII. p. 242. Written, in a petulant mood, by Drummond, when he saw himself compelled to subscribe the Covenant, in the spring of 1639 probably.

XXXV. p. 242, l. 1. *sitten* : p.p. of " to sit " ; a Scots and northern English dialectal form.

XXXVII. p. 243. *Zanzummines* was a nickname given by the Presbyterians to their enemies, in allusion to the giant Zamzummim of *Deuteronomy* ii. 20.

l. 4. *The king of Beane* : a " Bean King " is a king elected by ballot. The Greeks and Romans used beans in voting by ballot. Hence " *the king of Beane* " means possibly the " rightfully elected king." Or perhaps " *Beane* " stands for *Bene*, an obsolete word, meaning " prayer," especially a " prayer to God." The contrast with " *blake prince of Walles* " (*Hell*, rhyming with *tell*) favours the second interpretation. A third interpretation would be to take " *the king of Beane* " to mean the Twelfth Night King, the one who gets the bean in the cake on Twelfth Night, and is adjudged king for the evening ; hence, in this passage, " an unreal king," " a mock king." This is the simplest, and probably the correct solution.

XXXVIII. p. 243. A scornful allusion to the honours bestowed by Charles upon the Presbyterian leaders during his visit of conciliation to Edinburgh, in the autumn of 1641.

XXXIX. p. 243. The Scottish Parliament met at St. Andrews on November 26, 1645. The parliament could hardly be said with justice to be " *confined* " at St. Andrews through fear of Montrose, as his cause had recently been shattered on the field of Philiphaugh.

l. 3. *Pasquill* : " Pasquin " : the Roman Pasquino (man or statue), on whom pasquinades were fastened ;

hence the imaginary personage to whom anonymous lampoons were conventionally ascribed.

XL. Epitaph of a Judge, p. 243. Compare the " epitaph " in vol. i. p. 124.

XLI. p. 243. *turnores* : " turners," or " black farthings," were the small coins which William Alexander, Viscount Stirling, was allowed by royal prerogative to issue for circulation in Scotland at a rate over the intrinsic value of the metal, so as to yield him a considerable margin of profit.

XLIII. A prouerbe, p. 244. Relates to the first Bishops' War, and lines 3-4 more particularly to the Earl of Holland's march into Scotland (June 3, 1639), and his precipitate retreat as soon as he caught sight of the Scottish army encamped on Duns Law.

XLV. On Marye Kings pest, p. 244. An allusion to the plague which raged in Scotland in the year 1645.
l. 4. *Marye* : Henrietta Mary of France.

XLVIII. p. 245. On this piece see note on " Poems of Doubtful Authenticity," vol. ii. p. 424.
l. 1. *Flyting* : " scolding."

XLIX. On Pomponatius, p. 245. Pietro Pomponazzi (1462–1525), a famous philosopher of the Aristotelian school, author of a dissertation " On the Immortality of the Soul," in which he contested the doctrine of the soul's immortality save as a Christian dogma.
l. 1. *Trade* = " tread." On this form see note to l. 37 of " An Hymne of the Passion," vol. ii. p. 335.

L. On the isle of Rhe, p. 245. Refers to the Duke of Buckingham's ill-fated expedition to La Rochelle and his attack, in 1627, on the isle of Rhé. To understand properly the pun in the second line it is necessary to remember that a "*drake*" was a species of cannon, and that "*duck*" is the Scottish pronunciation of "duke."

LI. Epitaph, p. 245.   Robert Crichton, Lord Sanquhar, was hanged at Westminster on the 29th of June 1619, for the murder of a fencing master named Turner.

LIII. p. 246.   Andrew Ramsay, Professor of Divinity in the University of Edinburgh, who incurred the displeasure of his friends by his zeal for the Covenant.
l. 4. *rocket*: "rochet"; a Scots form chiefly.

LIV. p. 246, l. 1.   *Momus*: in Greek mythology the evil spirit of blame and mockery.
l. 2. *Mores* = Moors: "black."   Cf. note to l. 189 of "The Shadow of the Iudgement," vol. ii. p. 343.
ll. 13-14. *His Rome when Cęsare*, etc.: a reference to the great fire at Rome which happened in Nero's reign (A.D. 64).   According to some ancient writers, the city was fired by Nero's order.

LV. On a glasse . . ., p. 247, l. 4. *excep*: "except." After *c* and *p* a final consonant is not infrequently dropped in Mid. Scots.   Cf. *interrup*, ii, l. 86, p. 266.

LVI. Sextain, p. 247.   An unmistakable reference to Alexander Craig (*c.* 1567–*c.* 1627) of Rose-Craig, one of the minor Scottish poets of the early seventeenth century. His works were published in collected form in 1873, with an introductory memoir by David Laing, for the Hunterian Club.   The allusion in line 2 is to the second of his works, entitled *The Amorose Songes, Sonets, and Elegies of M. Alexander Craige, Scoto-Britane* (London, 1606), "*Kala*" being one of the eight fictitious damsels addressed by Craig in that collection.   Craig's exaggerated opinion of the value of his own poetic effusions, which are devoid of all literary worth, probably brought upon him Drummond's sarcastic lines.   In one of his sonnets to "Idea," for example, he says:

My flowing Songs I consecrate to thee,
Good reason were, that they should all be thine.
Thy presence creates all those thoughts in me,
Which mee Immortall, and make thee Diuine.

LVII. Encomiastike verses, etc., p. 248, l. 2. *Encomium Morie* : *Encomium Moriæ,* or "Praise of Folly," by Erasmus (1465–1536), composed in Thomas More's house on the third and longest visit of Erasmus to this country. In this witty satire, which Milton found "in every one's hands" in Cambridge in 1628, and which is read to this day, kings and princes, bishops and popes alike are shown to be in bondage to Folly.

l. 4. *Carowsd the Horses spring* : simply a way of saying that James cultivated poetry. The "*horse*" referred to is of course Pegasus, and the "*spring*" Hippocrene.

l. 6. *Jhon Maior* : cf. note to l. 198 of *The Entertainment,* vol. ii. p. 359.

l. 18. *Or like the french kings relicks at Saint Denis* : the famous Abbey of Saint-Denis, some five miles north of Paris, was during twelve centuries the burial-place of the kings of France.

l. 34. *pecorious,* or rather *pecorus* : properly "rich in cattle," but here, like the noun *pecus* ("cattle") in Latin, applied contemptuously, or as a term of abuse, to a person.

LVIII. To the Memorie of . . . Master, M. F. R., p. 249.

John Ray was Professor of Humanity in the University of Edinburgh while Drummond was a student there. He died probably about the year 1636. Whatever his powers as a Latinist may have been, it appears from a letter (*Lives of the Lindsays,* ii. p. 5) of Sir John Scott of Scotstarvet, addressed to Sir David Lindsay in April of 1615, that this John Ray had been charged, at the desire of Sir John Scott and Sir William Alexander of Menstrie, to make a collection of the Scottish poets who had written in Latin.

The scheme, however, dropped to the ground, and it was not till twenty-two years afterwards that the *Delitiæ Poetarum Scotorum* appeared at Amsterdam.

LIX. D. O. M. S., p. 250. The first part of this epitaph was first printed in Phillips's edition, the name Dalyell being omitted. The entire epitaph was first printed in *Archæologia Scotica* (iv. p. 113). The gentleman in question was Sheriff of Linlithgowshire, and his son became afterwards commander-in-chief in Scotland for Charles II.

LXI. To the Memorie of . . ., p. 251. The verses of this epitaph were first printed in Phillips's edition, and the whole epitaph in *Archæologia Scotica* (iv. p. 114).

LXII. To the Memorie of . . ., p. 252. Possibly Lady Jane Ker, wife of the second Earl of Perth.

LXIII. To the Memorie of . . ., p. 253. The lady addressed in these verses was one of the Prestons of Craigmillar near Edinburgh, possibly the mother of George Preston, Laird of Craigmillar, one of Drummond's most intimate friends.

LXIV. D. O. M. S., p. 254. The first four verses are borrowed from *Teares on the Death of Moeliades* (ll. 21-24).

POSTHUMOUS POEMS.

IV.

Eclogue I., p. 257, l. 12. *brunt*: " burnt " ; a Scots form. On the frequency of metathesis of *r* in Scots cf. note to l. 58, xix, vol. ii. p. 390.

l. 16. *Or*: " before." This use of the word is now

confined to Scots and to certain English dialects. Cf. vol. ii. p. 272, x, l. 1.

ll. 32-33.

> *vnder vhich doth grow*
> *The rose and lilie far excelling yours—*

A singular verb after two or more singular subjects is frequent in Elizabethan English. See W. Franz, *Shake-speare-Grammatik*, p. 396. Cf. vol. ii. p. 270, l. 11.

ll. 37-38.

> *Suouft vinged archers & ye sea-borne queene,*
> *In Mirrhas child if yee tooke ere delight—*

According to the common legend (cf. Ovid, *Metam.* x. 10) Adonis, the beloved of Aphrodite (the "sea-borne queene") sprung from the unnatural love of the Cyprian princess Myrrha (or Smyrna) for her father Cinyras, who, on becoming aware of her crime, pursues her with a sword; but she, praying to the gods, is changed into a myrtle, out of whose bark springs the beautiful Adonis.

l. 66. *hard*: an obsolete past of *hear*, still extant in Scots. Cf. vol. ii. p. 261, l. 131.

l. 85. *Earths best perfections doth but last short time*: "*doth*" might be explained (in the same way as *doth* and *hath* in the Shakespeare Folio) as a southern plural inflection, early southern English having the inflection *-th* for all three persons of the plural, but this seems hardly likely in the early verse of a Scottish poet. We have already noticed (cf. note to l. 16 of Sextain i, vol. i. p. 180) that in Scots the inflection of the present indicative is *-s* for all persons singular and plural, whenever the verb is separated from its personal pronoun. *S* being the typical inflection of the third person singular present indicative, it is not unreasonable to suppose that the equivalent form in *-th* came to be used, by analogy, for the form in *-s*, when the latter was really not a third person singular. Cf. *And fairest things doth last* (ii. p. 263, l. 18); *The Stars . . . doth rise* (ii. p. 265, l. 77); *ye fillet hath our*

eies, And fostreth vith beguiling hope our mind (ii. p. 266,
ll. 109-10). Cf. A. Montgomerie (ed. Cranstoun, p. 142) :

> Among the gods that sittis aboue,
> And *ruleth* in the skyis.

l. 104. *thow did* : cf. note to l. 8 of Sonnet xi, vol. i.
p. 170.

l. 125. *oke* : the MS. has clearly *oxe*, which is no doubt
a *lapsus calami* for *oke*.

l. 154. *strenhtes* = " strengthes." In Scots *ng* often becomes simple *n* before *th*. Cf. *lenthen*, vol. ii. p. 285,
xxxv, l. 7.

l. 158. *kendle* : an obsolete form of *kindle*, found chiefly
in Mid. Scots.

Eclogue II. p. 263, l. 26. *sights* = " sighs." Cf. note
to l. 77 of *Forth Feasting*, vol. i. p. 245.

l. 32. *Len* : " lend " ; a Scots form.

l. 34. *flourish* : " bloom." Cf. note to l. 28 of Song i,
vol. i. p. 171.

l. 36. *mids* = " meads." The form *mydde* is found in
sixteenth-century English ; the usual Mid. Scots form is
meid. Cf. " *Midows* " (l. 49 below).

l. 38. *Stracht* : a Scots form of *straight*. Cf. vol. ii.
p. 283, xxvi, l. 6.

l. 40. *heareefter* : *efter* is a Mid. Scots variant of *after*.

l. 50. *Venus deare delight* : the anemone, which
sprang from the blood of Adonis.

ll. 51-52.

> *The Hyacinth, & others vho var kings*
> *And ladies faire vhen thay enioyd this light—*

For l. 52 cf. the note to l. 7 of Son. xvii, vol. i. p. 184. The
" *ladies faire* " who were turned into flowers are Daphne,
who was transformed into a laurel-tree (Ovid, *Metam.* i.
12), and Clytia, who was turned into a heliotrope (*ibid.*
iv. 6).

ll. 53-54. These two lines, with a slight variation,
occur also in *Teares on the Death of Moeliades* (ll. 123-4).

l. 61. *sight* = " sighd," " sighed."

l. 66. *Syne* : " then," " next in point of time " ; M.E. *sin, sen,* contracted from the older *siþþen* ; O.E. siþþan = sīþ + þon (= þæm). Cf. vol. ii. p. 299, l. 79. *Syne* is now confined to Scots, and to certain northern English dialects.

l. 86. *interrup* : cf. note to l. 4, lv, vol. ii. p. 402.

l. 98. *I suld not beene oprest* : cf. note to ll. 7-10 of Sextain i, vol. i. p. 179.

l. 103. *embled = emled* (with a supporting *b* between *m* and *l*) : *amled = ameld,* from the verb *amel,* which was used in the sixteenth century by the side of *enamel.*

Sonnets and Miscellaneous Pieces, III. p. 268. This sonnet appears to be addressed to Pierre de Ronsard, judging by the title.

l. 4. *magnes* : cf. vol. ii. p. 78, l. 350.

l. 12. *sel* : " self " ; a Scots form.

IV. p. 269. This is acknowledged in the Hawthornden MSS. to be a paraphrase of Mirtillo's speech, at the beginning of the second scene of Guarini's *Pastor Fido* :

Cruda Amarilli, che col nome ancora
   D' amar, ahi lasso, amaramente insegni ;
   Amarilli del candido ligustro
   Più candida, e più bella ;
   Ma de l' Aspido sordo
   E più sorda, e più fera, e più fugace :
   Poichè col dir t' offendo
   I' mi morrò tacendo :
   Ma grideran per me le piagge, e i monti,
   E questa selua, a cui
   Sì spesso il tuo bel nome
   Di risonare insegno.
Per me piangendo i fonti,
   E mormorando i venti
   Diranno i miei lamenti,
   Parlerà nel mio volto
   La pietate, e 'l dolore,
   E se sia muta ogn' altra cosa, al fine
   Parlerà il mio morire,
   E ti dirà la morte il mio martire.

There is not the slightest doubt that this sonnet is by Drummond, yet we find it included among the poems of Sir Robert Aytoun in Charles Roger's edition of that poet (Edinburgh, 1844, p. 49).

l. 10. *pace* : " peace." This spelling indicates the Mid. Scots pronunciation of the word.

l. 11. *Suppone* : " suppose." The root consonant of the original infinitive is frequently preserved in Mid. Scots, in contrast with the southern adaptation from the past participle. Cf. *promou'd,* vol. ii. p. 270, vi, l. 7. Other such forms are : *propone, expone,* etc.

V. p. 269, l. 1.　*whom to* = " to whom " — one of Drummond's awkward inversions.

propine : " bestow," " give." Cf. note to l. 326 of " The Shadow of the Iudgement," vol. ii. p. 344.

l. 3. *braue but art* : " brave without art." *But, bot* was regularly used in Mid. Scots in the sense of *without* (*sine*). It is still used for " without " in Scots in speaking of place, and particularly of the parts of a house, when it is opposed to *ben, bæn* ; thus " gang but the hoose," which means " go into the outer apartments or kitchen." Cf. vol. ii. p. 276, l. 8.

VI. De Porcheres . . . vret this sonnet, p. 270. Of all the sonnets, still numerous in France at that time, penned during the reign of Henry IV., none caused so much stir in literary circles and at court as that of the poet De Porchères on the eyes of Henry's beautiful mistress, Gabrielle d'Estrée, Marquise de Monceaux. It was much imitated and translated in France and in other countries, and of the numerous translations that by Drummond is by no means the worst.

Curiously enough this sonnet of Drummond is also included by Charles Roger in his edition of the poems of Sir Robert Aytoun.

vret (in the title) : a Scots form of the past tense of *write.*

l. 1. The spelling " *de* " before " *dieux* " is no doubt

meant as a phonetic spelling for *des*. Cf. the spelling
" *vn* " for *vne* on p. 274, l. 6 below.

l. 5. *lest* : " last " ; a Mid. Scots form.

VII. p. 271, l. 4. *sprent* : " sprinkled " ; past
participle of the archaic verb *spreng*, " sprinkle " ; O.E.
sprengan, the causal of *springan*, to " spring." Cf. " *be-
sprent*," vol. i. p. 29, Son. xxxi, l. 3.

VIII. p. 271. Lady Mary Wrothe, to whom this
sonnet is addressed, was the daughter of Robert Sidney,
Earl of Leicester, and wife of Sir Robert Wrothe. She is
the authoress of a prose romance entitled *Urania* (1621),
written in imitation of her uncle's *Arcadia*, interspersed
with regular sonnets and other verses. To her George
Chapman also addressed a sonnet, as did also Ben Jonson
in his *Underwoods*.

X. p. 272, l. 4. *lacing* = laching : "laughing"; a Scots
form.

XI. Essay out of the Italien, p. 273. The title of
this sonnet would point to an Italian original. We have
not succeeded, however, in tracing back this sonnet to
any Italian source.

l. 2. *More sueter accents* : for the double comparative,
frequent in the Elizabethans, cf. p. 280, xix, l. 8 below.

l. 6. *thy heuenlie suannet* : presumably James VI. of
Scotland.

ll. 7-8.
     that faire vel
Vhich Horses haue from flintie rocke mad spring—

Hippocrene, or the " Fountain of the Horse," a fountain in
Mount Helicon in Boeotia sacred to the Muses, and said to
have been produced by the horse Pegasus striking the
ground with his feet.

l. 10. *To Monarks fals if y'il not giue such praise* :
an allusion to the *Monarchicke Tragedies* of Sir William
Alexander.

ll. 11-12.

> *Yet grant at least to them, in sueet sad layes*
> *Vho help faire Sions virgins, to lament—*

appears to be a reference to the translation of the Psalms which King James and Sir William Alexander were executing in partnership, but which was not published at Oxford till 1631, under the title of *The Psalmes of King David: Translated by King James.*

"*Grant*" might be taken as equivalent to *grand* = "grant it." In that case "it" would refer directly to "*praise*" in the preceding line.

l. 14. *Forth boasts of him vho song the Turquish vounds*: a clear reference to King James VI.'s poem on the battle of Lepanto (in which the Turks were defeated), which forms part of *His Maiesties Poeticall Exercises at vacant houres* (1591), and which had the honour of being turned into French verse by Du Bartas, the author of the famous *Weeks*.

XIII. Fragment, p. 275. This piece and the following are obviously early efforts—literary exercises with Sir Philip Sidney as the model.

ll. 5-8. These four lines, with the exception of the second, are identical with ll. 187-190 of *Forth Feasting.*

l. 20. *gueles* = gules : "ermine dyed red"; originally and chiefly heraldic. O.F. *goules, gueules*; Fr. *gueules.* The ulterior etymology of this word is uncertain, but may be the Persian *gul,* a "rose."

l. 26. *Liuing the heauen* = "the living heaven."

XIV. Fragment, p. 276, l. 8. *mids*: "midst"; now obsolete except in Scots.

ll. 9-10. These two lines are repeated in ll. 115-116 of Song i in the *Poems.*

l. 11. *jurie* = ivrie = "ivory."

ll. 13-14. Correspond to ll. 127-128 of Song i in the *Poems.*

l. 17. *each other*: "every other." Cf. vol. i. Sonnet xlv, l. 13.

XV. To my ladye Mary Wroath, p. 277, l. 18. *Nor blamé mee not* : *nor* followed by another negative is now obsolete.

XVI. Sur les œuures poetiques de Guillaume Alexandre . . ., p. 278. In these lines we see Drummond appearing in the rôle of a French poet, and addressing his friend and contemporary, Alexander of Menstrie, in a series of somewhat hobbling alexandrines. These verses, undoubtedly written in Drummond's hand, do not, it is true, bear his signature, but the very faulty versification (the elision of the *i* of *qui* in ll. 2 and 5, and the use of the lyric feminine caesura in ll. 9, 15, and 16) preclude the possibility that we may be in presence of a copy of verses by some unknown French poet. Defective as these lines are, they afford a further testimony to the Laird of Hawthornden's familiarity with French.

l. 4. *Terpandre* : Terpander, the father of Greek music and of lyric poetry. He was a native of Antissa in Lesbos, and flourished between 700 and 650 B.C.

l. 6. *fait reuivre les grands rois* : an allusion to Sir William Alexander's *Monarchicke Tragedies*.

l. 16. *ta belle Aurore* : Sir William Alexander's *Aurora* (1604), a collection of sonnets, interspersed with songs and madrigals.

Madrigals and Epigrams, XX. p. 280. Adapted from a madrigal by Mauritio Moro (*I Tre Giardini de' Madrigali*, Venetia, 1602, pt. ii. p. 96) :

> Lume fido, & amato,
>> Che miri i furti miei caldi, e uiuaci,
>> E godi al dolce suon de' cari baci,
>> Riman in uita ; e se 'l morir hai grato,
>> Spira all' hor, che 'l diletto
>> M' incatena di Lidia al caro petto.
> Anzi morir tu puoi,
> Che mi son chiare stelle i lumi suoi.

XXI. Amarillis to her dog Perlin, p. 281. Again adapted from a madrigal by Mauritio Moro (*ibid.* pt. iii. p. 121) :

> Perlino non latrar, mira, che fai ?
> Ah non conosci 'l mio
> Vag' Amante, e disio ?
> Frena i latrati, e care gioie haurai.
> Non ti basta del giorno
> Che fai meco soggiorno ?
> Cedi la notte, e taci,
> E prendi 'l sonno, a l' Harmonia de' baci.

XXII. p. 281. From a madrigal by Valerio Belli (*Madrigali dell' eccellentissimo Sig. Valerio Belli*, Venetia, 1599, p. 4^b) :

> Qui giace vn feritore
> Di quel petto, che mai
> Piagar non potè amore :
> Morì ; ma ben fù assai,
> Che Pulce inerme, sol d' ardire armato,
> D' offesi amanti, vindice sia stato :
> Amantes proprio ære,
> Militi bene merenti posuere.

XXIII. p. 282. A condensation from Horace, *Odes,* iv. 13 (" Audivere, Lyce ").

XXVI. p. 283, l. 2. *soume* : " swim " ; a Scots form.

XXXI. p. 284, ll. 3-4. These two verses are repeated from ll. 5-6 of piece xiii, vol. ii. p. 184.

XXXIV. Epitaphe on a Cooke, p. 285, l. 2. *wretched* : " niggardly," " miserly." Cf. note to l. 376 of *A Cypresse Grove,* vol. ii. p. 349.

XXXV. On a noble man, p. 285, l. 10. *to take's Death* : " to take his Death." The use of *'s* for *his* is found in the sixteenth and early seventeenth centuries. Cf. Marlowe, *Jew of Malta,* IV. iii. : " Look how his brains drop out on 's nose," and Shakespeare, *Cymbeline,* v. v. 294 : " I cut off 's head."

XLIII. p. 286, l. 1. *Zoilus*: a Greek rhetorician, born at Amphipolis, flourished in the third century B.C. From the bitterness with which he attacked Homer he was surnamed Homeromastix or Homer's Scourge, and has bequeathed his name proverbially for a malignant critic.

l. 2. *gree*: an aphetised form of *agree*; now obsolete except in Scots and certain English dialects.

XLVII. p. 287, l. 1. *cornard*: "cuckold"; Fr. *cornard*.

LII. Out of Passerat, p. 287. The original runs as follows (Passerat, *Poésies françaises*, ed. Blanchemain, ii. p. 137) :

> Qui est cocu, & n'en croit rien,
> Ie le pren pour homme de bien.
> Qui le sçait, & semblant n'en monstre,
> Pour homme accort passé à la monstre.
> Qui à son front taste s'il l'est,
> Ie le pren pour maistre Benest.

LIV. p. 288. We have been unable to trace the allusion in this piece.

LVII. Vindiciae against the Comones . . ., p. 289, l. 12. *practike*: now obsolete, and replaced by *practice*.

l. 14. The last word in this line is by no means certain ; the Hawthornden MSS. appear to read " *eʃe*." We interpret this, with considerable hesitation, to be a mistake for *esle*, a form of *easle*, a " hot cinder," " a live coal " or " ember," a word still used in Scots and in Northumberland and Cumberland. The usual Mid. Scots form is *isill*.

POEMS OF DOUBTFUL AUTHENTICITY.

I. Lines one the Bischopes, p. 293. These verses, ascribed to Drummond by his contemporary Sir James Balfour, occur in a manuscript (19. 3. 8) of pasquinades dated between 1637 and 1647 in Sir James's handwriting, preserved in the Advocates' Library, Edinburgh. They first appeared in print in the " Third Book " of James Maidment's *Book of Scotish Pasquils*, Edinburgh, 1827, and not in the Maitland Club edition of Drummond's *Poems* (1832), of which they form part, as Ward and Masson state.

l. 7. *lauch* : a Scots form. Cp. note to l. 4 of x, vol. ii. p. 409.

l. 10. *Ignatian Matchiuell* : probably William Laud, Archbishop of Canterbury (1573–1645), the upholder of absolutism in church and state, and the arch enemy of Presbyterianism in Scotland. He is doubtless called " *Ignatian* " in reference to Ignatius de Loyola, the founder of the Society of Jesus, and " *Matchiuell* " in allusion to Machiavelli, the author of *Il Principe* (1532), of which the central idea is, that for the establishment and maintenance of authority all means may be employed, and that the worst acts of the ruler are justified by the wickedness and treachery of the governed.

l. 36. *Marikin* : a variant of *Maroquin* (Fr. *maroquin*), " morocco leather."

ll. 53-54.

> *Had I bot halffe the spyte of Galloway Tom,*
> *That Roman snakie viper—*

a reference to Thomas Sydserff (1581–1663), successively Bishop of Brechin and Galloway. He took an active part in the introduction into Scotland of the English Prayer Book. This, and his intimacy with Laud, made him a mark for the violence of the Presbyterians. He became so unpopular that he was attacked by a Presbyterian mob at Stirling in February 1638, and only escaped severe injury through the intervention of the magistrates. A few days afterwards he was again assaulted in the streets of Falkirk and of Edinburgh, and in December of 1638 he was formally deposed by the General Assembly. On the Restoration he was appointed to the bishopric of

Orkney. Sydserff's name appears several times in the Presbyterian lampoons of the time ; in one of these, a pasquil against the bishops (see Maidment, *A Book of Scotish Pasquils*, ed. of 1868, p. 20), he is plainly called a " papist," and in another (*ibid*. p. 65) he is addressed as " Galloway Tam."

l. 59. *Johne de Koell* : we have been unable to identify this person, if indeed the name is not a sobriquet. As far back as 1868 a question was asked in *Notes and Queries* about this mysterious individual, but elicited no reply.

l. 67. *polypragmatick Macheuell* : possibly John Maxwell, Bishop of Ross, deprived in 1638, who in contemporary lampoons is sometimes styled " Bishop Mackivell " (cf. Maidment, *op. cit.* p. 65). He was the author of a pamphlet entitled *Sacra Sancta Regum Majestas*, in which he states that " Monarchy and Scotish Presbytery agree as well as God and the Devil."

II. For the Kinge, p. 296. We have recently discovered these lines in the manuscript referred to under the last heading. They are not however, as is the case with the " Lines one the Bischopes," expressly attributed to Drummond by Sir James Balfour. They were first ascribed to Drummond in the folio edition of 1711, and their authenticity has never, we believe, been questioned except by Ward, who nevertheless includes them among Drummond's undisputed poems. The same critic sees in this satire a severe exposure of the vices of King James (the very severity of the attack is Ward's reason for doubting Drummond's authorship), but the cap, it seems to us, fits Charles I. equally well, if not better.

l. 1. *quhois* : the *i* of "*quhois*" or *whois* is merely orthographic. This orthographic *i*, to indicate the length of the preceding vowel, is common in Mid. Scots.

l. 2. *souerainges* : the metathesis of *g* (with *n*) is frequent in Mid. Scots. Cf. *Reseinge*, l. 4 below.

l. 25. *nor* : " than." On this Scots use of *nor* cf. note to ll. 2-3 of Mad. iv, vol. i. p. 197.

l. 31. *canditis poysoned baittes* : "*canditis*" (= *candieds*) is a case of the adjective bearing the inflection of the plural, a Mid. Scots usage. Cf. note to l. 6 of xv, vol. ii. p. 369.

l. 36. *throngit* : p.p. of the verb *thring*, "press," "push," "squeeze"; O.E. *þringan*. *Thring* is now confined to Scots and the northern English counties.

l. 45. *nossethirle* : "nostril"; chiefly a Mid. Scots form.

l. 79. *syne* : "afterwards." On *syne* cf. note to l. 66 of Eclogue ii, vol. ii. p. 407.

III. Hymns, p. 300. These hymns were printed for the first time, as Drummond's, in the folio edition of his *Works* (1711). Mr. Orby Shipley, in the preface to his *Annus Sanctus* (1884), has proved that they were by no means printed for the first time in the folio edition of 1711 ; they had appeared, anonymously, nearly a century before, in *The Primer or Office of the Blessed Virgin Mary in English*, published at Saint-Omer by John Heigham in 1619. An earlier edition of this work was published in 1614, in which the hymns in question are apparently lacking. They are also wanting in the Hawthornden MSS. as they now exist, but they may very well have formed part of the manuscripts which the editors of the folio edition state expressly they received from Drummond's son. It has rightly been pointed out that though these hymns may have been comprised in the manuscripts such as the editors of the folio edition were able to consult, yet this would not be a proof of their having been composed by Drummond himself, as Drummond was in the habit of transcribing for his own edification passages and sometimes whole poems from all kinds of authors. On the other hand, the folio edition was prepared under the patronage and with the concurrence of Drummond's son, who can reasonably be presumed to have known what his father wrote, in spite of the fact that the editors of the folio edition did include, as we have already pointed out, two pieces which are known not to have been written by Drummond. Mr. Orby Shipley, who is inclined to reject the ascription of these hymns to the Laird of Hawthornden, observes that it is altogether untenable to admit that John Heigham, a Catholic publisher, should have addressed himself to Drummond, a Scottish Protestant. Even if Heigham obtained them from Drummond, which need not be admitted, Mr. Orby Shipley appears to us to overlook the fact that the Scottish poet was a very broad-minded man and a Protestant of a type very different from the normal Scotch Protestant of his days. Moreover, we may conclude from a letter of Drummond's, addressed probably to Sir Robert Kerr, and printed for the first time from the manuscripts by David Laing (*Archæologia Scotica*, iv. p. 92), that Drummond at one period of his life was engaged in writing Christian songs and hymns. This, we think, strengthens considerably the case for Drummond's authorship; but a still more important piece of evidence is advanced by Mr. W. T. Brooke (*Athenæum*, April 4, 1885), who points out the following statement in the preface to the 1632 edition of the *Primer* : " The Hymnes most of which are vsed by the holy Church in her publick Office ; are a new translation done by one most skilfull in English poetrie, wherein the literall sense is preserued with the true straine of the verse." Mr. Brooke remarks that it would be difficult to find a Roman Catholic poet of the time to whom these words are applicable, and concludes, somewhat rashly perhaps, that they are an obvious allusion to Drummond. Another correspondent in the *Athenæum* (March 21, 1885), arguing in the same direction, thinks that there is " almost intrinsic evidence that Drummond wrote these hymns." We think, on the contrary, that the somewhat colourless language of the hymns is the strongest argument against their ascription to Drummond, though it must be admitted that, on the whole, the evidence is in his favour.

vi. Dedication of a Church, p. 304, l. 27. *Paraclete* : a title of the Holy Spirit, representing Greek παράκλητος, in *John* xiv. 16, 26 ; properly an " advocate," " intercessor."

xii. Hymn for Wednesday, p. 310, l. 13. *lightsome* : " luminous."

IV. Polemo-Middinia. Drummond's name appears for the first time, as that of the author of *Polemo-Middinia*, in the edition published at Oxford in 1691, by Bishop Gibson. The first edition of his poems in which it appears is the folio edition of 1711.

As Professor Masson (*Drummond of Hawthornden,* pp. 482-484) has already stated the reasons for and against Drummond's authorship, without, however, coming to any definite conclusion, it will be sufficient to summarise his results, and add any further facts that may seem relevant.

In favour of Drummond the weightiest arguments are his intimate connection with the persons and localities mentioned in the poem ; and further, the fact that his authorship, when *Polemo-Middinia* was published under his name, was not only undisputed, but expressly asserted in the following terms in " The Author's Life " prefixed to the folio edition of 1711 : " For diverting himself and his Friends, he wrote a Sheet which he called Polemo-Middinia: 'Tis a sort of Macaronick Poetry, in which the Scots Words are put in Latin Terminations : Some Years ago it was Reprinted at Oxford, with an excellent Latin Preface concerning Macaronick Poetry : It is Reprinted here almost every Year, and is very Witty and Diverting, and suits mightily with the Humour and Genius of the Nation." On the other side, it has been objected that there is no record or reference in Drummond's lifetime, or immediately afterwards, of such a piece having been written by him ; and that *Polemo-Middinia* is too unlike anything else he wrote to have come from his pen. The

last argument has very little value ; though the bulk of
Drummond's writings are prevailingly serious, a not in-
considerable number show that he was not lacking in the
sense of the humorous. It may also be recalled, in this
connection, that Drummond had read and studied the
Macaronics of Folengo, otherwise known as Merlinus
Coccaius.

What appears at first sight to be a stronger argument
for doubting Drummond's authorship has recently been
put forward in *Notes and Queries* (Sept. 5, 1891). It is
there pointed out that *Polemo-Middinia* is mentioned, and
its author named, in Defoe's *Tour thro' the Whole Island of
Great Britain* (London, 1727), in these words : " The
People who work in the Coal Mines in this Country . . .
are well describ'd by their own Countryman Samuel
Colvil, in his famous Macaronick Poem, call'd *Polemo-
Midinia* ; thus,

Cole-hewers Nigri, Girnantes more Divelli."

Little is known of this Samuel Colvil, except that he is
the author of a piece entitled *Mock Poem, or Whiggs
Supplication*, published at London in 1681, not anonymously as Ward states, but with the initials " S. C."
(Samuel Colvil) only. The Edinburgh edition of 1687
bears the name " Sam. Colvil," and that of 1692, published
at London, has the extended title : *The Scotch Hudibras :
or, a Mock Poem . . . corrected and amended, with addi-
tions and alterations*. Colvil's satire turns upon the
insurrection of the Covenanters in Scotland in the reign of
Charles II., and, as the extended title indicates, is written
in imitation of Butler's *Hudibras*. The *Dictionary of
National Biography*, repeating an error in Chalmers'
General Biographical Dictionary, confuses this Samuel
Colvil with his eldest brother Alexander Colvil, a distinguished Oriental scholar and divine, who was Principal
of St. Mary's College, St. Andrews, where he died in 1666.
Both Samuel and Alexander were sons of John Colvil or

Colville, who succeeded in 1640 to the title of Lord Colville of Culross, but for some reason or other did not assume the title, though his wife, who wrote *Ane Godly Dreame,* is commonly called Lady Culross. If it be admitted that the earliest known edition of *Polemo-Middinia* falls within the years 1642–1650 (see Bibliography, vol. i. p. xcii), and account be taken of the fact that the *Mock Poem* did not appear till 1681, the large gap between the two publications is not easily explained. The difficulty of identifying Samuel Colvil with the author of *Polemo-Middinia* is further increased by the fact that he is known to have been alive in 1710, according to Chalmers' *Life of Ruddiman,* it being there noticed that the *North Tatler* was printed at Edinburgh that year by John Reid for Sam. Colvill. After due consideration we are inclined, in this case also, to favour Drummond's claim.

ll. 2-3. Pittenweem, Crail, and Anstruther are coast towns in the east of Fife.

l. 7. *breddum* : " broad " ; Scots *braid.*

l. 13. *Maia . . . Bassa* : May and Bass, islands in the Firth of Forth.

l. 14. *Edenum* : Edinburgh.

l. 26. *armati greppis* : " armed with pronged forks " ; Scots *graip.* Cf. Swedish *grep,* Danish *greb,* " a fork."

l. 35. *Oldmoudus* : Scots *auld-moud,* " old-mouthed " ; " sagacious in speech."

l. 36. *pleugham* : " plough " ; Scots *pleugh.*

l. 38. *plouky-fac'd* : "pimply-faced." The word *plouk, plook,* a " pimple," is now confined to Scots and to the northern English counties. Its origin is obscure.

inkne'd : " knock-kneed."

Alshinder : Scots form of " Alexander."

l. 40. *lethus* : " loath " ; Scots *laith.*

l. 41. *Nout-headdum* : a " blockhead." The word *nowt,* " cattle," is confined to Scots and to the northern English counties ; O.N. *naut,* " cattle," " oxen."

l. 46. *assam* : " ashes " ; Scots *ase, ass* ; O.E. *asce.*

l. 49. *crooksaddeliis*: a " crook-saddle " is a saddle for bearing panniers or creels.

heghemis: Scots and northern English *hames*; the two curved pieces of wood or metal resting on the collar of a draught-horse, to which the traces are attached. Cf. Low Ger. *ham*, " yoke for horses," and Mid. Dutch *hame*, " a leather or wooden yoke for horses."

l. 50. *Brechimmis*: Scots *brecham*, a " horse-collar " ; O.E. *beorg* (from *beorgan*, " to protect ") + *ham* (hom), " a covering," according to the *E.D.D.*

l. 52. *averos*: Scots *aver* or *aiver*, a " cart horse " ; O.F. *aveir* (*aver*) ; Fr. *avoir*, " property," " stock," " cattle."

l. 57. *flankavit*: this word apparently signifies " harnessed," but we can find no authority for that meaning.

l. 60. *swieros*: Scots *sweer*, *sweir*, " dull," " heavy " ; " lazy," " slow " ; O.E. *swǣr*, " heavy," " sluggish," " weak."

ll. 63-64.

Haud aliter quam si cum multis Spinola trouppis
Proudus ad Ostendam marchasset fortiter urbem—

a reference to the capture of Ostend by Marquis Spinola, on the 20th September 1604, after a siege lasting three years and seventy-seven days.

l. 67. *Incipit Harlæi cunctis sonare Batellum*: an allusion to the battle of Harlaw in Aberdeenshire, where the forces of the Eastern Scottish Lowlands met and defeated Donald of the Isles in 1411. The battle of Harlaw continued for several centuries to be the theme of Scottish ballads.

l. 76. *saltpannifumos*: " smoky salt - panners," or " salt-makers." A " salt-pan " is a shallow pond for making salt by evaporation.

l. 85. *gliedam*: Scots *gleid*, *glied*, p.p. of *glie*, *gley*, *glee*, " to squint." Of obscure origin.

l. 93. *riftos*: Scots *rift*, " belching," " eructation " ; O.N. *rypta*, " to belch."

l. 94. *Barmifumi* : " fuming with barm " ; " inflamed with beer."

l. 97. *goulæam* : Scots *gully*, " a large knife." Of obscure origin.

l. 98. *fleidos* : Scots *fleyd*, p.p. of *fley*, " to put to flight," " to frighten " ; O.E. *flēgan*, " to put to flight."

l. 101. *thrapellum* : Scots *thrapple* or *thropple*, " wind-pipe," " throat," " neck."

l. 102. *rivabo* : Scots *reeve*, " to split asunder," " to tear." *luggas* : Scots *lug*, or *lugg*, the " ear."

l. 105. *dirtfleyda* : Scots *dirt-fleyed*, " in excessive fear."

l. 108. *fleuram* = *fleure*, an obsolete sixteenth-century Scots variant of *flavour* in the sense of " smell."

l. 111. *shoollare* : Scots *shool*, " to shovel."

l. 112. *feire fairie*, or *feery-fary* : a Scots expression, meaning " a great hubbub," " an angry tumult " ; a reduplicated form of *fary*, " a state of tumult " or " con-sternation," of which the origin is obscure.

l. 121. *gutture* : Scots *gutter*, " mud," " mire."

l. 122. *Perlineas* : " made of perlin," a kind of thread-lace.

l. 123. *Vasquineam* : " petticoat " ; sixteenth-century Fr. *vasquine* ; Fr. *basquine*.

begariavit : Mid. Scots *begarie*, " to variegate," " to bespatter " ; Fr. *bigarrer*, " to variegate."

l. 128. *girnavit* : Scots *girn*, " to grin."

l. 129. *Bublentem* : Scots *bubbly*, " snotty," " drivel-ling," " dirty " ; from *bubble*, " to snivel," " weep," " blubber."

l. 131. *Gilliwyppum* : " a hard blow " ; from Northern *wipe*, " a blow," and *gilli* (of unknown origin), which appears to have an intensitive value.

l. 133. *gash-beardum* : " with a long or protruding beard " ; from the adj. *gash*, of unknown origin, " pro-jecting," " protruding " (of the chin), which itself is derived from the noun *gash*, " chin."

l. 134. *sneezing* : " snuff " in Scots.

l. 135. *swingere* : Scots *swinger, swingeour*, " rogue," ' rascal."

l. 136. *Gilliwamphra* : " a hard blow." The second element, *wamphra* (for which *wampla* should possibly be read), seems to stand for the Scots *whample*, " a stroke," " blow."

nevellam : Scots *nevel*, or *naval*, " a blow with the fist."

l. 139. *bumbasedus* : Scots *bumbaze*, " to bewilder," " stupefy " ; apparently a kind of intensitive form of the obsolete and dialectal *baze*, " to alarm," " stupefy," identical with the Dutch *bazen, verbazen*, " to stupefy," " to astonish."

l. 141. *nizavit* : Scots *neese*, " to sneeze."

l. 142. *Disjunium* : " breakfast " ; Fr. *déjeûner*.

l. 143. *Lausavit* : Scots *lowse*, " to loosen," " to break out."

l. 149. *Monsmegga* : Mons Meg, a large cannon whose origin is doubtful, stands on the highest part of the Castle Rock in Edinburgh. It is said to have been forged at Mons, Belgium, in 1476, while according to other authorities it was forged in Scotland by a Galloway blacksmith.

l. 155. *Sluissam* : refers to the attempted relief by Spinola of the town of Sluys, besieged by Maurice of Nassau, and captured by him on the 18th August 1604.

dingasset : Scots *ding*, " smash," " batter."

l. 156. *Ludovicus* : Louis XIII., who besieged the Huguenot town of Montauban unsuccessfully in 1621.

l. 158. *yerdam* = " yerd," a Scots form of *earth*.

l. 161. *wirriabo* : Scots *wirry*, " to worry."

l. 162. *seustram* : Scots *sewster*, " seamstress."

broddatus : Scots *brod*, " to prick," " pierce." Of uncertain origin.

l. 163. *stobbatus* : " stabbed " ; a Scots form.

greittans : Scots *greit, greet*, " cry," " weep," " lament "; O.E. *grǣtan* (past *grēt*), " to weep."

l. 164. *Barlafumle* : an obsolete Scots expression, found also in the forms *barla-fummil* and *barla-fumble*, " a call

for truce by one who has fallen in wrestling or play."
The first element is the exclamation *barley* ; the second
element is doubtful. The exclamation *barley*, still used in
Scots and in the northern English counties, is perhaps from
Fr. *parlez*, Eng. *parley*, and means " parley," " truce,"
" quarter," more especially a cry for truce in a game, used
by children when a short rest or break is wanted.

l. 165. *guisa* : Scots *guise*, " a masquerade " ; " a
merry-making," " frolic " ; Fr. *guise*.

V. To the Reader, p. 327. Dr. Rudolf Brotanek (see
Anglia, Beiblatt, v. p. 161), in a review of Hoffmann's
Studien zu Alexander Montgomerie (Englische Studien,
xx. 1), was the first to put forward the theory that these
lines are Drummond's. In his *Untersuchungen über
das Leben und die Dichtungen Alexander Montgomeries*
(Wien und Leipzig, 1896, p. 42) he explicitly ascribes them
to Drummond, without however bringing forward any
additional evidence. From ll. 17-18 it is evident that they
were composed for the first edition of *The Flyting*, which
appeared in 1621, but of which no copy is now known to
exist. In any case they appear in the second edition
(1629), and in subsequent editions, and are lacking in the
two manuscript versions (the Tullibardine and the
Harleian). Dr. Brotanek's main reason for ascribing this
preface " To the Reader " to Drummond is that the
Hawthornden manuscripts contain a kind of short sketch
of part of it by Drummond (see p. 245 of the present
volume). Dr. Brotanek likewise adds, and we share his
view, that the firm of Hart, who had all along been
Drummond's printers, may have asked him to supply a
preface to a work which they were also printing, and
which was from the pen of a fellow-countryman and poet,
the greater part of whose works Drummond possessed in
manuscript. Dr. Brotanek might also have added that
the verse preface of *The Flyting* is in English, while *The
Flyting* itself is of course in Scots.

Both Dr. Cranstoun, the editor of *The Poems of Alexander Montgomerie* (Edinburgh and London, 1887), and Mr. George Stevenson in the supplementary volume thereto, leave the question of Drummond's authorship untouched.

Without wishing to dogmatise, it appears to us that Dr. Brotanek's views are at least worthy of serious consideration.

1. 6. *Walk'd* : Dr. Cranstoun (*op. cit.* p. 57), who prints from the same edition as we do, writes "*Waked*," but "*Walk'd*" should be retained ; it is merely a spelling of "waked," the *l* indicating that the vowel is long. This intrusive and unsounded *l* is common in Mid. Scots, chiefly after *a* and *o*. Cf. such forms as *palpis*, " paps " ; *waltir*, " water " ; *rolkis*, " rocks," etc.

1. 18. *tholes* : " suffers." Cf. note to 1. 11, xxx, vol. ii. p. 399.

INDEX OF FIRST LINES.

THE END